THE DEFINITIVE GUIDE TO ENTERTAINMENT MARKETING

BRINGING THE MOGULS, THE MEDIA, AND THE MAGIC TO THE WORLD

Al Lieberman and Patricia Esgate

ISBN-10: 0-13-419467-5
ISBN-13: 978-0-13-419467-7

Pearson Education LTD.
Pearson Education Australia PTY, Limited.
Pearson Education Singapore, Pte. Ltd.
Pearson Education Asia, Ltd.
Pearson Education Canada, Ltd.
Pearson Educación de Mexico, S.A. de C.V.
Pearson Education—Japan
Pearson Education Malaysia, Pte. Ltd.

Library of Congress Control Number is on file.

Vice President, Publisher
Tim Moore

Associate Publisher and Director of Marketing
Amy Neidlinger

Executive Editor
Jeanne Glasser

Operations Specialist
Jodi Kemper

Marketing Manager
Megan Graue

Cover Designer
Alan Clements

Managing Editor
Kristy Hart

Project Editor
Elaine Wiley

Copy Editor
Chrissy White

Proofreader
Karen Gill

Indexer
Lisa Stumpf

Senior Compositor
Gloria Schurick

Manufacturing Buyer
Dan Uhrig

For Carol
And for Bren

Contents

Foreword

Entertainment is a technology-driven industry and, as such, is caught up in a disruption not seen in hundreds of years. The digital revolution has created exciting new pathways, but has opened the door to pirates. Traditional business models are under attack. One can barely keep up with the avalanche of hardware, all creating new ways to deliver the product to consumers hungry for more, now.

Preparing those who will create, manage, distribute, and market entertainment and media is no small feat, given this sea change. In the last two decades, Al Lieberman has overseen the creation and growth of the Entertainment, Media, and Technology Program at NYU's Stern School of Business, which now offers sixty sections and a curriculum that offers unique insight into the challenging and dynamic business of entertainment.

In *The Definitive Guide to Entertainment Marketing*, Al Lieberman and his writing partner, Pat Esgate, have created a must-read compendium of all the platforms that make up this exciting industry. While no one book can ever capture all that drives this fascinating and fast-paced business, Al and Pat have managed to encapsulate a mass of information, offering readers an excellent overview of the possibilities, the potential, and the pitfalls that face today's entertainment executives. They have woven them together through the prism of their own experiences, creating a guide that is not only useful, but a darn good read. After all, it's about entertainment. It *should* be entertaining.

I wish Al and Pat much success with this excellent effort and applaud them for their contribution to the current and future entertainment executives, entrepreneurs, and fans.

Craig Hatkoff
Co-Founder of the Tribeca Film Festival
Creative Director of the Annual Disruptive Innovation Awards

Acknowledgments

The authors would like to acknowledge the help of Dan Anagnos, Rob Moore, and David Polinchock, who provided invaluable insight into their particular platforms and the industry in general.

About the Authors

Al Lieberman is a Clinical Professor of Marketing and the Executive Director of the Entertainment, Media, and Technology (EMT) Program at the Stern School of Business, New York University, where he was awarded the first Albert Gallatin endowed Chair as Professor of Business. He has created a unique specialization curriculum with courses covering the marketing, professional management, finance, accounting, globalization, new media, and strategic development of the entertainment, media, and telecommunication sectors.

Professor Lieberman has extensive experience in the world of entertainment marketing. He served for over 12 years as President and founder of Grey Entertainment and Media, a wholly owned subsidary of Grey Advertising. Under his leadership, Grey Entertainment grew to become a leading specialized marketing and communications agency, servicing clients such as Warner Bros. Studios, Warner Home Video, ABC Entertainment, Harper Collins Publishers, Viking/Penguin, Murdoch Magazines, People Magazine, Universal Music, Radio City Music Hall, Madison Square Garden Network, Metro Cable Coop (1.800.OK.Cable), Celebrity Cruises, and Barbados Board of Tourism, among others.

Professor Lieberman also served as Executive Vice President of Simon & Schuster. As General Manager of the Silhouette book division, he played a significant role in launching the Silhouette paperback brand, which grew to over $250 million dollars in retail sales worldwide, with distribution in 90 countries and 16 languages.

His research involves film festivals, technology and its disruptive impact on media and entertainment, and global entertainment and media. He has worked and taught in Italy, France, Germany, India, Argentina, China, and Brazil.

Patricia Esgate specializes in strategic business development for market platforms that utilize dynamic experiences to build brand loyalty, drive repeat visitation, and increase revenue. Through the consulting practice of Esgate & Associates, Ms. Esgate's clients have included the Walt Disney Company, Sony, Universal Studios, Jim Henson Productions, and the McDonald's Corporation, along with an extensive list of individual projects both domestic and international. Ms. Esgate has had the pleasure of organizing several conferences focusing on the destination entertainment industry, including her own event, the Summit for Experience Creators, and enjoyed five years as the editor of *EM* magazine, a groundbreaking publication that focused on all facets of the experiential marketplace. Ms. Esgate has appeared at industry events as both a featured speaker and provocateur; she has also served as a faculty member for Harvard University's Experience Architecture Forum and Pine & Gilmore's popular Strategic Horizons thinkAbouts.

Introduction

Let Us Entertain You

I n the decade since *The Entertainment Marketing Revolution* was published, the impact of new technologies has been such that we might as well have chiseled our first book in stone and sent it out on dinosaur-back.

A little over ten years ago, the Internet was primarily used for email and very limited information search. Going on the Web at home meant tying up your phone line, as cable modems—*very* expensive—were only just appearing. "Mobile" was a word used primarily with transportation. "Google" was a funny little word associated with a cartoon character from the 1920s. And AOL and Time Warner were basking in the rays of their earth-shattering merger.

People were still replacing their vinyl or cassette music collections with CD versions, and the majority of people who cared about such things still owned collections of VHS tapes but were switching over to DVD. Downloading a song took 3.5 hours. A movie took 28 hours. Broadcast networks were TV royalty, surrounded by the serfdom of cable, which lived off of broadcast re-runs.

The only people who were digitally recording anything were the people who were inventing the technology. There was no HDTV, HD video, HDMI—no high-definition anything. Neither the product nor the technology existed in commercial form.

Print media—newspapers, magazines, books—was healthy. A struggling startup called Amazon tried to convince traditional booksellers that it was the World's Largest Bookstore. The only form of texting was a service called instant messaging. That was tied to your computer screen—which most likely was a large box that sat on your desk. Without an Ethernet cable (or a telephone line) to anchor you to the World Wide Web, you had to resort to a phone call, or—get this—a face-to-face conversation.

The death knell of movies was predicted. Again.

Flash forward to today. We are surrounded by innovative, mobile technology: smartphones, tablets, laptops. Every small device is now a center of the entertainment universe, bringing all the platforms—movies, publishing, music, sports, television—into the palms of the public, who wants it all, NOW—and gets it. Entertainment is streamed everywhere, at any time, pushed onward by the consumer, who burns with a desire to know more and have more, faster.

The opportunities for entertainment, and entertainment marketing, seem endless. But traditional business models are morphing daily.

The music industry writhes, as digital downloads become the norm. The entire concept of albums—compilations of several songs being sold in a package—is disappearing rapidly. New platforms threaten the very idea of music ownership. The Internet allows for self-distribution, allowing greater freedom for musicians and new approaches for labels.

Newspapers and magazines both strive to find ways to monetize what's been posted for free for nearly a decade, reversing a slide in advertising and subscriptions dollars. The book business wrestles with digital readers. Traditional distributors seemed destined to fail, while mighty Amazon has become a publisher.

The revenue from electronic gaming is now far greater than that of the theatrical box office and continues to grow, though primarily through mobile and social gaming. Game consoles seek to become the sole set-top box, while over-the-top distribution drains viewers from cable TV. Broadcast networks fight for relevance as the consumer finds great original content on 900 channels, more and more of it mobile.

But movies? Please. Did anyone really expect them to die? Movies are still the root of the entertainment industry. This platform is not simply about box office. Movies provide a marketing dream, with licensing, merchandising, sponsorship, and retail creating billions in revenue, across all platforms. And now, with mobile the new mantra, movies are always with us, digitally downloadable on every tablet, smartphone, laptop, gaming console, smart TV Internet, and pretty soon, your sunglasses.

Beyond the platforms, there's the growth of social networking, possibly the biggest harnessing of word-of-mouth ever. A marketer's dream, the proliferation of Facebook, Twitter, YouTube, Pinterest—and whatever's next—has connected consumers like never before. With the good comes the challenge: keeping control when bad buzz goes viral. Now more than ever, speed thrills... and kills.

So the world might have changed, but one constant remains: We, as a people, want more entertainment. We want escape, respite, drama, laughs, learning, and sometimes, simply something to blank out on. And now we have it all, everywhere, from big screen to small.

For entertainment marketers, it's a *huge* opportunity.

The Market for Marketing—and Marketing Professionals

Ten years ago, entertainment marketing was a relatively tiny, but growing, niche. At that time, consumer spending on entertainment was pegged at $150 billion, with additional revenue from associated advertising.

Entertainment spending now reaches into every corner of the developed world. Revenue growth is aided by new technologies, delivering content to the furthest corners of the world, not to mention every public space in America—including the back seat of taxicabs and restaurant booths, grocery stores, and gas pumps.

The consumption of entertainment creates huge streams of revenue. One source[1] pegs total global entertainment expenditures for 2012 as follows:

TV Subscriptions / Licensing:	$85 Billion
Music:	$17 Billion
Consumer Magazines:	$21 Billion
Video Games:	$15 Billion
Radio:	$22 Billion
Consumer and Educational Book Publishing	$32 Billion
Cinema (Box Office Only)	$34 Billion

This adds up to a whopping $226 billion. Keep in mind that these figures—with the exception of television—do not include the licensing, sponsorship, and merchandising that flows from the multi-billion-dollar monetization of content, revenue streams that we will discuss in later chapters. It also does not include the marketing spend associated with these platforms, a figure that, according to the same source, exceeded $165 billion all on its own.

By the time we add in similar ticketing, licensing, and merchandising revenues from sports (estimated at $464 billion[2]), we're exceeding $1 *trillion* in entertainment spending around the globe. But more than simply a huge stream of revenue, the business of entertainment—specifically, movies and television—is a significant contributor to the economy.

As the Motion Picture Association of America (MPAA) reports[3]:

> The production and distribution of motion pictures and television programs is one of the nation's most valuable cultural and economic resources.
>
> **The industry is a major private sector employer, supporting 2.1 million jobs, and nearly $143 billion in total wages in 2010:**
>
> - Direct industry jobs generated $42.1 billion in wages, and an average salary 32% higher than the national average:
>   - There were nearly 282,000 jobs in the core business of producing, marketing, manufacturing, and distributing motion pictures and television shows. These are high-quality jobs, with an average salary of nearly $82,000, 74% higher than the average salary nationwide.
>   - Additionally, there were over 400,000 jobs in related businesses that distribute motion pictures and television shows to consumers.

---

[1] *PwC Global Entertainment and Media Outlook: 2012-2016,* www.pwc.com/outlook.

[2] Plunkett Research, www.plunkettresearch.com/entertainment-media-publishing-market-research/industry-and-business-data.

[3] The Economic Contribution of the Motion Picture & Television Industry to the United States, The Motion Picture Association of America, Inc., 2012.

- The industry also supports indirect jobs and wages in thousands of companies with which it does business, such as caterers, dry cleaners, florists, hardware and lumber suppliers, and jobs in other companies doing business with consumers, such as DVD retailers, theme parks, and tourist attractions.

The industry is a nationwide network of small businesses:

- The industry is comprised of nearly 95,000 businesses in total, located in every state in the country.

- The industry made $37.4 billion in payments to nearly 278,000 businesses around the country in 2010.

The industry increases the tax base:

- The industry generated $15.6 billion in public revenues in 2010 from federal income taxes, including unemployment, Medicare and Social Security, state income taxes, and sales taxes on goods.

The industry is one of the most highly competitive around the world—one of the few that consistently generates a positive balance of trade, in virtually every country in which it does business:

- There were $13.5 billion in film and television services exports in 2010, down 2% from 2009, and up 6% over 2006.

- The industry had a positive services trade surplus of $11.9 billion in 2010, or 7% of the total U.S. private-sector trade surplus in services.

- The motion picture and television services surplus was larger than each of the surpluses in the telecommunications, management and consulting, legal, medical, computer, and insurance services sectors.

As entertainment reaches further into the global marketplace, its moguls continue to focus on issues of fair trade, including NAFTA, the European Union, and China's continuing impact in the World Trade Organization. And with information literally moving at the speed of light—bounced off satellites and fed along fiber optic cables—both domestic and international distribution are critical, and marketing even more so.

As all of this continues to morph, opportunities for marketing professionals continue to grow. Both the entertainment business and the marketing of it are the focus of course offerings at over 50 of the top U.S. universities and colleges, including New York University, Wharton, Columbia, Yale Management, UCLA, and USC. Some of these institutions offer Entertainment and Media majors or specializations with courses offered at both the undergraduate and graduate levels.

You, as one of these future marketing professionals, have picked up this book not because you want to know how movies are made—you want to know how *money* is made. In entertainment marketing, we do not make the original content; we *leverage* the original content through any number of products, experiences, sponsorships, licenses, concepts, and opportunities. In this new edition we discuss how each of the entertainment platforms addresses that concept.

But before we do that, let's take a broad look at this amazing business and the challenges you will face.

What Sets Entertainment Marketing Apart?

Ten years ago, it was estimated that the average city-dweller was pummeled with over 3,000 marketing messages per day. In 2007, Yankelovitch Research revised the number upward to 5,000.[4] The increase in technology, the growth of Web-supported ad strategies, and the proliferation of new ways to slap brand messages on every surface available have only added to that load in the last six years.

The simple fact is, the human brain can't keep up with the overload. Keep in mind, this marketing tsunami addresses every product imaginable, from low-cost divorces to high-end jewelry.

There's a *lot* of clutter out there, all of it competing for the consumer's time and pocketbook. But what's your single greatest challenge as an entertainment marketing professional? What makes it necessary for you to cut through all of this in order to reach your target audience—NOW?

Shelf life. The amount of time that your product is relevant.

The average entertainment product is an economic tsetse fly, living and dying in an exceedingly short time span. Although entertainment marketing shares the search for the right medium and consumer connection with its more traditional cousins, the product itself is quite different. Entertainment isn't some*thing*—like a home, a car, a financial institution, or a great restaurant—that can carefully build a relationship with the consumer over years or decades. Entertainment and all of the products associated with it must grab the attention and the wallet of the consumer before that fickle target turns to something else.

Entertainment *content* is based totally on creativity—a story, an action, something ephemeral that stirs the consumer. The creation and distribution of the end result is fraught with peril due to human frailties. Production and release dates can change with the sneeze of a star and require a fine balance of crossed fingers and creative finagling. As in fashion, trends and styles change. With the preproduction planning and strategizing of many forms of entertainment stretching out years before actual release, entertainment producers must strive to catch the wave before it crashes into the cliffs of consumer apathy.

The basis of all decisions rests on the whim of that fickle populace, and keeping in the forefront—especially in this technology-rich age—requires a stiff combination of market research, guts, and just plain luck.

Entertainment *marketing* requires the same focus on grabbing the wind. Rather than simply selling an object, entertainment marketing first focuses on selling an experience, convincing the audience to buy into the event before any sale of objects associated with that encounter can occur. It requires creating Wannasee-Have-to-Go-Have-To-Have in a population that is overwhelmed with choice—including not going at all.

---

[4] Louise Story, "Anywhere the Eye Can See, It's Likely to See an Ad," *New York Times*, January 15, 2007.

So marketing original content is consumed with speed—there is little or no time to test-market before release, before one source or another gets word of the buzz on a project and broadcasts it to the world at large. Every film is a new product, and each one is different: different content, different audiences, different deal structures. There may be two or three—or ten—of these products released every week, yet every campaign must hit the target on the money and on time. With film, any misfire, any hint of bad box office, must be counteracted immediately because the window of first-run distribution is only three to four weeks.

Budgets for initial marketing can be huge—for a film that costs between $50 and $100 million to produce, the average marketing budget is between $25 and $40 million—but the burn rate is extremely high, with much of the budget being spent during the six- to eight-week period just before and during the film's theatrical release dates. The stakes can be as proportionally high for any other fresh-release entertainment product—games, books, or music.

Additionally, the marketing of that original product focuses not only on the initial product itself—the movie, the CD, the program, the sports spectacle—but also on all the associated products spun off through licensing and merchandising. Each original concept can launch billions of dollars in revenue if carefully handled and strategized across all channels. In fact, licensing and merchandising revenue can widely eclipse the revenue brought in by the original event. Licensing is what makes movies the still-reigning champ of the entertainment world, regardless of box-office revenue that looks small in comparison to that of electronic games.

New Channels, New Challenges

Today, technology plays a huge role in the development and distribution of entertainment content. Marketing professionals must not only understand how to manipulate the available platforms; they must also be keenly aware of what technology might come next. Each new step brings scads of disbelievers—*Twitter will never amount to anything*—who may be right about the ability of the product to generate revenue, but deaf, dumb, and blind to the importance of a particular channel in acting as a conduit of influence. (To that point, Twitter-fed griping about the 2012 Olympics actually caused *more* people to tune into NBC's broadcast of the events.)[5]

Let's take a moment to ponder technology platforms in the twenty-first century, if only to understand how fast a new one might arrive.

Marketing to the Mass

Consider this: To have mass marketing, you need to have mass, defined as penetration of at least 50% of the market. When we view the penetration of technology—which can allow for the distribution of our product as well as our messages—we can start to understand just how important keeping an eye on innovation has become.

- Telephones took 35 years to reach 50% of homes.

- Radio took 20 years.

---

[5] "Despite #NBCFail, NBC and Twitter Say Partnership Was Success," *New York Times*, August 22, 2012.

- Television dropped the span to 15 years.

- VCRs ambled in over 8 years.

- Cell phones, 5 years.

- iPods went mass in 2 years.

And from that point on—smartphones, iPads, tablets—the ongoing flood seems never-ending, almost a yearly phenomenon.

The Digital Disruption

As nearly anyone who hasn't been stranded on some frozen tundra or desert island knows, the last decade has been all about the Internet, the phenomenal conduit that has opened the doors to the mass distribution of all digitized media, thereby creating a fertile ground for innovation. But as the invention of gas-powered engines set the mighty railroad industry on its ear, so the new democracy of digital has upended entertainment. We are involved in a disruption of existing entertainment and media business models not seen in hundreds of years, greatly transforming the traditional entertainment platforms and creating new ones.

As Plunkett Research, a firm specializing in the entertainment and media industry, so correctly points out, there are three basic issues related to the control of entertainment content[6]:

1. Pricing for content (including free-of-charge access versus paid, illegal downloads versus authorized downloads, and full ownership of a paid download versus pay-per-view).

2. Portability (including the ability for a consumer to download once and then use a file on multiple platforms and devices, such as tablets and smartphones, or the ability to share a download with friends).

3. Delayed viewing or listening (such as viewing TV programming at the consumer's convenience via TiVo and similar digital video recorders).

It would be nearly impossible to capture all that is happening in this disruption. As soon as we have discussed one platform, set it in stone, and moved on to the next, changes occur that send everything and everyone scurrying around once again. It is our intent, in this discussion, to capture the current situation in each platform as best we can, bringing you up to date to current standards. But be aware: This is a subject you must research every single day...change happens that fast.

Conveyance Versus Content

In a moment, we begin our discussion on the distinct elements that make up the entertainment marketing economy, but we'd like to clarify one thing first. In our industry, it is the *content* that

---

6 Plunkett Research, http://www.plunkettresearch.com/entertainment-media-publishing-market-research/industry-and-business-data.

has value, that can be monetized and extended across platforms. The carriage of that content—as in the Internet, or a broadcast network, or a radio station—is not entertainment. They are conduits by which various products are delivered to devices both fixed and mobile.

In that same regard, social networking applications such as Facebook and Twitter are not entertainment platforms (although many of the discussions that take place there are certainly entertaining). They are conduits that allow marketing professionals to reach audiences. In the case of Facebook, it provides an access point for a wide variety of games but is not a game in and of itself unless you're trying to figure out the latest value of its stock offering.

We will leave it to the social networking experts to discuss why the public seems to love congregating online. In the meantime, we offer discussion on how entertainment platforms are interacting with those sites and using them to monetize content.

We take this same approach with the move toward mobile. Mobile devices are allowing consumers to take their entertainment everywhere and as such are critical to our industry. We discuss how entertainment platforms are taking advantage of this access but leave it to others to define the actual technology behind it.

This evolution of technology carries with it ever-expanding opportunities. The rapid growth of mobile devices gives marketing professionals the ability to reach potential customers right at the moment of the buying decision. Social networking allows for far more buzz (essentially, free marketing) than ever before. All distribution channels and opportunities must be addressed. Marketers must be constantly aware of the demographics involved in every new format.

Technology Trends

From a global perspective, technology has brought massive expansion into new markets. Wireless technology forms the communication backbone in such rising giants as China and India. In many places, these countries have literally skipped the step of telephone lines, creating both a broad network and a consumer base that seems completely tech-savvy.

Data collection has exploded. Today's marketing professionals can reach hairs-width consumer slivers. This requires a thorough knowledge of what those consumers might want, along with a strategy for reaching across all platforms to have the greatest reach.

The great challenge is the public's ability to get far out ahead of any marketing effort. Social networking has made an insider of everyone. With bad buzz on Facebook, Twitter, or any other form of social networking, firestorms are created in a matter of minutes. Disney's 2012, $350 million film *John Carter* was basically dead on opening, with bad news reaching core audiences long before the first ticket was sold. Domestic box office was less than $40 million. Bad news no longer gets hidden in Hollywood, where, in the past, it might have been carefully massaged into something more palatable.

There's No Business Like Show Business

If anything, the rise of technology and the easy, fast reach of connection have created a consumer even more obsessed with stars—and the business itself. Entertainment continues to bring big press, from regular reports of box office revenue to bestseller lists to weekly ratings of network TV shows. All of this—and much more—is explored in the mainstream press, trade publications such as *Variety*, *Hollywood Reporter*, *Billboard*, *Broadcast & Cable*, *Electronic Media*, and hundreds of other magazines, websites, blogs, and Twitter feeds examining every aspect of each of the sectors.

And lest you think it's all about digital, old platforms still have an impact. Award shows, not within the control of the marketer, can still make or break entertainment products, at least in the longer term. The profitability—or failure—of a film, an album, or a Broadway show can still rest on the opening of an envelope one evening each spring.

So here we are in the twenty-first century, in a world well-schooled in the pleasures of in-home, out-of-home, and self-created entertainment, surrounded by a population that knows it runs the show. The marketing professional of today operates in an industry consumed by louder, faster, bigger, and brighter, attempting to reach an audience on choice overload. The global desire for entertainment requires a universal understanding of the language needed to promote the product, both locally and internationally.

In short, entertainment marketing is not a career for the indecisive, the incompatible, or the inexperienced. With over a trillion dollars in total revenue at stake, today's entertainment marketing professional must be fully aware of the mistakes of the past and the opportunities of the future to produce something extraordinary.

A Marketer's Manifesto

We, as marketing professionals, live in an age of seemingly unlimited reach and ever-more-specific information, with amazing new conduits to reach our target audience. But this cornucopia comes with a price.

We no longer have the luxury of a mass audience.

We must now understand every possible segment, every possible target, to reach an audience compatible with, or interested in, a given entertainment product while competing against a myriad of possibilities.

We must leverage original content in as many ways as possible to create the income streams that keep the industry healthy and happy. To do this, we must go the full length and extension of every possible tactic to make sure that the entertainment the customer is consuming is *ours*.

We must keep pace with constant innovation. We must understand and use every tool available to build the highest degree of loyalty and expand our share of mind and pocketbook to the greatest percentage possible. We must use all distribution platforms, all devices, and know how to connect all of them for the greatest exposure.

And in this new arena, once we achieve that loyalty, that share, we can *never* take it for granted. We live in a world of ever-shifting attention spans, with every new entertainment product competing with one another for a finite amount of time and money.

We face a *lifetime* marketing challenge, one that requires not only the classic reminder, but a constant catering, stroking, and branding whenever possible in order to make the content desirable and of value in the selection process.

Be warned: If you think the entertainment industry is a glitzy, fun business, full of ski-slope weekends and fabulous meetings with moguls, you're right—for one-tenth of one percent of the industry population. For everyone else, it's a shin-skinning climb up a greased power-pyramid, each and every one of the contestants willing to do what it takes to get to the top. Life at the top is high-stakes, high-speed, and high-risk—and for very few, high-rewards.

Still want to take the ride? Well, buckle up.

1

Begin with the Basics: The What and Where of Entertainment Marketing

Entertainment marketing, regardless of which platform we discuss, has some commonality with other industries. Licensing, merchandising, sponsorship, brand extension—all of these occur elsewhere, no matter what the product might be...that is, if you're fully exploiting the profit potential of your product.

However, entertainment has some unique properties that affect the use and distribution of the brand. Before we go deeper into the unique worlds of each entertainment platform, let's discuss the common threads that tie them all together.

The Four Cs

The structure that defines the whole of the entertainment industry can be described in four words, all of which begin with the letter "C":

- **Content:** The *actual entertainment product*, from the initial idea to the finished offering, always creative-driven or -derived and occasionally manipulated with technology. The book, movie, song, game, experience—even a software package from the likes of Microsoft—ready to be delivered to the consumer.

- **Conduit:** The *pipe* through which the entertainment product flows to get to the customer: coaxial cable, Ethernet, Wi-Fi, television receive-only (TVRO) dish, ultra high frequency (UHF), very high frequency (VHF), digital transmission, the Internet. These pipes are not limited to electronics. In the entertainment world, product also flows to the customer through movie theaters, arenas, stages, or brand experiences—anything that carries the product to the audience.

- **Consumption:** The form in which the consumer actually makes use of the product: the digital-download, CD, DVD, smartphone, tablet, personal computer, application, film, Internet-protocol (IP) enabled high-definition television, set-top box, the written page, or the live event.

- **Convergence:** The coming together of technology that enables the consumption of entertainment across multiple screens and venues, fed by digital transmission. Compressed data streaming everywhere, downloadable and consumable over a variety of devices. This might take place with an application that allows you to download a movie and send it to all of your devices—smartphone, PC, HDTV. Or in a digitally enabled theater, where you watch a live performance of the Metropolitan Opera while listening through the earbuds on your iPhone.

Each of the four Cs stands alone yet is fed by the others. Each of them offers a way to further exploit the initial idea, transforming that original thought into a product, a business, or a saleable commodity. Each involves some type of transaction with the consumer that calls for a well-developed, fully executable marketing strategy that will allow for the full capitalization of the idea.

The entertainment industry has a huge stake in each and every one of the Cs. Therefore, entertainment *marketing* must fully focus on

- What the consumer ultimately watches / listens to / reads / experiences

- What form the content takes to be consumed

- What conduit the consumer chooses

- What mix of technology and media the consumer might use to create his or her own personal experience

Think of it this way: It isn't just the movie. It's the consumer seeing it in a theater, on a DVD, via premium cable, or downloading it to a tablet. Or buying the electronic game based on it. Or purchasing the newly released Kindle version of the original book.

Entertainment is a hugely diverse industry with an equally huge opportunity to create income streams. And the marketing of that entertainment is the key to the vault. However, there is one huge challenge facing the entertainment marketing professional, a factor that is different from other industries: perishability.

Lightning in a Bottle

Entertainment is a luxury, not a necessity. Movies won't give you a dependable ride to work, and a downloaded song won't feed your family for a week. People will only consume entertainment when they have time, money, and the desire to do so. That desire comes about through any number of variables, but once it's there, you'd better deliver—*now*. Entertainment must be available to the public when the public wants it, not a minute sooner or a second later.

It is this perishability that poses the biggest challenge to the industry. Trends in automobiles or home furnishings—large investments—may ebb and flow over several years. Those industries can follow a linear path in the life of a product, taking more time to create the new version, model, style. Entertainment? Today's hot thing can be cold as a clam tomorrow. The consuming public is fickle, so if you want to take advantage of their interest, you need to mobilize *all* your forces immediately.

This wasn't always so. In the early days of mass entertainment, when a much smaller investment might have been at stake, products were often carefully nurtured, strategies tested and retested. But in today's incredibly fast-paced world—with consumers tweeting, YouTube-ing, and texting their opinions—managing buzz is like holding on to a lightning bolt. Every entertainment product is in a race to the finish line from the moment the light goes green.

That "wanna-see, wanna-read, wanna-watch, gotta-hear" marketing produced for the launch of a product can mark the difference between success and failure. To grab the public's interest, the promotions that create these compelling messages cannot wait until the launch of the product. They must simultaneously weave in and out throughout the process of production, distribution, and consumer transaction.

And, all of this must happen at every step of every extension of the brand to fully maximize the product's potential. Again, it isn't just the movie (song, book, team, electronic game); every other product associated with or spun off from the movie (song, book, team, electronic game) must be addressed as well.

So where do we start the process of creating entertainment? With *content*.

The First C: Content

If marketing is the key, content is the coin. *All* entertainment starts with content. The term "content" covers everything that happens to produce the actual entertainment product that is ultimately delivered to the consumer in one form or another.

Even though the *idea* for content might possibly come from the mind of one person, it takes an army of dedicated professionals to craft that idea into a product that hits the market at just the right time, in just the right form, with exactly the right buzz to grab the lion's share of the consumer's disposable income and discretionary time.

Creating content is a multilayered process, much like an onion. Like said onion, it's hard to peel one bit without grabbing part of the next, but in general, there are four elements in content, regardless of which sector of entertainment we're discussing. They include

- The development of a *creative idea* to prime the pump or start the production process

- The endorsement and utilization of *technology* to help complete the production

- The use of *talent* to act in or flesh out the idea and make it work

- The *perishability* of the product, given, as discussed, that time is always of the essence due to changes in consumer trends and tastes.

Planting the Seed: The Creative Idea

Without Walt Disney's initial creation of Mickey Mouse, there would be no Disneyland, Walt Disney World, Tokyo Disney, EuroDisney, Disney Cruise Line, Disney on Broadway, Disney books, videos, games, T-shirts, coffee mugs, designer furniture, stuffed animals, or Disney Happy Meal toys. Somewhere along the line, there has to be the heart of the movie, the book, the script, the score—the creative idea. Oh, and if there's a cute little furry something that can be morphed into a billion products, so much the better.

In today's entertainment world, the creative product is often an outgrowth of a strategic research process that has minutely identified a market, like a vein of ore waiting to be mined. The strategic development (SD) team at any major entertainment provider is often the initiator of what will ultimately become a new product or destination. Millions of dollars and thousands of hours might have been invested in a concept long before the actual creative process fully begins. SD, which typically has a full-time staff as well as outside consultants, carefully examine the market demographics, competition, impact on brand identity, development cost, and ultimate return on investment in a search for new revenue streams.

This initial investment, however, does not guarantee that a product will ever come to market. More often than not, a concept is shelved when the idea being researched proves to be either unprofitable or not profitable enough. Disney, for example, believes that a new product line (for example, a Disney Theatrical Group or Cruise Line) must ultimately become a billion-dollar—that's right, billion with a "b"—revenue stream to be seriously considered. Although some products and concepts might be launched because they extend the brand equity, each project is minutely researched and can even come to fruition in terms of a product rollout, only to be shuttered if full-profit expectations are not met.

But none of this investment—either from a strategic development perspective or the simple act of a singular idea that slips in as a no-brainer product—would be worth a cent if it could not be protected in some way. Thus, we come to the most important aspect of content: the ability to legally protect it and to create ownership.

The process of establishing ownership is known as *copyright*.

Copyright

In the late 1970s, when the movie industry finally awoke from its glitz-induced slumber (probably aided by the sound of a thousand MBAs thundering up the road, swarming to save several bankrupt studios from complete annihilation), the new business-based management focused its full concentration on copyright. The bottom line was this: Without copyright, there is no entertainment industry—for there is no legally protectable product that can be bought, sold, licensed, leveraged, extended, and otherwise shaken by the ankles until every penny drops out of its pockets into the hands of the investors.

This focus on copyright dovetailed with the passage of the Copyright Act of 1976, which gave creators and their assignees exclusive rights to reproduce, distribute, and make the most of other uses of their original works. With the passage of this act, made necessary by changes in technology and global usage, copyright also applied to much more than traditional writings; it now protected motion pictures, videotapes, sound recordings, computer programs, databases, and many other original creations, including artwork and sculpture. Additionally, certain works were now exempted from copyright protection—in particular, works of the U.S. government.

As a result, contracts flowing from within all areas of the entertainment world now contain phrases such as "intellectual property," "work product," and "work for hire." All of these terms define the who, when, why, and where of idea or concept ownership—that an idea itself can be owned by a person or an entity (and not necessarily by the actual creator of the same), and therefore not copied in any form or fashion by anyone else—including that creator—either for fun or for profit.

The ownership of ideas and concepts is a complex and important subject, given copyright allows for the syndication of TV shows, the licensing of brands, the sale of sports paraphernalia, or the inclusion of comic book characters on lunchboxes (or in mega-blockbuster movies and their endless string of sequels). Creativity might be the soul of entertainment, but copyright is the key to the cash.

The exploding growth of global entertainment creates new challenges to face in this area. Although digital streaming has allowed for faster transmission to markets around the world, it has also opened the doors to piracy. Copyright is recognized in the courts of many established countries, but emerging markets often lie outside those confines. In addition, the Internet has created a country of its own—the Wild Web—where nearly anything goes. Entertainment companies must be constantly on the alert for those who would steal their protected content and bootleg it.

From a marketing perspective, the ballyhoo has already begun at the creative stage of content—whether it's news about what major star has been signed for what upcoming blockbuster movie, which must-read author has holed up to pen another tale, what software giant is working on the latest version of the hottest game—the machine is cranked up to whet the consumer's appetite. This part of the campaign might be relatively low-key—a PR placement here or there, a one-sentence insertion in *People,* a small post on Facebook—in case the project takes a turn.

Now that the creative and copyright elements have joined together to begin the content process, the product must now be filmed, animated, scripted, recorded, promoted, and shipped out the door to be experienced by the customer. So on to the next layer of the onion.

Production

The production phase includes everything it takes to produce the best book, movie, home video, downloadable song, network TV or cable show, radio program, electronic game, or any other of a myriad of packaged or preproduced entertainment products. This would include the launch of a new ride or exhibit at a theme park, the completion of a state-of-the-art movie, or the final burnishing of live theater.

Again, this is not linear—the project can swing back and forth from the creative stage to production throughout these first two steps, whether for rewrites, legal challenges, or a change in players. This can be especially true concerning shifts in talent in film, given that each new player who comes to the table might require a slightly different approach to his or her character—and that character's interaction with other characters—both of which are highly dependent on that new player's position in the Hollywood pecking order.

Marketing is in serious swing by this point in the project, especially as production moves closer to release. The idea is to build up the desire of the public to see/hear/read the product so that by the time it's finally poured into its respective conduit, the public is in a lather, waiting at the other end to be showered with the latest release.

The Second C: Conduit

Conduit, the distribution of an entertainment product in a high-tech age, refers to two elements of the delivery process: the where and the how. In simple terms, the conduit is the actual process by which a product is distributed, as opposed to the consumption (coming later in this chapter), which is the final form in which the consumer receives the product. For example, think of a theater as the conduit and the exhibition of a movie as the consumable.

Ten years ago, when we wrote the first edition of this book, we wrote—with great sagacity—that big box retail was the big winner in the race for retail, severely damaging the Mom and Pop Shops. We believed that only the big chains would succeed with a public that wanted more, faster, at less cost.

Though we were smart enough to make a few prognostications on the Internet that did come to pass, we stand amazed by the speed at which this conduit has changed the industry. Tower Records? Virgin Records? Gone. Barnes and Noble? Still hanging on by its fingertips, but the competition—Borders Books—gone. Even Loews and the other theater chains are doing their best to keep people coming to the movies instead of waiting for the movies to come to them.

In their place we have Amazon.com, not only selling books by the zillions, but *publishing* them, both hardcover and Kindle versions. iTunes owns the music download business. Netflix is busy tucking everyone into their home media rooms with pay-for-play movies, broadcast network series, cable programs, and now, their own original content. Digital transmission, streaming away, is putting a whole new spin on all forms of retail, and UPS is having a field day.

The Internet has brought innovation to every corner of our lives, changing the way we do business, learn, and communicate in a profound manner. We have yet to know the full scope of its impact. But as we've said: the Internet is not entertainment. It's just another pipe. A really amazing pipe with an incredible reach, but a pipe, nonetheless.

Of course, the old conduits are still in place—movie multiplexes, broadcast and cable television, live theater, radio, satellite dish, direct marketing catalogs—and still deliver the lion's share of content to the consumer. But the Internet is more than a technology shift; it's a lifestyle shift, so we have yet to see how any or all of these traditional delivery systems morph.

The Third C: Consumption

The consumption phase is the point at which the finished entertainment product has been offered to the public. Effective advertising, as part of a fully integrated marketing program, results in a transaction—someone paying for and consuming the product. The consumption phase is when the marketing rubber really hits the road, where the marketing executive depends on his or her ability to successfully lure the consumer.

The transaction could be buying a ticket at the local cinema; viewing episodes of a TV series on Netflix; listening to satellite radio; clicking the channels on a set-top box; downloading a book to a Kindle, Nook, or iPad; or for the old-fashioned, purchasing a book at a local bookstore. Or it could be a visit to a live concert, where 100,000 fans are motivated emotionally and physically by pulsating laser lights, incredibly loud music, and the sense of sharing it all with their fellow devotees.

In the U.S., there are five major television broadcasting networks,[1] 1,781 television stations,[2] 280 cable networks,[3] 39,000 movie screens,[4] 15,256 radio stations,[5] 13,000 newspapers,[6] and 24,000 magazines[7] for people to consume. There are hundreds of electronic games, both hard copy and mobile. We have yet to identify the number of new, old, and classic CDs, books, newsletters, live concerts, Broadway shows, off-Broadway shows, summer theaters, nightclubs, and theme parks to enable the consumer to feed his or her entertainment habit.

The typical American annually watches 1560 hours of television (across all platforms),[8] listens to 880 hours of radio,[9] and spends 176 hours reading newspapers[10] and 120 hours reading magazines.[11] We are a consumer society, and we consume entertainment with abandon across a wide variety of platforms and technology.

But the most important point? *It's all available at the same time.*

This is the underlying challenge of entertainment marketing. Your target consumer is not simply waiting around for your product. Your consumer has literally thousands of entertainment choices to fill his or her time with. You are competing with each and every one of them, all the time.

After work and sleep, consumers have roughly 62 hours per week to spend on anything else—including entertainment. You are competing for every single second of that discretionary time.

And what's driving the number of consumer choices through the roof?

The Fourth C: Convergence

From both technology and content standpoints, convergence is the true wave of the present and the future. Convergence is the coming together of technology that enables the consumption of entertainment across multiple screens and venues, fed by digital transmission and compressed data streaming, which is downloadable and consumable over a variety of devices. This convergence has created a boom in the marketing of entertainment, and it has made the consumer king (or queen).

---

[1] http://benton.org/node/65435.

[2] http://transition.fcc.gov/Daily_Releases/Daily_Business/2013/db0412/DOC-320138A1.pdf.

[3] www.ncta.com/About/About/HistoryofCableTelevision.aspx.

[4] www.natoonline.org/statisticsscreens.htm.

[5] http://transition.fcc.gov/Daily_Releases/Daily_Business/2013/db0412/DOC-320138A1.pdf.

[6] www.stanford.edu/group/ruralwest/cgi-bin/drupal/visualizations/us_newspapers.

[7] www.magazine.org/insights-resources/research-publications/trends-data/magazine-industry-facts-data/1998-2010-number.

[8] http://blog.nielsen.com/nielsenwire/online_mobile/report-how-americans-are-spending-their-media-time-and-money/.

[9] www.radioinsights.com/2010/04/how-much-do-people-listen.html.

[10] http://paidcontent.org/2011/04/29/419-infographic-how-print-vs-online-news-consumption-compares/.

[11] http://techcrunch.com/2010/12/15/time-mobile-newspapers/.

According to Nielsen research, Americans spend more than 41 hours per week watching video across the screens.[12] But how they're consuming content—traditional TV and otherwise—is changing. Demonstrating that consumers are increasingly making Internet connectivity a priority, 75.3% pay for broadband Internet (up from 70.9% last year); 90.4% pay for cable, telephone company-provided TV, or satellite. Homes with both paid TV and broadband increased 5.5% between December of 2011 and December of 2012. This number continues to rise in 2013.[13]

At the heart of convergence is the ability to create, transmit, and capture all information—movies, art, music, news—in a digital format. After that information has been reduced to the ones and zeroes of the digital world, it can be transmitted over any available form of the latest technology via satellite broadcast or cable transmission. Wired or wireless, the ability to move information fluidly from point to point has created a new world of information, entertainment, and services.

With thousands of choices at their fingertips, fed through any number of devices, consumers now fully control their entertainment options. They decide what, when, and how. Gone are the days where a studio could assume that consumers will go to a theater to watch the latest release. Theaters are still holding their own, but there is a growing segment of the market who is happy to wait for the premium cable or Netflix release to view a movie in the comfort of their own super-charged media rooms, with mega-sized HD-3D TV, surround sound, theater-style seating, and really great popcorn (with real butter). Or on their tablet. Or on their smartphone.

Note that the consumer is still paying for the movie. The transaction is still taking place, but the venues and devices have changed, which opens whole new fields of discovery and opportunity for the entertainment marketing professional.

What does all of this mean to the entertainment world, outside of the ability to move content digitally? Most important is the variety of conduit channels that are now available. As a simple example, consider the following statement: "I watched ESPN last night." The entertainment marketing professional has to ask: Were you watching ESPN or ESPN2? Were you watching it on your television, or were you viewing it on a closed-circuit broadcast at the ESPN Zone down the street? Or were you viewing it on espn.com? On what? Television? Smartphone? Tablet? Laptop? And how? Via the Internet (either wired or wireless) or mobile?

Oh, and what other technology were you connected to while you were watching? Were you texting? Tweeting? Emailing? On Facebook, "liking" what you were watching, along with the rest of your friends?

Have I managed to reach you? The entertainment marketer ponders this question and more, trying to find the very best way to the pocketbook of that overloaded consumer. Riding the waves of discretionary time, disposable income, and expanding technologies, marketing teams must build brands, develop audience awareness, create need versus want, and leverage the brand to the *n*th degree, utilizing every avenue possible to create an ongoing income stream.

---

[12] "Free to Move Between Screens, The Cross Platform Report", Nielsen, March 2013

[13] http://blog.nielsen.com/nielsenwire/online_mobile/report-how-americans-are-spending-theirmedia-time-and-money

In fulfilling that mission, billions of dollars are spent to reach that coveted consumer (see Exhibit 1-1).

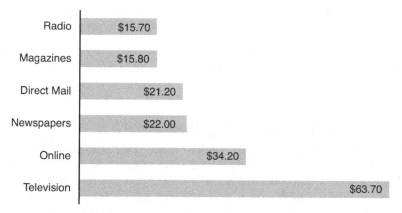

Source: Barclays Capital I Internet Data Book January 2011

Exhibit 1-1 Estimated media spending in billions

Do take note: Television spending is still—by a long shot—the big winner. The Internet is coming on strong, but it will take a bit more time to have the reach of TV. But another up-and-coming challenger is on its way. Mobile advertising topped $4 billion in 2012 and is expected to exceed $7 billion in 2013. If this trend continues, it may hit $21 billion by 2016.[14]

This is the heart and soul of entertainment marketing: identifying unmet needs; producing products and services to meet those needs; and pricing, distributing, and promoting those products and services to produce a profit.[15]

Successful marketing is the product of a carefully orchestrated attack, and often in today's entertainment industry, that attack comes from a multitude of directions, stretching the brand—the original idea, the original content—into a variety of products and revenue streams. Those streams spread across a wide web, producing returns at all levels, in all dimensions:

- **The marketing of the original content:** The movie, the book, the song, the game.

- **The development of the relationship between the consumer and the original content that helps to sell another product:** The sale of a McDonald's Happy Meal, driven by the *Finding Nemo* toy inside.

---

[14] www.emarketer.com/newsroom/index.php/unexpected-growth-facebook-google-lead-significant-uptick-mobile-advertising-us-market-share/

[15] This is opposed to advertising, which is a paid form of communicating a message by the use of various media, generally persuasive in nature, or public relations, which is a form of communication primarily directed toward gaining public understanding and acceptance, usually dealing with issues rather than products or services.

- **The utilization of marketing within the media:** The creators who make money from the original concept; the cohort that makes money from retailing (the toy company that makes the *Nemo* toy and McDonald's selling the Happy Meal); and the conduits that charge to carry the content and extract a fee from consumers to consume it (cable companies, Netflix, and so on). These are the people who *remonetize* the original content.

- **The use of entertainment to sell new hardware:** Hardware allows entertainment to be used anywhere, at any time, by any consumer, in any form that they want: televisions, tablets, smartphones, laptops.

Licensing, Merchandising, and Sponsorship

Whatever the approach, the ultimate payoff of this synergy is the creation of the three most conspicuous revenue streams evolving directly from the entertainment and media businesses: licensing, merchandise retailing, and sponsorship. Each acts not only as a revenue stream, but also as a marketing strategy—marketing that more than pays for itself. As always, there are several ways to measure the success of these supplementary revenues, either as separate categories related to the entertainment and media sectors or as a percentage of all sales, both domestic and international.

For example, worldwide licensing in 2010 was estimated at more than $192 billion.[16] Although this total represents a wide variety of market segments, entertainment companies rank high in the listings of the top 125 Global Licensors. Consider the estimated revenue licensing brings to the following entertainment brands, as shown in Exhibit 1-2:

Exhibit 1-2   Entertainment Licensing Revenue

Company	Revenue
Disney Consumer Products	$37.5 Billion
Mattel	$7 Billion
Warner Bros. Consumer Products	$6 Billion
Nickelodeon Consumer Products	$5.5 Billion
Major League Baseball	$5 Billion
National Football League	$3.25 Billion
DreamWorks	$3 Billion
LucasFilm	$3 Billion
National Basketball Association	$3 Billion
Cartoon Network Enterprises	$2.9 Billion
Twentieth Century Fox Consumer Products	$2.2 Billion

Source: *License!Global* magazine, May 2012.

Consider this: Licensing is profit, pure and simple. When the lawyers have agreed on terms, the money flows back to the owner, with no other real investment.

---

[16] *License!Global* magazine, May 2012.

Synergy also happens through deals with companies outside the parent company's umbrella. Additional licensing can come from other forms, including household products, general merchandise, packaged goods, private-label store brands, and fashion designers.

In fact, the fashion industry is often represented as a close cousin to the entertainment industry. Fashion shows are staged like Broadway opening nights, with fabulous sets and the most current hit music driving the display of beautiful models—some of whom eventually realize their ambition to act in major motion pictures. The fashion business has also been well-integrated into the media, as it uses public relations, music videos, magazine covers, and product placement to burnish the brand—while adding to the bottom-line profitability of the entertainment product being utilized.

Fashion circles back around to join the entertainment industry in the growth of entertainment-related sponsorship sales. We find fashion icons like Hilfiger, Lauren, and Armani sponsoring major music concerts, film premiers, sports contests, product placement within network TV and cable shows, film festivals, and Broadway openings.

Continuing in a synergistic vein, consider the liquor, soft drink beverage, and fast food industries, which are certainly interested in their stockholders' satisfaction and aggressively chase sponsorship and its important promotion subset, product tie-ins.

Most important, revenue from licensed products can cover the sins of box office failures, protect the funds needed to invest in new properties, and maintain shareholder value in a highly volatile and competitive segment of the world economy.

Another lesson to be learned from this group of self-promoting, income-generating vehicles is that licensing, merchandising, and sponsorship have the added benefit of being marketing tactics in and of themselves. Any marketing professional alive would give a year's salary to have millions of consumers wearing his or her brand to schools, to the park on weekends, while shopping in the malls, lying on sheets, using towels, drinking from glasses—all with brand reminders. The buying and wearing of licensed products promotes the movie, the series, the team. They also look good on special-events ties, T-shirts, and expensive jackets. These products are live billboards that provide an implied endorsement, maintaining brand awareness and credibility.

Branding is a serious program and a commercial support system that is well worth the planning and involvement of marketing teams that can envision the future, even in the face of artistic criticism. Herein lies the separation between the art film or independent movie made as a statement of the director's life view as contrasted with a film that is made for pure mass audience engagement with the prospect of a huge return on investment.

But branding is not only about momentary profits—it is a long-term strategy that can pay off handsomely over the years. A classic brand, sustained for 30 or 50 years, still as fresh and productive as when it was first invented, is a perfect example of value in equity. Franchises like Peanuts, Superman, Batman, and yes, all those Disney characters (we know you're tired of hearing about Disney, but did you notice who the gorilla at the top of that chart was?) are often the pillars of major media companies, or at least the support of a division. They can be expected to perform financially every time they are brought out and relaunched for a new audience.

The good times will continue to roll as long as there is disposable income to fuel the purchases and discretionary time to enjoy the ever-growing portfolio of entertainment choices. Although movies themselves may be a relatively small part of the overall revenue stream in the entertainment industry, films are still the center of the entertainment universe, creating the launch pad for the remaining platforms: video, retail, DVD, books, magazines, electronic games, and more.

Now that we've defined the structure—on with the show!

Summary

Content, conduit, consumption, and convergence: These four elements form the basic structure of all entertainment products. However, because entertainment is generally based on a creative idea, the glue that binds the industry together is copyright, which gives the content-holder the ability to create protectable revenue streams, such as licensing and sponsorship based on the product.

2

Getting the Product to Market: Who and How

In an industry that depends not only on getting to market before a trend has passed—and in some cases, even creating the trend in the first place—what does it take to create big box office, platinum records, bestsellers, and all the associated revenue streams attached to that original content?

The usual marketing questions are all present: where to market the product and to whom; how to price, package, and position; when to introduce the product; how to communicate the product's values, benefits, and availability.

But as discussed earlier, in entertainment the cycle is condensed. Entertainment products are of the moment. They are not investments, like cars or furniture. They are not consumables, like detergent or toothpaste. They are seasonal only from the perspective of blockbusters for the summer or family movie for the holidays. The content is ever-changing and, when successful, ever-growing.

This chapter examines what it takes to bring an entertainment product to market in today's world and the people and players who drive this enormous business.

Molding the Message

If entertainment itself can be broken into four Cs, the entertainment hierarchy can be defined by three Ps: people, power, and players.

Although many of the broad issues in the entertainment industry are the same as they might be in almost any business, the speed at which a product must be delivered, coupled with the budgets associated with the product, demand that hundreds of dots be connected in a very short time span. That level of play requires the power to make things happen, and people willing to do what it takes to make them happen in time.

With no creative production lines and no linear progression from start to finish, marketing must ride the development process, supporting all the products associated with the core content: soundtracks, electronic games, theatrical scripts, licensed merchandise—any intellectual property that will put the original product into the black. The marketing message must maintain crystal-clear consistency to reach these goals. Even the aspiring actor sweating under the Orlando sun inside a theme park character costume must deliver an experience that is harmonious with the consumer's expectation.

Entertainment starts as a momentary fancy in the public's imagination; the role of marketing is to carefully feed and water that fancy until it grows into something much larger, more extendable, and more profitable.

In most industries, marketing decisions are based on deep and thorough research, tied into short- and long-term planning objectives. Strategic planners have reams of data on what the other guys are doing, how the market is responding, what price points have been covered, market saturation, and how this year's new product introduction will open the door for something slightly more radical next year.

Although research plays a part in entertainment development, the entertainment marketing executive must understand the public's tastes and be able to guess where those tastes may be heading—often in the face of research or precedents that might say otherwise. After all, data doesn't become data until after a trend begins. Entertainment must exploit new veins while mining old ones.

The executive must know in his or her gut when to give the green light, that final nod of approval—knowing full well that his or her head may roll if that gut feeling is wrong. The associated marketing campaign must absolutely recognize all the factors, all the trends, and all the tastes to best position and promote the product while the product is still in the content phase. A wrong decision can destroy a major asset and the millions or billions of dollars in goodwill developed over decades.

Even as the core content is undergoing this gut-wrenching ride, the associated products—that which will feed the revenue streams—must undergo the very same rollercoaster. Missing the opportunity at the wrong time of the year—say, Christmas—can leave a gaping hole in the company's balance sheet.

Finally, the marketing of entertainment demands an approach that is entertaining in and of itself. Entertainment and marketing have become so incredibly intertwined that it is almost impossible to separate one from the other. Consider this: What is a T-shirt with the name of the latest hot band printed across the front? Is it a promotional item, or an extension of a revenue stream?

In the Good Old Days...

Regardless of the industry, product, or service, marketing is about brand development, customers, and matching one to another while motivating the prospects to make a purchase decision. This has been the province of traditional companies—the Coca-Colas, Fords, and Apples—throughout the twentieth century.

During most of this time—certainly up until the 1970s—entertainment remained a cottage industry developed by entrepreneurs and wheeler-dealers who had little use for marketing, other than an add-on when a film was ready for release. They spent money only on product production and the sales representatives they needed to close the deal and gain distribution. Entertainment and media had several things in common, but most importantly, they were all experiential businesses, simply giving the customers a good time or a break from their everyday problems.

This was relatively easy because the competition for discretionary time and disposable income was fairly uncomplicated. A simple announcement or awareness campaign would sell out movie tickets, sports events, rock concerts, Broadway shows, and most other entertainment options. The three television networks made channel switching a minor issue, and counter-programming was but a twinkle in the strategist's eye.

But in the middle of the twentieth century, the entertainment and media world took on a new look, with major corporations or investment groups buying up well-known studio brands that had struggled and were experiencing hard times. Some were bought for the glamour of the name. Some were bought for the real estate the studio was built on. The film libraries of these studios were of lesser concern—after all, the only way to remonetize those movies was to ship them off to the Million Dollar Movie, shown at 10:30 p.m. in metro marketplaces. There were no VCRs, DVDs, tablets, smartphones, or cable networks.

Yet.

By the early 1980s, a huge shift had begun to take place. Major brands gave the entertainment industry access to a world market. Competition between products and leisure services began to intensify as the consumer's available time became more compressed. A cultural revolution was opening the pocketbooks of women and teens. The need to refine the marketing strategy within the various entertainment niches became more apparent as more products competed for the same dollars.

Vive La Revolution!

Entertainment executives, eager to hold on to and increase their market share, overcame their earlier reluctance to expend time and resources on marketing. The pendulum now swung to enormous advertising and promotion budgets to attract and motivate consumer purchases.

Today, studios with 12 to 15 films releasing in one year mount a marketing war chest of $500 to $750 million. They work with leading global advertising agencies or media buying services, supported by in-company creative units and directed by experienced marketing professionals.

Television networks have also thrown their hats into the marketing fray. Having for years relied on free or unused airtime on their own networks to promote new programs, research showed that this form of promotion simply spoke to the same committed network viewers. Marketing plans for networks began to include the previously unmentionable or impossible idea of using print advertising in newspapers, magazines, TV guides, or even TV listing pages in local tabloids. They then expanded to using cable, outdoor billboards, and the ubiquitous subway and bus posters, where millions of urban workers spend their transport time to and from work.

Magazines, already in partnership with advertising agencies and advertisers, took some of their own marketing advice and developed dual-strategy marketing campaigns: one for the consumer to build awareness of upcoming magazine issues and the other directed at the business community to announce growing circulations. This enhanced the quality of their reader demographics in terms of age, family size, income, and even spending habits. Marketing campaigns based on special promotions encouraged readership trials.

Even cable TV, long a free-rider on network TV's coattails, came to the conclusion that effective marketing was necessary to brand new channels, build awareness, and stand out from a universe of exploding channel growth—hundreds of choices and still counting.

Radio, sports venues, electronic games, theme parks, blockbuster books, and unique imprints all rapidly joined this entertainment marketing revolution. Budgets expanded and new, sometimes outrageous themes and tactics were implemented to stand out in this fast-paced, perishable world of glamour, glitz, and blockbuster entertainment.

As all of this rolled along, the companies themselves became blockbusters, sprawling concerns stuffed with synergistic opportunities. The idea of using other media to market one's core concept grew into owning that other media, using it in the ever-widening battle for the consumer.

Super-Size Me

Today, in the place of the old-time studios, we have mega-entertainment and media companies built and nourished to capture every possible penny connected with their intellectual property. With this new beast came a breakthrough in marketing, a strategy known as *integrated communications*, which calls for all the various tactics in the brand or company's portfolio to work together under one umbrella strategy.

Originally, this approach meant that classic advertising—television, cable, radio, outdoor, direct marketing, sales promotion, public relations, yellow pages, skywriting—all worked in tandem and stayed on point toward the ultimate brand message. This was employed as the marketing machinery turned on behind studio films, major television shows, the launch of new electronic games and consoles such as PlayStations 1,2,3, Xbox, and Wii. The marketing of the brand or content continued throughout each of the windows: home video, premium cable, network TV, streaming video, Internet portals—and international repeats of these domestic windows. A whole marketing universe opened, extending the life of the otherwise perishable product for years.

Then came another breakthrough. The brand handlers (managers and chief marketing officers) found that content sectors such as animation, action adventure, and certain dramatic series could go *beyond* the windows of basic distribution and consumer consumption. These onscreen (large and small) brands could morph into games, books, toys, clothing, theme park rides, ice shows, Broadway events, and myriad products frequently manufactured offshore, creating tsunami of gain and profit. The revenue from these products was and is difficult to collect as data, but the revenue has a huge impact on the bottom lines of the media conglomerates and their suppliers.

The outcome of this strategy might be known as *compounded marketing*, given that it has the same effect as compounded interest, forever growing against the principal—in this case, the original content.

Today's mega-company looks something like what you see in Exhibit 2-1.

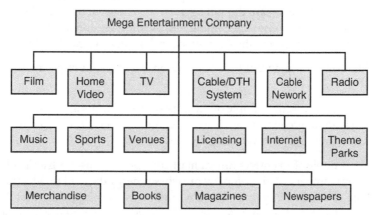

Exhibit 2-1 Mega-company structure

How does this come to be? Let's use Viacom as an example.

First, start with a chain of movie theaters for stability, then add a movie studio, a book publishing company, a cable operator (with several major cable programmers), and a leading video retailer. Next, sell off the cable franchises, add a retail store, close the retail store, acquire a national radio network. Add a billboard company and get a television network in the bargain. Sell off the textbook division of the publisher, trigger the option on acquiring the majority share of another television network, and then grab a wrestling franchise and incorporate it under the programming umbrella. Then go after a major studio in a world-class hostile takeover and add another publisher as part of the deal.

Viacom became a mega-entertainment company, owning Paramount Studios, CBS, MTV, Nickelodeon, and BET, among a raft of other acquisitions. This was big news back in 2002 when we published *The Entertainment Marketing Revolution*. But in true mega-entertainment company style, the show wasn't over yet.

In 2005, Viacom, interested in giving some oomph to a stagnating stock price, announced that it would spin off parts of the company. CBS Corporation would now own the CBS television network, CBS Radio, Showtime, CBS Outdoor, CBS Distribution, and Simon and Schuster. The new version of Viacom would own MTV, BET, Nickelodeon, and Paramount. Two rival executives, Les Moonves and Tom Freston, were put in charge of the two new companies, Moonves with CBS Corporation and Freston with Viacom.

It was thought that CBS would be the "slow growth" wallflower of the two, with the assumption being that cable would grab ratings share. But through retransmission, licensing, and great programming moves—with such hit series as *Survivor* and all the various *CSI* franchises—CBS and Moonves became the wunderkinds.

The other piece—the new Viacom—lost its way. Freston didn't do well in this spinoff. Only eight months into his tenure, he failed to purchase MySpace, which was snatched up by Rupert

Murdoch's News Corporation for $580 million, instead of the $500 million Viacom might have taken it for earlier. Freston's head rolled. Changes at the executive suite left management to newbies. The new management team did not aggressively continue their marketing posture and lacked clarity on their audience segments, muddying the message and losing viewers, while their competition—Cartoon Network and the Disney Channel mainly—came charging up from behind.

MySpace? Sold by News Corp. in 2012 for $35 million. Mr. Freston might have gotten one last laugh.

The Viacom story is an excellent example of the importance of keeping brand identity and brand equity. Marketing is about presenting the clearest communication of the corporate mission, along with the products, name, logo, and various divisions.

Probably the best example of an entertainment marketing powerhouse with a clear brand strategy is The Walt Disney Company. This company preaches synergy day and night, strategizing marketing and its halo effect, enabling one form of a product to morph into another. Think of their original products—*The Lion King* and *Beauty* or *the Beast,* for example—which have translated into hundreds of thousands of spin-off retail items. Both were turned into Broadway musicals, launching a whole new division of the company. Disney is able to stretch those brands into as many different successful products as consumers will accept and purchase.

Disney's success is not limited to feature films and animation. For example, Disney took a very successful cable channel, ESPN, and multiplexed that brand into ESPN2 as a platform for extreme sports and college games. Then it launched *ESPN* magazine, which is now considered a legitimate competitor to *Sports Illustrated*. Today's ESPN owns the rights to televise Major League Baseball, NFL, NBA, NASCAR, tennis, a host of college conferences, the Bowl Championship Series, and the new playoffs the BCS has just announced. ESPN and ESPN2 have 98.5 million subscribers and bring in more than $6 billion annually from subscriber fees alone.[1]

In 1995, Disney launched its cruise line business with the decision to build two purpose-built ships, designed specifically to accommodate both families and adult cruisers with no children. Although many wondered if Disney could pull this off—especially considering there would be no gambling, a cruise-line staple—the company has performed spectacularly. There are now four ships in the line, cruising around the world. It is estimated that Disney Cruise Line owns nearly 3% of the world cruising market.[2]

The Mouse also has a house in the interactive world, courtesy of Disney Interactive Media Group, which includes Disney Interactive Studios (offering games based on Disney franchises and new properties across multiple video game platforms); Disney Online Studios (immersive, online virtual worlds such as Disney Club Penguin and the World of Cars Online); Disney Mobile (mobile entertainment content, including music-based games, casual games, franchise apps, digicomics, and informational apps); Disney Online (access to Disney movies, television, games, music, travel, shopping and live events); and Playdom, which produces casual games for social networks such as Facebook and Mr. Freston's old nemesis, MySpace.

---

[1] "Fox to Create New Network It Sees as Rival for ESPN," *New York Times*, March 5, 2013.

[2] "2013 World Wide Market Share," *Cruise Market Watch*, 2013-4-29.

Within every branch of these mega-companies there are contingency budgets, teaser campaign budgets, tie-in product budgets, and (in the case of movies) budgets to encourage home video rentals and sales as well as pay-per-view cable viewing. The game of out-spending and out-marketing at the highest dollar level is played only by the leading studios, eager to take advantage of the various consumer viewing windows available to them in the entertainment universe.

But not everyone in the entertainment world is a major player with huge resources; companies with small or non-existent budgets are becoming more mainstream. Every aspect of the industry—faced with politics, budget cuts, forced retirements, and fallout from the vast quantity of consolidations—finds hundreds of talented youngsters and experienced professionals creating production companies and support businesses. These include advertising boutiques, public relations enterprises, media buying shops, and other opportunities built around the business.

From blockbuster extravaganzas to off-off-off-Broadway plays, the marketing team is an intrinsic part of the success, creating strategies that will develop awareness for the product and extend the brand as far as it can possibly stretch. On the awareness side, it could be major stars meeting the press at a five-star hotel or stenciled messages on a New York sidewalk. On the revenue side, it's licensing the brand in as many ways as possible.

Whatever it takes, entertainment marketers must focus the public's attention on their product above all others. Their ability to do so—and the revenue that results from their efforts—has led to a revolution in entertainment marketing.

Decisions, Decisions

Marketing professionals face a variety of decisions on each project, in no way limited to how much or where to spend, which define the nature of the message. How those decisions are made differs across the board. Some professionals pride themselves on seat-of-the-pants, nose-to-the-breeze, arbitrary guesswork, while others swear by the application of sophisticated analysis, feeding off the ever-growing mountain of information now known as *Big Data*. In any case, there is very little margin for error.

And yet error and the unpredictability can reign. With movies, slippage plagues the release of each film. No matter how careful the planning, there may always be the surprise that makes winners out of weak entries and losers out of sure things. As mentioned previously, social networking—that bonanza of buzz—can be a blessing or a curse.

Surprises may come from other corners of the marketing universe, especially with the constant stream of related decisions being made in other areas, decisions that are difficult to categorize or visualize until they are fully discussed, formulated, argued over, and weighed against the possible political repercussions. This keeps everyone on their toes, trying to predict the unusual or unpredictable—or at least being flexible enough to shift positioning if the circumstances require it. In the tightly wound world of entertainment, "positioning" could refer to the positioning of the product or the personal position of a team member savvy to the politics of the industry.

In any case, decisions can be broken down into three categories:

- Large decisions
- Small decisions
- No decision at all

Small Decisions

Small decisions include those that are recurring, consistent, must be made week after week, month after month, season after season, and usually look similar from studio to studio—or even from sector to sector. These decisions, formulated by the marketing team and signed off on by the executive in charge, include

- What is the marketing budget?
- When will we launch it in the marketplace?
- Who is the hypothetical target audience?
- Will we spend the advertising budget in network, Internet, mobile, cable, and print or use some other media mix?
- What is our fallback plan, and how fast can we employ it?
- What are the key elements for the visual aspect of the campaign?
- Which service organizations will be used for research and advertising?
- Is there a seasonal message as part of the marketing push?

There are hundreds of these small decisions that must be made, some with a planning timetable of 6 to 12 months and some that must be made with the snap of the fingers to respond to the particular situation in the marketplace at the moment.

Large Decisions

Large decisions, usually made by the leader or chief executive of the company with the brain trust of advisors and board members, include

- Should the company acquire a competitor or any allied company?
- If there is a merger or acquisition, what will its impact be on the marketplace situation?
- Will a merger or acquisition allow for a dominant share of market in the sector?
- What will be the expected impact on the competition's marketing practices?
- What will the government accept or reject?
- Is there potential for expanding global marketing clout?

- Is this potential ally going to provide access to a new audience segment?

- Will it provide marketing efficiencies that create greater returns on advertising and branding investments?

These decisions are generally made over a much longer period of time but may also appear quickly on the radar screen, depending on opportunities in the marketplace. They call for strong leadership and good instincts in the industry as a whole.

No Decision at All

The dreaded no-decision-at-all decision can happen when a process has gotten out of control, costs have skyrocketed, finished product has been delayed, and no one wants to take the blame for a bad call.

In still-entrepreneurial environments, the practice of avoidance and the seeking out of scapegoats for potentially bad decisions or inactivity are signals that the marketing and management processes have broken down, the organization is frozen, and the leadership is failing.

Relying on Research

To avoid the no-decision-at-all scenario, companies rely on research. Though this may sound at odds with the earlier discussion regarding shelf life, it's important to remember that entertainment doesn't just follow trends; it creates them. One of the jobs of the entertainment marketing executive is to understand where the zeitgeist might be heading and to license products around that.

Research can uncover new veins in the mother lode of consumer desires. With the dollars at stake, creating any kind of marketing plan without a carefully designed research program is a cardinal sin. This need for research extends to the introduction of a new product, the relaunch of an old product, the extension of a successful product line, or the capture of leadership share for a corporation or division.

But even the most hardened professionals will admit that research can only measure so many variables and give limited but reasonable direction. Industry stories abound of huge research projects, costing hundreds of thousands of dollars, that were ignored by the CEO—who put a finger into the wind and went with his gut.

These stories are usually told only when a project was ultimately successful.

Research now shapes television programs to meet market demand. The AC Nielsen companies provide the most comprehensive network/local television ratings and "share of audience" research systems, through diary panels and some recording boxes. Arbitron gives similar information for local and national radio stations, and Starch helps advertisers understand the influence of powerful ads in the magazine editorial environment. EDI-Neilsen is now one of two or three companies that specializes in the electronic transmission of audience ticket sales over a weekend, providing instant gratification—or the Maalox moment—to tension-stricken executives waiting for the results of a box office hit or bomb. Measurement also exists for music sales, cable audience penetration, and movie box office sales.

And of course, there's the set-top box: that black blinking thing that links you with your cable provider. That box sends back all sorts of information about who watches what during which time period. So does your smartphone, your tablet, your Roku, your Apple TV—any digital device that brings entertainment to you is capable of taking information from you. Your media actions and preferences are constantly tracked. This wealth of knowledge allows the entertainment marketing ecosystem to plan, target, create, and monetize new content.

The availability of finely tuned research has increased the number of decisions made in any entertainment sector. Product diversification, fragmentation, and a rapidly increasing population have led to a trend away from mass marketing and toward niche marketing. Just as Coca-Cola realized there are diet soda natural fruit-based beverage and just plain water market segments in addition to the classic cola segment, the entertainment industry has realized there are different demographic, age, gender, and other niche target markets for a variety of vastly different film, TV, sports, radio, and publishing genres. This is great for cross-media marketing but certainly creates even more decisions in an already pressure-packed industry.

Tailoring the Team

As mentioned previously, today's entertainment marketing team has become a key player in the development of the initial entertainment concept itself, molding concepts to fit demographic niches. The marketing team is now a standard fixture at the conceptual stage of product development in all entertainment sectors. The team's presence at this stage allows for additional time to develop a creative strategy, a marketing plan, a media schedule, and alternatives to each that take into consideration goals achieved, exceeded, or not reached.

There are those who sometimes decry the influence of the marketing team in the development stage, pointing to the reliance on research and data that can change quickly in today's fast-moving world. And, there are those who feel that content is better left in the hands of its traditional sponsor, the production team. On occasion, if the production team is under pressure to produce results, there is an adversarial atmosphere. In this case, if a movie is successful, it is the brilliance of the production team; if a film fails, it is the fault of the marketing team.

Roles and Jobs

In the best of all worlds, it is usually the excellence of the often hundreds needed to make it all come together. In this integrated environment, the questions of who is on the team, what they do, and how they work together tend to overlap in the process of creating a sustainable product that meets the marketing goals of the company.

The simplest way to explain the complex structure of the entertainment/marketing team is to make a distinction between roles and jobs. For example, the job of a talent agent or business manager may include the responsibility of assembling and packaging a team of talent for the production of a creative product. The agent's/manager's role might also embrace the marketplace positioning of the product, through the particular relationships with the team members he or she has helped assemble. Regardless of the task, the agent's or manager's goal is to make the product a "must see," a "must read," or a "must watch."

The titles of the marketing professionals reflect the intertwining of marketing and production. They may include the president of licensing and merchandising, head of home video sales, entertainment attorney (who could be in-house or at a firm), chief financial officer, talent agent, literary agent, and president of an independent production company.

Then there are the heads of subsidiaries that could provide synergy and develop supplementary income streams. These would include the head of television production, the head of cable and DBS licensing, the head of theme park ride conception, the heads of the music and publishing divisions, as well as their business development and marketing executives. And let us not forget the head of publicity, an executive who has moved up through the ranks of public relations and owns the fattest contact list in town.

All of these executives will not be found at every meeting. They are kept informed with daily and weekly updates on the progress of production, the market potential, and any audience research that has been done in the field. They are well aware of the usual "windowing" dates (the time gap allowed between the arrival of the film in theaters and the date on which the film should be released in each of the supplementary or ancillary distribution forms—network broadcast, premium cable, DVD, Netflix, and so on). They must know the final, or "drop dead," dates and which critical decisions must be made for the final and confirmed release dates of the entertainment products in production.

They must be fully aware of the various synergistic products that may have been created to grow the concept. If the marketing plan involves a CD with a soundtrack from the film, or a PBS concert features a major pop or operatic world star about to release a video, then everyone, in all jobs and responsibilities, must collaborate on a consistent message and audience target.

In each sector, the nature and job description of the teams may differ, but there is no doubt that the planning, strategy development, implementation, and measurement of success—or the learning experience of a failure—separate a superior marketing team and secure its place in the corporate environs. However, all of this presumes that business is careening along as usual. When business becomes "unusual"—a star is replaced on a film, the script goes through rewrite number 33, or the lead singer needs surgery on her vocal cords—the dates, the costs, and the marketing plans must be reworked.

In any case, keeping the marketing machine on track means managing myriad details, from concept to consumption. In some cases, major entertainment companies reach outside their own in-house teams for additional support and input. This often involves the use of an advertising agency.

The Role of the Outside Agency

Of the over 2500 advertising agencies listed in the Red Book (a major reference source in the ad business that provides information on clients, geographic concentration, specialties, global coverage, billings, revenue, and senior executives), most do not list an entertainment company as a client—for a variety of reasons. For some, it is lack of experience; for others, it is the challenge of the industry's volatility; and for others still, the unbundling of services makes the industry unaffordable to service.

The reported spending for this sector of the economy totaled well over $10 billion in measured media for the year 2000. The spending level has increased consistently over the last 10-plus years. As digital movies have reduced the money spent on prints, advertising budgets have ramped up. Over $100 million was spent in advertising on the worldwide launch of *Avatar* alone. With similar amounts for *Harry Potter*, *Pirates of the Caribbean*, *Spider Man*, and *The Avengers*, the figure for U.S. spending on advertising for entertainment products, across all platforms, rocketed to nearly $100 billion in 2012.

Agencies that have established a foothold in the industry find great loyalty and very little turnover of the account until there is a perceived client conflict or deep business decline. They also find a feeding frenzy when the mega-million-dollar media budgets and total marketing programs for Disney, Warner Bros., and NBC/Universal go up for periodic review.

Entertainment companies also frequently access other suppliers through advertising agencies, including research firms, consulting firms, data suppliers, direct marketing companies, trailer houses, media planning and buying specialists, public relations firms, Internet agencies, and lobbying firms. Each of these serves a different purpose in the development of an integrated entertainment marketing plan and implementation program.

Today's agency scorecard looks like what's shown in Exhibit 2-2.

Exhibit 2-2   Major Agencies Representing the Entertainment Industry[3]

Agency	Client Company
McCann Erickson	Sony Pictures
DDB Worldwide, Division of Omnicom	Universal Studios and Theme Parks
Grey Advertising, Division of WPP	Warner Bros. Studios, *Entertainment Weekly*, *People Magazine*
TWBA, Division of Omnicom	ABC TV Network
Young & Rubicam Division of WPP	Showtime, Viacom, Sony Electronic Games
Saatchi & Saatchi	News Corp.
In-House Agency	NBC Universal

There are also many small and mid-sized agencies handling diverse creative and media projects for entertainment companies. These agencies are finding new ways to showcase their other clients through their entertainment accounts. The entertainment companies are more than happy to help them out through lucrative sponsorship, licensing, and (in growing numbers) product placement deals.

In the entertainment marketing industry, large budgets and intense time frames call for seasoned teams of marketing professionals who have the right instincts, the ability to make quick decisions, the knowledge of when to rely on research, and great contacts both inside and outside their own companies. Making the right decision on a consistent basis—along with a healthy dose of hand-shaking, back-scratching, and the right moment at the right time—can propel a professional to the top of the heap, where he or she is recognized as a leader.

---

[3]   As of September 2012.

Movers and Shakers

Regardless of who he or she has placed on the team, the leader bears the ultimate responsibility for moving the entire process forward to the end result: a transaction for money—in fact, lots of transactions for lots of money. The successful leader accomplishes this task through a very fragile series of relationships and deals: some based on talent, some on money, some on power, and almost all (in entertainment) based on personalities. The people who rise to the top of the entertainment industry understand how to manipulate all of these factors to create a winning outcome.

Follow the Leader

While teams of experts assist with the various steps involved in the marketing timelines, including awards presentations, deal negotiations, and contract completions, they can only help the boss navigate the precarious grounds in the attempt to avoid disaster: cost exceeding revenue, or the other side of the creative-based coin of entertainment, nothing happening at all. Delays can come from a strike by writers, a concession demanded by a star, even a hurricane—either in the form of weather or a disgruntled studio executive.

In an industry based on human talent, the leader must be a consummate politician, a brilliant strategist, and a charismatic executive who can make things happen. He or she must lead, guide, direct, manage, support, compensate, build, and structure the creative process.

In the entertainment world, money is the ultimate report card—a report card that is published not only in industry magazines, but also in consumer periodicals ranging from *The New York Times* to *People* magazine. Entertainment leaders, who consistently make great bets for big studios, may make far less money than a film's superstar (though nothing to sneeze at), but they deal in a different reward: the power that allows them to make picture after picture, with greater long-term results for the leader. These leaders are known for their *development of value* in the market.

To develop value, it is important to make investments of three kinds of capital. The first, *financial capital*, are the funds needed to run a business. These funds are usually raised through public or private placements. The second is *human capital*—the individuals who create the ideas, make the decisions, and provide the professional services or selective experience to make a successful product launch through a disciplined marketing program.

But it is the third form that entertainment leaders use for exploration, analysis, and even implementation. It is called *social capital*—the relationships that exist among the veterans of the industry wars. Relationships are more important than title or money in the entertainment industry. Relationships create power and authority through the ability to get things done. Even when a recent project has failed, or a set of prior circumstances may not have been all they could have been, certain industry players can still get the green light based on who they know.

Nowhere is the old adage, "Be careful on your way up because you never know who you'll meet on your way down," more true than in this industry. A poker game at an executive's home can often be as important as a major staff meeting at the studio. More than one major project has come about after a Friday night discussion of what movie to make, who to hire, and how to craft the financials.

In entertainment, there is little formula to fall back on and even less insight to the rapidly changing tastes of the market. Yet the leader must make consistently successful decisions—while dealing with pop culture and fickle loyalties at the box office/retail outlets/broadcast distribution points. No one can rely on history to assess and create the direction for tomorrow's projects. The only history available is the amount of money a project made or lost, under whose guidance. Often, regardless of whatever may have come to pass during the actual production of an entertainment product, good or bad, it is that final report card—the money made—that makes the next project happen—that, and the relationships maintained.

The leaders that maintain these relationships manage the ultimate selection of the product. They employ vast numbers of creative people at salaries and perquisites that range from union-required minimums to the most extravagant levels that managers and agents can negotiate.

But it isn't an easy ride, all glitz and glamour. The president of worldwide marketing, the president of production and distribution, the CEO of the studio must all have the ability to develop marketing strategies and implement the marketing plan under minimum input situations. Often there is only bare-bones research and budgets and timetables that are out of control. There's often little room for error, careers on the line, and hundreds of millions at stake.

Yet decisions must be made and implemented—decisions that will make or break careers. When dollars are tight, some of these decisions may be affected by a true entertainment art form: the making of a deal.

Deal Me In

Deal-making is usually associated with the initial steps in formalizing a creative project and gaining financing. However, when it comes to creative marketing, deal-making proceeds as the producer or the director—or on occasion, the star—tries to usurp responsibility for the marketing message and even the selection of the media. If the team member has experience in this arena and knows when to push the right buttons, it can go very well. If nonmarketing professionals get involved with the marketing—to brandish their egos, burnish their images, or simply exercise power—the implementation can go wildly astray. This can lead to the wrong audience seeing a film. If that audience is disappointed and spreads negative word of mouth, a very big-budget movie can become a very big financial failure.

However, the right use of the deal is critical to success. Getting a star on the right primetime talk show requires deals to be made at the highest studio and network levels, especially when a star from one network is promoted on a talk show owned by another. Here is where contacts, relationships, experience, and public relations savvy become very valuable in the integration of the marketing communications plan.

Nothing in deal-making happens as a reflex. It is not "the way it has been done in the past" or "the way we have always done it." Everything is negotiated, starting with the time an event should begin, the size of the budget, the people to be involved, the expected outcome, the titles or credits, and the friends who will receive some form of participation. Even the promotions department requires deals to be made to get sponsors or product placement people to provide items for free, funding for contests, sweepstakes, wardrobe, air tickets, limousine services, hotels, and catering.

This is often where the true mettle of the marketing team member is tested: putting the package together with maximum effort and minimum cost.

Deal-making is also a specialty of the stars themselves. Big names can certainly have an impact on the green lighting of a project, but some ventures are still considered too risky for studios to undertake. When this occurs, there are other considerations that go into the making of a decision. If Barbra Streisand wants to make *Yentl* or Madonna wants to star in a third remake of *Evita*, the studio might need to maintain good relations with their music division and produce, finance, or at least distribute the project. It took almost 15 years for John Travolta, an acknowledged devotee of Scientology, to get a movie made from one of the books written by the deceased founder of the popular religion—a project that turned out to be a box office disaster.

The ultimate—and riskiest—type of deal-making is the grass-roots effort of an actor or actress who wants to promote him or herself in a personal project to increase his or her visibility. This is a labor-intensive, frequently frustrating experience for actors whose goal is to build a star role or platform. The actor may write the script and find the financing; that dedicated soul may also develop the marketing, advertising, and public relations in order to build an audience. *The Big Night*, written, produced, and starring Stanley Tucci, got Hollywood's attention and built a fan base for Stanley, who soon after won roles in several movies. This type of self-marketing may include everything from the occasional billboard to attendance at every possible function, including film festivals and charity dinners. And then there's the leading gossip columnists, who must be pampered.

If it works, it's golden. If it doesn't, it's history, as might be the actor.

Generally speaking, the true artists of the deal—and the legends of Hollywood—are those super-powers who rise to the top of the industry through a combination of deals, talent, experience, and luck: the moguls.

Top of the Heap: The Moguls

Entertainment moguls have always been with us—stories of Louis B. Mayer and Daryl Zanuck abound, kingpins of the studios in the early days—but in today's world, it takes a lot more than a studio chief to be considered a mogul. The growth of the entertainment industry, stretching out into all the platforms discussed in this book, has created a world in which true mogul-dom is conferred upon those who know how to tie it all together, creating endless streams of revenue for their mega-companies.

But it also takes a lot more than revenue to make an entertainment mogul. Apple may be on the brink of being the first company to be valued at over $1 trillion, but for the time being, its reach is well within the world of conduits, not content. Steve Jobs...rest his soul...would not be considered an entertainment mogul, though he certainly was a genius with technology, and understanding that design was the driver that whets the consumer's appetite.

No, moguls in this industry are people who wield enough power and vision to create the giant companies that feed the public's desire for all that drives the entertainment and media industry. But beware, you who aspire to these heights. The glare of fame and power can often hide the lights of the oncoming semi. Ask any one of the four moguls who were featured in the first edition of this book, a mere 10 years ago. All four powerful men, divining the future of the business, creating the very engines that have taken this industry to the over $1 trillion it takes in today, have fallen far behind the scenes.

Michael Eisner was booted from the board of Disney by angry shareholders, led by Walt's nephew, Roy Disney. Michael Ovitz, forever linked to Eisner in a disastrous run as president of Disney, never reattained his position as the most powerful man in Hollywood. Barry Diller, dreams of a fourth network long gone, is busy redistributing the intellectual property of those that do exist—and making no friends in the process. And Gerald Levin? Well, that Time-Warner/AOL merger did get approved—and flamed out in a spectacular super-nova. Far from his old corner office, Levin—a distant memory—publicly apologized for the merger as late as 2010.

So, who shall we choose this time? Who stands at the precipice of power now?

And how will *their* reigns end?

Mega-Moguls

The events of the last ten years have left two true moguls standing. These men—Sumner Redstone and Rupert Murdoch—are old-school. Though both inherited businesses from their fathers—Redstone a theater chain in the Northeast; Murdoch, a daily newspaper in Australia—each built his empire over time, mashing together all sorts of elements, bundling and unbundling as new opportunities presented themselves, rising to the very top of the entertainment and media pyramid. In literature, men like these form the basis for thinly disguised characters in sweeping family sagas. They are both billionaires many times over.

Redstone—the man who said "content is king"—practices what he preaches. Though he may not own or control all of the following now, over the course of his reign he has parlayed the many holdings listed in Exhibit 2-3, in addition to many others. He is the current chairman of both Viacom and CBS, which split from one another, as described earlier in this chapter. His personal chess game has knocked knights from their horses, and brought new kings to old networks.

Exhibit 2-3   A Partial List of Sumner Redstone's Media Holdings Throughout His Career

Mass Media Conglomerates	Viacom
	CBS Corporation
Television	Cable networks: MTV, MTV2, VHI, CMT, Nickelodeon, Nick at Nite, Noggin/The N, TV Land, Comedy Central, Spike TV, BET, and UPN/CW
	Pay television: Showtime, The Movie Channel
	Production companies: Spelling Entertainment, Paramount Television, Big Ticket Entertainment
	King World Productions (a syndication unit): *The Oprah Winfrey Show, Dr. Phil, Wheel of Fortune,* and *Jeopardy!*

Film	Columbia Pictures
	21st Century Fox
	Orion Pictures
	DreamWorks SKG
	Paramount Pictures
	UCI Cinemas (in 13 foreign countries)
Music	Infinity Broadcasting (radio)
	Famous Music (Paramount's music publishing division)
Publishing	Simon and Schuster
Sports	New York Knicks (NBA)
	New York Rangers (NHL)
	(both through Madison Square Garden properties)

A partial list of Rupert Murdoch's holdings includes filmed entertainment, television, online, and print media (see Exhibit 2-4).

Exhibit 2-4   A Partial List of Rupert Murdoch's Media Holdings

Television	20th Century Fox Television
	Cable: Fox Business Network, Fox College Sports, Fox Movie Channel, Fox News Channel, Fox Soccer Channel, Fox Sports Enterprises, FX Networks, National Geographic Channel, BSkyB (U.K.)
Film	20th Century Fox
	Fox Searchlight Pictures
	20th Century Fox Home Entertainment
	Blue Sky Studios
Online	Fox Interactive Media
	Fox.com
	Foxsports.com
	AmericanIdol.com
	TheXFactorUSA.com
	TheSimpsons.com
	Hulu.com

Publishing	HarperCollins
	The Wall Street Journal
	Barron's Financial News

Like the mega-moguls before them, neither has had an entirely smooth ride of all of this, notably Murdoch, with the *News of the World* phone-hacking scandal that shook the very roots of his British business dealings in 2011.

But we do not aim to add another commentary to the list of thousands that have been written on this situation, only point out that Redstone and Murdoch may be the last two men with such intimate knowledge and control of their businesses, having built them ground-up. They may be the very last of the old-style moguls, and for better or worse, they have changed the entertainment and media landscape forever.

Media Monarchs

Mogul-ness depends as much on personality as it does on holdings—the perception that this person has the vision and the nerve to create something bigger, shifting the destinies of the businesses and people they lead. To look for today's power brokers, we follow the intersecting paths of entertainment, media, and technology—or convergence, which was described in Chapter 1, "Begin with the Basics: The What and Where of Entertainment Marketing."

It is this intersection that creates the power that will continue to drive entertainment marketing. Content is useless without a conduit. Conduits are useless without content. Therefore, it is those industry leaders who bring the two together—the convergence—that get the nod for this edition.

Let's divide the players via three of the Four Cs (keeping in mind that one C, consumption, has to do more with the choices the end-user makes to consume the media).

Content

Top of the List: Bob Iger, Disney

Iger stepped in to the vacuum left by Michael Eisner and quietly—in comparison to the man he followed—took this entertainment monolith to new heights. While steering a steady course for the Mouse, Iger resolved the thorny relationship with Pixar by buying the company, providing an excellent return for the company. Iger then showed his gumption with the acquisition of Marvel Entertainment. Though many in the industry thought he had overpaid (at $4 billion), the skyrocket success of *The Avengers* silenced the critics. As of September 2012, *The Avengers* box office stands at $1.5 billion. Who knows what windowing will add to this pile, and there's no way to track the millions...or billions?...that licensing will bring. Iger then capped off his strategic run by buying LucasFilm, with all the glory of the *Star Wars* franchise, effectively buying a base of boys to complement Disney's long-standing hold on princess-loving girls.

Perennial Evergreen(s): Harvey and Bob Weinstein, the Weinstein Company

After a 26-year run with Miramax—the last 12 under the ownership of the content king, Disney, the Weinsteins moved back to independence, founding their eponymous company in 2005. It's hard to beat the brothers when it comes to sheer content, with their movies (*The King's Speech, The Artist, The Iron Lady, Silver Linings Playbook*) constantly winning awards and accolades, not only from organizations but from the stars who work for them. But it's more than their movie-making skill (and distribution deals, partnerships, and books); it's the outsized personalities that fill any room they enter, demanding respect from all directions.

Conduit

Top of the List: Tim Cook, Apple

Much like Iger at Disney, Tim Cook has been handed the reins of what is arguably the biggest conduit company in the world. Apple continues to change the way technology is used, and therefore distribution is enhanced (or threatened, depending on which side of the intellectual property being played on the iPad you might stand). With a new smart TV project on the horizon, a successful patent infringement lawsuit against Samsung's Galaxy on the books, and the continuing issuance of iPhones and iPads along with the sheer dominance of iTunes in the music distribution business, Apple—and Cook—may be on top for a long time to come. Can he out-Jobs Steve? Those are huge shoes to fill, and the competition is coming on *very* strong.

Finally Underway: Jeff Bezos, Amazon

In 1994, Jeff Bezos created an online bookstore, naming it Amazon partially to make sure the company name showed up early in alphabetical searches. When it went public in 1997, Bezos made it clear that he did not expect to turn a profit for several years. Stockholders complained that the company was moving too slowly, and when the dot-com bubble burst, all eyes turned to this upstart, wondering when the coffin would be carried out. Amazon seemed doomed to be just another punchline. But Bezos held on, broadening his offering beyond books, and turned his first profit in 2001—small, but a memorable milestone.

Today, online consumers can purchase nearly anything on amazon.com. Revenues exceed $47 billion, and the company is on track for $100 billion by 2015, mirroring the growth path of another American retail phenomenon, Wal-Mart. But more than this, amazon.com has defined online retailing, creating a comfort zone for consumers that has spread to other sites.

What truly brings Bezos to mogul status is his ongoing push into more than simply selling stuff. He pioneered e-books with the development of the Kindle and then decided to move past the middleman by developing online publishing, dealing a difficult blow to the already wobbling publishing industry. Amazon is also a major provider of cloud computing services, hosts websites for retailers such as Sears Canada, Marks & Spencer, and Lacoste, among others. The company also owns other online retailers such as IMDb (Internet Movie Database), Zappos (the shoe e-tailer), Reflexive Entertainment, a video game developer, and BoxOfficeMojo.com.

But in early 2013, Amazon announced its biggest entertainment venture to date. The company is now creating original content for its Amazon Prime Instant Video service, creating yet another competitor in the growing cord-cutting cable war.

Convergence

Top of the List: Jeffrey Bewkes, Time Warner

Like Bob Iger, Jeffrey Bewkes has come to his mogul-dom through a climb to the top of an already existing empire, and like his Disney counterpart, he's doing a steady job of steering this ship. Time Warner is a multinational media company, with major operations in film, television, and publishing, including HBO, Time Inc., and CNN, along with New Line Cinema, Turner Broadcasting System, The CW Television Network, TheWB.com, Warner Bros., Kids' WB, Cartoon Network, DC Comics, Warner Bros. Animation, and Castle Rock Entertainment.

We count Bewkes under convergence rather than content because Time Warner, up until Bewkes's reign, seemed more focused on the pipeline than the content (especially with the disastrous merger with AOL, which he finally cleaned up in the last spinoff in 2009). But now Bewkes has publicly stated that he wants the new Time Warner to be a content company. Spending on content has jumped 7% annually since 2008 as Time Warner has shed costs in other areas.[4] Given his track record at gold-standard HBO—his path to the top of the Time Warner ladder—Bewkes knows importance of content, so much so that he finally softened his stance on Netflix, putting together a deal with the streamer, even as his own HBOGo keeps its product close to home.

However, his focus on content will not be extended to the magazine that launched the company. In early 2013, TimeWarner attempted to sell off its magazines, including *Time*, *Sports Illustrated*, *Fortune*, and *Money*, but when the deal with Meredith fell apart, the decision was made to spin the magazines off into a separate, publicly traded company. The end of an era—and another toll of the bell for magazine publishing.

Coming on Strong: Brian Roberts and Steve Burke, Comcast / NBC Universal

The deal spun between Comcast and GE for NBC Universal nearly defined the term convergence. Comcast, which controlled a lion's share of the technology and conduit that feeds the American living room and home Wi-Fi networks, and NBC Universal, a top content provider, are now one company, an entertainment media giant with tentacles in all directions.

Brian Roberts, son of the founder, has spent his career with Comcast. Steve Burke came to Comcast in 1998, after a successful run with The Walt Disney Company (Disney Stores, ABC Broadcasting, EuroDisney). Under their watch, the company became the United States' largest cable company, largest residential Internet service provider, and third largest phone company. Roberts is the chairman and CEO of Comcast and serves on the Board of Directors for NBC Universal. Burke serves as executive vice president of Comcast and CEO/president of NBC Universal.

Moguls as Mentors

Throughout these relationships, it is not only the moguls that ultimately affect the direction of the entertainment industry, but the people they mentor as well. The entertainment industry has a long list of mentoring moguls, people whose reign ultimately ended, but whose influence lives on. There is a continuum in the industry that reaches far and wide. This relationship network

---

[4] "Time Warner Trims Its Excesses," *New York Times*, October 31, 2011.

continues to bear fruit in the ongoing convergence. In many cases, it is the long-standing relationships of the moguls that bring these packages together.

Summary

As the entertainment industry has grown and the synergy between sectors has increased, the ability to make things happen, to break logjams, and to build effective teams has become increasingly important. Although the players of early Hollywood reveled in their power in the domestic film business, today's mogul extends his or her reach well beyond the movies themselves. Through distribution, licensing, and sponsorship, entertainment moguls now direct international campaigns that move with the speed of an ever-widening pool of new technology.

But at the heart of it all, there is still that flickering image on the movie screen.

3

Marketing Movies: Building Wannasee, Haftasee, and Mustsee

amuel Taylor Coleridge called drama "that willing suspension of disbelief for the moment, which constitutes poetic faith." Most modern movie producers would probably call the act of financing and making a movie the willing suspension of financial sanity. With blockbusters running well into the multiple hundreds of millions of dollars, making a movie is a seriously risky business, full of potential pitfalls at every turn.

For producers and studios, movie *marketing* is the hedge against disaster and the support system for success. Marketing is the engine that drives public perception, creating "wannasee," luring people into the theaters and dollars into the box office.

Big Numbers for the Big Screen

Of all the platforms, the revenue for movies—the box office—may be the most misleading. When you stack up those ticket sales against those for other forms of entertainment, the revenue may not seem very impressive. But movies attract far larger audiences: annual movie attendance is estimated at 1,358 million versus 359 million for theme parks and 131 million for sports.[1] Given the far higher participation, there is a much larger audience for all the associated merchandising and licensing that flows from movies, not to mention the downstream revenue from the "windowing" that occurs after first release[2]: premium cable, home video (DVR), Netflix, streaming in Hulu, HBOGo, basic cable, U.S. network TV, Red Box, airplanes, cruise ships—more lives than your average cat.

So in the world of entertainment, movies are still the Big Dog.

---

[1] Motion Picture Association of America (Rentrak 2012 research).

[2] Windowing used to follow a fairly traditional schedule, spread across many months, with international release repeating the process outside the U.S. However, with digital piracy now a primary concern, windows have been compressed to a point of overlap in order to get the movie out as quickly as possible. Movies may now have a simultaneous release all over the world, with home video and streaming occurring quickly thereafter.

Movies are a marketing powerhouse. The so-called Big Six studios alone—outlined in Exhibit 3-1—average over $700 million per year on their marketing spend.[3] A conservative estimate for all other movie marketing, including independent films and home video, comes to $4.5 billion per year.[4] Add the marketing attached to all the associated licensing and merchandising deals for these films, and the number does nothing but climb.

Exhibit 3-1   The "Big Six" Studios[5]

Conglom-erate	Parent Division	Major Studio Subsidiary	Arthouse/ "Indie" Distribution Subsidiaries	Genre/ B Movie Distribution Subsidiaries	Other Divisions and Brands
Viacom	Paramount Motion Pictures Group	Paramount Pictures	Paramount Vantage		Insurge Pictures, Nickelodeon Movies, MTV Films
Time Warner	Warner Bros. Entertainment	Warner Bros. Pictures			New Line Cinema, HBO Films, Castle Rock Entertainment, Tuner Entertainment, Warner Premiere, Warner Bros. Animation
Sony	Sony Pictures Entertainment	Columbia Pictures	Sony Pictures Classics	Screen Gems	TriStar Pictures, Sony Pictures Animation, Destination Films, Triumph Films, Stage 6 Films, Affirm Films
The Walt Disney Company	The Walt Disney Studios	Walt Disney Pictures/ Touchstone Pictures (unified business with separate brands)		Hollywood Pictures	Pixar, Walt Disney Animation Studios, Marvel Studios, Disneynature
Comcast/ General Electric	NBC Universal	Universal Pictures	Focus Features		Universal Animation Studios, Illumination Entertainment, Working Title Films
News Corporation	Fox Entertainment Group	20th Century Fox	Fox Searchlight Pictures		20th Century Fox Animation, Fox Faith, Blue Sky Studios, New Regency Productions (20% equity), Fox Animation Studios

[3]   PwC Global Entertainment and Media Outlook: 2012–2016, www.pwc.com/outlook.

[4]   Marich, Robert, *Marketing to Moviegoers: A Handbook of Strategies and Tactics*, Third Edition, Southern Illinois University Press, 2013.

[5]   http://en.wikipedia.org/wiki/Major_film_studio.

The cost of advertising a mainstream movie has risen for blockbusters, from an average of $35 million in 2005 to over $50 million in 2012.[6] This includes network, cable, and satellite television; national and local newspapers; billboards; radio; online; and tie-in advertising. When a blockbuster goes global, that figure can rise to $70 million for publicizing and distribution.[7]

All that spending—on marketing as well as production—creates a huge risk, and that risk is exacerbated by a rule of thumb known as the *6-2-2 formula*, which states that out of a slate of ten yearly releases, six movies lose money, two break even, and two make the money that covers all the aforementioned losses. This is true for movies in general, both produced by the studio and independent films.[8] Although marketing is critical for all ten films, it will put those crucial two over the top.

You will note from Exhibit 3-1 that the Big Six studios are all part of large public entertainment conglomerates and as such, are expected to pull their weight in the battle to create shareholder value—in other words, to make money.

Film divisions are important to conglomerates because they create lucrative assets. Each new release is added to a film library, which enhances the value of a conglomerate's cable and television channels. But risk is hiding around every corner, and today's studio executives—a very risk-averse crowd—use many strategies to fund those blockbusters and alleviate potential bombs.

A Bit of Background

Toward the end of the last century, the explosive introduction of home video provided a new stream of revenue that grew so rapidly that all the studios were making money. Awash in profits, studios paid little attention to high expenses. Talent agents, who held the keys to the stars, and directors, who drove the audiences to the theaters, worked huge deals for their clients, resulting in lavishly paid talent—and a number of famous flops. Director Michael Cimino, hot off *The Deer Hunter*, crashed and burned with the never-to-be-forgotten *Heaven's Gate*. *Waterworld*, starring Kevin Costner, is still used as a punch line. (It didn't help that Costner followed *Waterworld* up with *The Postman*, another mega-flop.)

But even without grossly paid talent, big movies are always at risk of becoming big disasters. There are a raft of other potential pitfalls—location shooting, the addition of increasingly complex special effects and computer-generated imagery (CGI)—that adds to the bottom line and therefore the risk. Disney's *Mars Needs Moms* (2011; total cost $175 million against a worldwide gross of $39 million) and Warner Bros. *The Green Lantern* (2011; total cost of $325 million, worldwide gross $220 million) are more recent examples of box-office busts.

Wall Street analysts are unforgiving when movie divisions have a string of box office flops. With the boom of home video a thing of the past, executives are pressured to take a closer look at the

---

[6] PwC Global Entertainment and Media Outlook: 2011–2014, www.pwc.com/outlook.

[7] "Movie Ticket Prices Hit All-Time High in 2011," *The Hollywood Reporter*, February 9, 2012.

[8] Please note: We use the word "film" interchangeably with "movie," even though movies are now primarily digital transmissions—bye-bye 35mm film.

bottom line. One way to corral costs is to cut back on the number of films produced, but with fewer films in production, studios do not enjoy the benefit of cross-collateralized income, a phenomenon that occurs when a studio has a broad portfolio of films, allowing losses from one film to be offset by gains from another.

So before a movie gets made, studio executives must look for ways to reduce the uncertainty that accompanies the business.

Reducing Risk: High Concept Films

Studios take great care in considering what movies will get the "green light"—the go-ahead to start production. Many of these movies are specifically created under a formulaic model known as *high concept*. With high concept movies, studio strategists plug in a potential genre/storyline and add a projected cast, while considering what other ways the movie can be exploited. If the modeling spits out a large enough revenue projection, the project will be pursued.

High concept movies exhibit the following characteristics:

- Known stars and/or director
- Always a mass-market movie
- A storyline that can be rendered in a clear, simple sentence
- A recurring single-image marketing motif
- A connection to prequels, existing theatre, or established music
- Extensive merchandising of licensed products

Films with big names attached to them are still more "bankable" (some things never change), or appealing to larger audiences with more discretionary income. Big paydays still exist for evergreen names, such as Julia Roberts and Steven Spielberg, as well as those in the current crop of must-sees—George Clooney, Angelina Jolie, and a whole cast of twinkling new lights.

Dum-Dum....Dum-Dum...

The first breakthrough high concept blockbuster and the roadmap for dozens of hits since was the 1975 movie *Jaws*. The storyline came from a successful number-one bestseller novel by Peter Benchley. Universal added then-hot stars Richard Dreyfus and Roy Scheider and a young director with four television movies and one box office so-so, *The Sugarland Express*, but a lot of perceived talent: Steven Spielberg.

The marketing mavens created a campaign that still sticks in movie-goer minds. The single image used extensively in the highly-saturated print, trailers, TV commercials, and other media ads was an apparently naked woman lazily swimming across open water, with a gigantic, open-mouthed Great White Shark shooting straight toward her from below, providing a clear and arresting image of good and evil. Even children not born until 20 years later understand the tension behind the famous musical syllables that underscored the movie, *dum-dum, dum-dum* (a classic once again put in the limelight at the 2013 Academy Awards, to warn winners their thank-you time was almost up).

No wonder that *Jaws 2* also rang the box-office cash registers.

Extending the movie brand, Universal featured that famous white shark at its theme parks, drawing shrieks from visitors until 2012, a 22-year ride for the attraction in Florida. It is still a centerpiece at Universal Osaka (Japan).

Jaws set a standard for high concept movie characteristics still followed today. A high concept movie

- Takes any genre or idea and uses every extreme opportunity to push its point and image.

- Makes absolutely sure it relates to as many diverse and broad-based audiences as possible.

- Is packed with activity—not always just action, but rapid movement, with high focus on the current hot actor.

This highly stimulating experience is meant to motivate repeat visits to the theater by mass audiences. When it works, those happy movie-goers continue the cycle, providing excellent word of mouth (or word of tweet, email, or Facebook post), culminating in great buzz.

The successful high concept movie may not always be a blockbuster. It does not have to cost over $100 million or have marketing budgets over $30 million. But it provides a desire for repeat viewing, generating ongoing revenue in digital downloads or cable because it hits some emotional note or empathic button.

Samples of high concept versus not high concept films are found in Exhibit 3-2.

Exhibit 3-2 High Concept Versus Not High Concept Films

HIGH CONCEPT	NOT HIGH CONCEPT
Dark Knight (all)	*Bridesmaids*
Skyfall	*Silver Linings Playbook*
Mission Impossible (all)	*The King's Speech*
Spiderman (all)	*Hangover*
Lord of the Rings (all)	*The Artist*
Twilight (all)	*The Big Wedding*
The Hunger Games (all)	*Black Swan*

Marketing is a specific focus—indeed, central to the whole strategy—in high-concept films, right from the start.

Another offering central to studio strategy is the *tent-pole film*. This term is applied to a specific film that the studio has decided will be its lead picture for a given year or season.

A studio will place its production and marketing budget bets on its tent-pole film, riding it as long and as far as possible. The expectation is that the tent-pole film will generate huge box office returns and multiple supplementary revenue streams, becoming an "evergreen" product, earning licensing fees around the world, and returning for play several times over a decade.

As executives are plotting their strategies with high concept and tent-pole films, they are finding ways to finance the film through creative cofinancing deals. Here again, marketing enters the picture—this time bolstering the bottom line—in the form of *product placement.*

Reducing Risk: Hollywood Meets Madison Avenue

Product placement is a strategy that allows studios to gain revenue from the appearance of a specific product in a movie.

There is no simple way to calculate how many marketing messages consumers are exposed to daily. Numbers range from the low 200s (for specific commercials/print ads/radio messages) to the 1000s (for impressions made from the sheer glut of ads plastered on as many available flat surfaces—static or projected—as possible). But what we do know is, those 1,285 billion movie viewers are sitting in their seats for two hours at a time, creating huge opportunities to parade a product in front of them, little mini-commercials that associate the brand with the movie, the star, and the concept: adventure, danger, romance.

This connection has been in the movies forever (think what Humphrey Bogart did for trench coats), but savvy marketing executives realized there was a goldmine in placement. Today, it's a given that part of a film's financing will come through the sale of space on the screen. Film placement was estimated to reach $1.53 billion in 2011,[9] no small hedge against the huge cost of producing a movie. And when you consider the cross-marketing that occurs when the product (say, a Rolex) places the star and the watch on its own billboard, the symbiosis is perfect—and very cost-effective: millions more impressions reminding the potential audience to see the movie.

One of the most successful franchises in film history, the James Bond movies, is the acknowledged master of product placement, garnering hundreds of millions of dollars over the life of the franchise. 1997's *Tomorrow Never Dies* featured a full 22 minutes of product appearances, including BMW and Omega (a slap in the face to Bond purists, who expected Aston Martin and Rolex).[10] *Skyfall* in 2012—the twenty-third Bond film—garnered an estimated $50 million in product placement, against a $150 million budget.

Brand masters love the association with movies. Consider Apple, the creator of Macs, iPads, and iPhones. Apple has carefully nurtured its hip image over the years with those wonderfully creative ads, but they've also relied on the movies. Apple products appeared in 42.5% of the 40 number-one U.S. box office films in 2010. Apple-branded products appeared in more than one-third of all number-one films at the U.S. box office between 2001 to 2010,[11] and continued the practice into 2012, when they went public with their strategy in testimony related to a patent infringement suit with Samsung.

[9] "Global Product Placement Spending Up 10% to $7.4 Billion in 2011," *PQ Media*, December 4, 2012, http://www.pqmedia.com/about-press-201212.html

[10] *Handbook of Product Placement in the Mass Media: New Strategies in Marketing Theory, Practice, Trends, and Ethics,* Mary-Lou Galician, EdD, Haworth Press, 2004.

[11] Brandcameo.com, *Announcing the Brandcameo Product Placement Award Winners,* www.brandchannel.com/features_effect.asp?pf_id=521, February 22, 2011.

It's certainly difficult to compute the exact impact to Apple's bottom line, but there's no doubt it's putting its product in front of millions, if not billions, of potential buyers, in a medium that will continue to deliver impressions as those movies make their way through all the platforms available to them in windowing.

The catch with Apple? It claims to have never paid for placement, but it does furnish product—and a particularly hip cachet.

Another revenue strategy for movies comes in the form of product tie-ins. We take a closer look at specifics a little later in the chapter when we talk about the actual marketing of the movie, but for now, keep in mind that all those dollars generated through McDonald's Happy Meals and Omega watches fall right to the bottom line.

As an entertainment marketer, your job is to find every possible way to leverage and exploit your movie, through every single window it passes through. Product placement and tie-ins are just the beginning. These two strategies allow studios to reduce risk by bringing in outside funding for those ever-more-costly movies.

But it isn't just live action that packs the profits into the studio coffers (hopefully). Another type of feature that has gained presence is *animation*.

Another Profit Powerhouse: Animation

Animated films allow for huge merchandising and licensing deals, stretching the brand across the globe, while generating additional marketing support for the original product.

For most of the twentieth century, animation meant Disney. After all, Walt Disney founded his studio with Mickey Mouse and became known as the king of family fare with the vast stable of characters that followed Mickey. Even as he pushed forward with live-action film classics like *Old Yeller* and television staples such as *Zorro* and *Davy Crockett*, when you said "Disney," you thought "Mickey."

What Disney realized, very early on, was this: You don't make animated features for children. You make them for parents. Children do not drive themselves to the theater or pay for their tickets. If you add enough adult-level interest, humor, and morality to an animated feature, parents will gladly take their kids.

The multi-billion dollar empire that is now Disney, stretching from theme parks to cruise ships to live-action and, yes, animated films, owes everything to that squeaky-voiced mouse—oh, and Walt, Michael Eisner, and now Bob Iger. These three men, along with Jeffrey Katzenberg (who brought animation back to the forefront with *The Lion King*—the first billion-dollar animated feature, cross-platforming all the way to Broadway), created a powerhouse that seems almost a part of our DNA.

The reason for that deep, entrenched loyalty has as much to do with warm and fuzzy fare as it does with brilliant brand extension and licensing. The intellectual property owned by Disney seemingly stretches everywhere in the world, including English-as-a-second-language schools in China, featuring the characters—a brilliant move that will serve the brand well, as this enormous potential market comes to fruition.

And due to superb management of the brand, Disney's intellectual property is held for rerelease on a carefully timed schedule. Interested in owning *Fantasia*? Available for years, on Blue-Ray or DVD. *Cinderella*? Not rereleased until 2012. You can bet that the Disney coffers filled once again and not just from the animated feature. There was plenty of licensed merchandise to accompany it, once again supporting the phenomenal brand that is Disney.

Not that Disney has rested on those animation laurels, by the way. Disney's deal with Pixar, the early masters of computer-generated imagery (CGI)—creating such mega-successes as *Toy Story, Monsters, Inc.*, and *Finding Nemo*, eventually built some bad blood between Disney and Pixar, given the inequity of a split heavily weighted in Disney's favor. The solution? In 2006, Disney purchased Pixar, and the beat went on, leading to *Ratatouille, Up, WALL-E, Brave and Cars.*

But moving into the new century, other studios also realized the power of animation, extending and supporting their own brands through licensing and merchandising such well-known non-Disney franchises as *Ice Age* (1 through 4) from Blue Sky via 20th Century Fox; *Despicable Me* from Universal's Illumination; and *Shrek* (1 through 4) from DreamWorks. DreamWorks, of course, was the brainchild of Steven Spielberg, David Geffen, and Jeffrey Katzenberg (Mr. *Lion King*), who left Disney after the power plays left him out of the president's chair.

The ratcheting level of competition between all these studios creates the need for powerful marketing programs to gain attention and a share of parents' pocketbooks.

As a side note, the impact of CGI needs to be mentioned. Not limited to pure animation releases, CGI has become a staple of the film industry. CGI, also called computer animation, is essentially the next step on the ladder from classic frame-by-frame 2D illustrations (all original animated Disney features) and stop-motion 3D (think *Frankenweenie*). CGI has created the magic of *Avatar*, switching from live-action to fantasy, and the classic battle scenes of *Lord of the Rings* (not to mention Gollum).

Animation has grown as a genre not just because of its popularity with children and holiday-hassled parents. The genre has some major advantages for studios:

- Animated characters get no salary, residuals, or benefits.
- The characters are brands unto themselves and can be marketed through licensing toys, merchandise, and must-haves.
- Animation can be created by software, which is faster and cheaper than traditional frame-by-frame hand-drawn animation cels.
- Kids' word-of-mouth is strong, gaining the attention of their friends and their parents.
- Seasonal marketing is easier; animation peaks during holidays from school.
- Voices and animation are usually recognizable stars, but the features are not reliant on that star power.
- Animation is easy to market via TV and trailers.
- Most animation has a morality story—good versus evil—offering positive imagery for marketing to parents.

- The strongest of the animation brands are walking billboards on lunch boxes, backpacks, T-shirts, jackets, and every possible product you can mention. This creates both additional revenue streams and additional marketing support for the original product. Additional tie-ins—creating the same effect—include fast food (McDonald's, Burger King), beverages (Coke and Pepsi), cold cereals, and vitamins.

- Animation, in home video, has high sales and rentals and supports repeat viewing (often acting as a babysitter).

However, even with experts conjuring up complicated models and "can't miss" formulas, accurately predicting movie performance is virtually impossible. There is no machine, computer, abacus, or psychic connection that can create the concept, script, and direction to turn an idea into a blockbuster financial success or critical artistic achievement.

The industry's past, present, and future depend on writers, directors, actors, cinematographers, and all the other behind-the-scenes professionals—not the least of which are the individuals involved in marketing.

Behind the Scenes: The Producer

The marketing of a studio's film is generally presided over by the president of marketing and his or her staff. However, many phases of marketing individual films are handled by the *producer*.

There are two types of producers that are used by the major movie studios, and the responsibilities are different for each.

Every large studio has *in-house producers*. An in-house producer, on a "work for hire" arrangement as a salaried staff member, has restricted responsibilities primarily focused on controlling the budget, scheduling, and coordinating on-location staff with studio executives. Problems of any magnitude are usually discussed with the studio chiefs. The promotion of a film is overseen by the president of marketing.

However, studios might also work with *independent producers*. (Note that an independent producer is not necessarily working on an independent film, which we discuss later. In this discussion, an independent producer is working on a studio project, taking the place of the in-house producer.)

Independent producers are used for certain unique properties being developed by the studio. But an independent producer may also bring an idea to a studio—for example, Jerry Bruckheimer, who has his own production company—with many producers on staff—brought *Pirates of the Caribbean* to Disney.

In this case, the producer can option a property, book, or screenplay with personal funds and then hire the writers, director, star, and extras or work with a talent agency to package the talent for the film. It is frequently up to the independent producer to develop the treatment or write the script to build up both momentum and credibility for the product. The independent producer is usually also responsible for the functioning of the film: the complete agreements for distribution, casting, collaborating, and managing the process.

Little of this work is performed by the executive producer, who usually gets this title because of a majority or significant financial investment in the production of the film. Sometimes a star obtains the title of executive producer, either for his or her bankable nature or need for ego-stroking.

Ignoring the independent producer's role as a marketer would be tantamount to describing the cinematographer's role as merely that of a cameraman or the head of distribution at a studio as a sales clerk.

An independent producer must be a marketing generalist, working with advertising professionals when the budget for marketing exceeds $10 million. Even then, the independent producer is involved with all aspects of marketing, including strategy development, trailer composition, selection of key visuals for print and poster advertising, Internet and social networking applications, and negotiating agreements with the stars to do publicity stills.

The independent producer also works with the advertising agency or media buying service to ensure that the message is correct and that the media is effectively purchased and targeted at the predetermined audience. He or she also coordinates any licensing and merchandise contracts with the licensees, seeking an integrated communications image—an important goal, if the licensees are obligated by contract to spend advertising budgets in support of a new toy, publishing or music product, or other licensed item.

Regardless of whether the producer is independent or in-house, be assured that no one is surprised to see the involvement of the president, the CEO, and perhaps even the chairman of the studio when the initial production budget is $100 million or above and the marketing investment is $25 to $30 million.

When films spiral over budget—as they often do—there is a frequent need for top management to expand their share of voice against the competitive film offerings. When there is a summer of blockbusters, with five or more films at the $100 million level, management and the creative staff are in frequent discussion, working to ensure that the studio's product will measure up to the competition. When those films are all competing for the same audience, shifts in scheduling frequently occur at the last minute to create better windows of opportunity for the movie's opening weekend.

This movement is happening more often now, as production heads realize that movie openings are all about logistics.

All of this discussion can turn to major conflict when things begin to go wrong. Yet in the highly volatile, content-driven and risk-averse business of movie-making, the "suits" are often loathe to stop the creative process for fear that something magical will occur. Thus, there was no way to stop *Heaven's Gate* or *Titanic* once they were in full production.

Heaven's Gate grossly exceeded its budget and was a historic flop, setting a precedent for out-of-control production. The cost of *Titanic* was nearly double the initial projected budget but had a theatrical box office of over $1.5 billion and became such an evergreen product that it was rereleased in 3D format 15 years later, jumping over $200 million in only 12 days.

Out the Door and Onto the Streets: Distribution

Getting the film from the studio to the screen takes a big chunk of the marketing budget. This process is known as *distribution*. In the past, when movies were actually distributed as film in large canisters that went to the theaters for screening, costs to distribute could vary based on the initial number of screens (how "wide" it opened) and whether or not the film had "legs" (a long, successful run at the theaters, with many more screens added after opening weekend).

At $2,000 a pop, with a typical opening of 2,000 screens, the cost of prints added up. Add to that the initial advertising budget and a $100 million movie quickly added anywhere from $25 million to $50 million to the cost. With a successful box office run, that number no longer had any anchor holding it to the ground.

For a variety of reasons, not every studio handles its own distribution. Many studios cut deals to have other studios distribute their movies. And the studios are happy to have them. The industry metric for a distributor's compensation is one-third of a film's box office. In other words, potentially more profit for those major studio distributors without taking the risk of making the movie.[12]

Animated feature distribution is an especially nice niche for those studios without animated divisions of their own. Fox recently signed a distribution deal for DreamWorks—which created the multiple versions of *Shrek, Madagascar, Kung Fu Panda*, and *How to Train Your Dragon*—whose distribution had been previously handled by Paramount.

At the time of this writing, there are many in the industry wondering if Mr. Katzenberg might be bringing his magic to yet another animation division, a Fox combo of Blue Sky and DreamWorks. But the stated reason for DreamWorks's shift to Fox is the obvious cross-platforming with Fox's FX cable network, as well as that studio's concentration on digital distribution.

Digital Distribution

The advent of digital transmission allows the studios to reduce the costly process of producing and distributing prints. Not all screens have converted to digital, so some prints must still go out. As of 2012, the breakdown was as follows: regular analog screens, 6,423; digital and 3D, 14,734; digital and non-3D, 21,643; total screens, 42,803.[13] That's a 50% decline in analog screens in one year.

Digital transmission is clearly the wave of the future, with benefits for both the studios and the exhibitors. It is less costly for the studios, but having access to digital transmission opens the doors for exhibitors to expand their offerings—and their revenue—filling seats for live screenings of everything from boxing to opera.

Studios are now much more nimble, with the advent of digital technology, expanding their reach not just domestically but internationally. The increase in digital transmission created a big boost

---

[12] There are select independent distributors who may consider lower rates for particular movies. Bob Burney cut a deal with Mel Gibson to distribute *The Passion of Christ* for only 10%. However, Burney was willing to take a risk on a larger return, a bet that paid off. He took his 10% off a $400 million box office.

[13] Motion Picture Association of America (Rentrak 2012 research).

for international box offices in 2012, when the major international markets grew 35% over 2011.[14] The international box office adds a hefty amount to a movie's take. The year 2012 saw the international box office hit $23.9 billion compared to $10.8 billion in the U.S.[15]

Piracy

One of the most critical factors in digital transmission is the ability to get movies to screens immediately, everywhere. Piracy—the out-and-out stealing of copyrighted content for illegal resale—flourishes if the audience, whether in New York or New Delhi, cannot quickly and easily see the film.

This technological wonder doesn't end the threat of piracy; in fact, in some ways it can make it easier. The Motion Picture Association of America said that the movie industry loses billions of dollars every year to Internet piracy. The phenomenon is widespread in part because of file-sharing technology such as that utilized by BitTorrent.com, which allows computer users to copy large files—like movies—and share them.

Sides have been drawn on this issue, with the movie industry justifiably on the "con" side. Techies who appreciate the value of file sharing take an alternate view. In any case, we do have the ability to track the impact. TorrentFreak.com, which monitors and stores the data reported by different BitTorrent trackers, released this list, shown in Exhibit 3-3, of the ten most-pirated movies of all time, compiled from BitTorrent files since 2006.[16]

Exhibit 3-3   The Ten Most Pirated Movies of All Time

Rank	Movie (Year of Release)	Illegal Downloads	Worldwide Box Office	Estimated Lost Revenue
1	Avatar (2009)	21 Million	$2.8 Billion	$105 Million
2 (Tie)	The Dark Knight (2008)	19 Million	$1 Billion	$95 Million
2 (Tie)	Transformers (2007)	19 Million	$710 Million	$95 Million
4	Inception (2010)	18 Million	$825 Million	$90 Million
5	The Hangover (2009)	17 Million	$467 Million	$85 Million
6	Star Trek (2009)	16 Million	$386 Million	$80 Million
7	Kick-Ass (2010)	15 Million	$96 Million	$75 Million
8 (Tie)	The Departed (2006)	14 Million	$290 Million	$70 Million
8 (Tie)	The Incredible Hulk (2008)	14 Million	$263 Million	$70 Million
8 (Tie)	Pirates of the Caribbean (2007)	14 Million	$963 Million	$70 Million

Source: CNBC.com, August 2012

[14] Motion Picture Association of America (Rentrak 2012 research).

[15] Motion Picture Association of America (Rentrak 2012 research).

[16] CNBC.com, The 10 Most Pirated Movies of All Time, www.cnbc.com/id/48768803/10_MostPirated_Movies_of_All_Time.

Piracy is a phenomenon that attacks international box office revenue. That box office is growing every day. There are 300 million people in the United States and 7 billion people in the world with somewhere between 3 and 4 billion people who are considered middle income in their own environment. With the ever-increasing entertainment appetite of rapidly evolving countries such as China and India, global entertainment—and global entertainment marketing—is a huge market rapidly rising on the horizon.

Down the line in the life of a movie, broadband and wireless, hand-in-hand with all the new hardware these conduits feed—smartphones, TVs, laptops, tablets, airplane screens—have created huge new outlets of distribution. Now that digital information can be compressed and streamed, the consumer is king, choosing when to see the movie, on whatever size screen he wishes, at whatever hour of the day or night that is convenient to him. The number of distribution outlets that provide the full movie without any interruptions has climbed enormously. And the process of acquiring that movie has gone from a three-hour drag to a lighting quick download.

Theaters: Still Big Box Office

In a time when consumers have greater and faster access to movies than ever before—with home-theater systems to rival the sound and image quality found in small movie houses—it would seem as though marketers would face an uphill battle to lure audiences into the theater to view any one of the over-600 films[17] released each year.

And when you add the ever-increasing price of going to the movies—with almost $20 per ticket in major metropolitan areas, another $20 for popcorn and soda, one fistful of bucks for the parking lot attendant and another for the babysitter—you might think that the theaters would be pretty empty.

But here's the news: the U.S./Canada box office grew 6% from 2011 to 2012, with 225 million persons going to the movies at least once in 2012.[18]

Even though the domestic box office (DBO) only accounts for a percentage of total film revenue, it is the scorecard, the buzz-creator and sustainer that drives all other revenue that will be generated by a film, from downloads to licensed products. It is that ancillary business that often provides a major portion of a film's profits.

So with all the access to movies on other platforms and with a rising cost of a movie ticket, why are people still going to theaters, still creating that DBO? People are social by nature. Although social networking platforms provide a place to connect thought instantaneously, people of all ages still follow their instinct to herd. And young people, in the throes of mating, know that there is only so much that can happen when sitting home alone in front of a screen.

Entertainment is one of the primary opportunities to accomplish a connection with others, and in our present-day culture, movies still offer the chance to sit in the dark with 300 strangers (or

---

17 Motion Picture Association of America (Rentrak 2012 research).

18 Motion Picture Association of America (Rentrak 2012 research).

your date) and participate in laughing, crying, thinking—and touching—and generally being swept away by the entire experience.

This fact is not lost on exhibitors. AMC Loews, Regal Cinemas, General Cinema, Carmike, Mann Theaters, and others are focusing on the quality of the in-theater experience in an effort to shift movie-going from a commodity, competing with all the other viewing opportunities, gearing up for this battle by building newer, bigger, better, cleaner, multiscreen mega-plexes, most of them with best-quality surround sound and state-of-the-art image projection, including 3D.

Exhibitors are also utilizing online ticket purchasing, stadium seating, snap-in food trays, credit card kiosks, fancy coffee bars, high-priced but filling comfort food, bright clean bathrooms, larger inside waiting areas, and placement near other amusement areas for after-movie interests. In major market areas, movie-goers can reserve seats, just as they might at a live theater venue.

This is all part of the arsenal of the leading theater chains and has contributed to another phenomenon: consumer's inelasticity to ticket price increases. Even with some metropolitan areas reaching the $20 per ticket level, there has been relatively little reaction from the public.

All of this funnels back into the all-important opening weekend and the marketing that must be done to get the audience in the seats. In the short lifespan of a film's initial release, the most critical time period is that opening weekend because it accounts for 20% of total box office gross.

Therefore, marketers have an awfully short window of opportunity to create a brand image for movies—the image that will pave the way for the windfalls beyond.

Movie Marketing: Who Are the Targets?

Today's blockbusters, including the *Iron Man*, *Bourne*, and *Harry Potter* franchises, have all expertly used time-tested, high concept techniques to create huge box-office returns. Aimed at not only building excitement but also maintaining it, marketing campaigns use all forms of traditional media—print, cable and network television, radio, and billboards.

With the more recent addition of the Internet and all that it offers—social networking, dedicated websites, links to other websites, twitter feeds, and all forms of constant contact—studios now have multiple ways to quickly build huge interest in films.

And who's interested? One of the key market segments that still sweep into the theater are teens and young adults—a heavy movie-going group. Twelve-to twenty-four year-olds are the most frequent movie-goers, with an equal male/female split. Hispanics also enjoy movies more frequently. These two groups buy half of all tickets.[19]

Teenagers will always search for the one private place to congregate away from the eyes of parents, teachers, and other adults. Although online social networking sites allow for conversation, movie theaters allow for touch. Even as screen-time has more to do with computers and smartphones, 12–18 and 20–25-year-olds still head to movies in droves. This has made the teen and young adult demographic the most sought after by movie studios and their marketing partners. Whether or not they can be weaned from texting and tweeting while in the theater remains to be seen.

---

[19] Motion Picture Association of America (Rentrak 2011 research).

The presence of this tempting, free-spending demographic has had a dramatic impact on movie content, as studios churn out what seems to be an endless string of action and special effect-driven films that might or might not actually contain meaningful content.

But a new challenge has arisen in this important demographic: the rise of electronic gaming, especially among males ages 18 to 35. We cover this platform later, but in terms of movies, games have created a separate path in the entertainment experience.

The defining characteristic of gaming is the ability of the participants to actually change the story line based on their own moves and strategies. And as the technology of games has improved to the point of delivering high-quality imagery and sound, it has begun to challenge the in-theater movie experience for this age group. Studios are responding with action-driven movies that feature even more graphic images of mayhem, sometimes featuring a Web-based game as an appetizer in an effort to bring gamers to the theater.

However, one true-blue demographic has caught the eye of studios: Baby Boomers. Raised on the movie theater experience, Boomers have become a hot demographic for studios as some segments have begun to look elsewhere. Big releases in the first decade of the new century included *The Expendables* (one and two), *RED, Julie & Julia, The Exotic Marigold Hotel, Gran Torino*, and *True Grit*, featuring stars well into their 60s, 70s, and 80s. Names such as Morgan Freeman, Jack Nicholson, Meryl Streep, Helen Mirren, Tommy Lee Jones, and Arnold Schwarzenegger still attract the Boomer demographic, a group with tons of disposable income and discretionary time.[20]

Studios have also begun to offer a far different image to young girls and young women than the old princess-who-must-be-saved model, finally recognizing that girls are movie-goers (possibly even more loyal than the previously mentioned game-playing boys). Though there's still plenty of pretty pink, movies such as 2012's *Snow White and the Huntsman*—where the heroine does not break up her coronation by rushing down the aisle toward her true love, choosing instead an equal affirmation and a steely look across her subjects—heralds a new concentration on a demographic with spending power and word of mouth.

Finally, we have a phenomenon known as *crossover*. Although crossover is typically used in the music industry (covered in a later chapter), the concept has emerged as the standard for celebrities who extend their careers across movies, music, television, and Broadway. The marketing machine ramps up when Will Ferrell, who got his start in improvisational comedy (The Groundlings) and went on to television (*Saturday Night Live*), leaps from the small screen to the big screen (*Anchorman: The Legend of Ron Burgundy, Elf, Blades of Glory, The Campaign*) to Broadway (*You're Welcome America. A Final Night with George W. Bush*)—or when Grammy-winning Joss Stone takes a turn in Showtime's *The Tudors*.

This is brand extension, pure and simple. But that extension has a direct payback to the movies, for crossover works both ways, luring audiences from one medium to another after they've been introduced to the star.

Even more important to the crossover discussion is the ever-emerging mix between cultures and countries, with stars from particular niches (Jennifer Lopez, getting her start singing in Spanish

---

[20] "Old People, Old Stars: Hollywood's New Hot Demo Is Saving the Box Office," *The Hollywood Reporter*, August 22, 2012.

in *Selena*, or Dev Patel opening the big doors with India-based *Slum Dog Millionaire*) finding huge success across language and media platforms. What's particularly interesting about these two examples? Although entertainment audiences see both these stars as specific to an ethnic background, Lopez was born in the Bronx, and Patel is British, born in Harrow. But they both bring new, emerging audiences to the theater.

Make no mistake: Today's entertainment marketing executive had better have a crystal clear view of the global market. Despite whatever challenges there might be between countries politically, entertainment in all its forms rings cash registers around the world.

We touch on global entertainment in a later chapter, but now let's concentrate on the how-tos of filling seats.

Movie Marketing: Creating Wannasee

We have the film, and we have the audience. Now we need to bring them together.

The movie marketer's challenge is to create "wannasee" among consumers, creating enough buzz or word of mouth to drive viewers into the theater, resulting in the classic marketing outcome of turning want into need.

As mentioned earlier, marketers have an extremely short window of opportunity, with increasingly high competition. Remember: Movies aren't just competing against other movies; they are competing against every other form of entertainment out there (not to mention doing nothing). To create strategies that will drive audiences into theaters, movie marketers—like consumer product marketers—rely heavily on consumer research. Focus groups, surveys, and in-depth interviews help studio executives make critical marketing and production decisions. Among those decisions are the following:

- Is the target audience correct?
- Is the trailer compelling, creating "must see?"
- Is the marketing believable?
- Is the audience laughing at the right spots?

Like every other supplier in this age of risk reduction, studio executives want to have a guarantee that their films will appeal to wide audiences. Though there is no such thing as guaranteed success, consumer research can help ease the angst. But there has been more than one studio executive who tossed the research out the window, going on his or her gut instinct, and lived to tell the tale.

Being too cautious has its own risks. One famous example of this was the launch of the first *Toy Story* movie by Disney. This coproduction with Pixar was expected to be a more minor release but quickly blew up into a box-office phenomenon. Disney reportedly missed out on an estimated $200 million in licensing and merchandising revenue because insufficient licensed product had been prepared for the Christmas rush. It was an expensive lesson but one that wasn't forgotten for *Toy Story 2*, *3*, and whatever other number has yet to be introduced.

Marketing Methods

Regardless of the strategy or instinct, there are a variety of methods utilized in the marketing of a film. Some are actual processes; others are more conceptual in nature. The following are typical promotional strategies used in the marketing of movies.

Test Screenings

During the production and editing of a film, it is crucial to get a reaction from the target audience. Studios get this feedback via test screenings. Typically, passes will be randomly distributed in front of a movie theater. The pass entitles the respondent to see an unfinished version of a film. After the film, the audience is asked to fill out a lengthy survey, asking detailed questions about the characters, plot, and scenes. The audience reaction is reviewed, and appropriate changes may be made.

Although test screenings are a useful marketing tool, the growth of the Internet has created new risks. Information that leaks from tests can result in disaster. The studios got a nasty introduction to viral backfiring years ago when Warner Bros. had a test screening on a version of the big-budget *Wild Wild West* that had not been completely edited. The test went so poorly the audience actually booed.[21] Even though the audience signed confidentiality agreements, the news quickly spread via the Internet, where anonymity makes it easy to dish bad buzz. This proved disastrous. Warner Bros. was unable to control the negative buzz, and the movie was a box office failure.

Sneak Previews

Sneak previews can build buzz, but studios prefer to set them up if they are confident the preview audience will provide favorable word of mouth prior to opening. It is not unusual for studios to avoid sneaks if they know the film will generate bad buzz. In this case, studios will open the "flop" as wide as possible without any sneak previews. If the advertising campaign is successful, a significant audience will show up opening weekend to see the film, helping to cover some of the costs. But inevitably, the negative word of mouth will circulate, and the movie will be out of the theaters in less than the usual four-week window.

Movie Trailers

When the marketing juggernaut begins to move, movie trailers are must-haves. Although media and print are important to a movie marketing campaign, the movie trailer is the most crucial element. The best trailer is a tiny movie unto itself, telling a story and whetting the audience's appetite. The studio executive's challenge is to get people to see a film without telling everything about the film, and a successful trailer does just this.

Typically, two trailers are produced. The first is called the teaser trailer, which is shown in theaters six months before the film is released.[22] The second trailer tells more of a story and is shown in

---

21   Svetkey, Benjamin, "Even Cowboys Get The Blues," *Entertainment Weekly*, July 8, 1999.

22   Lukk, Tiiu, *Movie Marketing*, Beverly Hills, CA: Silman-James Press, 1997.

---

theaters ten to eight weeks before the film opens. With today's access to the Internet, additional trailers may also be produced. More about that in a minute.

Trailers have their plusses and minuses, depending on the movie as a whole and what's left on the cutting room floor. If handled by an expert, with the guidance of a movie marketing professional, trailers can hit a home run with the target audience. However, many studios allow the filmmakers to play a role in the marketing of a film, which can often lead to clashes. Marketers are trying to deliver what the consumer wants, while filmmakers can be concerned with the integrity of the story. The two don't always match.

The marketer isn't always in the right, though; too much creative license can be disastrous. To capture the attention of the appropriate segment of the audience, a trailer might focus on a certain element of a film, making the movie appear to be more of a solid representation of a genre than is truly deserved. The only slightly sensual, barely action-oriented, or vaguely funny comedy may utilize a trailer that exaggerates any of these elements. Consumers who have no other source of information can be disappointed when they actually see the movie, and thus negative word of mouth is created.

Then there's the question of giving away too much. A survey taken in April of 2013 by YouGov. com found that 49% of Americans feel that movie trailers give away too many of a film's best scenes. 32% felt that trailers gave away too much plot, while 48% disagreed. Would that stop audiences from seeing a film? 19% of respondents said that too-revealing trailers have deterred them from seeing a film, but 24% said it makes them want to see the film more. 35% said it has no impact at all.

In other words: it's pretty much a draw. Given the increasing attendance in movie theaters, it would appear that there's a fairly good balance in what trailers represent. However, the group that feels some trailers show all the best scenes may have a point. More than a few marginal movies make it to the theaters, and in those cases, those few best scenes are the only thing the film has going for it.

That same survey found that trailers play a huge role in getting people into theaters: Americans cite the two biggest factors in helping them decide which movies to see as trailers (48%) and personal recommendations (46%).

Trailers can also garner two different audiences for a movie that has a distinct but potentially dual personality. *The Adjustment Bureau*, a 2011 film starring Matt Damon and Emily Blunt, functioned both as a thriller and a romance. With the Internet offering a conduit for multiple versions of the trailer, potential audiences were able to make a decision regarding the film based on their own desired point of view. The trailers were accurate in their use of footage from the film but simply focused on the action and drama for the male audience and made the romantic scenes more prominent and expansive for the female audience. Neither audience was disappointed because both were satisfied by the story, content, and elements each was seeking. Women brought men, and men brought women, resulting in a great marketing success.

Trailer Distribution

Trailers can run a few minutes when shown in a theater, can be cut to a 30- or 60-second version for TV commercials, or can run as long as five to six minutes when placed as part of a rolling series of previews or display on social networking sites. In the past, trailers were seen in only a few places—the theater, a television commercial, at the beginning of DVDs, or a download from Netflix. But with the advent of the Internet, the marketing potential of trailers has exploded.

No longer confined to the movie theater or a television commercial spot, trailers are now available all over the Internet—Facebook, YouTube, the movie's website, associated websites, Fandango, Moviefone, IMDb.com, any link from any media source. Viewers can play them again and again (a marketer's dream!) and enjoy several different versions. The consumer is now in full control of how and when she or he wants to consume that little bit of movie.

The cost-effectiveness of the Internet is unlike anything in traditional marketing. Those who wish to view the trailer can do so as many times as they want and share it with as many friends as they like. On the happy chance that the trailer goes viral—spinning over the Internet to millions of eyeballs—the cost disappears into the ether.

Television Commercials

Even with the importance of trailers, television is where most of the media dollars are spent because unlike the Internet, the majority of television exposure must be paid for. Even with the rise of the Internet, television still has the most consistent reach for marketing movies.

No other vehicle, including cable television, can reach as many people with one trailer as broadcast television. One spot on primetime television reaches over 25 million viewers. Between networks, cable, satellite, and syndication, well over $70 billion is spent yearly in the U.S. alone.[23]

The goal of the commercial is to grab the audience's attention. Whereas a trailer (in the theater) has a captive audience, a commercial has to fight to keep the viewer from changing the channel. Because of this, most movie commercials rely heavily on good reviews and sexy images from the film—the type of content proven to keep viewers' fingers off the remote. Movie commercials are aired predominantly on Thursday evenings, when consumers are making their plans for the weekend.

Movie marketing strategies for blockbuster films—opening wide to over 2000 screens simultaneously—incorporate specific television tactics. The media plan is developed over months of planning, with backup options in place for signs of success or weak performance. The strategy includes local TV and cable to capture specific target audiences:

- Romantic films are advertised on Lifetime Channel, Women's Entertainment (WETV), Food Network, Oxygen, the Oprah Winfrey Network (OWN), and any other predominantly female conduit.

- Adventure films, spy stories, murder mysteries, sports films, and violent movies are advertised on ESPN, Fox Sports, *Monday Night Football*, Spike, and the traditional networks, adjacent to similar shows and movies.

---

[23] PwC Global Entertainment and Media Outlook: 2012–2016, www.pwc.com/outlook.

- The prime movie-going audiences (12–18 and 19–25) are reached on MTV, VH1, BET, and on situation comedies (sitcoms) popular with that demographic: *Modern Family, Two and a Half Men*, and all the clones of these shows, along with such reality television as *The Voice* and *American Idol*.

Newspaper Advertising

The local newspaper has always been a mainstay, an underpinning for all movie advertising. The big marketing blitz for a perceived or actual blockbuster will get a double-page spread and a teaser campaign in every local newspaper city by city, as long as there are screens in that area. Almost all "A" movies (big-budget, big-star films with an expected four-week run or better) will get at least one full page in the Sunday editions.

Most newspapers have either their own film reviewers or use nationally syndicated reviewers. If their evaluation of the movie is positive, they may even find their quotes picked up as part of the film's campaign. However, this tactic received a lot of press in the summer of 2001, when it was discovered that Sony Pictures had fabricated a reviewer, who, of course, gave great reviews to Sony films.

An important part of newspaper's support of the film industry are special issues. *The New York Times* and *The Los Angeles Times* provide a series of special film issues each year. These can include the following: *Spring Film Preview, Oscar Films, Summer Film Preview, Fall Film Preview, Holiday Film Preview,* and the Hollywood Issue in *The New York Times Magazine*.

Variety magazine provides an extensive movie description and analysis of every new movie.

Movie Tie-Ins

Earlier in this chapter, we discussed the financial impact of tie-ins and their importance to the bottom line of the film. From a marketing perspective, movie tie-ins create great symbiosis. The brand—McDonald's, BMW, Omega watches—gives films added exposure through their own ads and publicity, while films deliver the buzz that keeps the brand hip (or at least current). The list of products is nearly endless, as both partners strive to create "havetosee" and "havetobuy."

The most desired demographic is the teenage market, a demographic with plenty of disposable income and a desire to connect with a particular identity as they strive to create their own.

Association with popular movies has created marketing success stories for companies as diverse as Aston Martin and McDonald's (see Exhibit 3-4). All report increased sales during tie-in periods.

Exhibit 3-4   Movie Tie-Ins

Movie/Studio	Company	Product	Target
Dark Knight/Warner Bros.	Hasbro		Kids and Young Adults
Spiderman/Sony	Mattel	Spiderman Toys, Halloween Outfits	Parents and Kids
Harry Potter/Warner Bros.	Scholastic	Books, Paraphernalia	Potter Fans

Movie/Studio	Company	Product	Target
Lurex/Universal	Verizon	Triple Play	Adults
Ice Age/20th Century Fox	Power Up Toy Company	Plush Toys	Kids
Toy Story/Disney and Pixar	Mattel, McDonald's	Toys, Happy Meals	Parents and Kids
Finding Nemo/Disney and Pixar	Hasbro, Burger King	Rubber Fish, Drink Cups, Collectibles	Parents and Kids
(James Bond) Skyfall/MGM	Aston Martin, Omega	Cars, Watches	Adults
Avengers/Disney	Random House	Super Heroes Pop-Up Books	Parents and Kids
Transformers/Paramount	Hasbro	Toys	Parents and Kids

Ticket Presale Conduits

Ticket sales left the box office with the advent of Moviefone, which allowed customers to dial 777-FILM and purchase tickets in advance. After the service moved online to moviefone.com—tied in to the then industry leader, AOL—the ticket purchase process was forever changed.

AOL paid the two Moviefone developers and their original investors millions of dollars for ownership of this very valuable marketing tool. Moviefone offered direct access to customers, while providing another media platform. It generated massive advertising revenue from major studios and film distributors eager to reach various segments of the movie-going public.

Moviefone was eventually bought by *The New York Times*. AMC/Loews cloned their own product, available via the Internet. But the winner in this category is Fandango, which allows for advance purchase of tickets and features the all-important movie trailer. Fandango users can purchase advance tickets on both the Fandango website and the associated smartphone app. This mobile presence offers marketers a chance to build box office by catching potential moviegoers just as they make their plans for the evening.

These conduits are another example of powerful symbiotic marketing tools. Studios have yet another platform to create buzz, and exhibitors have an external box office.

The Oscars—A Powerful Marketing Tool

Everyone in the movie business knows the leverage a nomination at the annual Oscars can provide for a movie. The award ceremony itself is broadcast around the world, both live and taped for delayed broadcast, and is viewed by well over a billion people. This supports both DBO and foreign distribution.

Much has been said about the process of selecting the candidates for every award and the nature of the performance by the Master of Ceremonies, including Billy Crystal, Whoopi Goldberg, David Letterman, and Steve Martin. On Oscar night, it isn't just the movies that get the buzz. James Franco and Anne Hathaway, both talented actors in their own right, learned the hard way that a bad night hosting the Oscars can lead to an even worse morning.

In 2013, the Academy, looking to build ratings in the 18 to 34 male demographic, brought Seth MacFarlane in as host. He brought a new low to the evening, creating more of a sophomoric roast than a toast—not what the traditional Oscars fan expected. As actress Jamie Lee Curtis later commented,[24] what if the actors and actresses stopped coming to the ceremony, not enamored of being skewered by Hollywood footnotes? Building ratings has its challenges.

Additional coverage, all of it acting as additional marketing for the movie, includes widely distributed reviews of the acceptance speeches (which range from maudlin, tear-filled, and boring to hysterical and occasionally heartfelt or funny) and preshows that focus on the clothes and opinions of the stars.

However, the serious players in this event understand that a win, with careful promotion and competitive tactics, can add as much as $30 million to the DBO revenue and untold millions in foreign and supplementary revenue. So-called "smaller" movies—non-blockbusters—such as *The Artist*, *Iron Lady*, and *The King's Speech*, have all benefited from Oscar and his largesse.

The Oscars has become a must-see for movie fans and those who want a quick review of films they should see if they have limited viewing opportunities.

And what would the film industry be without the obsessed? Many films have enjoyed multiple visits by audiences captivated by award-winners. It is still a discussion of great wonder and envy that a portion of *Titanic*'s female teen audience members saw the film more than 10 times, with some memorizing dialog from the love scenes. These same fans probably made up the base for the 2012 3D relaunch as well.

Techno Tools

Today, no film is released without a website, and most have websites long before the movie is ready to be distributed. Websites built excitement, create interest, allow for multiple showings of those trailers, and due to data collection allow studios to get a feel for just how many people are connecting with the film.

A successful website is highly imaginative and engages the audience, really connecting them with the story and the characters. Often, the site will provide links to related political, financial, and historical issues and certainly to the product tie-ins discussed earlier. Seeking to actively engage the audience in an experience, many sites will feature interactive devices, such as games or contests.

Social networking—with its creation of buzz through Twitter, Facebook, and a variety of newcomers—has created yet another conduit for marketing movies. Along with the direct application of linking lookers to trailers or websites, these platforms serve to create a sort of backward spin that can encourage additional movie going, an opportunity to move the herd. Faced with a plethora of posts regarding hot new movies, social networkers can find themselves feeling out of touch if they haven't yet seen the film everyone else is talking about.

---

[24] Curtis, Jamie Lee, "And the Oscar Goes to...Hell," Huffington Post, March 1, 2013 www.huffingtonpost.com/jamie-lee-curtis/and-the-oscar-goes-to-hell_b_2793392.html.

The ever-evolving self-authorship of the Internet has also allowed for the actual individual marketing and initial success of a movie. *The Blair Witch Project* was made by a group of young adults for less than $65,000 and created great Internet buzz. Artisan Entertainment purchased the rights and continued to use the Internet, directly targeting teens (great horror fans). The film broke out to wider audiences and eventually generated $140 million.

However, the use of the Internet can also backfire. Marketing professionals learned a lesson back in 2001 when the Steven Spielberg/Stanley Kubrick film *A.I.* was released that summer. The combination of these two geniuses created huge expectations. The studios created additional buzz through an interactive game placed on the film's website. The game achieved cult status, with buy-in from a highly interested audience base. However, the game also created high expectations of the movie. When the film failed to match those expectations, the game players, a very Internet-savvy group, created huge negative word of mouth among the very base of potential movie viewers the studio was trying to reach. As a result, *A.I.* failed to achieve its expected box office returns.

Planes, Trains, Automobiles—and More

Once limited to tiny airline drop-down screens several rows from your seat, offering one movie per flight, feature films have now found a home on all sorts of personal screens—on the back of the airline seat and the car seat; in your cruise-ship room; and thanks to Netflix, on laptops in the quiet car on the Acela. Although the viewing experience may still feel less than theater-perfect, these new conduits provide yet another revenue stream and are so popular with travelers that some people book certain airlines based on the entertainment equipment featured on particular models of planes.

Most major carriers now offer a selection of movies, and with the advent of DirectTV and its satellite feed, travelers now have the choice of several recent releases, along with evergreen favorites presented by various movie channels mixed in with television offerings. On most airlines, first class views films for free; back in steerage, one swipe of the credit card, and it's all yours.

The films are highlighted in the airline's magazines, giving each of them additional marketing exposure. The quality of the viewing may also drive later downloads by those who decide they'd like to get a better idea of what it was they just watched.

Independent Films

Not all films are produced with lavish budgets, extensive promotional departments, audience testing, and second-guessing. Independent films—films that are made outside the studio system— form a major segment of the motion picture industry.

Independent films often focus on genres, social issues, or classics, niches that might not carry the same broad-market appeal sought after by major studios. With the cost of advertising a mainstream Hollywood movie increasing from an average of $35 million in 2005 to over $50 million in 2012[25] (including network, cable, and satellite television; national and local newspapers; billboards; radio; online; and tie-in advertising), the breakeven point for blockbusters is climbing to the stratosphere.

---

[25] PwC Global Entertainment and Media Outlook: 2012–2016, www.pwc.com/outlook.

With this kind of financial burden, major studios find it difficult to turn a profit on genre and classics films—the mainstay of independent movies—because their overhead is much higher than an independent producer's.

Studios can increase their profit margins by cutting the number of films they produce, holding down production costs, and sharing more risk with financial partners. This cut in releases opens a door for the independents. Even a modest cut in output by the majors can result in about half a billion dollars in incremental box office revenue for independents.

Independent filmmakers, expert at making films on tiny budgets, can take advantage of this opportunity by making films that appeal to their target markets. Hollywood studios, spending millions to make the most broad appeal films possible, often wind up with a few big hits but plenty of boring, bland misses—not necessarily losers, just not the gains of the blockbusters.

So studio executives can't help but lick their chops when they see the profit margins of low-budget films such as *Juno* (budget: $6.5 million; worldwide gross: $230 million) or *Slumdog Millionaire* (budget: $15 million; worldwide gross: $365 million). Creating distribution deals with independent films allows the studios to potentially reap a portion of the profits—important, when you're also stung by big-budget flops such as Disney's *John Carter* ($250 million versus a take of $72 million). Independents can take advantage of this opportunity by making films that appeal to their target markets.

The Market for Independent Films

Independent films represent about 40% of total releases, yet they only account for about 20% of total revenue. Why is there such a significant disconnect?

- Independent films tend to have narrower audience appeal than Hollywood films.
- There are fewer screens dedicated to independent fare than to Hollywood.
- Independent films may be of lower quality than major Hollywood releases simply because their production budgets are a fraction of Hollywood releases.

Independent films tell stories that might only appeal to a narrow audience. Because the potential audience for independent films is smaller, it is even more difficult to get them into the theater.

And traditional big-studio marketing isn't necessarily the answer, even if the independent had the money for it. One of the most unique aspects of the independent filmgoer is that he or she enjoys discovering a movie for him or herself. The independent audience does not like in-your-face marketing. Independent marketers are challenged to reach their audience without the audience knowing and simply can't do a Happy Meal tie-in and expect to fill the theater.

Marketing the Independent Film

Optimally, movie producers should enlist marketing experts to consult them in every stage of production. The marketer should envision a marketing plan as soon as a project has the green light, an industry term that means the movie has been given the go-ahead.

Some examples of the value that a marketer would add to an independent production are

- The incorporation of market research and industry trends.

- The use of focus groups to gauge audience perceptions of the film/scenes.

- The formulation of an advertising and release strategy to increase the chances that the film will not only have a successful opening, but will have legs—that is, will go on to earn millions of dollars.

This approach, referred to as the *studio model*, is virtually shunned by independent producers. They are very different from mainstream producers and are *independent* from outside interference. Independent filmmakers will not change the way they tell their stories and make their movies because studio executives tell them to. Independent filmmakers only care about getting their movies made. Advertising and marketing are afterthoughts. After all, the independent filmmaker believes that it is the quality of his or her film that will take market share from the majors.

So faced with smaller marketing budgets and far less marketing personnel—and openings that may consist of only three or four cities or three or four theaters—the independents must use aggressive marketing techniques to generate buzz, with the hopes of picking up a distribution deal from the studios. As discussed earlier, in the "Out the Door and Onto the Streets: Distribution" section, the studios are happy to have them—and that one-third of the film's box office. Again, more profit for those major studio distributors without all the risk of making the movie.

Like all entertainment, independent films are faced with a limited window of opportunity. But unlike the major studios, they have a particular fan base. The average independent moviegoer is urban, well educated, with a white collar career and at a median age of 35 and a median income of $40,000 per year. Independents also enjoy a growing over-50 demographic.[26]

Independent movies find homes close to their base demographics, with screens often located near college towns. In addition, these films are finding increased bandwidth on cable, with channels such as Sundance, IFC, and the specialized HBO and Showtime multiplexed channels. Independents are also available through Netflix streaming and other online sources.

Word of Mouth

Independent fans are proud of "discovering" films and enjoy spreading the word. Independent filmgoers rely heavily on this word of mouth. Marketers can capitalize on this by staggering a film's opening. A classic example, *The Blair Witch Project*, only opened on a handful of screens before opening wide two weeks later on July 30. Artisan knew the film would generate good word of mouth, so it opened the film in select key markets. The more people buzzed about *The Blair Witch Project*, the better its grosses were. In fact, the buzz was so strong, people camped outside to get tickets to the limited release. The lines themselves created such positive buzz that the *Wall Street Journal* called it "fierce."

---

[26] PwC Global Entertainment and Media Outlook: 2012–2016, www.pwc.com/outlook.

The "new" *Blair Witch*, a 2009 movie called *Paranormal Activity*, followed the same footprint. Made by young filmmakers on a shoestring, the movie blew up (to use the vernacular of the film's audience demographic) all across the industry, generating $108 million. That success led to 2010's *Paranormal Activity 2*, which took in $85 million; and 2011's *Paranormal Activity 3*, $104 million.[27] *Paranormal Activity 4*, released in 2012, has done over $140 million to date, globally. To paraphrase Walt Disney, it would appear a scream is a wish your pocketbook makes.

Internet and Independents

Independents favor the Internet because of its "discovery" aspect versus "in-your-face" marketing, again playing to the desire of the independent film fan. Websites are a crucial tool for independent films, but in keeping with the fan's desire for something less "Hollywood" than a major film release, the website might need to be less glitzy and more unique.

Additionally, social networking sites such as Facebook allow those fans to "like" the movie, setting up another terrific word-of-mouth source. Throw in tweets by the cast, the moviemaker, or the fans, and viral marketing takes over—lots of eyeballs with no cost.

And just as with major studio releases, there are countless websites with film reviews. These reviews, with trailers either on the site or linked for viewing elsewhere, give the potential audience another link to the movie they're hearing about.

Film Festivals

Film festivals are to independent film what power lunches are to Hollywood: a place to see and be seen, establish status, and make deals. There are nearly 300 film festivals, both competitive and noncompetitive, in the U.S., with new ones arriving every year.

The goal of the competitive film-festival entrant is to have his film picked up by leading independent distributors such as Lionsgate, The Weinstein Company, Focus Features, Fox Searchlight, or Sony Pictures Classics. Today, even cable channels like Sundance and IFC are looking for new films.

More than half of the films shown at these festivals never get theatrical release. Some go direct to home video through the remaining retail video outlets or stream directly to the consumer over Netflix. Festivals are important for showcasing new talent, testing marketing programs, gaining research, building word of mouth, garnering awards, and finding distribution deals. Every successful independent film, released in either narrow or rolling wide distribution, has been launched or shown at one or more film festivals.

The most famous of the festivals that focus on independent movies, Sundance, was founded as the Utah/U.S. Film Festival in 1978, with then-hot young star Robert Redford as its chairman. Fast forward to 1984, and the management of the festival is taken over by the Sundance Institute, a training facility for newbie writers and aspiring directors founded by Redford in 1981. Sundance set the standard for independent film festivals and continues to enjoy its prestigious rank.

---

[27] Boxofficemojo.com.

Though Sundance began as a place for non-Hollywood filmmakers to show their work, the festival became a scene, drawing Hollywood by the private jet-load. But the festival has recently reset its course, adding a competition, Next, for microbudget films, staying true to its roots.

Drawing from thousands of submissions, the festival chooses 110–120 feature films and 70–80 short films to be shown.

Notables who got their start at Sundance include directors Quentin Tarantino, Steven Soderbergh, and Jim Jarmusch. Films that started successful runs via Sundance include *Saw*; *The Blair Witch Project*; *Reservoir Dogs*; *Little Miss Sunshine*; *Sex, Lies, and Videotape*; and *Napoleon Dynamite*.

The Tribeca Film Festival, held in New York, was cofounded by Robert de Niro, Jane Rosenthal, and Craig Hatkoff, as a response to the 9/11 tragedy. The intent was to help rebuild Lower Manhattan while offering a different film festival experience from Sundance.

Now in its eleventh year, the Tribeca Film Festival draws filmmakers, as well as artists and musicians.

There are also noncompetitive film festivals that cater to viewers, including the New York Film Festival, begun in 1963 by the Film Society of Lincoln Center. (Interesting factoid: Lincoln Center, built in the early 1960s, is located in the area *West Side Story*, one of the most significant movie musicals of all time, took place. Thus, Lincoln Center literally has its roots in the movies.) The phenomenon that is the New York City Film Festival is replicated in over 50 cities and states across the U.S.

In addition, there are niche festivals like the African-American, Asian-American, Gay, Lesbian, Transgender Film Festivals, along with many more. One or two seem to be added every year. South by Southwest (aka SXSW) in Austin, Texas, has emerged as a successful film festival inside an extraordinary music, technology, and art festival.

Of course, we cannot talk about film festivals without mentioning the grand daddy of them all, Cannes. Cannes, a by-invitation-only competition, is as important to traditional studio films as it is to independents, with the prestigious Palme d'Or—the grand prize—awarded to the best film, regardless of budget or provenance. It is, without a doubt, the place to be for the entire international film industry every spring. It draws film producers, distributors, and even nontheatrical entrepreneurs from around the globe.

The international spotlight continues to shine on festivals held in Berlin, Venice, Rome, and Toronto, as well as Dubai, Qatar, and Abu Dhabi.

And tying back to the Internet, most major film festivals now stream selections from the festival, giving movie-lovers almost immediate access.

Wild Postings

Another time-honored method to reach an independent audience is the movie poster. While Hollywood studios pay to have their posters displayed on bus stops and in subway stations, wild postings appear in places where you are not supposed to put posters (such as construction sites).

There is an underground organization referred to by independent marketers as the "poster mafia." Independent marketers use these "snipers" to hang their posters around a city. Posters for independent films tend to be more mysterious and cutting-edge than Hollywood movie posters—and certainly more subtle.

Independent Screens

Independent film is supported by a network of independent theaters dedicated to what were once known as *art house movies*. Independent theaters have sprung up around the United States, and owners now have their own event to mirror the studios' ShoWest: The Art House Convergence, held each year in participation with the Sundance Institute.

Sundance stretched its brand a bit more in 2006, opening Sundance Cinemas. These facilities are designed for the classic independent audience, with an emphasis on unique design that blends with the Sundance aesthetic. Popcorn and other food is served in recycled paper products and "spudware" made from potatoes.[28]

Sundance Cinemas came about as a result of the efforts of Paul Richardson and Bert Manzari, the founders of Landmark Entertainment, the largest and most successful independent film circuit in the country. Eager to bring the Sundance brand into the exhibition world, they approached Robert Redford, and Sundance Cinemas was born.

Landmark was purchased by Mark Cuban, the Internet billionaire, and his partner Todd Wagner, who also created the first high-definition network for television, HDNet. It also prompted them to open their own independent film production companies, Magnolia Films and 20/20 Films.

Exhibitors are not ignoring the growth in the independent film segment. In the past, exhibitors had fewer screens and would not risk putting a specialty film onscreen. With the advent of large multiplexes, exhibitors are more likely to dedicate a screen or two to independent films.

The growth in the number of screens dedicated to independent films has created a demand for more product. The lower cost of technology allows more potential filmmakers to exercise their creativity. This increase of competition in the marketplace creates an even greater need for savvy marketing of the independent product. Independent film marketers will have to be more aggressive to increase market share.

Summary

The movie industry—both mainstream and independent—continues to be the central focus of the entertainment business. It is the engine that drives the entertainment and media industry, given that movies are ubiquitous to all platforms.

Though other segments of the business may have surpassed movies in overall revenue, it is impossible to say how much of this additional revenue depended on the marketing done for the original film. Movies are still the King of Content.

---

[28] www.sundance_cinemas.com.

Further Reading

Anderson, John, and Laura Kim, *I Wake Up Screening*, Watson-Guptill Publishing, 2006.

Bart, Peter, *Who Killed Hollywood—and Put the Tarnish on Tinseltown*, Los Angeles, Renaissance Books, 1999.

Cook, David, *A History of Narrative Film*, Fourth Edition, W.W. Norton, 2010.

Crabb, Kelly Charles, *The Movie Business*, Simon & Schuster, 2005.

Craig, Benjamin, *Cannes: A Festival Virgin's Guide*, 5th Edition, Cinemagine Press, 2006.

Durie, Hohn, Annika Pham, and Neil Watson, *Marketing and Selling Your Film Around the World*, Silman-James, 2000.

Epstein, Jay Edward, *The Big Picture, The New Logic of Money and Power in Hollywood*, Random House, 2005.

Gore, Chris, *Ultimate Film Festival Survival Guide*, 4th Edition, Watson-Guptil Publishing, 2009.

Hall, Phil, *Independent Film Distribution*, Michael-Wiese Productions, 2006.

Marich, Robert, *Marketing to Movie Goers, A Handbook of Strategies and Tactics*, 3rd Edition, Southern Illinois, University Press, 2013.

McDonald, Paul, and Janet Wasko, Eds., *The Contemporary Hollywood Film Industry*, Blackwell Publishing, 2008.

Puttnam, David, *Movies and Money*, Knopf Publishers, 2000.

Reiss, Jon, *Think Outside the Box Office, Ultimate Guide to Film Distribution and Marketing for the Digital Era*, Hybrid Cinema Publishing, 2010.

Simon, Deke, *Film & Video Budgets*, 5th Edition, Michael Wiese Productions, 2010.

Magazines to Devour

Entertainment Weekly

Hollywood Reporter

Premier

The Industry Standard

Variety

4

The Business of Broadcasting: Network TV, Syndication, and Radio

I n this chapter, we take a look at broadcast media—that is, content that is delivered to the consumer through a signal that is broadcast via radio waves versus cable. The business model for this conduit, be it television or radio, is based on delivering content to the consumer at no charge, earning revenue by selling advertising space to businesses eager to reach those consumers. This platform is undergoing some serious assaults, but for now, broadcast still delivers the maximum reach.

Broadcast Basics

Even with the proliferation of other conduits—Internet, cable, and satellite—broadcast has the widest consumer reach by a wide margin. Though many in this Internet day and age might find that statement hard to believe, consider these ratings for total television viewership in 2012, shown in Exhibit 4-1.

Exhibit 4-1 Top 5 Television Shows, 2012, Total Viewership[1]

Broadcast TV					Ad-Supported Cable TV			
Rank	Program	Network	Total Viewers		Rank	Program	Network	Total Viewers
1	NCIS	CBS	20.7		1	The Walking Dead	AMC	11.8
2	NCIS LA	CBS	17		2	The Closer	TNT	8.7
3	American Idol (Wednesday)	Fox	13.3		3	Rizzoli & Isles	TNT	7.4
4	American Idol (Thursday)	Fox	12.6		4	Major Crimes	TNT	7
5	60 Minutes	CBS	12		5	Pawn Stars	History	6.3

---

[1] Nielsen, 2012.

The traditional broadcast networks beat the top ad-supported cable networks by a margin of nearly two to one. Though viewership is changing as consumers choose new ways of viewing television (over-the-top, Internet, mobile), for the time being, for marketers, broadcast still rules in terms of overall reach.

Basic broadcast facts:

- There are 16,400 broadcast stations in the United States—1,781 broadcast television outlets; 14,619 broadcast radio stations.

- 46 million viewers receive television exclusively through broadcast television (as opposed to satellite, cable or mobile).

- 241 million people listen to radio each week.

Furthermore, there is still a big difference in the time spent by consumers in front of their televisions, although the Internet is coming on strong. When we break down overall consumer use, it looks like what's shown in Exhibit 4-2.

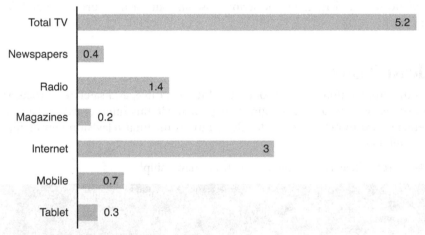

Exhibit 4-2 Average hours of daily use, 2012
Source: Television Bureau of Advertising, Inc., 2012

For other forms of media to overtake broadcast, especially broadcast television, as we discuss next, there will need to be a large investment by the viewing public in new devices; a radical shift in viewing habit; and a commitment by alternative conduits in new and better content. In other words, exactly what is happening now, as you discover as you move through the following chapters. To have mass marketing, you have to have mass, and each form of technology in current use has reached that mass with an ever-increasing rate of speed.

But for the time being, in marketing, nothing beats broadcast in reaching a mass audience.

Broadcast Television: The Networks

Broadcast media, both television and radio, is highly regulated by the Federal Communications Commission (the FCC), which grants the rights to the specific spectrum used by broadcasters in exchange for public access to programming at no charge—thus, the familiar designation of "free TV" or "free radio." Under federal guidelines, 75% of the local population must have access to this service.

Network TV has remained a staple in the entertainment industry for over 70 years. Although it has been pummeled by basic cable, pay-per-view, home video, premium cable, video on-demand, multi-billion dollar sports franchises starting their own networks, a mix of TiVo, digital video recorders (DVRs) something called the Hopper, and of course, the Internet, the networks still out-deliver. Broadcast reaches 20 million households—an average of 40 million consumers—for a 30-second commercial.

As a marketing professional, it is critical to know and understand the workings of this global media staple.

What Makes a Network Work?

All of the stations affiliated with the networks broadcast over what is known as *terrestrial television*; that is, the signal is broadcast via microwave radio relay networks and requires some type of tuner to receive the signal.

Network television as we know it today is an outgrowth of the earlier mass medium, radio. Some of the same businesses that built networks of local radio stations—the Columbia Broadcasting System (CBS), the National Broadcasting Corporation (NBC), and the American Broadcasting Corporation (ABC)—jumped onboard the television train, applying the same business model that had proven successful: selling programming to local stations to bring them under the network umbrella; selling advertising to companies that wanted national reach. Though local stations continued to produce some of their own local content, purchasing network programming was more cost effective.

What's critical to this discussion is the ability of the networks to hold the *interest* of those viewers. Though the government mandates that the viewer must have access, it does not mandate that the viewer must watch what the networks are delivering. As always, it all comes down to content. Each and every show must deliver an experience that will keep the viewers coming back for more and the advertisers paying for those 30-second spots.

In today's highly competitive media world, audiences expect high-quality content with great production value. Gone are the days of grainy black-and-white images, filmed in studios against simple, hand-painted backdrops. Today's programming is an expensive venture, featuring costly productions with expensive talent. For the time being, networks are the only entities that can consistently produce this level of programming (or afford to buy it from other production houses), although cable networks and over-the-top providers, which are discussed in the next chapter, are certainly making a play on quality.

How do the networks pay for content? Advertising revenue drives network television. That revenue depends on a network gaining and maintaining a significant share of the available market. That share is then captured through the development and broadcasting of content that will attract viewers—not just any viewers, but viewers in the specific target markets found most desirable by advertisers.

For decades, the Big Three networks—ABC, CBS, and NBC—delivered those viewers by creating entertainment that captured a mass audience. Entire families watched the same shows, a phenomenon that worked just fine—after all, programming reached the breadwinners (men) and the influencers (women and children). Anyone under the age of 18 didn't have enough money in their pockets and so weren't much of a market.

Today, we now refer to the Big Four networks, with Fox having gained enough market share to deserve that designation. Women are in the labor force in huge numbers, with far more disposable income. Children have become a huge market, if not for their money, for their influence on buying decisions. Tweens and teens, now with more discretionary income of their own, are ground zero for mass consumption. This last group is a huge target for marketers wishing to build brand loyalty early, strong enough to tie their target to products for a long, long time.

The after-shock of this culture change has been the primary force in the growth of the cable industry, with its ability to provide niche programming. We take a look at cable in a later chapter, but first let's look at the mechanics of "free TV" as it does have application to cable: Regardless of how the programs are delivered, network or cable, commercials are what create the primary revenue stream.

A simple set of numbers give a broad overview of the state of broadcast television today:

- Over 97% of households own at least one television, accounting for nearly 115 million viewing households.

- What are now the Big Four networks—ABC, CBS, NBC, and Fox—reach nearly 70% of those households weekly. (None of the cable networks even come close to 40%).

- If any given network—or any given network show, be it *The Voice* or any of the *CSIs*—grabs 10 to 12% of those viewing households—12 to 14 million consumers are delivered for a 30-second spot.

Regardless of all the hoopla over all the other potential conduits, network television is still the undisputed leader in reach, motivating advertisers to air their product messages on the Big Four.

The Bones of the Business: Programming

To lure advertisers, networks create content that will attract viewers, tailoring that content for particular dayparts and particular demographics. Between 1950 and 2000, the three traditional major networks—ABC, CBS, NBC—all had a turn at leadership in this very competitive arena, vying for a rapidly growing TV public with news, daytime programming, talk shows, evening dramas, and sitcoms.

CBS, for instance, dominated the 1950s and early 1960s with number one-rated programs like *I Love Lucy, Gunsmoke,* and *The Beverly Hillbillies* until NBC's *Bonanza* and *Rowan & Martin's Laugh-In* took over through the rest of that decade early into the 1970s. Then CBS charged back with *All in the Family,* which held the number-one spot for five years. ABC, determined to reach the top of the pile, got serious with comedy in the late 1970s when *Happy Days* and *Laverne & Shirley* helped propel the network to number one. CBS fought back with *60 Minutes* and *Dallas.* ABC took the "If you can't beat 'em" approach, mimicking *Dallas* with its own *Dynasty.*

NBC finally got back on-board with *The Cosby Show,* which maintained its position as the number-one show for five years. When Bill Cosby bowed out, CBS's *60 Minutes* took the top spot until NBC's *Seinfeld* and *ER* dominated the late 1990s.

All of the networks have moved on, with each of them having moments of ratings glory, but these early programs helped feed the growth of competition—the newer networks that proliferated in the last two decades.

The Upstarts: Newer Networks

Fox (20th Century Fox) was the first channel to challenge the entrenched trio, initially purchasing many of the proven sitcoms just listed in order to lure advertisers. However, original content is always the key to success in this arena. Fox made its biggest gain with shows like *Married With Children, The Simpsons,* and sports events like college and professional football—the latter featuring insightful voices such as that of former coach John Madden, along with the then-innovative technologies: the computerized first-down stripe on the field and the information-laden scorebox in the corner of the screen.

Fox also developed its identity by pushing the envelope on semi-nudity and coarse language. At the time of Fox's entry into network TV, those characteristics had been more consistent with some cable channels. But as the network grew, the quality of programming increased. Staples such as *24, Bones,* and *House* gave the network a glossier look; *American Idol* sent it over the top, spawning a whole new form of amateur talent-based shows.

Today, Fox Broadcasting is known as much for its news outlet, Fox News, as it is for its prime-time programming.

Other entries to the network steeplechase were not as successful. WB (Warner Bros.) and UPN (Viacom) both went the purchase-proven-sitcoms route and followed up with original programming, but neither generated enough critical mass or innovative programming to continue. The two were merged into CW.

Pax, a network started by NBC, ran into a number of problems and disappeared. But NBC, intent on gaining more clout, accepted an offer from cable giant Comcast to buy them out. In a complicated deal, NBC is now part of a joint venture between Comcast and General Electric (the former owner) known as NBCUniversal.[2]

But no network would survive without framework that supports the entire business, the local stations.

---

[2] Comcast had previously tried to buy Disney but was thwarted in the attempt.

Local Television Stations

What we now refer to as the Big Four—ABC, CBS, NBC, and Fox—sell their programming to over 1,700 stations in America and 21,500 television stations worldwide.[3] Although the viewing audience may think of their local network affiliates as being owned by the network itself, this is not always true. These stations are grouped into three primary relationships with the television networks: owned and operated, affiliates, and independents.

Owned and Operated

For the networks to ensure they can provide coverage to the federally mandated 75% of U.S. TV households, they have acquired local television stations in major cities and leading U.S. markets with substantial TV household populations. These stations are referred to as *owned and operated* (O&O) because they are, in fact, considered to be divisions of the networks and must carry the programming dictated by them.

Although the station's marketing management typically reports to the network's divisional marketing executive, the stations have a responsibility to create their own local marketing plans and put forth consistent efforts to brand their stations within their markets' (usually crowded) spheres of influence. This can mean having a helicopter that delivers local traffic conditions—weather, news, sports, and the occasional local programming—or syndicated programs, which the stations purchase on their own.

The stations share in national advertising revenue generated by the networks and pay for the rights to carry national programming, thus helping to defray some of the expensive marketing costs at the network level.

Affiliates

Well over 800 stations fall into the category of affiliates. Affiliates have contracts with the network broadcasters that run for a period of years. In this relationship, the station has a responsibility—a commitment—to run programming supplied by the network, giving the network the increased TV household population it needs to fulfill the FCC-mandated 75% requirement. In return, the station benefits from the promotional efforts of the network on a national level, driving viewers locally.

On occasion, when a network goes through a pre-season exercise to gain clearance for a soon-to-be-televised new national program, an affiliate can decide not to carry or clear that program. It could be for any reason, including having an important local program to put in its place or a concern over content that might not be acceptable to local viewers. The network, requiring coverage on a national basis, can then go to an independent, which is not affiliated with any network, to see if it wishes to carry the program in direct competition with the network's own affiliate. Sometimes a single episode of a national program might be pre-empted to allow for a locally produced program, such as a town hall meeting or a local retail-supported event.

---

[3] The National Association of Broadcasters' Information Resource Center (www.nab.org).

Independents

The third group of stations, known as independents, consists of two types of station ownership: *corporate (or group) ownership* and *mom-and-pop entrepreneurship*. These stations have no contractual relationship with any network and are solely dependent on their own programmers to fill the stations' airtime with programs that appeal to viewers in their own markets. They are in direct competition with in-market O&O stations as well as affiliate stations.

Station groups balance the cost of programming against locally generated advertising revenue by using original programming in several markets. They can also make advantageous license or rental agreements for syndicated programming in multiple markets. Single stations, or mom-and-pop stations, usually operate on tight budgets in much smaller markets. They are often good takeover targets for corporate groups eager to assemble that 75% population coverage, enabling them to become strong affiliate contenders when groups switch their alliances.

Switching of alliances does occur. One example took place in 1996, when a group of CBS affiliates who had reached a contract renewal period (in those days, every three years) decided to join with Fox on what they decided would be a more advantageous and productive basis.

Local Programming

Regardless of how well it may market and promote itself, every television station's success is directly attributable to the quality of its programming. Today's growing number of channels provides a home for a wide variety of content, servicing a range of niche audiences. Not only does this diversity make the audience happy, but it provides a direct path to certain viewing groups that marketers may find desirable.

Local programming typically consists of news, documentaries, and sports. In most markets, one or more independent stations produce a daily newscast, which must compete with at least two daily newscasts from the ABC, CBS, NBC, and Fox affiliates. There is significant preparation necessary for everyday newscasts, which generally run for a half-hour to an hour for early-morning, noon, afternoon, and evening program slots. Many stations also provide five-minute local cut-ins.

Because local news is *local*, news can be a big factor in branding the station. After all, if you live in Tuscaloosa and you want to know why the sirens are going off, you aren't going to switch to the national news.

Viewership of local broadcast news is strong: 19.7% for Americans over the age of 18. Cable news channels only garner 10.2% of public viewership (see Exhibit 4-3).

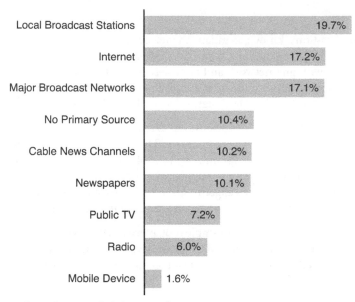

Local Broadcast Stations	19.7%
Internet	17.2%
Major Broadcast Networks	17.1%
No Primary Source	10.4%
Cable News Channels	10.2%
Newspapers	10.1%
Public TV	7.2%
Radio	6.0%
Mobile Device	1.6%

Exhibit 4-3 Primary choice for news of adults over 18[4]

Some local stations' news departments also produce weekend news programs, news magazines, news/talk shows, public affairs programs, and documentaries. Oprah Winfrey made her initial appearance on a local show called *Chicago A.M.*

Local sports programming is somewhat limited. Professional football and basketball are only sold to networks on a national basis, making it difficult for local stations to provide coverage. The NBA, however, also sells rights for local coverage to individual stations. Baseball is sold similarly to basketball. College football may be broadcast on both national and local stations, provided they are not aired at the same time. Amateur and community sporting events are usually aired on local stations.

Cable has made huge inroads in sports coverage, which is discussed in a later chapter.

Regardless of how commercially driven television is delivered—network or local, O&O, affiliated, part of a group, or a mom-and-pop operation—as always, content is king. It is content that attracts and holds viewers, and holding viewers is crucial to market share, the guiding force behind the revenue generated from advertisers.

How is that share determined? Through ratings.

The Basics of TV Ratings

Ratings are essential to commercial television and are the root of all advertising dollars. They are the starting point for negotiations between networks and local stations for the price of

---

[4] TVB Media Comparisons Study 2012. Knowledge Networks Inc. Custom Survey.

commercial time. When you mention ratings in respect to advertising-supported media—television and radio—the name most often mentioned is Nielsen Media Research.

Nielsen was founded in 1923 by Arthur C. Nielsen, Sr. It was one of the first research companies to measure the audience for the burgeoning radio broadcasting and advertising industry. The company has expanded its reach into all media, but for now, we focus on the mechanics of network TV.

How Nielsen Ratings Work

Nielsen uses a recruited sample group of 5,000 households, representing 13,000 people (an average of 2.6 people per home), to get a perspective of viewing habits in the over 100 million homes with TVs in the U.S. Nielsen does not accept volunteers for its ratings service; "Nielsen families" are recruited through random selection to be statistically accurate. Every household in the U.S. has an equal chance of being selected, no matter where it is located. The random nature of the sample ensures that people of all backgrounds and ages can be included; however, it can only happen from Nielsen contacting them.

Every effort is made by Nielsen to ensure that a thorough cross-section of ethnic and income groups is represented. In 1991, Nielsen expanded its monthly national reports to include data specifically on the viewing of African-American households, and in 1992, it expanded its reports to include specific Hispanic ratings. The firm also checks its samples against U.S. Census Bureau data. On occasion, Nielsen even does special studies it calls telephone coincidentals, in which the firm seeks to double-check its data against a random sample of direct telephone calls to homes.

To confirm exactly what shows are playing and when, Nielsen tracks more than 1,700 TV stations and 11,000 cable systems so it can properly credit viewing habits. In some specially selected homes (in the 48 largest markets), Nielsen technicians install metering equipment directly on TVs, VCRs, cable boxes, or satellite dishes, with all the meters connected to a centralized computer. The data collected through this system gives advertisers a clear picture of who is watching and when, helping guide the decision of where to best spend their dollars.

Key Terms

Nielsen uses the following terminology to describe ratings data:

- **Sweeps:** Periods in which local markets are simultaneously measured. Nielsen surveys all 210 local television markets during what are known as "sweeps months": November, February, and May; in July, Honolulu, Fairbanks, and Juneau are excluded. The data collected during sweeps is the basis by which local stations and cable systems make program decisions and set local ad rates.

- **Designated Market Area (DMA):** Nielsen's research divides the entire country into DMAs, or nonoverlapping areas used for planning, buying, and evaluating TV audiences. Each DMA consists of a group of counties in which stations achieve the largest audience share. Each county in the U.S. is assigned to one DMA.

- **Metro Area:** The central part of the DMA, or the most densely populated portion of the market. Metro areas are helpful geographic breaks for local advertisers, given Nielsen provides detailed ratings and demographic information on metro areas as well as DMAs.

- **Households Using Television (HUT):** The percentage of all TV-owning households that have at least one TV set in use during a specific time period. During a typical weeknight, HUT levels tend to peak at about 60–70%, meaning that 60% to 70% of TV-owning households have at least one set in use.

- **Rating:** A Nielsen rating point flexes with the population (that is, the number of households that own TVs). Early in this millennium, the number crossed the 1,000,000 household mark and will continue to grow.

- **Household Rating:** The estimated percentage of all TV-owning households (or persons) tuned into a specific station or program at a given time. For example, if an episode of NBC's hit series *Friends* achieves a household rating of 12.5, this means that 12.5% of households that own TVs are tuned into this program.

- **Share:** The percentage of HUTs tuned into a specific station or program at a given time. If a *Friends* episode achieves a 25 share, this means that out of households with a TV in use, one-quarter of them are tuned into *Friends*. This would correspond to a HUT level of 50%, given the HUT level is simply the rating divided by the share.

Who Advertises?

Major advertisers shift by the year, but generally the same players remain in the top 10 (see Exhibit 4-4). One very notable exception is political advertising. In today's highly competitive political arena, political advertising can be a real bonus for both network and local stations—with local stations in hotly contested presidential races seeing huge dollars come their way.

Exhibit 4-4   Top Ten Spot Advertising Categories: Full Year 2012

Rank	Category	Full Year 2012
1	Automotive	$3,117,937,900
2	Communications / Telecommunications	$1,423,780,400
3	Restaurants	$1,181,139,600
4	Political	$1,025,964,500
5	Car and Truck Dealers	$999,141,100
6	Government and Organizations	$894,144,800
7	Furniture Stores	$677,444,800
8	Financial	$640,438,200
9	Legal Services	$604,161,400
10	Insurance	$539,312,700
	TOTAL	**$11,103,465,400**

Source: Television Bureau of Advertising, Inc. 2013

Key Demographics

When considering where to place their advertising—and therefore their dollars—decision-makers focus on what programs/time slots are most frequented by the particular demographic group to which they wish to sell. For example, placing an ad for a product mostly used by 18- to 24-year-old females in the middle of Monday Night Football probably isn't going to give an advertiser the best bang for its buck. Demographics are the key to matching the right wallet with the right product.

Demographics are also key factors in the conceptualizing and production of the programming available on both network and cable TV. In the age-old chicken-or-egg argument, networks search for content that will lure advertising dollars to their coffers. The producers of this content are more than happy to oblige. With any luck, the viewing public happily tunes in, week after week, presumably unaware that their favorite show has been developed from a carefully crafted formula, not so much to enrich their minds or entertain them as to sell advertising space or drive subscriptions. After all, it is a business.

Network TV, with its broad base of viewership, tends to focus primarily on two key audience demographics:

- Adults, men and women, 18–24

- Adults, men and women, 25–49

Cable TV is a different story. The ever-growing number of cable channels creates a scenario in which niche marketing is much more successful than mass-reach. Cable programming tends to drill down even further into particular age, race, gender, and economic variables. In fact, certain channels—Lifetime (women), BET (Black Entertainment Television), ESPN (sports)—are devoted to particular audiences to drive subscriptions and advertising. Niches can be divided into even tighter age segmentation. For example, a product looking for the 18- to 24-year-old market may head directly to MTV.

Time Slots

Simply having the content and knowing who wants to watch is not enough. The third important variable in selecting spots is knowing who is available to watch the programming at what time of day. Sections of the advertising clock are divided into what are known as *dayparts*. The key demographic for daytime TV is women, 25–54. Prime time tends to be adults, 18–49.

The principal dayparts used in TV ratings are

- Early Morning (5 a.m.–9 a.m.)

- Daytime (9 a.m.–3 p.m.)

- Early Fringe (3 p.m.–5 p.m.)

- Early News (5 p.m.–7 p.m.)

- Access (7 p.m.–8 p.m.)

- Prime (8 p.m.–11 p.m.)

- Late News (11 p.m.–11:30 p.m.)

- Late Fringe (11:30 p.m.–1:00 a.m.)

- Prime time on Sundays runs from 7 p.m. to 11 p.m.

It is difficult to match a "typical" audience profile to each of these dayparts because the demographics are driven by the programming. For example, the typical audience watching CW or Fox at 8 p.m. is likely very different from the audience watching a PBS station. Programming is created to capture the audience for the advertiser, not vice versa.

Ad Spends

Of course, the goal is to wrap all of the elements—age, gender, interest, economics—into programming that will attract the most viewers to the advertisers willing to spend the most money. To do that, the programming typically must be made available during the time of day when HUT levels are highest, the aptly named *prime time*, which is 8 p.m. to 11 p.m. The six broadcast networks (NBC, ABC, CBS, Fox, CW, and Univision) compete for the key 18–49 demographic during this essential time slot.

Local stations enter the fray as well, with what is known as *spot advertising*, which allows advertisers to select particular markets and time slots. When combined with all other forms of television, ad expenditures provide a huge revenue stream, as shown in Exhibit 4-5.

Exhibit 4-5   Ad Spending, First Half of 2012 Versus 2011, Television

	Spot TV	Network TV	Syndication	Cable TV	TV Grand Total
Jan–Jun '11	$7,145,786	$12,437,858	$2,287,819	$11,017,701	$32,889,164
Jan–Jun '12	$7,397,870	$13,236,646	$2,580,458	$11,654,124	$34,869,098
Change (%)	3.5	6.4	12.8	5.8	6

Source: Television Bureau of Advertising, Inc. 2012

However, for television advertising to be effective, it has to be watched, preferably without any device that allows the viewer to skip the commercials.

The Impact of Technology

Much like the movies, the end of broadcast television has been forecast every decade or so as new technologies have appeared. Basic cable was supposedly going to deliver a death blow; subscription-based premium cable was supposed to dig the grave; and streaming is supposed to put the last nail in the coffin.

We would be disingenuous to say that new technology is not having an impact on the traditional broadcast business model. Even though television still delivers, by far, the greatest reach of any medium, the battle is raging. Broadcast viewing is still holding its own, but all manner of platforms—cable, mobile, Internet TV—are tugging at those numbers as streaming takes hold in the marketplace.

The single biggest threat to the revenue stream is time-shifting, specifically through those devices that allow the consumer to skip through the commercials. The most commonly used is the DVR, either through TiVO, which the consumer purchases, or the DVRs that the cable companies provide for an upcharge. DVRs are now in 46% of households.[5]

Nielsen reports, however, that although time-shifting has increased, it is still a very long way from taking over live viewing. According to Nielsen, viewers spent 4.38 hours per day watching live TV in the first quarter of 2012, only 6 minutes less than they spent in the same quarter in 2008 and still over *4 hours* more than they spent watching DVR playback.[6]

There is an age factor in this shift. Nielsen reports that adults 65 years old or older consume the most traditional TV, at nearly 48 hours in a week, also watching 1 hour and 54 minutes of time-shifted TV per week. People ages 35 to 49 watch just over 35 hours of traditional TV per week plus roughly 3 and a half hours of time-shifted TV.[7]

DVRs are also improving ratings, as shown in Exhibit 4-6. According to Nielsen, new shows are seeing increases of 50% or more from three-day DVR playback. Now that DVR usage is tracked, shows that might have gotten the axe are now getting orders for additional episodes.[8] Note: Each increased rating point means additional advertising revenue for these shows.

Exhibit 4-6   Top 10 Live-Plus-Seven-Day-DVR Viewing Adults 18–49 (Ranked on Percentage Gain) / Week Ended September 30, 2012

Rank	Program	Network	L+7 Increase in Rating Points	L+SD to L+7 Increase
1	*Grimm*	NBC	1.2	75.00%
1	*Supernatural*	CW	0.6	75.00%
3	*Revolution*	NBC	2.1	65.60%
4	*Private Practice*	ABC	1	62.50%
4	*Parenthood*	NBC	1	62.50%
6	*Glee*	FOX	1.6	61.50%
7	*Fringe*	FOX	0.6	60.00%
8	*The Mentalist*	CBS	0.9	56.30%
9	*666 Park Ave*	ABC	0.9	52.90%
10	*Castle*	ABC	1	52.60%
10	*Last Resort*	ABC	1	52.60%

Source: ABC Networks, based on data from Nielsen Media Research, October 23, 2012

Another interesting fact in this discussion is the data gathered on consumer decision-making. Although commercial skipping is on the rise, consider what you see in Exhibit 4-7.

---

[5] www.medialifemagazine.com/the-dvrs-huge-impact-on-this-season/ October 12, 2012.

[6] "Live TV Still Overwhelmingly Dominates TV," *Ad Age*, September 11, 2012.

[7] Ibid.

[8] www.medialifemagazine.com/the-dvrs-huge-impact-on-this-season/ October 12, 2012.

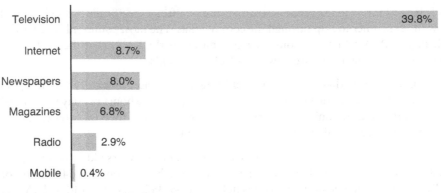

Television	39.8%
Internet	8.7%
Newspapers	8.0%
Magazines	6.8%
Radio	2.9%
Mobile	0.4%

Exhibit 4-7 People who learn about a product they would like to try or buy from a commercial

Source: Television Bureau of Advertising, Inc. 2012

Broadcast television needs to find an answer to the commercial-skipping dilemma to maintain the revenue that supports this business model. In the tradition of the movie industry, one answer could be product placement. This practice is already becoming part of the answer to this challenge (see Exhibit 4-8).

Exhibit 4-8 Primetime Shows with the Most Product Placement

Program	Network	Number of Placements	Number of Episodes
American Idol	Fox	577	39
The Biggest Loser	NBC	533	34
Celebrity Apprentice	NBC	391	12
Dancing with the Stars	ABC	390	29
The X Factor	Fox	312	26
Extreme Makeover: Home Edition	ABC	224	31
America's Got Talent	NBC	220	32
Friday Night Lights	NBC	201	13
America's Next Top Model	CW	178	26
The Amazing Race	CBS	111	11

Source: CNBC, 2012

Licensing and merchandising are also a part of this strategy.

Finally, there's certainly room for improvement in commercials themselves. Content is king. Commercials are just as much about content as anything else that the public indulges in. Don't think so? Two words:

Super Bowl.

As much as there is a dedicated fan base that tunes in to this event every year—so popular that some have called for making the Monday after a national holiday—the commercials are what get the most press before and after the event, garnering commentary from all corners of the world.

Clever, interesting commercials go viral over the Internet via all forms of social media. They become part of our jargon, adding shorthand to our vocabulary.

The theory is, if the creators of commercials recognize them for the content that they are and don't insult the intelligence of the viewer, those 30-second spots will still be viewed, even by those who might quickly bypass lesser ads.

Will this save the industry we know today? Hard to say. But it certainly won't be part of the funeral cortege, will it?

Promotion and Marketing

There is no better way for a major advertising brand to reach critical viewership than through broadcast television. What is surprising is that despite an overall decline in total ratings of network viewership, due to the loss to cable, pricing for commercials continues to rise due to the efficiency in reaching desirable demographics among Nielsen's 115 million TV households. Although overall shares decline, total television viewership has increased as more people watch more television than ever before.

To maintain this stature, networks and local stations must promote themselves along with promoting their individual programs and series. Audience ratings and share reflect programming viewership, which drives advertising rates. Nielsen sweeps monitor these metrics, which attract advertisers, ad agencies, and media buying services.

A network or station must be able to maintain and build its audience. Though a certain amount of this viewer loyalty will (hopefully) result due to the content aired, networks and stations as individual entities must also recognize the need to build and promote their own specific brands.

A base of regular viewers is built through

- Viewers who are loyal to particular shows on the network
- Viewers who buy into the holistic messages of "Must-See TV" or "Come Home to CBS," choosing that network for their primary viewing
- Viewers who choose the local station due to self-marketing at the local level

Network television remains a powerhouse because of its ability to deliver a mass audience of 5 to 10 million viewers for most shows, 20 million for the best shows, and over 111 million for specials like the Super Bowl. Each and every one of these viewers must be wooed by more than just the actual broadcast of the event or show.

Network Self-Branding

Network self-promotion takes many forms and utilizes all available media. Banner ads flash across websites. Pop-up ads interrupt your mobile viewing. Billboards tout local radio stations, television sitcoms, news broadcasts, or the launch of a coming season's new shows. Bits and pieces show up on YouTube. Radio airs sound bites of hit shows, while radio personalities show up in television commercials, giving listeners a glimpse of people they have only known as voices.

Social networking builds "personal" relationships between consumers and the brand. Websites and Facebook pages give fans a place to get the latest news. Every network has its own website, where fans of particular programs can log in to get the latest news. Boxed sets of DVDs promote the show and the network.

Networks know that to build audience share for a program, they must steal viewers from other broadcast networks, cable networks, and streaming media. Because networks do not permit advertising from competitive networks—ABC cannot advertise on Fox and vice versa—careful selection of basic cable shows with compatible audiences becomes an important part of the network's media plan, along with all other forms of non-network media. Cable ads are an enhanced revenue source for cable programmers and operators and may often be synergistic; the show being promoted may someday become a syndicated property for that very cable network.

On-Air Self-Promotion

Self-promotion also takes the form of advertising aired on the network or station itself. Airtime on television networks is perishable; if it isn't sold to advertisers, it runs the risk of simply disappearing into the ether. Rather than have this happen, unsold time is utilized in a variety of ways, all of which build goodwill for the network or station in one form or another. Public service announcements (PSAs) are given to not-for-profit organizations. Government institutions may also benefit from unsold time, an act smiled upon by the FCC. Commercials touting the benefits of not smoking, just saying no to drugs, and not burning Smokey the Bear out of his habitat fall into this category.

The remainder of the available time may be used for promotion of the carrier itself. This is not "free time," but it certainly is more economical than spending promotional dollars on other media. Every minute of available advertising time has a dollar value attached to it. However, as networks and stations build their sales forecasts and operating budgets, they build in certain amounts of time they know will be used to carry their own message. Broadcasters will always prefer to sell any and all time over and above that which they have budgeted for self-promotion or PSAs, for it is the sale of that time that makes self-promotion possible and keeps the broadcaster profitable.

But why use on-air promotion to ask viewers to continue watching a station to which they are already tuned? To remind them to *stay* tuned—to not touch that dial, remote, DVR, mobile device, laptop—all the other conduits of this day and age. All forms of media are interested in holding their audience and doing it in the most economical way possible. As is true in any sales process, it is *always* easier and far less expensive to harvest existing customers than to grow new ones. The existing customer only needs a focused reminder now and then, while the new customer warrants an all-out attack, utilizing other forms of media not necessarily controlled by the station or network.

Vertical, Horizontal, and Standard Cross-Plugs

On-air promotion takes the form of TV spots (known as promos) usually running 30 seconds and, on occasion, 10 or 15 seconds (known as IDs). Networks also implement strategic devices that build off of successful shows in specific time slots. These can include vertical cross-plugs, which are commercials touting the show in the next time slot. The show receiving the promotion is usually new or has a similar demographic but weaker audience share. Vertical cross-plugs can hold viewers who are known to surf stations and may be willing to give the next program a trial viewing.

If the show of choice seems to be losing its Nielsen share or ratings, or if it is so strong that there is a chance of capturing new tiers and making fresh viewers loyal to the program, a standard or horizontal cross-plug provides a quick snapshot of the next program in the series. This is similar to a movie trailer or a "coming attractions" format, which maintains interest and builds buzz. This is most frequently used for daytime series and weekly primetime sitcoms.

Social media has become crucial to the promotion of shows, using Facebook, Twitter, Google+, and any proven conduit for reaching the potential audience. Home pages exist for each show, usually as an offshoot of the network's web page. Fans of shows can get sneak peeks at new episodes, updates, and interviews on stars and links to purchase merchandise connected with the show. These sites also allow a voice for viewers who want to make their preferences known, especially if a favorite series seems destined to be dropped. In general, the Internet has allowed for a much more highly personalized experience of television programming, which is a huge plus when it comes to building brand loyalty.

Intra-Industry Marketing

Each of the media rolls up its sleeves and sells when it sells within the industry itself. Trade magazines, promotion booklets, direct mail, and program sales conventions like the National Association of Television Programming Executives (NATPE) and MIFED (international film) or MIPCOM (international TV, video, cable, and satellite markets) are all vehicles through which the industry markets itself. It is here that network and station executives are treated to clear outlines of consumer advertising campaigns, including the media schedule, station clearance line-ups, and the size of the marketing budget in minute detail.

In addition, associations like TVB, which focuses on local broadcasting, and the National Association of Broadcasters (NAB) have created deep-bench Internet presence, creating newsletters, blogs, market research—all manner of support material for members and parties interested in the health and well-being of the business. Although these two associations do not focus on any specific network or station, they provide excellent information for the savvy marketing professional.

Relationship Marketing and the Halo Effect

What takes a program from mere flash-in-the-pan popularity—or on the flip side, utter unwatched disaster—and turns it into a long-running hit and syndication star? The answer is loyal fans—an audience that reserves the time slot every week so that they can become one with their program. In the best of all possible marketing worlds, the relationship these fans have developed with the program extends to the products, services, and brands offered during the commercial breaks or linked to the home page. This is known as a *halo effect*; taking advantage of the halo effect is known as *relationship marketing*.

Most people who hate a program switch the channel or turn the set off, the advertising just a distant dream in some media buyer's brain. On the other hand, loyal viewers of any of the *Real Housewives* or the *CSIs*, for example, may never move from their seats during the entire program. It is the hope and intention of the advertisers that the fan will not only see the commercial but also associate it with their preference for the show. The goal is to create a consistent relationship between the program and the consumer. Although the new trends in technology may someday make this goal obsolete, at the time of this writing, more than 50% of households are still watching television without the aid of a DVR.

Within the entertainment industry, relationship marketing is often called the development of a fan. Fans are frequently known to purchase merchandise or licensed products that relate to stars and programs in almost any medium. Viewers of the game show *Jeopardy* purchased enough copies of the software version of the show to justify bringing out *Jeopardy 2*.

Send in the Clones

The success of a new program or format can have a decided impact across the airwaves. The Fox Network's *American Idol* launched a whole new genre, "the search for performing talent," which now includes *Dancing with the Stars* (ABC), *The X Factor* (Fox), and *The Voice* (NBC).

When broadcasters find a successful formula, they have to maximize its success immediately and invest in a marketing budget to expand awareness and maintain loyalty: two classic marketing techniques. But beware the semi-clone that attempts to trade on the popularity of a concept.

Several years ago, borrowing on the public's fascination with ABC's *Who Wants to Be a Millionaire (WWTBAM)*, Fox took a slightly different angle with *Who Wants to Marry a Millionaire*, a program that caused embarrassment, potential lawsuits, and a decline in credibility for Fox—and risked a negative halo effect for advertisers. But ABC fell victim to its own greed. Running *WWTBAM* five times a week after its initial success, ABC managed to burn out the audience, and the program was cancelled.

The Fall Launching Season

When shows are launched each fall, nervous executives stand by with their fingers crossed. Enormous effort is made to create a huge opening audience tune-in, setting the tone for the early purchase of advertising schedules by advertisers. This is known as a *strong up-front*. Network marketing departments are in full swing, working with their own in-house teams as well as external agencies to fashion the season's marketing plans, create the advertising messages, and provide the rationale for placing percentages of the marketing budget in cable, print, outdoor billboards, radio, Internet, mobile, and promotions.

On-air advertising activity falls into its own category. Print advertising includes full-page ads in local newspapers seeking tune-in for the networks as well as affiliate stations and the use of standard ads in entertainment-oriented magazines like *Entertainment Weekly*, *US*, *Rolling Stone*, *People*, *InStyle*, and many others. The use of Internet, social networking, and mobile strategies allows for the placement of trailers, whetting the appetite of potential core audiences.

Just Like in the Movies

Networks have learned from movie advertising, no surprise since ABC, CBS, NBC, CW, and Fox all have movie studios as sister divisions. This movie-based strategy includes the use of significant promotion and merchandising events. For example, CBS has created effective promotions and tie-in programs with major advertisers such as Kmart, Coca-Cola, and McDonald's. The product-specific sweepstakes and contests developed with these synergy partners have driven consumers to participate with both the program and advertiser's products. ABC was one of the first networks to utilize mall promotions that presented daytime television stars up-close and personal. Fans were able to meet them and get autographs; the stars often participated in fund-raising for local charities, driving further goodwill.

ABC's soap opera supermarket magazines, following in the long tradition of movie monthlies, are particularly effective. The magazines provide inside gossip on the daytime shows stars, helping fans stay involved while building interest in additional daily tune-in. The magazines also generate revenue.

Finally, as we mentioned earlier, product placement has built additional revenue for programs while also creating a halo effect for advertisers. As in the movies, viewers see products consumed or used by the characters of their favorite drama or sitcom and (hopefully) make a mental note to rush right out and purchase them.

Syndication

A television station or network is like a grocery store with empty shelves, needing product to draw customers to the aisles. And like the grocery store, those networks and channels get their product from mostly outside sources.

Television programs are produced by independent production houses, network production divisions, or movie studios with television production arms. Shows may also be produced by foreign companies—*Survivor* is an example—producing for their own networks and interested in licensing the concept. Finished programs from English-speaking networks like the BBC, Canadian Broadcasting Corporation, and Australian Television networks are further examples of internationally produced content.

Syndication is the method by which local stations, less affluent cable networks, and some international networks fill their shelves, stocking them with programs that were originally produced for the major networks or programs that have been produced specifically for syndication with no prior network attachment.

Syndication was the mainstay of all cable in the early years, providing content to build viewership. It has been the vehicle through which new television networks have emerged, including the beginnings of Fox (and later, Fox's FX) and CW. It has also been the primary building block of such "classic" cable channels as TVLand and Nick at Nite, along with many of the less affluent cable channels.

From a marketing perspective, syndication is how existing product is remonetized and repurposed, adding millions of dollars of value to the original network's bottom line.

Dealing for Dollars

In the early years of syndication, the government set out to protect the independent television production enterprise and restrict the all-powerful Big Three (ABC, CBS, NBC) from gaining even more power. In 1970, the FCC imposed the *Financial Interest and Syndication Rules*, which came to be known as Fin-Syn. These rules restricted the power of the networks by not allowing them to participate in syndication revenue after the programming came off network TV airing.

Fin-Syn caused a huge shift in the financial balance of the TV world, moving the money from networks to the production companies. One of the first winners was Carsey-Werner, a small television production company that had developed *The Bill Cosby Show*, featuring an African-American family in a situation comedy. The show starred a popular comic named Bill Cosby as the head of the household. *Cosby*, as it was known, ran for eight years with excellent ratings.

When the time came to end the show, there was such a strong interest in syndication that Carsey-Werner decided to put the syndication rights into an auction. Local stations went into a feeding-frenzy. The show quickly cleared more than 80% of the country's designated marketing areas (DMAs) and generated $1 billion in revenue. This was split, by contract, between Carsey-Werner and Bill Cosby, making him (at that time) the wealthiest actor in Hollywood.

This encouraged Carsey-Werner to continue the auction process with Tim Allen and *Home Improvement* and Rosanne Barr's *Roseanne*. Other independent production companies followed suit, allowing stars and production companies to reap huge rewards.

The rise of the Fox network (originally built on syndicated programs) and cable television altered the original landscape of television, creating huge competition for the Big Three. Declining ratings gave the FCC a reason to provide additional revenue opportunities to network television by allowing them to own or share off-network syndication license fees. Controversial from the beginning, Fin-Syn was abolished in 1993.

Today, depending on the deal made between the production company and the network, revenue is split between parties, a true case of risk and reward.

Types of Syndication

Regardless of where they are produced, syndicated programs fall into three categories: first-run syndication, off-net, and syndicated product in-auction.

First-Run Syndication

First-run programs are shows that are developed directly for syndication to local networks or cable channels. They may also be programs that were originally developed and broadcast overseas and offered for syndication elsewhere. Some of the best examples include *Hercules*, *Xena: Warrior Princess*, *Star Trek: Deep Space Nine*, and *Babylon 5*. Those dramas had great appeal to an attractive audience, young males and females 18–24.

First-run syndication has also been a popular niche for animated series, going all the way back to such classics as *Speed Racer* and *Scooby Doo* and to hundreds of present-day series. Talk shows also provide local stations with fresh, never-before-seen programming. *Entertainment Tonight* and *E!* have built and retained loyal audiences, but one of the best examples was the early *Oprah*, which launched the phenomenal career of Oprah Winfrey, who now has her very own cable network (OWN) and media empire.

On occasion, some network television pilots, initially well considered, fail in audience research or are yanked out of the line-up in midseason due to poor ratings. These would still be considered (under the original definition) first-run programs but are never commissioned for a full season. Instead, the programs are brought to the attention of local stations, eager for new, unexposed programming and given a second life. If this "almost first-run" programming builds audience interest, full 13-week schedules are purchased and sold to the thousands of television stations across the country that need to fill time slots on empty dayparts.

One of the most successful examples of an almost first-run syndicated show is the evergreen *Baywatch*, still seen around the world. *Baywatch* originally aired on NBC, was dropped after one season and put into syndication, and has never looked back. It has spawned several look-alike shows based on the production companies' belief that imitation is the sincerest form of flattery.

Off-Net

Off-net ("off network") programs are originally created for the major networks, where they have built loyal followings over many seasons. In general, 100 episodes, or roughly eight seasons (four years), is the magic number that allows for successful syndication, although a few programs have been syndicated successfully with slightly less than that number.

The most famous of these is *Star Trek*, originally aired on NBC, which threatened to cancel it after two seasons and pulled the plug after three. The series went into syndication and has spawned several new spin-off series, as well as movies, merchandise, and all the assorted hooplah that goes into creating a multi-billion-dollar bit of intellectual property.

Off-net shows began their licensing surge when the Fox network discovered that no more than 30% of the TV viewing population had ever seen every first-run show of each series—even the successful shows. Because these shows had been massively popular in their first incarnation, it followed that there was an audience eager to catch those shows the second time around. That hunch proved to be true then and continues to this day. Consider this data in Exhibit 4-9.

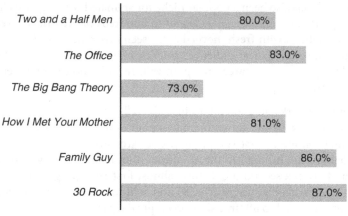

Exhibit 4-9 Percentage of those who have viewed only the syndicated program

Source: Syndicated Network Television Association, *Advantage Syndication, Top Ratings and Reach,* 2012

Off-net shows are created based on a successful pilot, which usually costs in the area of $1 million. Additional episodes are generally budgeted at $500,000 and upwards. The "upwards" can occur when a series has reached such levels of success that the star—or stars—begin to demand higher salaries, knowing full well that the show will eventually be syndicated, reaping huge profits for the network. Remember: The cost of an episode is born during the original production and airing and is offset by advertising. After a show is licensed into syndication—for millions of dollars—that revenue is pure profit for the network; there are no more production costs as the series goes into syndication.

A recent example is the series *Two and a Half Men (TAAHM)*, which originally starred Charlie Sheen, Jon Cryer, and Angus T. Jones. *TAAHM* had already gone into syndication after five seasons. During its eighth season, Sheen—who had negotiated for partial ownership as part of his original contract—went into a world-class meltdown and eventually went into rehab, shortening that season. Although he was replaced by Ashton Kutcher in the ninth season, Sheen continues to make millions as the show runs in syndication around the world.

Syndicated Product in Auction

The purpose of syndication is to maximize the income and returns to the syndicator, whether it is the production company, the network, the studio, the participating stars, or all of the above. With certain programs, the potential outright purchase price of the syndicated rights may seem too low. To maximize the potential, these programs may be placed into auction by the syndicator's representative or sales agent. This is similar to what happens in the publishing industry with a particularly tasty concept—Hillary Clinton's memoirs, for example.

If the program is hot enough, the auction typically entails a rash of bidding or an escalating price war, with the rights going to the highest bidder. In the business, this is a way of separating the seriously interested parties from the lesser stations; some of these packages can rise into the billions. It clearly places deep-pocket stations at an advantage and motivates station *groups* to bid for all of their stations as a package. The result is a higher price and greater profit for the syndicator.

There is a marketing implication, however: The higher the cost of the syndicated product, the more important targeted and effective marketing becomes to reach and motivate the viewing audience, building ratings and audience share. It is the advertising that flows as a result of these ratings that pays for the program in the first place.

Stripping

When a program, such as a talk show or a personality show with a growing local or national audience following, becomes extremely popular, it is sold as a *strip*. Strips have segments, which means they usually run for one half-hour every day of the week in the same time slot. *Law and Order* is an example of stripping; the show runs every day on local channels around the country. If there is a major blockbuster TV hit like *Seinfeld* or *The Simpsons*, with several seasons of completed show segments, a local station or station group might decide to lock up an important time slot by stripping, or scheduling a segment every night during prime time. This provides continuity, important in the process of securing a major advertiser to sponsor the program.

Selling and Licensing Programming

The value of any syndicated show is in its ability to attract big dollars from big advertisers. The goal of syndication is to link enough stations cleared for a given show to be able to sell to major advertisers or a low-cost national buy, for advertisers such as Coke, Pepsi, or McDonald's. For some programs, the package price can reach billions of dollars.

The process of selling or licensing programming to local stations has several recognized methods of transaction, including all cash, barter, or a mix of cash and barter. Few people need an explanation of cash, but, as mentioned earlier, in some of the major auctions where five or more successful seasons are available for syndication, the stakes are very high (and growing all the time).

Cash Deals

When the deal for a license to run a show is all cash, the production company or studio that has developed, produced, and syndicated the show usually provides commercials and print ad slicks at no additional cost to the station. On-air promotions, which run as much as $30,000 to $50,000 for a 30-second commercial, plus residual costs, are covered by the production company as a form of co-op advertising. After all, it is just as important to the production company as the station that the program be successful; success means more sales of the program in other markets, as well as the enhanced reputation of the production company.

The licensee runs TV spots on its own station(s), websites, and mobile apps and works out a separate barter arrangement with local newspapers. The newspaper gets free advertising spots on the station and possibly the station's websites or mobile apps; in exchange, the newspaper runs strips on its television tune-in page, promoting the local syndicated show, as well as providing some full-page ads or website links at the beginning of a new season. Everyone wins, and very little cash changes hands, except to the original syndicator.

Barter

In the case of small-market, cash-poor television stations, a programming schedule might be negotiated through a barter arrangement. Barter is based on the station's ability to sell local advertisers for supporting the show. The originator of the program contracts to receive half the income from the advertising time slots, with the local station receiving the balance. However, the owner of the program receives the owner's funds from the first sales. After the originator has been paid his or her share, the balance goes to the station. In this way, a poor advertising season or selling performance does not jeopardize the producer's possibility of getting paid, and the station has not lost anything except the airtime provided. A combination of cash and barter is usually preferred, even from small markets, so the downside risk is minimized.

What's Mine Is Not Yours: The Impact of Technology

As of this writing, there are any number of new and developing methods by which content is distributed to viewers, and, if society continues its current love affair with mobile technology, many more may occur. We discuss this at length in Chapter 6, "Digital Disruption."

Gone are the days when anyone is tied to TV. The term *appointment TV*—saving the date and time to watch anything—sounds like something from the age of dinosaurs. Today's consumer wants what they want when they want it, and many entrepreneurs are working to find ways to deliver: TiVO, Apple TV, Boxee, Slingbox, Aereo, possibly a Google/Android product, and the DVR available through your cable provider.

And conduits? Networks, cable, satellite, Internet, mobile transmission. Makes one wonder if it's time to start wearing those tin-foil hats kooks wear in the movies to fend off the invisible waves of programming scurrying around in the air. You pay your money, you get your program, and you get it on any size screen you want—the one in your hand or the projection screen in your media room, many now bigger than the small dark boxes that used to be known as *art theaters*.

But there's a dark side to all of this, at least for the business of entertainment, those folks who actually create content. Key to syndication is the concept of intellectual property, copyright, and ownership. As discussed in Chapter 1, "Begin with the Basics: The What and Where of Entertainment Marketing," ownership is what allows the business of entertainment to survive and thrive. Simply put, it pays the bills for the development of new programming.

With the advent of streaming, content suddenly became easier to manipulate. The major achievement or breakthrough on the part of Hulu, YouTube, and other technologies/conduits that allow for the distribution of copyrighted content may be the usurping of available television programming with no payment to the networks or the syndicators.

What is in contention is the fact that the intellectual property is not being monetized. Running that content, either with or without the advertising and without payment, is an issue that will be settled either by court or by contract. For now, the upside can be construed as having added exposure for network programming and gaining some support for the continuation of loyal fan interest.

Advertisers, up to a point, have had little complaint, given that their ads are repeated along with the programming. Though the DVR has allowed viewers to skip ads for some time, it calls for the viewer to actually take the time to fast-forward the recording, something that doesn't always occur. But new technologies now allow for automatic skipping, jumping from one section of content to the next as though the ads never really existed.

Beyond the legal and moral implications of this activity—and programmers are winning some legal suits, with some small IP income coming back—the battle is giving Internet conduits some important motivation to begin to build their own TV-style channels, which will become more lucrative as the next generation continues its move to mobile. And where will they eventually get their content to begin the channel? The same place Fox did so many years ago—from existing providers. It would be a rare thing indeed to find a startup that can afford all new content.

There are other angles to this story, chief being what are known as retransmission fees. But we cover that in the next chapter, under cable, where it belongs.

The bottom line is this: Although disruption is changing the business models of one entertainment *platform* after another, it is not changing *business*. Entrepreneurs and companies exist to make money. The system might wind up looking very different than it does today, but money will still flow from one hand to another. Watching how that happens will make for an entertainment experience all on its own.

Noncommercially Driven Broadcasting

There is still one small island of culture in the sea of commercial- and subscription-driven content: the Public Broadcasting Service (PBS). In the last two decades, however, PBS channels have come to resemble their competitive network TV counterparts more and more.

Public Broadcasting: The Evolving Picture

PBS has its roots in the FCC's Sixth Report, issued in 1952. The Sixth Report focused on the allocation of stations in the UHF and VHF frequencies, in an attempt to ensure that all communities would have access to the airwaves—not just the powerhouse networks. At the same time, the FCC also allocated one-tenth of the assigned channels to noncommercial TV. Communities with one or two VHF stations currently in operation automatically won an educational television frequency. This was the beginning of government-supported public television (PT), which led to the organization of PBS in 1969.

The evolution began in the 1980s when Lawrence Grossman became president of PBS. Prior to that, public television was known not only for government-supported, commercial-free broadcasting, but also for an eclectic program mix that varied from station to station. This mix led quite naturally to smaller, though loyal audiences—but loyal as they were, they were untouched by advertising in any way other than the sponsorship companies might provide to certain programs.

Of the four basic types of PBS stations (state, university, school, and community), the community stations became national leaders in the 1970s by contributing to the production of critically acclaimed original series such as the National Geographic Specials, Nova, and Evening at the Pops.[9] Grossman's arrival on the PBS scene marked the arrival of the *core schedule*. PBS then began to focus on consistent evening schedules, which were nationally advertised. Furthermore, promotional campaigns led to PBS having a clearer identity and an expanded audience.

With government support dollars eroding, becoming inadequate to satisfy the needs of local stations, PBS learned to reach out for viewer support dollars, market by market; some began to take on barely conspicuous advertising.

On the national front, the unity of the PBS platform kicked in as a marketing-driven force with several key marketing strategies:

- **Signaling value:** The use of consistent taglines nationwide, such as "Public television is made possible by the support of viewers like you."

- **Branding:** The use of an outside creative or advertising agency and the application of a gradually increasing marketing budget. Through the use of press releases, PBS mounted a national branding campaign in the 1990s to reinforce its consistent and educationally entertaining content. PBS logos were consistently positioned beside those of local stations, with taglines such as: "If PBS doesn't do it, who will?"

- **Pop-ups:** One or two programs a year were chosen to get premier promotional pushes, usually with major performers such as The Three Tenors or BBC programs such as *Sherlock* or *Downton Abbey*.

- **Maintaining and expanding viewership:** The addition of support programs that rewarded contributors with program mailers, mugs, cloth bags, T-shirts, videos, and other tokens of appreciation that signaled product loyalty.

- **External promotions:** The introduction of national, direct mail, and common carriage advertising in *TV Guide*, public radio advertising, and websites that provide additional content.

- **Mobile applications:** PBS now has its own mobile app, allowing on-the-go viewing of the most popular and current PBS offerings, along with promotional messages.

- **Licensing:** Among a bevy of licensing deals, PBS has created revenue streams with children's products such as those based on Barney or the Teletubbies, a British import; licensed PBS Learning Media, which provides "trusted, classroom-ready, curriculum resources"; and a 2011 licensing deal with Amazon for 1,000 programs that would be made available to Kindle Fire owners.

On the marketing research front, PBS identified the Discovery Channel, Arts & Entertainment (A&E), the History Channel, and the Learning Channel (all supported by commercial advertising but focused on educational content) as chief competitors. PBS has fought back with quality original programming, including the well-received Ken Burns' series on the Civil War and

---

[9] Stations like WNET in New York, KCET in Los Angeles, WTTW in Chicago, WGBH in Boston, WETA in Washington, and WQED in Pittsburgh.

baseball. Even details such as viewer turn-off during lengthy post-program credits were considered; those credits have been shortened considerably. In short, PBS has rolled up its sleeves and gotten competitive and continues to do so by emphasizing itself as a leader in technological shifts that include multimedia, HDTV, and the newest trends of education, information, and entertainment.

Summary: Network TV and Syndication

No matter how it gets to the consumer, content remains king. Marketers continue to seek out programming that will deliver loyal audiences in the largest numbers available. Production houses and networks count on syndication returns from years of successful ratings. For the time being, the mass reach of traditional broadcasting still offers the quickest path to the most viewers. The disruptive factor of new technology may make inroads on traditional forms of broadcast advertising, but the technology must become affordable, functional, and used by a mass audience. For the time being, commercial messages are alive and well in TV World. If anything, technology will only drive the marketer's message further into the actual content through product placement.

Radio

Radio is alive and well on the national marketing scene, although it certainly has gone through its changes since the days of *The Shadow* or smoky-voiced deejays in the early days of frontier FM. But regardless of new conduits, radio has a distinct place in our lives. It is personal, portable, and available constantly in our homes and automobiles. When the power goes out and the Internet and television shut down, radio is still there, battery-powered, a soothing voice in the dark, be it due to disaster or simply a storm-tossed power outage.

Radio is a marketing medium in flux. Ten years after we mentioned the advent of satellite radio, traditional broadcast radio has broken through the boundaries of the airwaves and has leapt into the digital age. Digital offerings—expanding the reach of local stations and in some cases, creating nationally known brands—include over 6000 streaming stations; 2100 stations broadcasting in HD (allowing for not only clearer sound, but visual content); and podcasts, with over 36 million Americans downloading podcasts monthly.[10]

Of course, the medium faces challenges from digital competition. Services such as Pandora are luring away those who traditionally listen to radio for the music. Satellite radio and the Internet have chipped away listeners who have depended on radio for news and information, such as traffic and weather. But here's a radio fun fact: A recent study found that recall of advertising was enhanced (27% vs. 6%) when a mix of radio and Internet ads was used compared to website ads alone.[11]

---

[10] Radio Advertising Bureau, Radio: On Air. Online. On Target, 2012.

[11] Radio Ad Lab, Radio and the Internet: Powerful Complements for Advertisers, conducted by Harris Interactive, Inc.

As Mark Twain might have said, the reports of radio's death are exaggerated. Listenership is up over 5 million since 2006,[12] and radio is still second only to television in adult reach—95% to 77% (see Exhibit 4-10). The Internet may be catching up, at 64%,[13] but radio is tagging on to that medium, as we discuss in a moment.

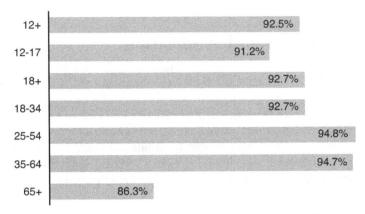

Age group	Reach
12+	92.5%
12-17	91.2%
18+	92.7%
18-34	92.7%
25-54	94.8%
35-64	94.7%
65+	86.3%

Source: RADAR ® 114, September 2012 © Copyright Arbitron (Monday-Sunday 24-Hour Weekly Cume Estimates)

Exhibit 4-10 Radio's reach by age group

Don't Touch That Dial: The Basics of Radio Marketing

Every radio station has a cumulative rating (*cume*), which is defined as the number of unique people tuned into a program or station at a given time for at least 5 minutes within a quarter of an hour. Those 15-minute segments are used to create the average quarter-hour ratings (AQH). When the AQH is combined with the overall time spent listening (TSL), advertisers have a clear picture of how long specific listeners are tuned into a station during each segment. It also gives station management a marker for improvement, where work is needed to keep listeners from shifting away.

Stations are constantly working to improve ratings to increase the amount of time listeners will tune in. A station might reach this goal through a variety of methods. Promotions such as community events, call-in contests, publicity, word-of-mouth campaigns, onsite broadcasts at events, giveaways (CDs, T-shirts, mugs, bumper stickers, and so on), and cross-promotion between daytime and evening audiences as well as between commonly owned sister stations can add listeners and increase TSL. In addition, *recycling audiences*—luring listeners back on a regular basis for regular weather or traffic updates, as well as news—helps build ratings.

---

[12] Radio Advertising Bureau, Radio: On Air. Online. On Target.

[13] Radio Advertising Bureau.

Radio marketers use those ratings to reach a plethora of major advertisers, as described in Exhibit 4-11.

Exhibit 4-11   Top 10 Radio Advertisers by Industry, in Millions

Rank	Industry	2012 Total $, Network and National Spots
1	Retail	$535.8
2	Communications	$309.2
3	Insurance and Real Estate	$225.2
4	Government, Politics, & Organizations	$209.9
5	Automotive, Automotive Accessories, & Equipment	209.4
6	Financial	$207.6
7	Media & Advertising	$188.0
8	Miscellaneous Services and Amusements	$167.5
9	Restaurants	$151.5
10	Department Stores	$87.0
	TOTAL	**$2,291.1**

Source: Radio Advertising Bureau, 2012

But today's radio marketer is also responsible for organizing and implementing other nontraditional revenue sources (NRS)—in short, revenue that comes from something other than selling airtime. For example, many stations are recognizing a natural fit between the Internet and radio and capitalizing on that relationship by creating their own web pages where they stream their programming. This allows for a visual experience for advertisers as well as an auditory experience, creating an opportunity to sell "print" (or screen) advertising as well as spots.

In short, the marketer's job is to gain new listeners, keep regular listeners tuned in, recycle the audience (for instance, by mentioning upcoming weather reports, road conditions, or features of interest to the listeners), and run promotions. All of this serves to motivate advertisers to buy airtime. Today's radio marketers have the same kind of rating information in their toolbox as their not-so-distant TV relative. An excellent example of the data available can be found at www.rab.com, the home page of the Radio Advertising Bureau.

Audio Diversity

Radio programming has evolved into so much more than syndication and has cross-pollinated into the new technology, increasing its reach and its offering to marketers. Today's radio—network, local, digital, satellite—goes nearly everywhere, reaches nearly everybody, and creates content specific to nearly every niche possible. Exhibit 4-12 gives a list of radio programming genres and their corresponding number of stations in the U.S.

Exhibit 4-12 Radio Station Formats, U.S.

Program Format	Number of Stations	Program Format	Number of Stations	Program Format	Number of Stations
Country	2001	Rock	295	R&B Adult/ Oldies	52
News/Talk	1488	Adult Standards	249	Variety	48
Spanish	824	Black Gospel	226	Pre-Teen	38
Sports	681	Southern Gospel	176	Jazz	36
Classic Hits	668	Contemporary Christian	161	Gospel	25
Oldies	607	Soft AC Lite Rock	155	Classical	22
Adult Contemporary	601	Urban AC	152	Easy Listening	19
Contemporary (CHR Top 40)	542	R&B	134	Modern AC	19
Classic Rock	480	Ethnic	133	Rhythmic AC	15
Hot AC	423	Alternative Rock	98	Other/Format Not Available	5
Religion (Teaching, Variety)	336	Modern Rock	93	**Total Formats**	**10807**

Source: Radio Advertising Bureau. 2012

To maximize marketing efforts in such a diverse land (or, more precisely, sound) scape, it is important to know how to reach the right "who."

Identifying Target Niches

The proliferation of niche radio has had a decided impact on the once-robust practice of mass marketing. Godfrey and Ashley Herweg, in their book *FutureSell: Radio's Niche Marketing Revolution*, discuss several tactics appropriate to researching and identifying target markets.[14] Though the book was written prior to the digital disruption—and therefore has no mention of social networking or any other opportunities of the digital age, the basic structure is still helpful.

For radio stations to have better relations with advertisers in an era of shrinking ad budgets and increasing means of advertising, the book makes a strong argument that mass marketing techniques are dead and that today's success story is built on better information and the implementation of that data.

Among the techniques they encourage are

- **Know your audience:** Supplement rating information with surveys by mail, by phone, and through focus groups.

- **Listen and analyze:** Seek to establish a more realistic picture of a station's audience (that is, more accurate age, interest, and income ranges) and establish the what, when, how, and why listeners tune in to a station.

- **Use better data:** Utilize acquired data to adjust programming and skew to pitch accurate and documented information to advertisers and to copyright ads designed to best use the station's strength.

- **Partner up:** Seek effective partnerships with ad agencies and dedicated advertisers. For example, have onsite promotions, seek survey information, and offer specials at bookstores, car dealerships, or at any other advertiser that can provide a two-way marketing advantage.

For advertisers, following these steps can mean that the job is easier if you're selling Coca-Cola or pickup trucks (big with that big country number), but the going gets tougher with products that must span across several niche types.

Case in Point: Americana Radio

Did you notice which format was number one in Exhibit 4-12? That's right—country. Also known as *Americana radio stations*, these outlets span broad niches of potential consumers, most of whom tend to be a very loyal lot. Americana offers prime radio marketing for a broad range of products.

Gavin,[14] a radio trade magazine, describes four subgroups within this particular niche:

- Older country stations, with up to a 30% mix of the newer alternative sounds.

- Noncommercial stations, usually college-oriented or listener-supported, featuring an eclectic mix that may lean toward insurgent country sounds such as Alejandro Escovedo and Lucinda Williams.

- Outright Americana stations, like KNBT (New Braunfels, Texas).

- Adult Album Alternative (AAA)/Americana mixes—AAA sounds with varied mixes, usually noncommercial radio.

Of the over 2000 country radio stations on the daily airways, at least 91 qualify for the Americana label. Three of the better-known examples are KFAN (Fredricksburg, TX), KPIG (Monterey, CA), and KHYI (North Dallas, TX). The actual music mix may vary from one Americana station to another—thereby grabbing different demographic groups station-by-station—but each of the stations reflect the cadence of their geographic region, often showcasing regional talent.

One of the chief marketing thrusts of Americana radio stations remains word of mouth. Performers showcased on the stations as well as faithful fans rigorously promote the stations; advertisers on these stations could very well benefit from the halo effect. Americana stations have been around since the 1970s but have gained a lot of their marketing momentum through Internet radio.

As a side note, it is also worth noting that the Talk/News format category has grown by 150% in the last decade.

---

[14]Also available on the Internet at www.gavin.com.

Radio: The Original Social Network

There are those who say that the Internet is the first medium to facilitate both conversation and community—that is, creating a meeting place for both individual interaction and group transactions. It's a good theory, especially when it comes to the idea of scale—the ability to reach huge groups of people, quickly and with a visual/written record (as most smart college students now consider before they post the naked-with-bong photo on Facebook).

But radio has been facilitating two-way communications for both individuals and groups for a very, very long time, with programming that reaches across territorial borders and facilitates basic communal connection. How has it managed to survive? By always finding a way to utilize new or existing technologies to facilitate new and innovative programming.

Radio bonded with the telephone long ago, opening up the airwaves to callers. Teenagers still call in to dedicate songs. Q & A shows still offer listeners the chance to talk with experts. And what is talk radio but a literal chat room? Radio joined forces with television to simulcast any number of television transmissions, from soap operas to news broadcast. And once again, with the Internet, radio is in the process of reaching out, creating a new, transitional medium that combines the auditory experience with the visual, with stations creating web presences.

These websites provide space for additional ad revenue and community connection, local sources of entertainment and information that can be accessed all over the world, extending the reach of the station—and the advertisers—as programming is streamed. The weary traveler connects with home. The one-time resident gets his or her local fix. Sports fans bond with their far-away teams for the game not picked up on the national screen. And the station is able to record every unique view.

Satellite Radio

When introduced over a decade ago, satellite radio was touted as the next Big New Thing that would kill traditional radio. Music would be offered (largely) commercial free, but some of the news and talk stations would offer spots. For marketers, it would seem to be a natural, given the conduit to the many niche markets satellite serves.

Ten years later, satellite radio still struggles to crawl above 14% reach in any major market (even after the two pioneer providers, Sirius and XM, merged in 2008) while traditional radio skates along at 93 to 95%.

Though it would seem to have great potential for growth—many new automobiles now include a satellite radio receiver—the subscription fee for the service is off-putting to many listeners, regardless of the wide variety of choice the service offers. In addition, the ads that do run seem to be off-putting to those who believe that once you've paid a subscription, there shouldn't be advertising. Finally, satellite radio faces competition from other music technologies, including cable television (which also offers music channels), mp3 players, Internet radio, HD radio, and so on.

Internet and Mobile Radio

Internet and mobile radio include but are not limited to local stations that stream their programming over the Internet via their websites or via a mobile application. More prolific from a popularity standpoint are the sites and applications that offer continuous music, tailored to the listener's taste. Providers of streaming music include Pandora, iHeartRadio (owned by Clear Channel), Spotify, and Songza. Vevo offers both the music and the music video, a non-stop audio-visual experience.

Internet and mobile radio as a business model has its own complexities. Remember our conversation about copyright and intellectual property? These nonterrestrial radio formats—unlike traditional radio—must pay performance royalties as well as the publishing royalties paid by traditional radio, as a result of the Digital Millennium Copyright Act of 1998. This adds a layer of cost onto the business, which must be paid for. Therefore, services such as Pandora offer a commercial-free version for a subscription fee and a free version that contain ads. The free version is a far more popular choice.

The use of alternate radio continues to grow, hand-in-hand with the use of the Internet and mobile communication. As of October 2012, over 50% of Americans[15] owned at least one mobile device, and by the time you are actually reading this paragraph, that number will have risen dramatically, as it continues to do on a weekly basis.

And, of course—as is usually the case with new technologies—many of those devices are found in the hands of the youth market, a particularly fertile ground for radio. They are finding their music online and will continue to drive this transition.

Exhibit 4-13 provides a visual tracking the growth. Note how the usage has been spiking since 2010, a key growth period for smartphones.

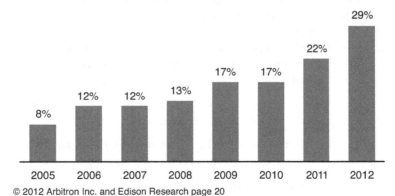

© 2012 Arbitron Inc. and Edison Research page 20

Weekly Online Radio Audience Jumps Dramatically Year Over Year
Estimated 76 Million

Exhibit 4-13 Percentage of people who have listened to online radio in the last week

Source: Radio Advertising Bureau, 2012

---

[15] "The Future of Mobile News," October 1, 2012, www.journalism.org.

As a final example of the impact of online listening/streaming, it's interesting to compare detected airplay (traditional radio) versus online downloads. First, consider the data in Exhibit 4-14 from 2012:

Exhibit 4-14   Top Streamed Songs, 2012, in Millions

Title	Artist	Total Airplay (in Millions)
Call Me Maybe	Carly R. Jepsen	119.8
Payphone	Maroon 5	62
We Are Never...	Taylor Swift	61.1
Mirror	Lil Wayne	53.5
As Long as You...	Justin Bieber	51.9
Boyfriend	Justin Bieber	51.2
Wide Awake	Katy Perry	49.8
Party Rock Anthem	LMFAO	48.4
Lights	Ellie Goulding	48
Starship	Nicki Minaj	47.2

Source: *New York Times*, February 4, 2013

When comparing streamed plays to detected radio airplay, the shift in listening becomes readily apparent. According to the *New York Times*,[16] "Call Me Maybe," for example, had 459,000 detected airplays against almost 120 million streams. "Payphone" had 480,000 radio airplays versus 62 million streams. Justin Bieber—himself a product of the online world, originally discovered on YouTube—did not make the top 10 for radio play but has two songs on the top-10 list for streamed music.

As a side note, this transition is the latest in an interesting trend that began in the very beginning of the 1970s, back when music was something one merely listened to. Any visuals were a product of the listener's imagination, a lovely way to daydream. Along came *Sesame Street* (late 1969) and with it a generation of children, plopped in front of the television, learning their ABC's via catchy animation set to music. As this cohort aged, they found a new way to enjoy music, again in a visual manner: MTV and the birth of music videos, song-turned-to-story.

Now a new generation has found the next step, linking their personal music experience to a constant stream of highly produced music videos, streamed directly to their mobile device.

It does make you wonder what this means to the long-term health of creativity and imagination. If every image is presented fully framed, do you ever develop any of your own?

We talk more about music in its own chapter.

Crowdcasting

In the quest to take on online/mobile music challengers such as Pandora, terrestrial radio is taking advantage of new technologies that allow the station to further bond with the listener. Radio

---

[16] "Most Wanted: Not Your Parents' Radio," *New York Times*, February 4, 2013.

has long served as the curator of popular music, bringing new songs in, moving old songs out, and now, with Listener Driven Radio (LDR), stations have a way to further cement the bond they have with local listeners.

This technology allows for a variety of audience input, from voting on favorites all the way to dayparts in which the listeners actually program the music (within guidelines set up by the station's programming director). The platform allows listeners to move songs in the playlist queue; recommend songs for airplay; receive SMS text messages, IMs, or emails when their favorite songs play; and dedicate songs to friends via Facebook. LDR Takeover also has a built-in music recommendation engine to introduce listeners to new music.[17] All of this serves to recycle listeners, giving added exposure to advertisers.

Podcasting

Where Internet radio depends on streaming, podcasting (the term that applies to digitized radio downloaded to a listening/viewing device) brings convenience to the listener, allowing him or her to consume the content at a time of his or her choosing. Podcasts might or might not include marketing messages, based on the original broadcast of the program. In this regard, podcasting is more akin to television content that has been recorded via a DVR in that fast forwarding or pausing may be possible.

Podcasting can be considered part of the disruption of contemporary media in that podcasts can be created and distributed by individuals outside of the traditional broadcasting structure. Theoretically, a podcast producer could align him or herself with advertisers, assuming that the podcast reached a worthwhile level of distribution.

HD Radio

One of the most significant steps in broadcast radio technology is the advent of High Definition (HD) Radio, which allows stations to broadcast multiple programs over the same spectrum at the same time. Sound quality is also enhanced. In addition, many user- (and marketer-) friendly features are a part of the HD package, including

- **Program Service Data (PSD):** Provides song title, artist name, station ID, HD2/HD3 Channel Guide, and other relevant data streams
- **iTunes Tagging:** Allows the listener to "tag" a song for future purchase through iTunes
- **Live Pause:** Allows listeners to pause programming and listen at another time
- **Bookmarking:** Allows the listener to save a song—or an advertisement—for consumption at a later time
- **Traffic:** With real-time traffic delivered both in audio and visually in the form of highlighted maps

---

[17] www.ldrradio.com/ldrtakeover.

HD Radio, with its interactive features and visual content, provides some challenges. Stations must invest in transmission technology, and listeners must invest in receivers. Although the technology has yet to make the big leap to big reach, many automobile manufacturers are now offering HD receivers. It isn't just the hip kids—Tesla, Porsche, Mercedes—it's nearly everyone, from A (Acura) to V (Volvo). According to a 2012 U.S. Automotive Emerging Technologies Study released by J.D. Power and Associates, HD Radio technology was ranked the most desirable emerging technology consumers want when purchasing a new vehicle,[18] with 52% of respondents saying that they would "definitely" or "probably" purchase their next vehicle with this feature.[19]

At the time of this writing, 2,000[20] of the current 14,000+ radio stations now offer HD Radio. Though it may take time for the medium to develop legs, it will offer marketers an intriguing platform when it does.

Finding Your Way Through the Thicket

The proliferation of niche radio has had a decided impact on the once-robust practice of mass marketing. This raises the obvious issue of how to identify and reach today's more diversified target markets and the opportunities they present. Today's radio marketing requires a new mindset, one that goes beyond the traditional mantras of "know your audience." The rise of technology now demands that the radio marketer fully understand the entire landscape and how his or her medium fits into it.

Mark Ramsey, of Mark Ramsey Media, is a consultant who blogs at www.markramseymedia.com. In response to a radio manager's comments about the business they were in—"not necessarily the page-view business"—Mr. Ramsay responded that managers should regularly repeat the following:

> I am in the page view business. I am in the Internet business. I am in the text messaging business. I am in the mobile audio business. I am in the social networking business. I am in the streaming audio business. I am in the content business. I am in the business of leveraging relationships between consumers and advertisers which can be mediated by my station and its content in any and all of its forms.

Well said, Mr. Ramsey. The best way to defend against innovation is to mine it, use it, build on it, and create new opportunities by joining it. Radio is in a particularly unique position to do this in the digital world, and the savvy marketer will do well to remember Mr. Ramsey's words.

---

[18] Radio Advertising Bureau, HD RADIO BROADCASTING: A Primer into Radio's Digital Technology, July 2012.

[19] www.hdradioalliance.com.

[20] www.hdradioalliance.com.

Summary: Radio

The traditional medium of radio broadcasting, often counted down as a marketing medium but never out, is finding new ways to utilize and partner with the Internet and mobile providers. Radio's ability to offer mass reach, along with a continued focus on niche markets, offers marketers new ways to reach target-specific audiences—not unlike cable TV, whose ever-expanding slicing and dicing will be discussed in the next chapter.

For Further Reading

Television

Blumenthal, Howard J, and Oliver R. Goodenough, *This Business of Television*, Watson-Guptill, 1998.

Eastman, Susan Tyler, Douglas A. Ferguson, and Robert A. Klein, Eds., *Promotion and Marketing for Broadcasting and Cable*, 3/E, Boston: Focus Press, 1999.

Litwak, Mark, *Dealmaking in the Film & Television Industry: From Negotiations to Final Contracts*, Los Angeles: Silman-James, 1994.

Parson, Patrick R., and Robert Frieden, *The Cable and Satellite Television Industries*, Boston: Allyn & Bacon, 1997.

Resnik, Gail, and Scott Trost, *All You Need to Know About the Movie and TV Business, Fireside*, 1996.

Radio

Eastman, Susan Tyler, Douglas A. Ferguson, and Robert A. Klein, Eds., *Promotion and Marketing for Broadcasting and Cable*, 3rd Edition, Boston: Focus Press, 1999.

Herweg, Godfrey W., and Ashley Page Herweg, *Futuresell: Radio's Niche Marketing Revolution*, Boston: Focus Press, 1997.

Magazines to Devour

Broadcast & Cable

Electronic Media

Entertainment Weekly

TV Guide

5

The Rising Tide of Technology: Television Content Delivery in a Digital Age

I n this chapter, we discuss the traditional and emerging platforms, including multichannel video platform distribution (MVPD), covering those providers who utilize set-top boxes as their primary link to the consumer, delivering basic, premium, pay-per-view, and on-demand services. This includes cable and direct broadcast satellite, as well as wireline (telco) video providers. This discussion includes Internet-protocol television, which delivers live and time-shifted television and video-on-demand and so-called "over the top" content, delivered via the Internet through third-party services such as Netflix and Hulu and received on devices such as smartphones, personal computers, smart televisions, and gaming consoles.

But beware: All of this is changing by the hour. Although the (fading?) standard of the industry is the set-top box, new advances in technology, along with the big data gathering ability of the Internet, have the television industry in the midst of a tectonic disruption, with marketing professionals welcoming an avalanche of new ways to identify, reach, and track consumers.

The Multichannel Video Universe

Historically, media content was designed for a single platform set—movies for the theater and television shows for the small screen. That paradigm was broken long ago, as movies became a prime piece of the cable television experience.

Now, with a proliferation of platforms—cable, satellite, Internet, mobile devices—the game is different. Technology is changing by day, disrupting the business models of content deliverers. And it is no easier for content providers. They must start each project with a strategy that addresses all the platforms, all the possible interactions, and all the sequencing to optimize both the content experience and the business outcome. The consumer is now king. They will watch where they want to, when they want to. If you can't keep up, you're dead. Marketing professionals must understand all of the options to fully exploit the product's potential, leading to full monetization of the brand. It is one hefty chunk to chew on, but what we cover here is central to your understanding of what is happening in the entertainment marketing ecosystem.

Let's start at the beginning: cable television.

Over the Cable or Through the Box

Few consumers today think of roof-mounted antennae bringing signal to their televisions, although HD signal can still be delivered to your living room for free, as long as you buy an HD antenna (possibly the best-kept secret in television-crazy America). As of 2012, 86% of American households subscribe to some kind of pay television, whether it is delivered via cable, satellite, or telephone wire.

This extraordinary penetration offers marketing professionals a direct conduit to specific audiences via an ever-growing array of content specifically developed to appeal to particular market segments. MVPD—what we often refer to generically as "cable television"—is currently the primary battlefield for the control of entertainment consumers and their pocketbooks, utilizing the set-top box as the centerpiece of data transmission and collection.

As we discuss later in this chapter, the set-top box is meeting many emerging challenges. But at the time being, cable is still the second-leading distribution point of television programming and is still hot on the tail of network broadcasting.

The simplest way to think about the business of MVPD versus traditional network broadcasters is this:

- *Network broadcasters* send 24 hours' worth of specific programming—one program per viewing segment of the day—to the local stations and affiliates we spoke of in the last chapter, via over-the-air digital radio signal. This content is supported by advertising, so viewers pay nothing to receive the signals. The only equipment necessary is the receiver in the form of a television set and an HD antenna.

- *MVPDs* deliver many different networks and services to paying subscribers. This includes the traditional network broadcasts, along with hundreds of different programs and non-broadcast networks, all packed into that same 24-hour period. MVPDs also offer additional consumer-chosen products and services. The offering is delivered via two primary modes:

  - Fiber-optic cable, buried below ground or strung along the road with telephone wire, then connected directly to the subscriber's location

  - Satellite transmission, with content downloaded to a dish mounted on the side of the house, building, or boat

The channel lineup delivered by cable or satellite may be somewhat similar—though each has its own claim to unique features—but the businesses are different.

- **Cable operators** work within specific territories, based on deals worked with various municipalities to deliver content to the local citizenry. These U.S. operators install and maintain a vast infrastructure of connectivity, centered on over 7,000 *headends*, the central receiving point where programming is delivered via satellite, fiber-optic feed, and/or antenna.[1] All programming—including broadcast networks received and retransmitted to cable subscribers—is then delivered to the subscriber over thousands of miles of cable.

- **Direct broadcast satellite** companies, a niche primarily served by DirectTV and DISH, send digital signals to subscribers all over the country (and the waters surrounding the country). There are no specific municipal boundaries. Content is uploaded and downloaded via satellites to the subscriber's satellite dish. The company's infrastructure costs are tied up in the transmission and reception of signal—the satellites—versus the fiber-optic highways of the cable companies.

- **Telco** companies—AT&T and Verizon—utilize existing telephone wire and fiber optic cable to deliver their full-Internet protocol television products and DSL Internet.

Together, these three forms of MVPD reach well over 100 million subscribers.[2] Though there are over 800 cable companies throughout the United States, the industry is dominated by Multiple Service Operators (MSOs), which operate many cable systems in many different municipalities (see Exhibit 5-1).

Exhibit 5-1   Top 10 Multichannel Video Programming, 2012

Rank	MSO	Basic Video Subscribers
1	Comcast Corporation	22,002,000
2	DirecTV	19,981,000
3	Dish Network Corporation	14,042,000
4	Time Warner Cable, Inc.	12,344,000
5	Cox Communications, Inc.	4,595,000
6	Verizon Communications, Inc.	4,592,000
7	AT&T, Inc.	4,344,000
8	Charter Communications, Inc.	4,197,000
9	Cablevision Systems Corporation	3,247,000
10	Bright House Networks LLC	2,038,000

Source: NCTA, 2012

The industry as a whole generates an estimated $150 billion,[3] including video subscriptions, advertising revenue, and a variety of services that we address later.

The continuing growth in content consumption—the ever-expanding entertainment marketing phenomenon—along with mind-boggling shifts in content delivery, is opening new profit pathways, and it seems that everyone is trying to get a piece of the action. As we put this chapter together, there are a number of technology companies—including Sony, Intel, and Apple, which

---

[1]   National Cable & Telecommunications Association (NCTA).

[2]   National Cable & Telecommunications Association (NCTA).

[3]   The exact revenue of what we call the cable industry is difficult to pin down, as some companies are not publicly held and therefore do not release revenue data.

---

have traditionally been involved in creating devices—that are seriously considering entering the world of the conduit, joining the systems described here in delivering content. How might that happen? Read on. We get to that in a bit.

Before we move into the finer points of this key entertainment universe, it's important to understand a bit about the background of cable, for buried in its history are regulations that will define the future of broadband and its new hot competitor, mobile content delivery.

The Link Between Then and Now

John Wanamaker, a nineteenth-century titan of retailing (often referred to as one of the fathers of modern-day marketing) once said, "Half the money we spend on advertising is wasted. The problem is, we don't know which half." Mr. Wanamaker would have loved set-top boxes, those winking, blinking basic-black receivers connected to your television, delivering more channels than you can watch—and providing the operators with specific audience data sliced and diced to the slimmest of profiles.

"Cable television" originally referred to a service that was literally linked, by a cable, to a tower or antenna tall enough and powerful enough to grab the radio signal of the nearby television stations and broadcast networks. The collected content was delivered to local subscribers by what was known as Community Antenna TV (CATV). In the earliest of cable days, this linkage may have been put in place by a local entrepreneur—a television repairman, an appliance salesman—who saw the business potential of creating a community network in any of the hundreds of towns and villages hidden behind mountains, down in hollows, or behind any structure that blocked signals.

Cable television is a sterling example of necessity birthing invention, leading to easy access, wide selection, vast wealth, and continuing controversy. Those canny pioneers, having created a healthy cash cow in their local community, looked for ways to fatten their business. Once they found the technology that allowed them to grab the distant signals of the network broadcasters, it didn't take long for the networks to start crying foul. After all, those then-tiny cable companies were grabbing the signal and redistributing it to the community for a fee—and the networks weren't getting a penny out of that.

The networks did not sit still, busying their lawyers with lawsuits and lobbying. The FCC responded, issuing rulings in 1962 that limited cable's reach.

You may be wondering why the FCC would take such a stance, especially if you've never known anything *but* cable television. The crux of the matter was this: originally created to sustain and promote broadcast radio, and later, broadcast television, the FCC had spent the better part of the 1930s, 40s, and 50s creating a regulated broadcast industry that would serve the best interests of the public. Remember, the programming that was broadcast was free—paid for by the advertising sold by the networks. Along came cable, making money by utilizing those signals and now trying to move into markets recently cleaned up by the FCC.

In a nutshell (although it is certainly far more complex than this), the FCC decided it was its duty to protect the consumer and the investment of the networks, which were serving the people. To do so, it had to regulate certain aspects of cable as well.

Over the next two decades, the legal battles raged. The FCC handed down policy statements and rulings that

- Forced cable to carry local programming (known as "must carry," which pops up later in our discussion), a move that was meant to underscore cable's role as a local, not a national, provider.

- Made cable companies provide channels that were known as local access, requiring them to provide studios and equipment for programming created locally.

- Limited cable from importing anything that duplicated what was carried on local stations.

- Kept cable from entering the top 100 markets.

- Prohibited cable companies from showing movies that were less than five years old or sporting events that had been broadcast within the previous five years.

Yes, all of this is true, and certainly a little hard to believe in the current environment. But all of this served to advance the FCC's policy that cable should be a local presence and that the networks should be protected.

In the end, the legal battleship was turned around. As reported by the Museum of Broadcast Communications,

> ...think tanks such as Rand Corp. heralded cable television's potential for creating a wide variety of social, educational, political and entertainment services beneficial to society. These constituencies objected to the FCC's policies because they seemed to inhibit the promise of the 'new technology.' Ralph Lee Smith's 1972 book, *Wired Nation*, captured many people's imaginations with its scenarios of revolutionary possibilities cable television could offer if only it were regulated in a more visionary fashion, particularly one that supported developing the two-way capabilities of cable and moving it toward more participatory applications. The discourse of cable as a cornucopia, as progress, as an electronic future captivated many. Interest in new technology and a concerted effort by the industry spurred a national debate, advancing the idea that cable must be allowed to grow in order to deliver consumers a wide variety of social, educational, political and entertainment services beneficial to society.[4]

Regulations began to relax, but it wasn't clear sailing quite yet. Cable was still limited or denied in its ability to carry the distant microwave signals of the broadcast networks, as well as recent movies and sporting events. Two landmark events finally brought this stranglehold to an end.

Beam Me Up, Scotty: Cable Enters the Satellite Era

The first significant shift began with the creation of Home Box Office, originally billed as the Green Channel, by Charles Dolan, owner of Manhattan Sterling Cable, a New York City provider. He approached publishing giant Time-Life (now morphed into Time Warner) with the idea of a subscription service that would show movies and sporting events. Time-Life took a chance on the idea, launching what came to be known as Home Box Office in 1972. HBO's original

---

[4] www.museum.tv, the Museum of Broadcast Communications, *United States: Cable Television.*

programming consisted of movies and sporting events and was only broadcast nine hours a day, utilizing a series of microwave towers.

Time-Life acquired control of Sterling and renamed it Manhattan Cable Television, replacing Dolan with Gerald Levin as president of HBO. (Don't feel bad for Mr. Dolan; he went on to organize Cablevision, now one of the top 10 MSOs. In 1980, he also spearheaded the creation of AMC Networks Inc., which today includes AMC, WEtv, IFC, and Sundance Channel, as well as the independent film business, IFC Entertainment.)

Levin built HBO into the fastest-growing pay TV service in America, and in 1975, he blew the doors open by switching the transmission process from microwave antenna to commercial telecommunications satellite. This was a critical move, for the capture of broadcast's microwave transmissions was no longer an issue. HBO and soon other programming from other entrepreneurs could now be beamed around the country. Time-Life/HBO furthered this leap by paying for the large satellite dishes that were needed for capturing the signal.

Now comes the huge leap forward: HBO, tired of being limited in content and hours, took the FCC to court—and won. In a landmark decision, one that continues to create mega-waves in the industry today, the court ruled that cable television resembled newspapers more than broadcasting, in that it "packaged content for publication," and therefore deserved more protection under the First Amendment.

This electronic publisher status was reaffirmed in another case in 1979, *United States v. Midwest Video Corp.* The cable industry continues to argue its legal cases based on this ruling today. You'll see how this has come to the forefront once again when we discuss new technologies entering the marketplace.

FCC regulations were now falling on a consistent basis. Satellite transmission opened the door for programming. The next decade saw the uplink of Ted Turner's Superstation WTBS, later to become TBS; Mr. Turner's entry into the news market, CNN; The Christian Broadcast Network (CBN), now ABC Family; Showtime; Nickelodeon; MTV; The Movie Channel. Getty Oil launched the Sports Programming Network, which is now Disney's ESPN.

But the biggest shift came in the 1990s.

Telecommunications Act of 1996

Prior to 1996, the FCC felt restrictions on *broadcast* station ownership would provide greater competition and therefore a greater diversity of voices and programming choice. This was determined to be in the best interests of the public and suggested the possibility of an increase in the quality of entertainment offered. Although the FCC had picked away at *cable* with new regulations here and there, the Telecommunications Act of 1996[5] was the first wholesale update to telecommunications law in 62 years—amazing given the rapidity of change within the industry. The implications to cable and satellite TV were significant.

---

[5] A complete copy of the law can be downloaded in Adobe PDF format at the Federal Communications Commission's website (www.fcc.gov).

With the passage of the Act, the broadcast networks were able to expand their owned and operated stations from coverage of 25% of U.S. households to 35%. This 10% increase encouraged some consolidation and motivated significant station sales. The changes wrought by the Act included allowing for multiple radio station ownership in a market and cross-ownership of several media in one market, such as newspapers, radio, and TV stations, a huge shift in a previously monopoly-adverse stance.

Take a moment to consider this: Markets that were once served by several independent outlets, over several platforms, providing different views on important issues, could now be relegated to having one large conglomerate who could basically own broad swaths of that market's media. This may be good for business, but to this day, there are those who decry the independent thought that flourished prior to cross-ownership.

The Telecommunications Act was very good for marketing. It eliminated the long-standing restriction on network ownership of cable television systems. This opened the door for media companies with multiple stations to blanket a local audience on behalf of their advertisers with efficient cost-per-thousand media planning offers. Media companies could now provide both in-depth coverage of a local audience and synergy between their properties, making for enormous competitive clout.

Continued support of the first amendment's "Freedom of Speech" enabled the cable industry to enjoy enormous freedom in selection of content, as well as adding services that would be governed by free-market competition. By providing a strong force for deregulation, the Act also set the groundwork for the combination of cable operators and Internet suppliers. Companies could now plan the marketing and sale of converging media vehicles.

Furthermore, the Act allowed for interactive programming and the ability of cable and telephone companies to offer voice and video transmission on the same wire. It also required any sexually explicit service to be scrambled to prevent reception by nonsubscribers but allowed this content to be available between 10 p.m. and 6 a.m. Most important to the cable companies, the Act eliminated any control over the rates for service tiers, packages, or single-channel services or discounted rates for multiple dwelling units, as long as it was not construed as predatory pricing designed to push all other competitors out of the market—this, in an era of rate regulation of public utilities.

All of this left cable in a terrific position, but it also left the business with an element that continues to have an impact on both the bottom line and the programming offered to the subscriber: the retransmission fees operators must pay to programmers to carry the programming the subscribers most want to see.

Retransmission Consent

As a provision of the 1992 Cable Protection and Competition Act, all MVPDs must obtain permission from broadcasters before carrying their programs. This typically also involves a fee being paid to the broadcaster (the "retransmission fee"). The MVPD may choose not to carry the programming but must always take into account the desire of the subscriber base in making those decisions or risk losing those customers.

The constant push-pull between the cable operator and the cable programmer often plays itself out in public. The programmer may ask for more money than the operator would like to pay, and then one or the other decides to take the fight to the public—the subscriber. Full page ads start to appear, blaming the cable network for getting rid of an audience favorite; the programmer will attack with their own salvo, telling subscribers what impact the increased costs will have on subscription fees.

One of the most famous cases of this nature occurred between Disney and Time Warner in May of 2000,[6] a knock-down-drag-out that affirmed the power of the Disney brand while blackening the eye of Time Warner. A more recent example occurred between Time Warner and AMC, home of the popular *Mad Men* series. Fox also battled with Warner Cable; ESPN slugged it out with Comcast. The result of these battles is pretty much the same: Negotiations ensue, agreements are reached, but the battles are rarely ended quickly.

What's at stake in all of this is a huge amount of money. Retransmission fees are projected to skyrocket in the coming years, for all three modes of delivery: cable, satellite, and telco, as demonstrated in Exhibit 5-2.

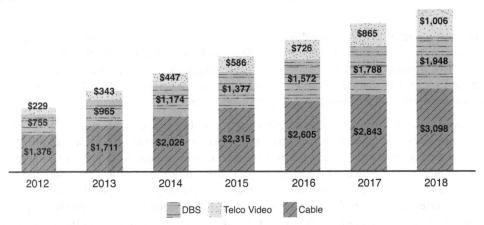

Exhibit 5-2 Estimated future growth in retransmission fees, in millions
Source: SNL Kagan, 2012

This, of course, is huge for the broadcasters. SNL Kagan analysis indicates that by 2018, the projected $6.05 billion of retransmission revenue would be approximately 23% of the expected $26.2 billion in TV station ad revenue.[7]

The fees may seem staggering, but the content—the programming—is the heart of the cable business model. The depth and breadth of the product offering is what brings subscribers by the millions. The ability to reach those subscribers is what brings the advertisers, who spend billions.

---

[6] For much more detail, see Stewart, James B., "Mousetrap: What Time Warner didn't consider when it unplugged Disney," *The New Yorker*, July 31, 2000.

[7] "Retrans Fees Seen Hitting $6B By 2018," *TVNewsCheck*, November 5, 2012.

Cable's Marketing Advantage: Reach and Segmentation

The heart of cable marketing is its reach and ability to cozy into niche markets. Before we describe the channels by category and examine their marketing philosophy, consider the range of coverage provided. Cable offers advertisers the opportunity to reach over 280 million men, women, and children in about 100 million television households. Once seen as an exclusively mass audience with a singular mentality and a plain-vanilla entertainment orientation, cable channels deliver advertisers a diversity of age, race, religion, country of origin, intellectual leanings, and genre of entertainment.

In terms of general categories, cable offers a doorway into some very specific and desirable markets:

- The executive or family that has a strong interest in the financial markets, managing its own portfolios, or staying ahead of the vast quantity of business news has a choice of CNBC, CNNfn, MSNBC, and Bloomberg via DIRECTV. In addition, each of these channels offers constant connectivity through its own websites, mobile apps, and email streaming to hard-core viewers.

- Women are at least 50% of the U.S. workforce and are major decision-makers in the purchase of new homes, cars, family market-basket products, and clothing. Though they are certainly a part of the audience watching any of the business cable channels, they will also be found viewing the Food Network, Lifetime, and WE (Women's Entertainment).

- Teenagers, who form an audience with significant discretionary time and disposable income, are drawn to MTV, VH1, Nick at Night, and the various movie channels. All are strong platforms for the 16 to 25-year-old demographic, with Comedy Central expanding the upper end to 35+ years of age with some of the more sophisticated and graphic-language programs.

- Although broadcast television has an obligation required by law to provide a certain amount of educational programming for children, basic cable provides the Cartoon Network, Animal Planet, Discovery, Fox Family, and Nickelodeon. Premium cable provides The Disney Channel for an extra charge.

- Adults from ages 25 to 45 interested in less-than-intellectually-challenging entertainment are drawn to A&E, with *Duck Dynasty* and *Storage Wars*, or Bravo, which has become the home of such cultural fare as *The Real Housewives* series.

- If you want to reach males 18 to 49—or almost anyone with a sports interest—advertise on ESPN. Clearly one of the most valuable properties Disney obtained in the acquisition of ABC, ESPN has been one of the most widely watched basic channels and a leader among sports channels in general. Others have followed in ESPN's financially rewarding footsteps, including the Golf Channel, NBCSports, Fox Sports, Madison Square Garden Network, and Sports Channel from the Rainbow Programming division of Cablevision.

Minority Reach

One of the defining characteristics of cable television is that it can attract and appeal to the ethnic and minority segments of television-viewing households. The Hispanic and African-American populations represent two specific focus points for the cable industry:

- Hispanics, one of the fastest growing populations in the U.S., will soon represent one-third of all television viewers. Hispanics have an acknowledged high interest in entertainment. Many family members speak predominantly Spanish, and, taken as a whole, the national demographic of Hispanics has a significant gross disposable income as well as a household budget in the billions-of-dollars range. The population growth is in major metropolitan areas in parts of Texas, California, Florida, and New York. Univision, the fifth most important network in the U.S., and SIN networks provide quality programming from Mexico, Latin America, and Spain. These networks use Spanish-language newspapers, magazines, and public transportation posters to identify Spanish soap opera stars and historical documentaries for their countries of origin.

- Robert Johnson launched his dream in 1980 with a cable station dedicated to entertainment skewed to an African-American audience: BET. By the year 2000, the station was reaching 60 million total households in the U.S. and had twice been ranked by *Forbes* among "America's best small companies."

What are the implications for marketers in attempting to reach ethnic and minority segments? Understanding the slang or language is a necessity, as it is in any global marketing. Additionally, the use of ethnic and minority actors and actresses or distinctive voiceovers in radio, television commercials, and print advertising is often the difference between success and embarrassing failure.

More and more communication companies have developed specialty advertising and public relations agencies whose management and staff are from minority groups, who speak the language and understand the mores and culture of these valuable audience segments. Young & Rubicam (Y&R), now part of a global communications company based in England, has two such specialty units. The Bravo group works only on Hispanic advertising to run in targeted media; they educate their non-Hispanic advertisers eager to reach these markets about the difference between Mexican, Cuban, Puerto Rican, and other subsegmented forms of the Spanish culture. Chang and Lee, another Y&R unit, specializes in advertising to various Asian audiences on cable channels that reach Chinese, Japanese, Korean, and other important ethnic groups.

Case in Point: Viacom Takes the BET

The success of minority-focused cable channels did not go unnoticed by the Big Brands. Within months after BET's anniversary celebration, it became clear the network was about to change ownership. The announcement that Viacom—the third largest media and entertainment conglomerate—had plans to purchase BET and turn it into a powerhouse brand was met with mixed reviews. The primary concern was a backlash from BET viewers, given that the largest African-American owned and operated media company was about to be acquired by a predominantly white company.

In acquiring BET, Viacom saw an opportunity to provide proven marketing success in the ethnic audience sector and expand BET's distribution. The marketing synergy and understanding of this demographic were based on current success within the various operations at Viacom. CBS had the highest ratings of any network in black households, UPN had an entire evening of black-themed shows, and Showtime had made a commitment to African-American programming.

Viacom, with many cable programmers under its umbrella, could provide clout in marketing BET to the MSOs and independent cable operators in ethnic communities. It also provided the resources needed to develop quality programming for a rapidly growing middle-and upper-class African-American community. The advantage of Viacom for BET's consumer marketing was the use of its varied media ownership, including billboards, radio stations, broadcast networks, and other cable programmers.

Viacom made an excellent wager on BET. Black middle class households (average income of $50,000 and above) have increased by 358% since 1990, while black upper class households (average of $100,000 and above) have increased by 128%.[8] Viacom reached an underserved market, while balancing existing synergy within all brand units—an excellent long-term strategy.

The Universal Audience

Cable is certainly not entirely focused on niches. There is a strong universal audience, as basic cable reaches 86% of television households. Many viewers simply shift their allegiance from network to cable. They have become a displaced mass audience shared by TBS, American Movie Classics, TNT, Fox Family, and the other basic channels.

One of the major breakthroughs in cable was the launch of USA Network, with Kay Koplovitz as the CEO. Koplovitz, one of the first women to reach a senior management position in the cable industry, came from a strong programming and marketing background. She was one of the first to capture valuable programming from the syndication auctions by the broadcast networks and ran many seasons of *Murder, She Wrote*; *M*A*S*H*; and other mass-appeal products. She also gained a significant male and teenage audience with expanded coverage of the World Wrestling Foundation.

One of the difficulties—and strengths—behind USA's growth was its ownership, divided equally between Universal and Viacom. In only a few years, USA Network became the leading cable channel, with over 26 million viewers at the height of its success. In its search for channel expansion, USA management recognized the value of a special-interest audience that would allow them to use their marketing muscle and cable affiliate relationships. From information shared by their Universal parent, USA Network's marketing management became aware of the strong following for *Star Wars*, *Star Trek*, and other science fiction films. It was no surprise when USA Network launched the SciFi Channel and built it a great audience following by marketing to "Trekkies" and readers of science fiction literature.

Universal, of course, was purchased by NBC, which then merged with Comcast. And what did SciFi finally realize? That to grow, it had to expand past science fiction programming. The channel

---

[8] "In Plain Sight: The Black Consumer Opportunity," a special supplement to *Advertising Age*, April 23, 2012.

changed its name to SyFy in 2009. One other advantage of the name change? "SciFi" was too generic and could not be easily trademarked. Not the case with SyFy.

Business Building: Stretching the Brand

Strategy is an important element of the cable industry. With so many niches to service, operators and programmers alike find themselves in a constant chess game. Part of the game includes a classic marketing technique: *brand extension.*

There are several examples of this maneuver in the cable industry. A&E, which originally stood for "arts and entertainment," focused on PBS-level programming in its early years. The network created *Biography*, an internally developed product directed at a segment of the basic network audience. From research of the unique interests of their viewer constituency and the acquisition of book club lists, A&E identified another target audience, an enormous population of history buffs. This led them to the next successful brand extension, the History Channel. The network cross-promoted these new channels on the mother channel, A&E. As we mentioned earlier, A&E now focuses on less high-toned entertainment. The network is now primarily known for programming that would make Newton Minnow—the FCC Chairman who, in 1961, proclaimed that television was a "vast wasteland"—say, "I told you so."

But business is business. A&E's new approach has shifted its average audience age a remarkable 19 years younger—to age 40—than it had been in 2003.[9]

Bravo originally focused on a menu similar to A&E. The network added town meeting discussions with actors and actresses in their Actors Studio program, especially geared to film buffs interested in anything about movies. When Bravo management (within the parent company at Cablevision) established this Actors Studio brand, Kathy Dore, then president, and her marketing executive (now president), Ed Carroll, set to work building their own line extension. The rumor that Sundance Institute was searching for a home for its independent film cable outlet, the Sundance Channel, motivated Bravo to quickly launch its own independent film channel, aptly named IFC. Sundance Channel arrived on the cable spectrum soon after.

Bravo is now the home of reality television, including franchises such as *Top Chef* and *Real Housewives*. Eleven new Bravo reality shows were announced at the 2012 upfronts.

ESPN also recognized that discrete audiences existed within its loyal sports-addicted viewership. Thus, ESPN2 and ESPN Classic were born to meet the demands of special audiences, including college football, basketball, international soccer, the WNBA (women's basketball), and the Gen X (and onward) craze, extreme or X-sports. Sponsors were prepared to advertise and market their products to these special audiences. For instance, Pepsi's Mountain Dew brand built an impressive soft drink market by becoming the lead sponsor of extreme sports competitions.

Live sports are one area where commercials are still relatively safe. The value of this niche has skyrocketed as new technologies have allowed viewers to record and time-shift programming, opening the door for manipulation of advertising—as in, just plain skipping past the commercials. There is little to be gained from recording a live sports event, unless you truly don't care about

---

[9] TVbyTheNumbers.com, "A&E Announces 2010–2011 Original Programming," May 5, 2010.

the competitive aspect or have no problem with watching the event even though you may already know who won.

This desire to have a bulwark against commercial-hopping has resulted in some extraordinary contracts being put together between conduits and teams/leagues. The most recent eye-popper is the deal announced in January of 2013, between the LA Dodgers and Time Warner Cable, for $7 billion over 25 years.

What makes this deal particularly interesting to our discussion is that it frames the ever-growing value of entertainment brands in relationship to content conduits. The Dodgers were sold in 2012 for an astounding $2 billion-plus, almost double the earlier record of $1.1 billion paid for the Miami Dolphins. Around the country, the immediate reaction was, "You have GOT to be kidding me." However, most of those folks, we would assume, may now be thinking differently—some happily so. After all, if the Dodgers are now worth $2 billion-plus, what does that mean for other major market teams?

The chart in Exhibit 5-3 demonstrates some of the most recent broadcast sports deals that have been inked in the last few years. Keep in mind that most of the following deals are for entire leagues, not just one team, with the exception of the deals with the LA Lakers (basketball) and the LA Angels (baseball). Perhaps it's just too difficult to actually drive to an LA sporting event.

Exhibit 5-3   Recent Major Sports Deals

Deal	Amount ($ Billions)	Date	Term (Years)	Increase over Prior Deal
CBS / Fox / NBC - NFL	$28.0	2011	9	63%
ESPN - NFL	$15.2	2011	10	73%
Fox / Turner	$6.8	2012	10	100%
ESPN - MLB	$5.6	2012	8	100%
ESPN - BCS	$5.6	2012	12	100%
Time Warner Cable - LA Lakers	$3.0	2011	20	400%
ESPN / Fox - Pac 12	$3.0	2011	12	320%
Fox - LA Angels	$3.0	2011	20	200%

Source: Will Richmond, 80 Billion Reasons Why Pay-TV Will Become Even More Expensive, www.videonuze.com, 2012

This increased value of sports programming is leading to increased subscription fees. Multibillion dollar cable contracts with local or national sports teams must be paid for somehow. An additional $3 to $5 per month, per subscriber—whether you watch sports or not—is often the answer.

Beyond Basic

New technologies now allow consumers to receive state-of-the-art services, including digital video and audio, HDTV, broadband Internet, pay-per-view events, and on-demand and premium programming, with over 900 channels available. So-called "triple play" packages bring television, Internet, and telephone into the home.

All of this brings fees well above the base rate. These important sources of revenue include the following products.

Premium Cable Channels

Cable packages offer a plethora of premium viewing, with several choices of all-movie channels, as well as selected children's channels offered by most cable operators either individually or as a package for a discounted fee. These include HBO, HBO2, HBO3, Showtime 1, Showtime 2, Cinemax, Disney, Encore, Starz, The Movie Channel, Sundance, and the Independent Film Channel (IFC). In some markets, the two "arts" movie channels, Sundance and IFC, are offered as premium channels because of the often violent or sexual nature of the movies. And speaking of sex, the once-discrete Playboy and Spice listings have been joined by many more channels with far more graphic titles, now shown on home cable guides.

Digital Video Recorder (DVR)

As we discussed in the last chapter, DVRs have had a significant impact on viewing habits.

At one time, home viewers needed to purchase a DVR device/service such as TiVo to time shift, but cable providers saw the wisdom of keeping control and added the technology to the set-top box, for an additional fee. DVRs also offer the viewer the ability to fast-forward through commercials. A recent development introduced by DISH, the Hopper, allows viewers to record entire prime-time schedules of all four major networks. Though the viewer still needs to fast-forward the commercials in the first 48 hours, after that time, the commercials simply disappear from sight, replaced with a brief black screen. DISH executives claim a high demand for the service but are unwilling to go on the record with specific numbers.

On Demand/IPTV

On-demand offers streamed programming, available at the viewer's discretion. Products offered include both movies and television shows. Viewers might or might not be charged, depending on the genesis of the programming. For example, Showtime shows may be free to Showtime subscribers but not to those who haven't paid for the Showtime channels.

Pay-Per-View

Pay-per-view (PPV) was the original conduit for alternative time-viewing, with recently released movies offered to cable customers for a charge slightly less than the cost of a movie ticket— without the fee for a babysitter, parking, and popcorn. Cable battled the rental industry for control of this segment, but all of the players—cable, Blockbuster, Netflix—saw their business models morph dramatically with the introduction of IPTV, just mentioned. Cable grabbed hold of the technology; Blockbuster saw its dominance crumble and its stores close, and Netflix—well, you'll be hearing more about Netflix in a bit.

PPV still brings in sizable chunks of cash in the area of boxing and extreme sports. In 2007, HBO sold 4,800,000 PPV buys for the Mayweather-Hatton fight, with $255,000,000 in sales.[10] The World Wrestling Foundation (WWF) has also built its business on PPV but has recently seen the Ultimate Fighting Championship (UFC) match their numbers. As a whole, HBO Boxing, WWF, and UFC are the bulk of today's PPV.

Cable Radio

Over 100 radio stations are making their way into households today through an entirely different conduit: cable. Among the benefits are

- Clear, static-free, commercial-free, digital-quality sound on today's higher quality home entertainment systems

- The name of the artist, label, and song scrolling on the TV screen

- Focused listening selections from music channels specializing in jazz, rock, country, alternative country, Tejano, salsa, metal, classics, oldies, and many more

Each channel offers music not often available on commercial radio stations. This music is sometimes packaged as a unique program. However, as you might imagine, new mobile music services such as Pandora present a strong challenge to this concept.

Media, Marketing, and Money

Control of the airwaves is just as important on cable as it is on network TV. Channels must fight the continuing battle for the cable version of "shelf space." Regardless of the discrete audiences attracted to an individual station or a group of stations, it is important to note that every channel competes with every other channel.

The difference is that on cable, a media conglomerate may develop and control many different channels, as opposed to one network. Successful media marketing in the cable industry is driven by MSOs that can package a variety of channels—reaching a variety of audiences—so that advertisers can expand their reach beyond the mass appeal of networks.

Think of it this way: A broadcast network might have 20 primetime shows hitting four demographic groups in the course of a week, in perhaps 5 primetime slots. The theory behind cable niches is that advertisers can hit those same demographics all day, all night, all week by buying a *package* of channels. Because repetition is the soul of advertising, MSOs that can offer these kinds of packages find themselves in the driver's seat of cable revenue, making it difficult for independent channels to get a share of the revenue.

Consider MSO Time Warner Cable: It has many cable programming niches in-house, including HBO, Cartoon Network, truTV, CNN, CNNfn, and Sports Illustrated. Time Warner is therefore in a position to leverage its audience clout in favor of its own new cable startups by adding those

---

[10] "Mayweather-Hatton Pay-Per-View a Smashing Success," http://sports.espn.go.com/sports/boxing/news

startups to a marketing package that includes many of the heavy hitters just referenced. Similarly, Viacom and Disney have vertical and horizontal integration that promotes this kind of power play.

Cable Carriage

Operators are reluctant to take on new channels—known as *carriage*—unless they provide access to a brand-new audience. Remember, it's all about how the channels can pull in additional advertisers/audiences or help keep the existing. It usually takes a new channel about 36 months to reach breakeven (where income equals cost of operation). When Fox News was launched, the Murdoch-owned channel wanted to get carriage on as many operators as possible. Instead of waiting to reach significant audience levels, Fox paid a "slotting" or "carriage" fee to gain entrance. Though the early cable dream might have included easier access to the airwaves for startups, the realities are the same as in any other business: He who has the gold gets the goods.

A serious cable subscriber in a major metropolitan market can be worth between $500 and $1000 each year he or she remains connected. This comes from a combination of monthly charges, including basic package fees, additional premium channels, and about $250 over the year for selected movies and sports events, streamed on-demand or pay-per-view.

In addition, programmers pay the operators for each subscriber they can authenticate as connected and tuned in to their channels. BET, for instance, pays about 23 cents per subscriber per month and collects about 50% of the advertising dollars that are attributable to their programming. Programmers also earn revenue by licensing their programs to other channels via syndication or international sales.

Curious as to who the top programmers are? Take a look at Exhibit 5-4.

Exhibit 5-4   Top Cable Programming Networks

Rank	Network	Subscribers
1	TBS	102,800,000
2	Discovery	101,900,000
3	USA Network	101,800,000
4	TNT (Turner Network Television)	101,700,000
4	The Weather Channel	101,700,000
6	Nickelodeon	101,600,000
7	Food Network	101,400,000
8	ESPN2	101,000,000
8	C-Span	101,000,000
8	CNN	101,000,000
11	TLC	100,800,000
11	ESPN	100,800,000
11	HGTV	100,800,000
11	Spike TV	100,800,000
11	A&E	100,800,000

Source: NCTA, 2011

Operators also derive income or participate on a per-inquiry basis with the television direct sales packagers of music compilations of catalog recordings or collectibles, gifts and gimmicks sold via info-commercials. Operators collect advertiser revenue on each basic channel that provides commercial airtime as well.

The most profitable carriage for an operator is the "selling up" of a subscriber to take a premium package and/or pay-per-view or on-demand programming, given the operator receives nearly 50% of the monthly fee. Because there is no advertising on these channels, the revenue split is of necessity greater than with basic channels.

However, to create revenue streams from any of these sources, a virtual maze of marketing must first take place. The cable industry must market both internally and externally, just like the networks. Cable programmers must sell their wares to cable operators as well as to viewers; cable operators must market their programs and services to their subscribers. Both must market themselves to that critical source of revenue, the advertiser.

Marketing Content: Cable Programmers

Each cable category and channel has a designated target audience. The marketing strategy for these channels is usually three-pronged:

- First, they must convince the viewers that the channel will provide them with exactly the information and entertainment that suits their lifestyles, their interests, their values, and their entertainment requirements.

- Second, the channels must maintain a market presence with cable operators all across the U.S.—and in some cases, around the world—to ensure carriage and basic cable package support.

- Third, in anticipation of each programming and advertising planning season, they must convince current and prospective advertisers and their ad agencies that they can deliver viewers of the greatest value to this business community.

Cable channel sales and marketing professionals must support their ability to attract the customers of greatest demographic appeal to the advertisers, providing customer viewer profiles developed through proprietary or omnibus research.

The efforts of the programmers to reach their specific targets—viewers and advertisers—flow into the greater stream of the conduit itself, the cable operators. The operators provide the mass reach that allows for niche marketing, which is the heart and soul of cable.

Conduit Marketing: Cable Operators

Because cable TV, unlike network TV, is a service to which one must subscribe, it is at some level directly marketed, whether by a salesperson or through an individual's contact with one of the nation's nearly 12,000 local service providers—the operators. These operators target new subscribers, existing subscribers, and advertisers. Many of these 12,000 providers are owned by MSOs such as Time Warner, Comcast, Cox Communications, and Cablevision. These companies possess the resources to mount slick campaigns featuring print, audio, and video media use.

In the late 1990s, this advantage became increasingly more apparent as MSOs began to build brand images, one of the best modern-day ways to increase satisfaction and product loyalty. The MSO brand images focused on reliability, customer service, and technological leadership. MSOs also developed distinctive branding techniques as well as promotional strategies that included cooperation with frequent flyer programs, fast food industries, and cross-promotions with radio and network television stations. The target of these strategies is the subscriber, both new and existing. Dealing with subscriptions means dealing with *churn* (or turnover). Remember that as with any marketing, it is easier and less expensive to retain an existing customer than to acquire a new one.

The Search for Subscribers

The last two decades have been the era of big cable growth. The cable industry, once populated by small-town operators and mom-and-pop stations, bought-sold-merged-acquired its way into that list of MSOs we discussed earlier. This cumulative-cable distribution—cable, satellite, and telco—now dwarfs traditional broadcasting, as demonstrated in Exhibit 5-5.

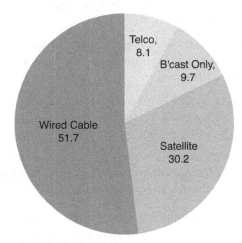

Exhibit 5-5 Television Programming Distribution 2012

Source: Nielsen, State of the Media / The Cross Platform Report 2012

Over 90% of all homes in America have easy *access* to cable, which means almost all households are potential cable consumers. Those not already subscribing to cable represent the greatest growth area. This includes new housing developments, apartments, and condos. Then there are those who already have access but are not currently using cable, split by cable salespeople into "nevers" and "formers." The nevers have, as the word implies, never subscribed to cable, even though the service may be already installed in their dwelling. Formers include transient users, such as apartment dwellers.

To reach potential subscribers, the cable and satellite industries use direct marketing, banner ads, outdoor billboards, radio spots, door-to-door salespeople, and network television spots. Although

TV networks and stations don't accept advertising from direct competitors, they do willingly take the advertising dollars cable companies offer.

Small and independent cable operators that have resisted being bought out depend on their relationships within the community for marketing to their customers. Their major marketing efforts are directed at maintaining the goodwill of the customers they have, reducing churn, connecting new homeowners, and massaging the programmers who pay them for carriage of programs by selling their content.

The local operator bombards the community with coupons in local newspapers and "penny-saver," free-circulation tabloids (sometimes owned by the local cable company), offering free installation. One of the most important aspects of his marketing program is "selling up"—marketing premium and PPV services to customers with basic cable. Bill stuffers, sent out in every monthly billing invoice, offer one month free of a premium channel or one or two free PPV movies to build trial.

The MSO uses many similar marketing tactics, with two major differences: bigger audiences in each of its locations and bigger marketing budgets. On occasion, an MSO simply unencrypts its premium channels and announces that this is its gift to loyal customers—another form of trial, without request. A certain percentage of basic cable viewers may then "convert," purchasing the premium package. MSOs also frequently send out glossy, four-color booklets announcing upcoming movies and special programs, engaging the customer and building a "must have" sensibility.

However, MSOs have had one specific hurdle to cross in building their subscription base. The early days of cable conglomerates saw a distinct lack of service, turning off many subscribers and, in part, forcing the passage of the Telecommunications Act of 1996, deregulating the cable industry to put pressure on the MSOs. In response, the leading cable operators focused on the service side of their business, both from the marketing and results standpoints. The results were lower churn and longer retention rates.

On the advertising side, the media company that owns the MSO can offer packages that include a cable media plan, magazines ads, radio commercials, posters at theme parks, ads on home video cassettes, and ads in cable bill enclosures. If the company owns a broadcast network, that too is factored into the package offering. Great examples of this are Comcast/NBC and Disney/ABC. Time Warner Cable/HBO used to be in that same mix, but the cable company was spun off from the parent Time Warner in 2009. Time Warner retained HBO, which it cheerfully sells to other MSOs.

There are ways for small, independent operators to gain a share of the market: the marriage of cooperation and competition known as co-opetition.

Cable Cooperatives

On occasion, a number of independent and MSO systems in a given regional territory may band together and form a marketing co-op. An example of this strategy is the Metro-Cable Marketing Co-Op, covering approximately 40 or more cable operators in the neighboring states of New York, New Jersey, and Pennsylvania. In their first joint effort, the co-op took advantage of critical mass to develop cost-effective mailing pieces offering a package of specials during one or two annual marketing periods. Potential subscribers were called to action with a 1-800-OKCable phone number.

Funding for this offer came from the combined pool of independents and MSOs. Though the average yearly budget for an individual operator might be as low as $10,000 for a small mom-and-pop and as high as $200,000 for a larger system or MSO affiliate, the co-op budget initially totaled over $1 million. This pool was matched by the programmers, with funds and film footage. The combined budget then grew to over $2 million.

The 1-800-OKCable calls were fielded by one bank of telemarketing personnel, who received the calls and dispensed the orders to the appropriate members. The marketing effort was totally accountable, measuring both cost per inquiry and cost per actual subscriber.

In the first three years, the co-op membership saw year-over-year growth of 15% in basic cable subscribers, and some systems added nearly 20% in premium and PPV revenue. The marketing budget has since grown to over $5 million. This case was reviewed at the annual Cable Tactical and Marketing (CTAM) conference; many of the strategies and marketing materials were acquired for use in other regional co-op markets.

Cable Television: A Marketing Powerhouse

Let's take a moment to review the key attributes of cable television:

- Because the cable industry is both local and highly targeted, the advertiser can reach the smallest demographic, even psychographic cohort, finding like-minded folks who love history, biography, opera, sports—a seemingly endless palette of prospects.

- Metrics prove that cable viewers are loyalists, maintaining monthly subscriptions and operator revenue.

- Unlike broadcast television—which has only a general idea of who is reached—cable operators have supporting information on every single cable household, right down to payment method.

- With the ability to match channels with customers and advertisers at far lower cost-per-thousand impressions (CPMs), it is a still a boom time for the cable industry.

- Cable's infrastructure is in place, leaving more funds for original programming, a huge drawing card for consumers. The attendant marketing by each cable network creates symbiotic marketing advantages for cable as a whole.

But new technologies are threatening this business model. In a moment, the rest of the story.

Summary

As with other entertainment media, multichannel marketing executives in cable and the newer technology, satellite TV, are continuing to explore ways to reach further into the discretionary time and disposable income of today's marketplace. Although their content beginnings played off the success of old stand-by movies, today's multichannel media boasts some of the best original content on the airwaves, driving both advertising and subscription revenue, and challenging programmers to continue pushing the envelope.

For Further Reading

Galland, Tom, *Dump Cable TV: Cut the Cord and Get the Most for Your Entertainment*, TG Digital Services, 2012.

Hofer, Stephen F., and Michael Davis, *TV Guide The Official Collectors Guide: Celebrating An Icon*, Bangzoom Pub., 2006.

Palmer, Shelly, *Television Disrupted: The Transition from Network to Networked TV*, Focal Press, 2008.

Tarvin, Neil, *Cutting the Cable TV Cord for Non-Geeks*, 2012.

6

Digital Disruption

D igital technology has created gigantic shifts throughout the business world. The full impact has yet to be seen, as it is still morphing—by the minute. In this chapter, we start our discussion of the challenges rattling the entertainment ecosystem by examining the impact on film, broadcast, and cable television. Although the disruption is not limited to these platforms—as you will clearly see in the following chapters—much of the new technology is taking aim at these major content providers, warranting this singular discussion.

Cable Levels Off: The Era of New Challenges

The changes wrought by digital technology have been especially vexing for all forms of television. Even with all of the marketing strategies discussed at the end of the last chapter, cable television subscriptions have dropped off, starting in 2012. Though there are those who say that this is primarily related to the economic downturn and cautious recessionary spending, there is also data that points to an ever-increasing number of people who are either "cord cutting" or, as mentioned earlier in the book, "cord nevering."

Exhibit 6-1 gives a visual representation of how this fall-off may occur.

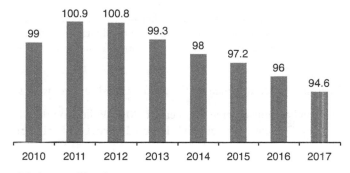

Exhibit 6-1 Projected decline in cable subscriptions

Source: TDG Research

Although the current cable business model still has television—as opposed to Internet or telephony—as the top consumer buy from cable companies, Internet access is quickly moving toward the top of the charts. As of early 2013, more than 81% percent of households have access to broadband Internet.[1] But the rising tide of Internet growth might have a huge impact on the current cable business model in the coming years. If certain shifts in viewing continue to happen, multiple system operators (MSOs) could be sowing the seeds of their own demise—though said demise won't be happening in the in the next five minutes.

Exhibit 6-2 demonstrates the explosive growth of the broadband buy over the last ten years.

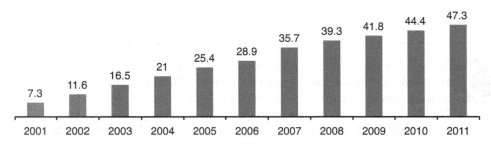

Exhibit 6-2 Total number of cable customers adding Internet, in millions

Source: NCTA, 2012

The cable companies that provide Internet service to their subscribers should erect a monument to whomever created that strategy, for if cord-cutting becomes the norm, that Internet attachment could be the saving grace of the business.

The Government Steps In

This growth of broadband access has not gone unnoticed at the highest levels in Washington. President Barack Obama, in signing an executive order that would allow for faster and more inexpensive construction of broadband pathways through properties controlled and managed by the Federal Government, stated:

> Building a nationwide broadband network will strengthen our economy and put more Americans back to work. By connecting every corner of our country to the digital age, we can help our businesses become more competitive, our students become more informed, and our citizens become more engaged.[2]

We might also add, create a wider audience for the products and services we discuss in this book.

Government influence had already entered the scene in 2011. Following the $13.75 billion take-over of NBCUniversal by Comcast, the country's largest Internet and cable provider, Comcast

---

[1] Nielsen, Cross Platform Report Q3 2011.

[2] "We Can't Wait: President Obama Signs Executive Order to Make Broadband Construction Faster and Cheaper," The White House, Office of the Press Secretary.

began a program called Internet Essentials in Chicago. The program is focused on underprivileged families, giving them access to the Internet for $10 per month. This was not entirely altruistic; the FCC had made access for the poor one of the requirements for approval of the deal.

The program offers slow access—3 Mbps, nothing that will allow for speedy download of the latest HD movie—but it does address an interesting issue facing the future growth of full-price Internet subscriptions: saturation in higher income households. Access in poorer households is one of the few growth areas left to providers. And in the classic camel's-nose-under-the-tent strategy, a little access may lead to a lot later.

There are some who view access to the Internet as a "natural monopoly,"[3] one that stands in the way of equal opportunity, one that demands government subsidization. In September of 2012, the FCC helped set up Connect2Compete, which gathers pledges from broadband providers and software companies, all directed at getting computers and access into the hands of the underserved.

The Consumer Steps Out

Cable television's business model is firmly based in the ability to deliver niche programming, which gives marketing professionals a clear entrée to the homes of the viewers they would most like to reach in a wide range of demographic slices.

But what if you, the consumer, didn't need cable to watch the content provided by cable channels and networks? Didn't need to have that set-top box winking at you? Could decide what and when you watched?

Well, you can. And that's what's giving the cable industry the chills.

Cutting the Cord

Up until now, the challenge with wirelessly connecting mobile-downloaded entertainment and your television has been the inability to "throw" huge chunks of data without the use of either fiber optic or HDMI cables. Therefore, even though we might have movies on the small screen, the attempt to link them to the big screen leads to fits and starts in picture and sound, fracturing the experience. But as we keep saying, technology is changing by the minute, and as of January of 2013, a breakthrough occurred in image compression that will eventually—within two years, if not sooner—allow all that data to be compressed in such a manner that fracturing will become a thing of the past. The only thing between your mobile device and your television will be a wireless connection, and the only thing coming from your TV will be seamless picture and sound.

Just like cable now delivers to you—but with no subscription fee.

"Ah!" you say, "but you'll still pay a fee for the content you're downloading to the mobile device, won't you?" Of course; this is still America, after all. Land of the free, home of the business. What will become possible is a choice that many cable subscribers are already clamoring for: the ability to pick and choose their content without paying for a whole package.

---

[3] "Mixed Response to Comcast Expanding Net Access," *The New York Times*, January 21, 2013.

A La Carte

As cable menus grew—in advertising-supported, public, and premium channels—cable subscriptions began to change. Customers could originally pay for basic cable plus individual premiums—say, just HBO or Showtime—creating a package that suited their own viewing desires. But the cable companies changed the game to create a more complex menu. Current subscribers now must pay for packages that may contain literally hundreds of channels they don't want in order to get one or two that they do wish to tune in to.

Cable operators claim they must do this in order to pay for the stations that don't have as many viewers (but create better packages for the operator to sell to advertisers, reaching all those niches we spoke of in the last chapter). Because of carriage fees, the cable provider's cost of content offerings does vary. HBO costs Comcast more to carry than, say, the Iguana Channel. Cable providers argue that if they were to offer a la carte pricing, allowing subscribers to simply put together their own list of channels, the operator's ability to average the cost of all these offerings into reasonable subscription fees would be severely limited. There wouldn't be enough subscribers to HBO and Showtime to spread the carriage cost over all subscribers. Prices would shoot through the roof.

Or so say the operators.

But this inability—or perhaps, plain stubbornness—to provide more flexible subscription plans could actually push the disruption of the cable business model over the edge sooner than later. Economics work in all directions, and it is feasible that enough potential subscribers, simply unable or unwilling to shell out, could eventually walk away. The cable companies would be left with pretty shaky ground under their feet. The golden goose could eventually wind up cooked.

Throughout this book, you have heard us say that content is king—that people will find a way to pay for the content they want to watch, listen to, or read. As long as the content is good enough to appeal to enough consumers and can be limited to as few access points as possible, the market stays steady.

But as Harold L. Vogel so succinctly points out in his book, *Entertainment Industry Economics*, the Internet is fundamentally changing and transforming many industries—not the least of which is entertainment—and certainly cable.

Vogel states that the Internet

- Redefines and rearranges (but does not wholly eliminate) the functions of the middleman or wholesale distributor.

- Changes the nature of customer relationships by altering the proportion of total revenue derived by advertising, subscriptions, and sales.

- Increases the amount, variety, and accessibility of entertainment program content and related products and services.

- Opens the way for new forms of entertainment products and services to be developed.[4]

---

[4] Vogel, Harold L., *Entertainment Industry Economics*, 8th Edition, Cambridge University Press, 2011.

This, then, is the crux of our discussion. How are the delivery systems changing? Where is the content coming from? And when do we hit the tipping point? This is a $150 billion industry. We're talking a *significant* disruption in the world of entertainment marketing.

Like the technology that drives this disruption, this is a highly complex transformation that is taking place. It is impossible to provide every last detail in this discussion with the speed at which things are changing. As before, we urge you to stay on top of this seismic shift. It is critical to your career in entertainment marketing.

That being said, let's at least start the conversation.

Over the Top

In discussing cable's challenges, the best place to start is with what is commonly referred to as *over the top* (OTT)—meaning without the use of the set-top box that delivers cable programming to your television. OTT means, as long as you have access to the Internet, you can stream content directly to whatever viewing device you choose to use: television, tablet, laptop, smartphone—or whatever new device might come along.

This provides opportunities for both the consumer and the providers. While consumers have more freedom to find much of the content they desire, content providers benefit through both transactional- (you pay only for the one-time content you want) and subscription-based (you pay a monthly fee) models.

But some of this creates odd gray areas. Case in point, HBO GO. HBO did a very smart thing when it began expanding its content offering: It made a decision to be its own production house. HBO *owns* its original programming, which gives it the ability to reuse it as it sees fit without having to worry about working any deals with any outside production houses, as we discussed earlier in Chapter 4, "The Business of Broadcasting: Network TV, Syndication, and Radio."

In 2012, HBO launched HBO GO, which allows subscribers to the premium service to access HBO's original programming on all devices, anywhere in the U.S. It's a great service for HBO subscribers, but what impact does it have on the cable companies?

Consider this: A Comcast customer in Florida subscribes to HBO. But that customer may be a "snowbird," someone who has a home up north for the hot summer months. Instead of paying Time Warner Cable or Cablevision a fee to watch HBO in New York, the customer simply accesses it through HBO GO. Have these other cable companies lost access to a possible customer?

And while we're on the subject of this very popular premium service, why doesn't HBO simply offer its content for a fee separate and apart from cable companies? Does it need the cable cord any longer? It's an interesting question, given, as we said in the last chapter, that Time Warner Cable and Time Warner have been two separate companies since 2009.

Here's the thing: For the time being, HBO can still reach far more viewers/subscribers via traditional cable than it can via the Internet. The percentage and demographics of cord cutters simply haven't moved far enough in that direction.

Yet.

Like we said, it's all a part of a complex conversation. Let's keep going, looking at some of the hardware that's driving this potentially game-changing shift.

Disruptive Hardware

The biggest challenge facing cable's content delivery is the new technologies that are taking advantage of mobile broadband. These are chiefly provided by cellular telephone providers but certainly including any Wi-Fi network with which the user can connect. *Mobile broadband* is exactly what it says—a service that allows you to access content anywhere you go, at any time, with any number of devices—all while your television and set-top-box are sitting at home, alone and lonely, like some poor kid who was left off the list for the hot party in town.

There are three primary forms of hardware that are driving disruption.

Smart TVs

There was a time when a television was nothing more than a receiver, a device that allowed content to be viewed. That content came via antenna (free) or set-top box (subscription), so the broadcast networks or the cable companies determined the overall viewing menu. TVs were therefore dumb, nothing more than an adjunct to the content conduit. Like much of everything else around us, the Internet has changed this scenario. Today, TVs are equipped with their own technology, allowing for connections to both the Internet and/or HDMI cables—the cables that deliver high-quality digital images from whatever receiving device you are using.

These TVs deliver the traditional broadcast media you may be watching via your cable provider. However, they also allow the viewer to consume a variety of products that are not managed by the Internet service provider (which in most homes typically the cable provider). In short, the cable provider, in selling you broadband service, is giving you a way to work around the television service it would like to sell to you. (How long do we think *that* is going to last?)

If you're not interested in trading up to a smart TV, you can accomplish the same reception goal by purchasing a game console. Xbox and Wii both utilize Ethernet connections to deliver content to owners. Or you can use an Internet-enabled Blu-ray player, which also delivers content.

An interesting outgrowth of this technology leap is a movement in the hardware—specifically television—world to actually *become* the conduit. After all, if all the technology is built into the box you're selling to consumers, why not get a piece of the content delivery yourself? Again, an exceedingly complex discussion, with no real footholds to date, but a subject of much discussion in 2012. Keep an eye on companies such as Intel, Sony, and LG, who produce a huge percentage of the smart televisions now available.

Smartphones and Tablets

Who can get along without that handy little device that seems to have attached itself permanently to your palm? Smartphones of all varieties—be it Apple, Android, Windows, whatever—now allow users to transfer content from that small screen to the big one in the living room, courtesy of any number of connective devices, with the simplest being an HDMI cable.

Apple, being the tech genius that it is, offers an easier solution, if you're already invested in the Apple environment. Connecting your iPad or iPhone to your television via an Apple TV receiver by way of the AirPlay network bypasses that cable. More on Apple in a moment.

Laptops

This one has been around for some time. Again, an HDMI cable between your laptop and your television allows you to throw the picture on your laptop screen up to the big device in your living room. In addition, hardware such as Slingbox allows you to connect into your home TV anywhere in the world, enabling subscribers to take their content with them.

Disruptive Conduits

When you have the hardware in place, entertainment content still needs a way to reach that screen, be it big or small. This is where the action is really happening. Because alliances and allegiances are changing constantly, no one really has a clue as to what's next, and everyone is trying to create the best business strategy possible to keep the revenue flowing in. It is an *amazing* whirlwind to watch.

Netflix

Long ago and far away, we started our whole discussion of entertainment content with movies—and here we are again. The rental business for movies has morphed into streamed content, and the prime mover in this area is Netflix. Originally started as a home delivery alternative to Blockbuster, the one-time VHS/DVD rental king, Netflix subscribers could order new releases and old favorites, delivered to their doorstep for just a few dollars a month. But as technology progressed, Netflix kept ahead of the curve by developing the on-demand streaming side of their business. At this point in time, streaming far outweighs disc-driven delivery and includes movies as well as television content.

Netflix has put more than one provider's nose out of joint. HBO refuses to license any of its content to the service. Cable networks have put together huge deals with studios to keep first run movies from appearing in the Netflix library before the premium services have had a go at them. This has left Netflix's library with more holes than their marketing might suggest, but the company continues to chip away, doing deals with television content providers such as Disney-ABC, CBS, and 20th Century Fox Television. Movie studios providing content to Netflix include DreamWorks Animation, The Weinstein Company, Open Road Films, and Relativity Media.

In late 2012, Netflix announced an alliance that stunned many onlookers, wresting Disney away from Starz, the cable channel that previously had an exclusive deal with the Mouse. Netflix now has the exclusive, gaining access to Disney's vast library of classics and new releases—as Disney sees fit to release them. Remember, Disney carefully strategizes the release of its classic content.

Even more important, Netflix has made sure that ease of access remains supreme. It provides free applications for smartphones and tablets and integrates click-through with peripherals such as Blu-ray players and smart TVs, where that familiar red icon shows up nicely on the home screen, and in some cases, right on the remote.

But Netflix also provides a word of caution to those who might believe that streaming is supreme. In 2012, Netflix suffered severe customer backlash when it tried to spin off its DVD line into a new brand, Qwikster. The plan was dropped like a hot potato when subscribers who wanted access to both streaming and DVDs howled. The company recovered and then some, beating growth projections by a mile in late 2102 and now serving 27.15 million subscribing households.[5]

Hulu

Hulu, a joint venture of NBCUniversal Television Group (Comcast/General Electric), Fox Broadcasting Company (News Corp), and Disney-ABC Television Group (The Walt Disney Company),[6] streams free, advertising-supported video, with programming provided by over 410 content companies. This includes television programming, movies, and documentaries from providers including FOX, NBCUniversal, ABC, The CW, Univision, Criterion, A&E Networks, Lionsgate, MGM, MTV Networks, Comedy Central, National Geographic, Digital Rights Group, Paramount, Sony Pictures, Warner Bros., and TED conferences.

Hulu Plus is a premium version of Hulu, streamed to any device, with limited advertising, for a subscription fee of $7.99 per month.

An interesting element of both Netflix and Hulu is what has come to be known as *recommendation TV*. Because both services know exactly what you're viewing, they can utilize an algorithm to suggest other shows or movies you might enjoy, driving additional purchases.

Digital Media Receivers

There are several digital media receivers out there, including Roku and Boxee. These devices provide access to streaming media content via high definition television, with interactive capabilities. This content might or might not (depending on the licensing deal) include Netflix, Hulu Plus, Amazon Instant Video, HBO GO, Angry Birds, NBA Game Time, and Pandora Radio. It is nearly impossible to fully define each device, as they continue to change as new opportunities arise, technology changes, and software is updated. In the interest of providing a snapshot in time, here are a few of the current offerings:

- **Vudu:** Owned by Walmart, allows users to rent or purchase films as well as watch streamed content.

- **Boxee:** Allows users to view, rate, and recommend content to their friends through included social platform applications.

- **Roku:** A digital media receiver that allows users to view streamed content through high definition TVs.

And while we're on the subject...

---

[5] "A Resurgent Netflix Beats Projections, Even Its Own," *New York Times*, January 24, 2013.

[6] "How Much Extra Cash Does Apple Really Have?" *Forbes*, December 12, 2012.

Apple TV

Grounded in iTunes, Apple TV, also a digital media receiver, offers access to the iTunes library of movies, shows, games—all forms of digital content, available on a transactional basis. It also offers Netflix, Hulu Plus, YouTube, Flickr, iCloud, MLB.tv, NBA League Pass, NHL GameCenter, along with content from Mac OS X or Windows operating systems.

But wait: there's (potentially) more. The early 2013 rumor mills have been heating up with conversation regarding Apple actually producing a television, not just a digital media receiver. Some say that it will help Apple lock consumers into other iOS-based devices (iPads, iPhones), even as competition from other tablet and phone providers heats up. After all, people replace their televisions an average of every eight years, while other devices, such as phones, may be changed out every two years. If that little device in the palm of your hand allows you to seamlessly interact with content in your living room, you might be less willing to move out of the iUniverse.

Apple is an 800-pound gorilla lurking in the background of the entertainment business, and not just because it launched the smartphone revolution with the sleek and stunning iPhone. Apple is a company that could forever change the hardware/content game in a few simple moves. The company is sitting on a pile of cash that could be worth as much as $158 billion by September of 2013.[7] That is a *lot* of buying power.

Apple already has a stake in content. It certainly has a stake in hardware and software. So what if it used a bit of that cash and purchased Disney—who has made several stunning moves of its own, purchasing LucasFilm (*Star Wars*, et al.) and Marvel? Or Time Warner (HBO, Cinemax, Turner Broadcasting, CNN, and much, much more)? What if Apple suddenly locked up all of it, together? They could do that with less than half of that pile.

Don't laugh. Stranger things have happened.

Gray Area...Errr, Aereo

You will note that most of the conduits we have described so far have found some way to play nice in the business model sandbox. Some devices are actually owned by media companies; others pay fees. Now along comes Aereo, and the whole world starts to tilt one more time.

Launched in 2012, backed by Barry Diller's IAC/InterActiveCorp, Aereo allows subscribers to watch both live and time-shifted over-the-air broadcast content on Internet-connected devices. Aereo launched its service in New York City in 2012 and was immediately the target of a pile of lawsuits, from both broadcast networks and cable providers.

Aereo sits in a strange gray area. It is perfectly legal for any person to purchase an HD antenna and capture broadcast signal at no cost—but that antenna is a fixed device. Aereo has set themselves up as the middleman, capturing those broadcast signals on antennas that are leased to each subscriber, then delivering that content to the subscriber via the Internet. Voila! The subscriber no longer needs to be near their fixed antenna.

Broadcasters are screaming because Aereo circumvents the very healthy retransmission fees cable pays to broadcasters—estimated at 10% of broadcast's yearly revenue. Cable companies are screaming because consumers can receive and time-shift content without paying cable fees. In an interesting "Huh?" moment, Federal Judge Alison Nathan tossed out a preliminary request for injunction, filed by a consortium of network broadcasters, with the decision based on a case that had established Cablevision's right to cloud-based streaming and DVR services—in effect, also undercutting any argument cable might have *against* the service.

In early 2013, at the yearly Consumer Electronics show, Aereo announced that it would be launching service in 22 American cities in 2013. This is about to get *really* interesting.

Google TV

Google TV integrates Google's Android operating system and Chrome browser to create a 10-layer overlay on the consumer's smart TV. Through multiscreening, it allows the viewer to access Internet-based content, including Netflix, HBO GO, and other streaming content currently available (all subscription fees are still in effect; you cannot access on-demand HBO programming if you haven't paid for the service through your cable provider). While watching content, viewers can also access all other content normally available through the Google browser.

This sets up an intriguing opportunity for content providers to create highly interactive programming. Imagine watching the Masters Golf tournament while simultaneously clicking through to order that new set of Ping clubs. This gives the term "recommendation TV" a whole new—and to marketers, exciting—angle. It could take product placement to a hugely profitable new level.

The multilayer function of Google TV allows for personalized viewing experiences, where viewers can put together their own "home screens"—particularly advantageous for parents who might want to set up a lock-out for their children, keeping little Justin and Tiffany from channels that aren't allowed.

Disruptive Content

So we have the hardware; we have the conduits. Now we need something to watch. There's certainly more than enough available through the traditional providers, all of it streaming nearly everywhere. And it's getting better all the time. Cable networks and channels have been on an original-content rampage over the last several years, ever since AMC's *Mad Men* (a program offered to but turned down by HBO) turned into the breakout, break-away hit of the decade, influencing everything from clothing styles to political debates and proving once again that content is king.

HBO, of course, is the reigning champ of original content, showing up at the Emmys, Golden Globes, and Cable ACE awards with a wheelbarrow, every year. But what used to be the also-rans—Showtime, Starz—have been launching their own media missiles of late, with great success. Content comes from everywhere. A small example: *Bomb Girls*, a program dealing with the lives of World War II Canadian factory workers, originally aired on Global TV, a Canadian broadcast network with 12 outlets in Canada. The original season of six episodes was picked up by Reelz, making the program available to American viewers. The show has developed a loyal and growing following, crossing international lines.

It seems that nearly every outlet with an eye toward eyeball-grabbing is in the hunt now. It isn't enough to stream just anything anymore. It has to be something unique, something that will sway the consumers to your site, to your subscription package, and original programming is the answer du jour.

Part of what's moving this forward is the leap in digital technology. It is estimated that the cost of a typical television pilot runs in the neighborhood of $3 million for a 30-minute show. The traditional system gets that pilot on the air for one viewing. If it sticks, great. If it doesn't, it's gone.

But the digital universe has delivered both the hardware and the software to the masses. A 30-minute show can be produced for $5,000. It can be launched on the Internet, where it can be viewed, reviewed, tweaked, and relaunched for less than nothing. It can be allowed to grow, gain viewers and traction, and turn into a modest hit on a not-so-modest medium. Are we talking broadcast television numbers? Of course not. But we're at the root of the revolution, the very start of the seedling.

That nursery is being fertilized by some very large dollars. Hulu now has original programming. YouTube has launched original programming, courtesy of the $100 million YouTube Original Channel Initiative. Why the push? YouTube is now owned by Google—and those original channels will kickstart that same Google TV we just discussed.

Even Netflix has joined the revolution and may have started a new one. In February of 2013, Netflix launched its own *House of Cards*, a 12-chapter series dealing with skullduggery in Washington (talk about your easy targets). What sets the series aside from the typical launch is this: They made all 12 episodes available immediately.

This is potentially game-changing. Netflix recognized a trend in consumer behavior: *marathoning*. With all the content now available on the stream, many consumers will simply wait until a series—from any of the networks, broadcast or cable—is available as a whole and then watch it all at once. No commercials, no annoying wait at the end of the cliffhanger—just a straight-through "read," like a novel. Another interesting feature of the launch is the episodes have no opening flashbacks—those bits and pieces of the previous episode supposed to bring viewers up to date. Marathoners don't need them, don't want them, and can give their fast-forwarding thumbs a break.

This might turn out to be the golden age of viewing. As each network ups the ante with new content, every other competitor must rise to the occasion, pumping out even more and faster. The consumer is being treated to a fresh content buffet unlike anything we've ever seen.

TVEverywhere

So here we are, with broadcast television, cable television, and now online television. The response from traditional providers has been an initiative called TVEverywhere, launched by Comcast and Time Warner. TVEverywhere is an authentication service that checks to make sure that online viewers accessing streaming content have paid the necessary subscription fees to access said content. In short, it's a way to make sure that providers who pay networks for the carriage of their shows are not undercut by those same networks placing that content online for streaming.

Summary

Today's entertainment marketing professionals *must* stay current with the rapidly evolving digital disruption. Hardware and software are changing by the nano-second. Though digital delivery offers great opportunities to entertainment marketing professionals, it also offers plenty of pitfalls. Read everything that you can in print, digital, or online; attend conferences and conventions; follow the trends; stay informed of new technologies. In the digital world, not doing so could lead to career death.

Before we explore the marketing of some very important entertainment content, sports and music, let's examine the first mass media: publishing.

For Further Reading

Iordanova, Dina, and Stuart Cunningham, *Digital Disruption: Cinema Moves On-line*, St Andrews Film Studies; 1st Edition (March 1, 2012).

Vivian, John, *The Media of Mass Communication*, 11th Edition, Pearson, 2012.

7

Publishing: The Printed Word Goes Digital

In this chapter, we explore the world of the printed word and how it comes to market, investigating books, newspapers, and magazines. Like many other entertainment platforms, publishing is in the middle of its own protracted drama, this one centered on the influence of digital technology—a villain to some and a hero to others. We leave it up to you to decide which it is. In any case, it is redefining this critical business segment.

In the Beginning...

At the heart of all that enchants and engages us—movies, music, television, and art—there is story. Story reflects our innermost yearnings and our greatest fears, allowing us to experience them in a safe place, far from whatever messy business might occur in real life. This is as true in nonfiction as it is in fiction; in orchestral music as in opera. Story is the emotional tagline that pulls us into and through any creative endeavor.

Story does not turn into revenue without some kind of controlled effort at distribution and monetization. Publishing is what takes the author—be it novelist, journalist, or blogger—from simply getting attention to making a living...maybe. The making a living part is rarely based purely on talent. It is, in fact, based on the business of publishing.

Marketing is the underpinning of the entire effort, regardless of the delivery: hardcopy or downloaded digital. This is as true for a single online blog as it is for the millions of Harry Potter books, as applicable to the self-publishing author as it is to the biggest names in the business. The advent of digital self-publishing makes cutting through the clutter more important than ever. The digitization of media has turned this, the first mass medium, into a Wild West never seen before.

From its very inception—the moment Johannes Gutenberg pulled the first page from his printing press—publishing has had many forms of control, some of them socio-economic (not everyone could own a printing press; not everyone could read); some of them governmental (censorship and regulation). But the digital disruption has literally opened the floodgates of access, control, monetization, and marketing, turning the world of publishing on its head.

The traditional model of publishing relied on trained individuals to vet content, controlling the product as it came to press, ushering it out to the market in a specific set of steps. Today, with self-publishing, blogs, and "citizen journalists," supported by technology that puts the process in the hands of both the creator and the consumer, publishing is battling for survival, in a war that sometimes feels like the French Revolution, complete with mobs of the digerati mounting the barricades of the Internet.

Even the simplest of concepts—the formation of opinion as a tool to grade quality—has been handed over to the masses, especially in the world of books. Good? Bad? Two sides to every story, one that we investigate as we touch on each platform.

So let's begin with books, starting with the traditional structure of the business.

Books

Book publishing covers a wide landscape: hardbacks, e-books, paperbacks, pocket-sized books, and coffee table books (not to mention books that could serve as coffee tables, given their size). Also, professional publishing, religious publishing, and educational publishing (texts, professional references, workbooks, and support materials developed specifically for elementary, high school, and college).

For basic reference, the following is a quick look at the terminology[1]:

- **Books:** All nonperiodical hardcover volumes regardless of length, excluding coloring books, and all nonperiodical softbound volumes over 48 pages.

- **Trade Books:** Books designed for the general consumer and sold primarily through bookstores, online retailers, and to libraries ("trade," then, is in reference to the traditional trade markets these books are sold in). Though trade books were traditionally hard cover, in recent years more soft cover trade books have been common. Adult trade books include fiction, poetry, literary comment, biography and history, the arts, music, theater, cinema, popular science and technology, cookery, home crafts, self-help, business, how-to books, popular medicine, sports, travel, gardening, nature, social issues, and public affairs. Many of these books are reprinted in lower priced editions called trade paperbacks or quality paperbacks. Often their original or only appearance is in a paperback edition.

- **Mass-Market Books:** Books sold predominantly through mass channels that extend beyond traditional trade outlets, such as book and department stores, to include newsstands, drug stores, chain stores, and supermarkets (often the same channels that distribute magazines). Mass market paperbacks are usually printed on less expensive paper than trade paperbacks, and their covers are more likely to attract a mass audience. Mass-market paperbacks are reprints of hard-cover fiction and nonfiction books, some original fiction (some are published only in this format), and original nonfiction. Mass-market books are often sold though the channels that distribute magazines and can also be found online.

---

[1] Woudstra, Wendy J., "Trade or Mass Market?," www.publishingcentral.com.

- **Textbooks:** Books designed for classroom use rather than general consumption. This category also includes workbooks, manuals, maps, and other items intended for classroom use. Textbooks usually contain teaching aids, such as summaries and questions that distinguish them from consumer-oriented materials (like trade books). These books are generally sold through college bookstores and are also available online.

Please note that for the purpose of this discussion, "e-books" refer to any of the types of books just listed, repackaged and sold as a digital version to be consumed via a digital reading device. The same holds true for "audiobooks," which are recorded and distributed whether in hard copy (DVD) or as digital downloads.

In the entertainment field, the two most common types of books are trade books and mass-market paperbacks. In North America, the trade publishing world is currently dominated by the Big Six: Hachette, HarperCollins, Macmillan, Random House, Penguin Group, and Simon & Schuster. We say "currently" because at the time of this writing, at least two mergers seem to be in the works, possibly leading to a "Big Four."

The fiction category of books represents the greatest percentage of books sold in any category. These are books identified as appealing to a mass audience and providing relaxation and engrossing reading. They are often described as "mental transportation"—escapism in a small package.

As entertainment, fiction is the focus of the book portion of this chapter

Something for Everyone

Within trade and mass-market publishing, books are further defined by the audience they serve. The term "genre" is used across the entertainment world to describe particular categories of writing, music, movies, television, and radio content. It helps content providers in all areas understand and measure the popularity of one genre against another, as well as strategize marketing plans for the audiences they serve. In publishing, the tracking of genres guides the decision-making process for allocating scarce resources, especially when it comes to paying advances or creating marketing support.

Some literary critics have been quick to attach a stigma to the marketing-driven concept of genre. Writers like Raymond Chandler and Dashiell Hammett created original, high-quality works but were never widely considered to be "literary" by American critics of their day, though others have ranked them in the top 100 American writers. Publishers catering to mass audiences and pop culture seem to care little for literary appellations, given that genre publishing has been very good to the whole industry.

Many genres have no clear-cut single descriptive but instead have major and minor subcategories. There is science fiction (sci-fi), which splits roughly between futuristic (Herbert's *Dune*) and sword-and-dragon fiction (Tolkien's *The Lord of the Rings*). Mystery books also fall into several popular and even niche subgenres. These include cozy reading (Agatha Christie, Nora Roberts), noir (Jim Thompson, James Ellroy), hard-knuckle (Mickey Spillane), and a number of other categories of distinction. Westerns still have their own shelves. Also, books of humor, poetry, plays, and African-American and gay literature find room on separate bookstore shelves, reaching for separate and distinct audiences.

Case in Point: Romance Publishing

Romance publishing continues to be evergreen, maintaining a hardcore group of readers that other genres envy. Consider these stats, courtesy of the Romance Writers of America[2]:

- Romance fiction revenue increased from $1.355 billion in 2010 to $1.368 billion in 2011. It remains the largest share of the consumer market at 14.3%.

- Thirty-one percent of the romance book buyers surveyed consider themselves avid readers (almost always reading a romance novel), and 44% are frequent readers (read quite a few romance novels). Only 25% are an occasional reader—someone who reads romance on and off, like when on vacation.

- Fifty-seven percent of avid readers and 43% of frequent readers have been reading romance for 20 years or more. Even 41% of occasional readers have been reading romance for 20 years or more.

- On the digital side, e-book sales of romances have proportionally doubled in one year, up from 22% in the first quarter of 2011 to 44% in the first quarter of 2012. This is in comparison to the total market, where only 26% of books are purchased in e-book format. Ninety-four percent of romance buyers read romance e-books (includes purchased and free titles).

When the term "romance publishing" comes up in conversation, the imprint most people think of first is Harlequin Romances, and with good reason. According to Harlequin's statistics, the Toronto, Canada-based company publishes over 110 titles a month in 31 languages in 111 international markets on 6 continents. These books are written by over 1,200 authors worldwide. Harlequin had 390 bestseller placements in 2010 that enjoyed a total of 1,048 weeks on bestseller lists. Since its inception, it has sold approximately 6.05 billion books.

The umbrella of Harlequin Enterprises' yearly releases includes at least six titles from Harlequin, several from Silhouette, Steeple Hill (Christian Romance), Mira (longer brand-name romances), and Gold Eagle, an action-adventure series described as romances for men.

In considering crossover appeal, one should note that romance—stories of love with a happy ending—was the inspiration for *The Bachelor* and *The Bachelorette*, the competitive dating reality television series.

Speaking of inspiration, every writer sitting in Starbucks, toiling away on his or her laptop, dreams of one day being published. That particular romantic dream has kept more than one scribe working toward completion of the marathon known as a novel. But long as it may take, writing turns out to be the easy part. Getting published? A journey all its own.

In the age of digital disruption, writers have a choice in how they might bring their books to market: They can follow the traditional route, or they can self-publish. It's a safe bet to say that many writers would prefer to be picked up by one of the Big Six, but there have been some breakout successes in the self-publishing world.

Let's start the discussion with a look at the tried-and-true method.

---

[2] http://www.rwa.org/.

Getting Published: The Traditional Route

How does a manuscript even reach the stage of consideration for publishing?

In years past, publishers had staff employees called "readers." Their job was to screen manuscripts, many of them unsolicited. In the 1980s, to cut overhead costs, publishers dispensed with the role and began to return unsolicited manuscripts unopened. The "readers" were replaced by authors' agents. The agents, at no cost to the publisher—but with the speculation of 10%–15% of an author's royalty—screen manuscripts for quality and anticipate marketing considerations of the appropriate publishers of each manuscript. A successful agent follows the publishing industry, usually focusing on a particular segment or two. They know the patterns, trends, and personalities of the publishers. Some agents even act as packagers of books, going so far as to deliver a book ready as a specific type or genre to an appropriate publisher.

Before a publishing contract is extended to any author, someone has made a considered study of the proposed book to determine the return on investment (ROI). The acquisition editor, the person who most often signs an author, considers several cost factors, including plant costs (overhead of running the business), physical costs (such as PPB—printing, paper, binding), author royalty, and marketing. Increasingly, one of the key ingredients of this study is whether the product will bear its own marketing cost. All of this is factored against the discounts that must be extended to wholesalers and retailers. The editor then makes a calculated guess as to whether a proposed book will meet or exceed sales goals based on the company's capacity to sell within a reasonably defined market.

But how does the editor know the size of each book's market? Trade and mass-market book editors do not have the luxury of a somewhat predictable market segment, as in some educational or technical/trade markets. In college textbook publishing, for instance, the market segment is decided by how many students are sitting in classes that focus on that subject. In addition to this total size of the market, the college text editor must know the competition—the other books currently used in that market segment, their strengths and weaknesses, and whether the author or authorial team has the background, credibility, and knowledge to author a book able to displace that competition. In short, there is a relatively forecastable market with some finite and promising parameters.

This is not the case for the riskier area of trade or mass-market books. An acquisition editor of these books must consider the author's reputation and quality of the manuscript. If the author's name is Stephen King or John Grisham, the reputation part is a no-brainer. But if it is an emerging author like Donna Tartt, who, in 1992, received a $450,000 advance from Knopf for her first book, *The Secret History*,[3] then the quality of the writing must speak for the book's potential—and then some. In today's more protracted publishing world, such advances for a new author are the stuff of dreams.

In times past, it was common to bring a book out first in hardback, and if it did well, it would appear about a year later as a paperback. By late in the twentieth century, it had become more common to bring an emerging author to the public through a series of paperbacks before shifting

---

[3] "Tartt's Content," *Sun Sentinel*, September 27, 1992.

to hardback status. Many emerging authors no longer have their first books come out as hardbound, but must earn that status.

Or they can self-publish.

Self-Publishing

So, you're a writer. You've managed to publish in print and online, in journals such as *Third Coast*, *Storyglossia*, *Timber Creek Review*, *34th Parallel*, and *Rubbertop Review*. But no matter how many queries you've sent out, you get nothing more than "looks good, keep trying." Convinced that you have something to say, you decide to take matters into your own hands and self-publish.

While self-publishing has always been with us, the reach of this approach used to be highly limited until the Internet came along. But that only opened the door—the self-published writer still needed to invest in printing, storage, and marketing. It was the advance of print-on-demand, allowing for high-quality end-product created order by order, that broke the door down.

Today's writers have hundreds of resources for getting their books to print and to market. Sites like Lulu, SmashWords, and BookBaby take writers through the paces. The finished product might be hardcover, or it might be an e-book, meant to be consumed via any of the growing number of tablet devices: Nooks, Kindles, iPads, and so on. Amazon has become a prime mover in this area with CreateSpace, offering design, editing, marketing, and direct links to the Amazon empire, including Amazon international sites as well as the Kindle store.

The number of self-published books produced annually in the U.S. has nearly tripled, growing 287% since 2006, and now tallies more than 235,000 print and e-titles.[4]

Self-publishing has its pros and cons. It's time-consuming; it demands knowledge of good visual design; your book still needs to be discovered. And there's the not-so-simple task of getting past your own ego regarding not being good enough to make it with the Big Six. But there have been breakouts, including a series written by E.L. James that took the world by superstorm in 2012, beginning with her first book, *Fifty Shades of Grey*, and followed by *Fifty Shades Darker* and *Fifty Shades Freed*.

This trilogy had even humbler beginnings than many self-published novels. It started off as online fan fiction, based on the popular *Twilight* series. Originally titled *Master of the Universe*, the fanfic was met by protest from enough *Twilight* fans that James removed the story and placed it on her own web site. She eventually reworked the piece, renaming the characters so as not to run afoul of copyright with *Twilight*, and released *Fifty Shades of Grey* through the Writers Coffee Shop, an Australia-based virtual publisher. It was originally released as an e-book and a print-on-demand paperback.

The book—poorly written and heavy on what has come to be known as "mommy porn"—took off via word of mouth and was picked up by Vintage, an imprint of Random House. To date, it has sold more than 65 million copies worldwide. Movie rights have been picked up by Universal Pictures.

---

[4] Self-Publishing in the United States, 2006–2011: Print vs. Ebook, Bowker, October 23, 2012.

Success by sex, we say. Never doubt the power of porn, like it or not.

When, Where, and to Whom

Meanwhile, back at the traditional publishing route.

The publishing of trade books happens in selling seasons. The spring release of titles anticipates the selling window of July through September and is heavily weighted to beach reading and light summer reading. The anticipation of Christmas season sales leads to a fall release of books. The fall list is heavier, especially in the nonfiction genres and specialty books arena. Each year, the NPD Group, an international provider of marketing information, makes available a Consumer Research Study on Book Purchasing, which is published by the American Bookseller's Association (ABA). This report confirms that most books are sold in the second half of the year and that the Christmas sales window shows the most aggressive growth. However, some publishers are even going to three-season and monthly selling.

The NPD report also confirms a demographic shift in book buying. The Pacific region and Mountain region combine for almost 30% of all books sold, while the New England states, including Boston and New York, command only 5%. Even with 15% more sales from the Mid-Atlantic States, the east coast must bow to the west when it comes to book sales.

Who is the average book buyer? Not surprisingly, it is someone with disposable income. The greater proportions of books were purchased by those individuals with the largest incomes, most of whom are Baby Boomers. The increasing number of individuals receiving college degrees since the 1960s has encouraged book sales, while also contributing to the information explosion that led into the new millennium. Once a book is ready to release to the public, it must find its way to consumers.

Distribution Channels

In the past, wholesalers such as Ingrams and Baker & Taylor were the prominent middlemen in the distribution chain. Because it consumed too much time—and too many inventory dollars—to keep books in stock, retailers would order and reorder from the wholesalers. However, Barnes & Noble and Amazon.com order most of the books stocked directly from the publishers, thus enhancing their margins. Today, wholesalers have yet to diminish in importance, having created their own print-on-demand divisions, such as Ingram's Lightning Source. This service is especially important to independent booksellers, who cannot hold large inventories of books (see Exhibit 7-1).

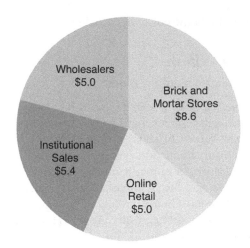

Wholesalers
$5.0

Brick and
Mortar Stores
$8.6

Institutional
Sales
$5.4

Online
Retail
$5.0

Exhibit 7-1 Channels receiving sales directly from publishers, 2011

Source: Bowker, 2012

The rise of online retailing began with Amazon.com.

Amazon Changes the Game

Ten years ago, Amazon billed itself as the "world's largest bookstore," angering—to the point of lawsuits—the traditional brick-built stores that laid claim to that title. Amazon has since gone on to be one of the world's largest stores, period, upending not only the Borders (now defunct) and Barnes and Noble chains, but the publishing industry itself.

The most significant step in this process was the introduction of Amazon's e-reader, the Kindle, quickly followed by products developed by others, including the Nook (Barnes and Noble) and applications for tablets such as the iPad, Surface, and various Android-based devices.

Today, an increasing portion of the U.S. population reports using e-reading devices as the primary way they consume books (see Exhibit 7-2).

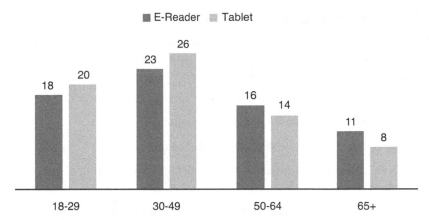

Exhibit 7-2 Percentage of Americans using e-devices by age group

Source: Pew Research, 2012

It follows that if books are no longer printed, the supply chain that provides that service might or might not be necessary—at least in the eyes of Amazon. Their part in the disruption of publishing is to become the publisher—and the distributor, and the agent, and the reader, and the marketing department, all through its previously mentioned self-publishing application.

It remains to be seen how the rise of e-books will play out. Actual sales of e-books are hard to track. Publishers and distribution outlets are not the most forthcoming when it comes to sharing this information. No one has any full knowledge of what is being self-published. But in 2011 the Association of American Publishers (AAP) and the Book Industry Study Group (BISG) joined forces to compile better sales data on the publishing business in their BookStats project,[5] with much of the information based on statistical modeling.

Results from the BookStats study demonstrated that, based on publisher's receipts, 2011 trade publisher e-book revenue was at an estimated $1.97 billion, comprising almost 16% of trade dollars. E-book totals in 2010 were $838 million, accounting for 6.7% of trade sales. Adult fiction drove the e-book gains, more than doubling to $1.27 billion from $585 million in 2010 and comprising 31% of dollar sales within that category.[6]

These figures do show a leveling off from prior years. There could be a variety of reasons for this: The market of those who would be considered users of that device might now be saturated. The novelty may have worn off. And it simply might be that no matter what, the feel of a book in your hand—and the ability to tell how far you've gotten in reading it simply by looking at the bookmark—may prove to have some value yet.

---

[5] "Looking at US E-book Statistics and Trends," www.publishingperspectives.com, October 3, 2012.

[6] Ibid.

Listen Up: A Word about Audiobooks

One fast-growing segment of the publishing industry is audiobooks, the digitized versions of bestsellers old and new, that are available either via download or on CD. To no one's surprise, Amazon is also a big player in this niche, having purchased Audible.com.

Consider this data from the Audio Publishers Association, published in 2012:

- The estimated size of the audiobook industry is now $1.2 billion.

- The total number of audiobooks being published doubled over the past seven years.

- Audiobook downloads continued on a growth trend representing 42% of dollar volume (up from 29% in 2009).

- In the past 5 years, downloading has grown 300% by dollar volume (from 9% in 2005) and 150% in terms of units (from 21% in 2005).

- The CD format still represents the largest single source of dollars but showed slight declines overall in 2012—54% of revenue (down from 58).

- The majority of sales (90%) continue to be in the unabridged format.

From a business perspective, audiobooks have their challenges. First, there are the copyright laws, which protect newer books, but many of the classics fall outside of these regulations. And then there are the complexities brought about with the production of the recording. Audiobooks, by and large, are not just simple recordings of someone reading from the original text. There may be some editing involved, and then there is the addition of the "voice"—the person who actually does the recording, often a fairly well-known actor or actress who brings his or her own contractual agreements into the mix. Add the studio time and the recording artists who heighten the tension with the background music, and you have full-scale production.

From the consumer's perspective, audiobooks are a great way to catch up on classics and new releases, providing hours of listening pleasure via iPhone or Galaxy or car stereo systems.

Other Retail Outlets

Anyone who has visited a Walmart, a Sam's Club, a Target, or a host of other such stores has seen whole skids of books available at tremendous discounts. Grocery chains have sections dedicated to books; gourmet groceries have health and cookbook sections. In mass marketing terms, it's easy for people to buy books in a place where they already shop. Drugstores and supermarkets are naturals for mainstream entertainment products.

What do the huge purchases of books by all of these retailers mean for publishers? A greater laydown (the number of copies of a book that can be presold and ready to ship the day of the book's release) for books already destined to succeed, primarily. Buyers committing discount resources to this kind of product tend toward the no-brainer books—those by Stephen King or John Grisham or books already enjoying long-term status on *The New York Times*' bestseller list.

But getting a book into distribution does little for its sale unless the public has been thoroughly made aware of its presence.

Marketing Books

The marketing of each book usually depends on a marketing professional who's intimately aware of the best and most cost-effective methods for a publisher in a marketplace that is changing rapidly.

The Book Release

As with many entertainment products, the debut of a new product is trumpeted through a release process.

Until recently, trade shows and book fairs were highly significant events in the release cycle. The ABA's annual event was once a premier launch spot, as were the Frankfurt, Bologna, and Peking book fairs. But the one-third drop in small store membership in the ABA—severely hit by the economy and the Internet—lowered the impact of these events because buyers at major chains and wholesalers are handled by specialized representatives of major publishers. The cost of attending such meetings is high; in some cases, it becomes more economically feasible to merely court the big buyers of chain stores directly. Book fairs such as BookExpo America and regional festivals like the New York City Book Fair continue to have an impact on a book's release but have nowhere near the drum roll of previous days.

Because bigger, entertainment-savvy companies have begun to show dominance, the publicity and promotion of a major book release has come to resemble the release of a movie, with a fanfare of reviewing, space ads, and high-profile signings in large cities. But you don't have to visit many bookstores to figure out that not every book is a bestseller. In fact, a significant portion of the trade book business, including profits, is composed of midlist and other levels of books. Like books that sell in bigger numbers, books that sell only a few thousand copies also have to be marketed. Momentum-building is even more important for these books but must be accomplished on a smaller budget.

In any case, there are several marketing approaches that are common to all types of books.

The Classic Approach: Sales Calls

A portion of book marketing has been consistent through the years. Major publishers staff sales representatives who call on bookstores before a book is released. These reps seek to reach an expectation about each book's laydown. For the large chains, there is often a separate, more-experienced rep assigned the task of dealing specifically with their needs.

A marketing staff or marketing manager supports the sales reps' effort by considering the market position of the book, examining the competition (whether direct or nearly direct), and preparing a tip sheet about the book that reduces its salient features to a selling format. These tasks may have already been anticipated at signing by the acquisition editor; in that case, the marketing manager acts as a facilitator and communication link to the sales force.

In the case of trade books, the tip sheet is often composed of the same sorts of comments a reader sees on the back cover or inside the dust jacket of hardbound copies. The marketing department is responsible for the preparation and dissemination of all such book descriptions, as well as press releases (where appropriate). Marketing also coordinates the timing of the book's release with events like meetings, festivals, a breaking news story, a film release—any event that can substantially support the book.

Backlist Sales: You Oughta Be in Pictures

Backlist books (those formerly published by an author) can become another important marketing tool. The moment a new book by a well-known author is released, the distribution machinery goes into gear. All of the author's former novels are rereleased—often with new covers—and either packaged as a set or displayed next to each other. This strategy is based on a critical tenet of successful entertainment marketing: No one can see or read everything when it is first available. Thus, every entertainment product needs multiple "windows of opportunity" to be seen and enjoyed by the widest possible audience.

Movies based on books are terrific for this second round of selling. According to Nielsen,[7] Elizabeth Gilbert's memoir, *Eat, Pray, Love*, saw a spike in sales in mid-2010, just prior to the August 13 opening of the Julia Roberts movie of the same name, with 94,000 units sold in the week ending in August 1 alone. This was the same number of total units sold for the entire 2006 year, when the book was first published. In 2010, the book sold more than twice as many copies (721,000) as all of 2009 (333,009).

In the same article, Nielsen pointed out two other book-to-movie titles that got a bounce from movies:

- *Dear John* by Nicholas Sparks saw an uptick in book sales concurrent with the February 2010 release of the movie, contributing to over 1 million units sold during 2010, nearly half of the book's 2.4 million total sales.

- *My Sister's Keeper*, based on Jodi Picoult's 2004 book, was released to theaters in June 2009, five years after the original publication run. This novel achieved its highest weekly sales number during the week of the film's release, with 81,000 units sold.

In addition, titles can enjoy repeat sales when a picture of the star of the movie replaces the original cover. Tom Cruise on the cover of *The Firm*, Julia Roberts on the cover of *The Pelican Brief*, and Danny DeVito on the cover of *The Rainmaker* all built additional sales for author John Grisham. Leonardo DiCaprio is driving new sales of The Great Gatsby in 2013. All served to build the identity of these authors as stars—and brands—in their own right.

---

[7] Nielsen Wire, "Book, Movie, Love: Best Sellers and the Hollywood Bounce," August 10, 2010.

The tie between Hollywood and publishing is deep and strong, but sometimes it may feel like a chicken or egg relationship. As intellectual property (IP) has gained more and more value—thanks to the copyright/IP battles of the late twentieth century—recent moves in branding have created even tighter linkage.

For example, James Frey might have found himself in very hot water after exaggerating claims in his 2003 memoir *A Million Little Pieces*, but he found a new niche in the publishing world with his venture, Full Fathom Five, a self-labeled "IP factory." Full Fathom Five works with a stable of (some say grossly underpaid) writers, many fresh from MFA programs, to package multimedia deals. What may first appear as a book has already been wined and dined in TV, animated features, movies, coloring books—you name it.

The first successful Full Fathom Five package began with the I Am Number Four blockbuster, a Young Adult (YA) sci-fi novel that went from bestselling book to series to the big screen as a collaboration between Disney and DreamWorks. Recent efforts are focused on *Little Shaq*, an early-reader series being developed with Shaquille O'Neal, the basketball great. Along with TV, Full Fathom Five sees even bigger potential, expanding the concept into a Little League-like youth basketball program.[8]

This type of packaging isn't new, of course. Much hullabaloo occurred in 2000, when then-editing superstar Tina Brown teamed up with Harvey Weinstein of Miramax and Hearst Magazines to launch *Talk* magazine, ostensibly to create multiplatform stories. The project flamed out two years later, with nothing much to show for the effort.

Direct Marketing

Direct marketing, while one of the most expensive ways for publishers to market, can be effective if the target marketing is accurate, the numbers are significant enough for the advantages of a bulk mailing, and the price point is high enough to make the return hit a breakeven point as early as possible. Direct mail typically is now done only on niche books, and those are almost exclusively high-price books because a good response rate can be in the area of 2%.

However, books purchased through direct marketing account for a higher profit margin because customers pay list price and no discount is needed for a wholesaler or large retailer. An additional advantage for the publisher is that sales of the book through regular channels will also benefit because a mailing will help drive those sales through regular retail and Internet channels. These additional sales usually offset any concerns by vendors or reps who do not receive commission on books sold through direct marketing means. In fact, a direct mailing can be billed to reps as an additional advantage to their sales effort.

Some of the best ways to identify a target market for direct marketing are through magazine subscription lists, which have usually already identified a niche that corresponds with the book's

---

[8] "How James Frey's 'IP Factory' is Re-imagining Book Packaging," www.publishingpersectives.com, January 17, 2013.

subject. In the case of a nonfiction mainstream title, there may be meetings, conferences, or special interest groups (SIGs) that can be approached by mail. Email outreach is done through "permission marketing," in which the e-vendor first asks if it is okay to send such emails and provides easy means to be removed from lists for such solicitations. Email marketers report response rates equal to or higher than regular mail approaches for considerably lower costs.

The Importance of Reviews

When the subject of book reviews is mentioned, *The New York Times* book review always seems to come to mind first. For years it has enjoyed a prominence that belies the fact that, according to U.S. Department of Commerce Bureau of the Census information, more books are now sold on the Pacific coast than in all the New England and Mid-Atlantic states combined. Almost every Sunday paper offers book reviews in a Living or Entertainment section, and free-circulation papers (those that thrive on advertising dollars while listing local entertainment) also include book reviews. *The Los Angeles Times* book review has also established itself as a pillar of early insight, while whole magazines are dedicated to books, among them *Publisher's Weekly*, which also provides advance book reviews.

But it is *The New York Times* book review list that has become the "no-brainer" marketing signal for vendors to buy—and buy in quantity. As such, it receives a stupendous proportion of advance copies, or *cranes*, of all books published. This advance version of a book is sent to newspapers, magazines, and Internet review sites before the book ever rolls off the printing press and is bound in its final form. In some cases, the advance copy is nothing more than a bound manuscript copy, often with errors still in place. In other cases, "folded-and-gathered" sets of galley proofs or page proofs are bound and sent, these too often containing errors that the authors and editors hopefully weed out before the book is published. The object for a publisher is not only to gain momentum, but also to get lines from the reviews—"blurbs"—that can appear on the jacket of hardbound and paperback copies.

Blurbs can also be requested from other established writers. There is usually an *honorarium* (paid fee) associated with these, although some authors are quite willing to promote their fellow authors. A blurb also helps the reader decide to buy a book—if Stephen King liked it, then I will. That became so true that Stephen King now draws an almost unflinching line against doing any more blurbs.

The Power of Publicity—The TV Talk-Show Circuit

Book promotion helped supply content for early television talk shows—Jack Parr's hour-and-a-half version of *The Tonight Show* featured thoughtful conversations on new releases by a wide range of authors—but the medium has long since given way to book conversations limited to film and TV personalities plugging their own works.

However, other talk shows emerged. An established author—or one with a unique spin—might sit with Ellen DeGeneres or Charlie Rose and build the audience's awareness of the author's work. The talk-show format lends itself well to this type of promotion because the author's appearance also constitutes an endorsement by the talk-show host or hostess.

By far, the show with the most impact on book sales was *Oprah*. Oprah Winfrey brought books back into American conversation, choosing titles for her Book Club that ranged from new releases in the early goings to old favorites and classics in the later years. Getting Oprah's imprimatur was golden. The 70 titles selected for her O-branded special editions sold 22 million copies in the decade leading up to 2011, when Oprah moved from her daily show to her own network.

Although some might argue that certain books might have done well on their own, there is no disputing the impact her imprint had. Consider the following: chosen as Oprah Pick #63 (September 17, 2009), *Say You're One of Them* by Uwem Akpan (Hachette) sold 47,500 units together in trade paperback and hardcover. The Oprah trade paperback sold 405,000 units—an 853% increase.[9]

Oprah promises that her new OWN network will continue to feature book conversations and selections. In any case, shows such as Oprah have a narrow window of opportunity for the number of guests per year. Therefore, publishers tend to promote only their top books on the show. This makes local and regional shows a much more commonly used media for the majority of the business.

Radio Interviews

One proven way to get exposure for a book is for the author to be a guest on a radio talk show. The audience for these shows fill particular niches, each with its own interest in reading material. Howard Stern has a slightly lower income following; Dr. Laura Schlesinger reaches over 20 million listeners on more than 450 stations. Sixty percent of NPR listeners read books for leisure, in contrast to 38% of the general U.S. population.[10]

Radio stations with an all-news or talk format are always hungry for guests. Regional format shows are often eager to bring a local author's work to light. But how to cast beyond that? A good publicist will be aware of all promotional opportunities and will include radio among the early targets for exposure and momentum-building. A great example of the power of radio is the phenomenon of *Chicken Soup for the Soul*, which was first advertised in *Radio-TV Interview Report*. It climbed to number one on *The New York Times* bestseller list and has engendered a family of clones the likes of which publishing has not seen in a while: Over 200 titles extend the *Chicken Soup* brand. There are over 100 million copies in print in 54 languages.[11]

Book Awards

Awards sell books. A few of the publishing awards given each year include the Man Booker Prize, the National Book Award, the Caldecott Medal, the Newberry Medal, the National Book Critics Award, the Circle Awards, the PEN/Faulkner Award, the Macavity, the Edgar, the Anthony, and the Shamus (the last three are all given to books in the mystery genre). Oddly enough, the Nobel Prize in Literature seems to mark the death knell of a writer—many who receive this distinguished

---

[9] "The Oprah Effect: Closing the Book on Oprah's Book Club," *Nielsen Wire*, May 20, 2011.

[10] NPR.

[11] www.chickensoup.com.

award rarely ever write another significant book. However, the sales of all that author's books get a boost that usually exceeds beyond the author's lifetime.

Can a publisher help an author win an award? In most cases, the integrity of the award dictates that the nomination and decision process be made by impartial judges, members of the award-granting organization. But a top-flight trade acquisition editor knows when he or she has signed a book capable of winning an award and will take every step possible to see that copies of the book reach those who nominate or judge such annual award events.

Some emerging publishers have cut several steps from the process by using a contest to select books for publication and then promoting the book with the publisher's award. This is a particularly—ahem—novel concept, but only one of many new approaches to entice readers.

Discoverability

Beyond the commercial sale of books to distribution outlets and the mass marketing that occurs for certain titles, the life of a book is driven by the number of consumers that buy. But with all the books in print or in e-form—and it is a number that grows exponentially, given self-publishing—how does a reader actually find the right book to read? Readers—especially voracious readers, the ones always on the lookout for something new and engaging—discover books in many ways.

Populist Reviews

Digitalization has brought consumer dominance to much of the media, and this certainly is true in online book reviews. And of course, given its presence in the publishing world, nowhere does this command bigger attention than on amazon.com.

As helpful as some might find Amazon reviews, they have lately come under attack. After all, it doesn't take much more than a few of your best friends' opinions to light up the ranking chart. Amazon has stated that it is taking steps to police this, but it's hard to imagine how they might do so. In addition, the site gained attention shortly after the release of a biography on entertainer Michael Jackson, when fans of the Gloved One stormed the listing for *Untouchable: The Strange Life and Tragic Death of Michael Jackson*, by Randall Sullivan. Swarming, the fans peppered the site with one-star listings, managing to erase several favorable reviews. This ravaging horde took credit for Amazon halting the sale of the book for a short time.[12]

Social Networking

Social networking sites are hot in the book world, offering readers more than just a review. Facebook, of course, gets lots of attention as a way to reach out to readers. Goodreads, an online site (with the ubiquitous, and some would say, annoying tie-in to Facebook), offers members space to chat about their favorite authors, rate books, write reviews, and interact on topics of the day ("readers: do you highlight?"). It also offers the ability to interact with the authors themselves, many of whom have their own pages at the site, filled with photos, blog-thought, and tweets.

---

[12] "Swarming a Book Online," *New York Times*, January 20, 2013.

And then there's Pinterest, which in many ways feels almost antithetical to the idea of marketing a book. The site is like stepping into a howling mass of visual screaming, with everyone clamoring for their bit of attention. Is this really where book lovers go to find the next great read?

No, says Peter Hildick-Smith, founder and CEO of the Codex Group, specializing in book audience research and prepublication testing. According to a presentation made by Laura Hazard Owen of paidContent, presented at the January 2013 Digital Book World conference and quoting Hildick-Smith, while 61% of book purchases by frequent buyers may occur online, only 7% of those buyers said that they had *discovered* that book online. Brick and mortar bookstores account for 39% of purchase, with a 20% discovery share.[13]

This, then, is the true problem facing marketing professionals who turn to the Internet. It is by no means the be-all-and-end-all and in fact, offers far more pitfalls than promises. Although the Internet offers much to many, it can simply be noise personified. Trying to thread your way through the din is tricky. Yes, it's helpful—even wonderful—once the book has gotten a following, but as a discovery tool, it has yet to level off.

What does continue to work is good old-fashioned word-of-mouth, delivered through hundreds of thousands of casual book clubs scattered across the United States. On any given night of any week, hundreds of people are sitting in living rooms or bars or restaurants, talking about this week's book and picking another for the next. Being discovered—and passed along as a favorite—by these groups can accomplish a lot for independent marketing efforts.

Finally, a bit of insight from the Romance genre. According to Bowker Monthly Tracker (New Books Purchased, Q1 2012),[14] buyers become aware of romances through the following ways:

- In-store display/on shelf/spinning rack
- Read an excerpt from the book online
- Received recommendation from a friend/relative
- Author's website
- Read a teaser chapter from forthcoming book in a book they were reading (print)
- Online retailer recommendation on a retailer website

Less influential awareness factors included online customer reviews, best-seller lists, e-mails from retailers, a teaser in a book read online, a book review, and direct mail/catalogs.

Author as Marketer

Today, it's not enough to write the book (or even self-publish it). If you want to build sales, you need to build relationships with your readers, and, unlike the olden days, when that might mean book tours or public appearances, today you must add blogs, author websites, and tweeting.

---

[13] Abrams, Dennis, "Is Online Book Discovery Broken? Here's How to Fix It," www.publishingperspectives.com, January 18, 2013.

[14] As reported by Romance Writers of America.

You might, in fact, wonder when you will actually have time to write.

Small publishers, some emerging publishers eager to fill niches left behind as too midlist by larger houses, and even the larger houses themselves are encouraging authors to become part of the marketing push. Today's authors are asked to initiate book-signing tours, create websites with links to the publisher or booksellers, and/or their agents or hire publicists[15] to help coordinate events and promotion.

These publishers either make their preference for proactive authors clear early or bring up the subject during the book-signing process. In some instances, however, the authors themselves may become the focus of the publisher's marketing spotlight.

Branding

As in most entertainment sectors, niche marketing has played a role in expanding the business of publishing. For example, westerns, action-adventure, and spy novels have always been a hit with a male audience from 25 to 65, while romance books, both contemporary as well as historical (known in the business as "bodice-rippers"), have appealed to women readers from 25 to 65. Mystery books, with many subgenres, have some crossover appeal to both men and women. Vampire novels—from Anne Rice to the *Twilight* series—have a consistent following within the category, including line extensions or follow-stories arising from the original story line.

So, how does a publisher build an "evergreen," or sustained revenue stream, in these reader favorites? The answer is through marketing—more specifically, through brand marketing.

Branding the Genre and the Author

Many imprints have grown an identity that has become part of the public's brand sense of that line. Knopf and St. Martin's have carved names for themselves as publishers of solid mystery fiction. When Otto Penzler first formed Mysterious Press, he wanted to leave no room for confusion about the brand focus of that imprint. Likewise, TOR made its brand presence known with a focus on science fiction.

However, it is usually the author rather than the imprint that becomes the brand. A customer falls madly in love with an author's style and storytelling technique, building a need to read another of the author's books. The beauty of this phenomenon is that older titles gain as much as do new releases; when a reader gets hooked on an author, he or she will search out all of that author's work.

The responsibility of the publisher is to manage the production or writing of the popular author's next book and to build awareness among the readers that a new book is on its way. All of this is performed successfully when a publisher builds the author into a celebrity, surrounding the author's books with a blockbuster halo and building the author into a recognizable and ever-present brand.

---

[15] A "publicist" fulfills a different role than an agent and is often more responsible for promotion, including the building and maintaining of momentum. Self-published authors and authors of books published by small presses can find the hiring of a publicist a huge boost, though the significant cost may offset some of the advantage.

The author as a brand is similar—though not identical—to the movie or TV star as a brand. In either case, the audience finds sufficient areas of appeal and the desire to spend time and money on products attached to the star brand. These industry icons are described as *bankable*: having the ability to take a subject and turn it into a money machine rather than a loss leader. James Patterson, David Baldacci, and Robert Ludlum are spy-thriller series brands; Stephen King and Dean Koontz are giant horror series brands; Janet Dailey and Nora Roberts are superstars of the contemporary romance novel; while Larry McMurtry and Louis L'Amour are primarily bestselling western writers and Elmore Leonard and Sue Grafton are detective brands.

The marketing of an author as a brand includes the occasional purchase of relatively inexpensive 30-second local market spots on television, using the author's story line as a mini-movie. On occasion, a simple voiceover on a still frame of the book cover with some tantalizing copy, a few reviewers raves, and a reference to other successful books from the same author can build a groundswell.

Cable TV advertising allows for more direct, targeted access to the audience for a given genre. It is relatively inexpensive to reach the perfect female audience with Lifetime, the Food Network, and WE. The male audience is available through ESPN, CNBC, or the local transmission of any major sports event.

The branding approach is not foolproof, however. As with any product, after an audience has been groomed to a brand's particular attributes, those attributes cannot be toyed with. In the case of publishing, authors occasionally write in several genres, either under pen names (pseudonyms) or using their own names. Ed McBain, author of the *87th Precinct* novels, also has separate literary reputations under his real name, Evan Hunter, as well as Curt Cannon, Hunt Collins, Ezra Hannon, and Richard Marsten.

The most important objective is to avoid "unselling a brand" by confusing the fan of one author/genre with other works by the same author in another vein.

Branding the Character

Many fictional characters have served as stars of entertainment content—Snow White, Winnie-the-Pooh—but most of these have become star brands over long periods of time, moving from the page to the screen as entertainment sectors found that the content they represented could be stretched into other profitable areas. However, few characters represent the modern-day approach to the whole of entertainment marketing—books, film, licensing—as well as a certain young wizard with a lightning bolt scar on his forehead.

Case in Point: Harry Potter

On a train trip from her small village in the countryside of England to London, a single, unemployed mother began to daydream about a young boy with big eyes, round glasses, a very high IQ, a quirky sense of humor, and the ability to use magical powers to make exciting things happen. With the launch of J.K. Rowling's first book, a paradigm shift occurred in children's book publishing. Harry Potter was truly magical.

Rowling was rejected by 12 publishers before Bloomsbury, a small U.K. publishing house, secured the first rights to the first novel. Barely realizing what it had in its hand, they offered the U.S. and worldwide rights to Scholastic, Inc., the leading global children's book and educational materials (newsletters, classroom newspapers, textbooks, early readers, and video and audio tapes) publisher, including stakes in some highly acclaimed children's theatrical and home video films. Scholastic snatched up the rights for $105,000.

Though typical hardback or trade format fiction books sell under 200,000 copies, blockbusters (Clancy, Turow, Sheldon, Collins, Fleming, Le Carre, and so on) sell close to a million copies or slightly more. Harry Potter hardbound books one through four sold in excess of three million copies *each*. Young Mr. Potter has repeated or exceeded those numbers in the paperback versions. A focus on the contributions of great marketing explains why and how this happened.

First, as soon as the book went into circulation among the literary agents and those knowledgeable about children's publishing, the marketing machine was set to work. An all-points alert went out to every possible promotional opportunity available, including global talk shows and interviews with the still-dazed-but-delighted Ms. Rowling.

Second, the popularity—as built through marketing efforts—of the brand reached a near frenzy with the publication of book four. Demand was built by artificially limiting the supply for a sold out or possibly unattainable product. This created an atmosphere of "must have." The launch date was a preannounced event, and the books were rationed by geographic area and store location, thus putting into place a master marketing tactic. The need—or perceived need—for advance orders or prepaid reservations for the book was trumpeted with stories in national consumer, business, and trade press, including *Time, Variety, Publisher's Weekly*, and a cover story in *Newsweek*. Seemingly overnight, Harry Potter became a brand in the same children's book solar system as Dr. Seuss, Maurice Sendak, and even classics like the Hardy Boys and Nancy Drew.

The third marketing hurricane was the decision by Warner Bros. studio to option the book for a film and start a global search for the young actor to play Harry Potter. Meanwhile, the studio's licensing, merchandising, and sponsorship magicians went to work. They strove to make the Potter character a marketing icon that would shake Disney's ownership of the licensing marketing crown and provide a true battle for domination of the children's entertainment sector.

In the end, Harry Potter won the battle with Voldemort and made J.K. Rowling a very wealthy woman. But even more important, Harry cast a spell on young children, turning them into readers at a time when publishers worried about whether the next generation would ever break away from television.

The Changing Publishing Environment

Publishing has been in the spin cycle for well over a decade, buffeted by the digital disruption and a shift in the public's reading habits. As mentioned previously, the advent of Harry Potter was a golden moment for the publishing business, creating new readers in the younger age groups—a hopeful sign for the future, given the falling numbers of adult readers.

Consider the statistics from the Association of American Publishers in Exhibit 7-3.

Exhibit 7-3   Trade Book Sales, 2010–2011

TRADE	August 2011	August 2010	Percent Change
Adult Paperback	$118.2	$125.3	–5.7%
E-Books	$88.8	$41.0	116.5%
Adult Hardcover	$74.5	$83.9	–11.2%
Religious	$66.0	$67.3	–1.9%
Children's YA/Hardcover	$58.7	$77.8	–24.6%
Children's YA/Paperback	$46.1	$58.5	–21.2%
Adult Mass Market	$34.9	$54.9	–36.4%
Downloaded Audiobooks	$8.5	$6.6	30.2%
Physical Audiobooks	$8.2	$8.4	–2.9%
TOTAL TRADE	**$503.8**	**$523.6**	**–3.8%**

Source: AAP, 2012

Do take notice of the increase in audiobook sales, as mentioned previously—another sign of the digital disruption.

This slide in sales has traveled downstream, creating an equally difficult time for distributors. The giant Borders chain disappeared altogether, and last-giant-standing Barnes and Noble posted declining sales in both bricks and mortar and their digital device (the Nook reader) sales in 2012.

Independents still struggle, with many shuttered over the last decade and many more struggling to hold on. The math is simple. Trade books are sold with what is known as a *long discount*. That means wholesalers and major retailers demand 50%, 55%, and even 60% discounts to handle trade books. Most independent bookstores must buy their books from major wholesalers, like Ingrams and Baker & Taylor, and the discount the independent stores see is less than if they bought direct. But it is not discounts that killed the independent; it was the inability of independents to put enough books into their bookstores (too little cash flow, no access to large capital markets) and their linked inability to discount to the customer—along with what was often a 1960s temperament about business and business management.

The old "gentleman's game" of the publishing world—brandy and tea in the conference room, tweed jackets with patches on the elbows, risk-taking with unknown authors—is either long gone or barely breathing. It's been replaced by merger mania and the gimlet eye of the media mogul. In the late 2000s, Penguin merged with Putnam, Random House combined with Bantam Doubleday Dell, and HarperCollins took over Morrow and Avon. Now Random House is in discussion with Pearson for a merger with Penguin. Penguin Random House will become the world's largest trade book publisher.

Will it mean better books? More bestsellers?

Publishing has never been about homeruns. It is truly a bunt/singles/doubles world, with the occasional big blow bringing big dollars to the lucky imprint. Creating bigger and bigger publishing houses will not guarantee more bestsellers—editors and agents can only find and vet so many books at a time. When corporate giants go looking for cost cutting, it's payroll that always leads the way. Can any publisher create more books with less of the front-end skills? Can publishing survive by cutting out midlist sales? What good does more economical distribution do if there's less quality product?

The money people point to the rise of Amazon and say that mergers must happen, that economies of scale are the only hope for the industry. The rise of Amazon has grabbed profit margins by the throat, creating new price points that hover at $9.99. If digital sales continue to rise, it means more books sell—but at fewer dollars.

Worst of all, shuttering stores shuts down the single-best mode of discovery for any book. So, if there was ever a time when savvy marketing was needed in this industry, it's now.

Small Publishers in the Mix

While big publishers get bigger and big bookstore chains stutter-step, there are still a number of small publishers and small, independent bookstores fighting the good fight. Several small press magazines—both print and digital—and the Small Publishers Association of North America (SPAN) serve the growing number of small publishers, which includes traditional imprints, university presses, and newer imprints that have surged to fill the niches left uncovered by publishers grown too big to sign marginal or midlist titles.

In fact, given the tightening focus of major publishers, many niches are left open as new frontiers for entrepreneurial publishers with start-up companies. Whether it is the intention of these companies to rise to become major forces themselves or to merely create enough of a presence to tempt the acquisitions unit of a major house remains to be seen. But, for many, the opportunity to grow in a robust market is aided by digital technology.

Global Reach

International sales account for as much as 40% of most good publishers' income. Additionally, the growth of e-tailing (which accounts for as much as 30% of most publishers' domestic income) has forced global pricing into the book business. No longer is a book published in the U.S. at $30 and sold in Europe at $90; the Internet has leveled pricing. Check out Exhibit 7-4 to see where the world's top publishing companies are based.

Exhibit 7-4 Top Ten Global Publishers

Publishing Company (Group or Division)	Country	Mother Corp. or Owner	Country Mother Corp.	Revenue in $B
Pearson	U.K.	Pearson	U.K.	$8,411
Reed Elsevier	U.K./NL/U.S.	Reed Elsevier Corp.	U.K./NL/U.S.	$5,686
Thomson Reuters	U.S.	The Woodbridge Company Ltd.	Canada	$5,435
Wolters Kluwer	NL	Wolters Kluwer	NL	$4,360
Hachette Livre	France	Lagardère	France	$2,649
Grupo Planeta	Spain	Grupo Planeta	Spain	$2,304
McGraw-Hill Education	U.S.	The McGraw-Hill Companies	U.S.	$2,292

Publishing Company (Group or Division)	Country	Mother Corp. or Owner	Country Mother Corp.	Revenue in $B
Random House	Germany	Bertelsmann AG	Germany	$2,274
Holtzbrinck	Germany	Verlagsgruppe Georg von Holtzbrinck	Germany	$1,952
Scholastic (Corp.)	U.S.	Scholastic	U.S.	$1,906

Source: Publisher's Weekly, 2012

Summary: Books

Another battlefield in the digital disruption, book publishing continues to morph into a new business model. Still the gatekeeper of story, books continue to create great starting points for many other forms of media, including movies, television, and Broadway shows. This synergy helps create continuing sales by opening doors to new consumers unfamiliar with the original work. The impact of digital publishing, e-readers, and the distribution giant Amazon—now a publisher itself—continues to play out, forming the impetus for continued mergers and acquisitions. Marketing professionals can find great opportunities in this platform but will need to be nimble as the industry changes.

Newspapers and Magazines

For the purposes of our discussion regarding entertainment marketing, we include the following commentary on newspapers and magazines as it relates to their role as a marketing platform. Entertainment vehicles of all types still rely on these traditional print models, whether for reviews or for advertising. However, we urge you to dig deeper on the subject of traditional print and the challenges it faces. There is much to be learned about consumer behavior in doing so.

Newspapers

When it comes to print publication and the decline in traditional business models, newspapers are the niche most under assault today. The decline in readership has as much to do with shifts in consumer lifestyles—more interest in broadcast media, viewable on smartphones and tablets—as it does with the speed of information delivery. Let's face it: News coverage happens faster when it can be broadcast directly, skipping the time-consuming steps of printing and distribution. Ours is a faster-paced society, and print has a hard time keeping up.

Unfortunately, speed often means less time spent on fact-checking and objectivity, but in an age of "citizen journalists," the entire news-gathering/dissemination business is in a whirlpool. Reader beware.

Early on, many papers, struggling with the leap to the digital age, simply posted content online for free, hoping to attract enough eyeballs to create better advertising revenue. Though the readers did come, the dollars didn't—at least, not enough dollars to make up for the loss of the print ad revenue.

What appears to be a turning point occurred in March 2011, when *The New York Times* announced a metered system for charging for the digital version of the paper. Although it is still possible to download articles for free, the *Times* limits the number within a given time period. The Old Grey Lady, as she is affectionately known (even though she is no longer grey, bowing to color in the 1990s), has once again proven her popularity, reporting more than 560,000 paying digital customers.[16] The additional good news here? Print subscriptions have held their value, as they allow for free digital access. Ads can be seen—and sold—in both formats. Though it remains to be seen how newspapers will weather this very dire turbulence, digital growth is occurring across the country as demonstrated in Exhibit 7-5.[17]

Exhibit 7-5   Growth in Digital Editions, 2010 to 2012

Paper	2010	2012
New York Times	71,697	896,352
Wall Street Journal	449,139	794,594
Denver Post	31,965	176,446
Los Angeles Times	41,601	151,577
Houston Chronicle	50,078	91,331

Newspapers continue to be a viable entertainment marketing platform, with wide reach into important demographic segments, and are still a source for local information. Consider the data in Exhibit 7-6 and notice how, while broad, general interest issues such as elections and disasters are the key storylines for other media, newspapers still excel at reaching readers who are interested in subjects that hit them close to home: business, lifestyle, health, education, and economy.

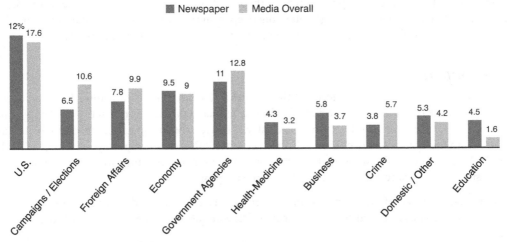

Exhibit 7-6 Newspaper topics differ from media overall

Source: Pew Research Center's Project for Excellence in Journalism, The State of the News Media 2012

---

[16]   Rieder, Rem, "Get Ready to Pay for Online News," *USA Today*, January 22, 2013.

[17]   2010 data: Pew Research Center's Project for Excellence in Journalism, The State of the News Media 2011. 2012 data: "Circulation Numbers for the 25 Largest Newspapers," *Denver Post*, October 30, 2012.

Magazines

As with newspapers, magazines have been buffeted about in the digital storm. The difference is, this platform seems to be finding stable ground faster than its newspaper cousins. Newspapers, by and large, are vehicles for news coverage, published daily and focused on specific events and trends. Magazines, on the other hand, focus more on feature-length writing, diving deeper into the subject matter, and are designed for specific niches. If media executives could determine by demographics, geography, occupation, or any of the other determinants of special interest that demand for a magazine on underwater basket weaving existed, you can bet one would be woven right into the fabric of the market.

Even in this day of disruption, magazines—both print and online—continue to grow in popularity. Ten years ago, we reported that there were over 20,000 magazine titles in circulation. Data published by the Association of Magazine Media[18] shows that as of 2010, there were over 24,700 magazines being published, addressing 280 different categories, from accounting (55 magazines) to zoology (12), with stops in between at baseball (58), energy (50), oil and fats (6), and unidentified flying objects (3). More to our subject, there are 171 entertainment magazines, 88 publications for fans of movies, TV, and radio, and 96 that focus on film.

Of all these, approximately 160 magazines account for 85% of the revenue generated by this industry. The names of the companies generating the most revenue from magazines include Time Warner, Hearst Corporation, Reed Elsevier, Advance Publications, International Data Group, Thomson Corp, Ziff Davis Publishing, Reader's Digest Association, News Corp, and Meredith Corporation. Among the giant media companies mentioned earlier in the book, Capital Cities/ABC, Tele-Communications, Inc., CBS, Inc., Gannett Co., General Electric Co., New York Times Co., Viacom, Knight-Ridder, Cox Enterprises, and Turner Broadcasting all have stakes in the magazine industry.

Off the Page and Into the Ether

Many of these magazines have migrated to the Web, where they offer subscribers (and readers, if they aren't charging) an interactive experience that binds reader and magazine even tighter than before, with clickthroughs to advertisers websites, special offers, and social networking to compare notes with others like themselves.

Growth isn't limited to the Web. Revenue continue to be aided by impulse purchases at drug stores, book stores, and airport concessions. Many magazines have extended their brands into television and vice versa. Consider *National Geographic* and the National Geographic Channel; The Discovery Channel and *Discovery Channel Magazine*, ESPN and *ESPN The Magazine*. Magazines create content for television, and television creates content for magazines. It's a great relationship for the consumer and a great marketing platform for reaching specific interest groups.

---

[18] "1998–2010 Number of Magazines by Category," the Association of Magazine Media at www.magazine.org.

Magazines can also thank the explosion of tablets and other mobile devices for this growing popularity, although that golden goose does produce some challenging eggs. Every new platform requires a new investment in staff and software, all to keep up with the changing needs/wants of the consumer. But digital devices are a great boon to magazines. Pew Research reports that as of December 2012, 45% of American adults had a smartphone. As of January 2013, 26% of American adults owned an e-book reader, and 31% owned a tablet computer.[19] Even more important, the Association of Magazine Media also found high levels of engagement with tablet publications. According to their research, 70% of readers want the ability to purchase products and services directly from electronic magazines. 73% read/tap on advertisements appearing in electronic magazines, and 86% access the same electronic magazine issue two or more times.[20]

The magazine platform is an area where brand supremacy is finding interesting challenges. Consider *Better Homes and Gardens* (*BH&G*), for years a leader in the home/lifestyle segment, a well-established brand that millions of women (and men) have turned to for advice on cooking, home design, and home style advice. The advent of the digital magazine has brought such newcomers as Houzz.com, a cross between a social networking site for home renovation enthusiasts and a tremendous home design resource, with literally millions of photographs, searchable by style, function, and form—in all combinations. Want a hundred ideas for a corner fireplace in a contemporary home? Or a thousand thoughts about front entrances for a traditional place? It's all there, and more, at your fingertips, in a constantly growing database.

We use this example to demonstrate the rising development of online magazines that allow the readers to create the content, while the online editorial staff adds short features that engender conversation. Quite different from the old days, where editorial content was served to the reader monthly in a format determined by a hopefully far-sighted staff.

Magazines still appear to be the Little Engine That Could—or at least, wants to be. Far from disappearing, new magazine launches happen yearly. In the first quarter of 2012, 52 new magazines appeared. The top category was "restaurants," with five new *DiningOut* guides from Pearl Publishing. The other top categories for new launches were "hunting & fishing," with four new titles from J.F. Griffin Publishing, and "lifestyle," with four new magazines, including Bloomberg Pursuits. There were 12 magazines that folded in that same time span.[21]

Like every other platform under attack from the disruption, the future is still a long way off; much will happen before it all settles out. But when it comes to magazines, there's a moral to the story: Next time you think magazines may be dying, don't. Just because you're not interested in a subject doesn't mean a whole lot of other people aren't. Just like you, they want their own little media home, be it online, in print, or cross-platformed with a cable station. And if you want to reach them, magazines offer a great way to do that.

---

[19] www.pewinternet.org/Trend-Data-(Adults)/Device-Ownership.aspx

[20] "Magazine Media Factbook, 2012–2013", www.magazine.org/sites/default/files/factbook-2012.pdf

[21] "Magazine Launches Outpace Closures in First Quarter of 2012," PRWeb, April, 2012. www.prweb.com/releases/2012/4/prweb9361089.htm

Summary: Newspapers and Magazines

Newspapers continue to battle with changing technology, with many folding and most dealing with ongoing staff layoffs. The tide could be turning now that there is more acceptance of paid content, but that change is still underway. Magazines continue to be the leader in niche marketing opportunities in regard to the entertainment sector of publishing. With an estimated 24,000+ titles in the marketplace, there are few audiences that cannot be reached via this medium. Furthermore, the expansion of magazines onto the Internet and mobile devices will continue to offer opportunities to reach an even wider audience.

Summary: Publishing

Publishing, like all other platforms, has felt the brunt of digital disruption. Publishing houses continue to merge and contract. E-books and digital devices are causing inroads into revenue but appear to be leveling off as the market becomes saturated. Bookstores are under assault by online distribution, specifically Amazon, who is now also acting as a publisher, while self-publishing continues to grow.

Although newspapers have contracted sharply, the ability to charge for online versions appears to be finding a foothold. Magazines continue to grow in number, offering both print and online versions to what seems to be an ever-increasing variety of niche markets.

For Further Reading

Books

Davis, Gill, and Richard Balkwill, *The Professionals' Guide to Publishing: A Practical Introduction to the Working in the Publishing Industry*, Kogan Page, 2011.

Forsyth, Patrick, and Robert Birn, *Marketing in Publishing*, Rutledge, 1997.

Grecco, Albert N., *The Book Publishing Industry*, Allyn & Bacon, 1996.

Kleper, Michael, *The Handbook of Digital Publishing*, Pearson, 2000.

Picard, Robert G., and Jeffrey H. Brody, *The Newspaper Publishing Industry*, Allyn & Bacon, 1996.

Thompson, John B., *Merchants of Culture: The Publishing Business in the Twenty-First Century*, Polity Press, 2012.

Other Resources

Gale Directory of Publications & Broadcast Media (published each year by Gale Research).

LMP: Literary Market Place: The Directory of the American Book Publishing Industry (published each year by Bowker).

Publishers, Distributors & Wholesalers of the United States (published each year by Bowker).

Ulrich's International Periodicals Directory (published each year by Bowker).

8

A Handful of Content: Games, Mobile Applications, and Mobile Marketing

Electronic gaming has continued its rapid rise, now claiming more revenue than either movies or music. However, gaming faces challenges. Classic video gaming, focused on a specific sector of the population, must widen its base while also battling the prime concerns of consumers: which device, what type of access, and how about that content? In the meantime, social and mobile gaming are charging up from behind, riding the wave of smartphones and tablets, changing the gaming and the marketing landscape. This ever-increasing interest in gaming is causing many products and services to include gaming in their marketing efforts.

Where devices go, marketing is soon to follow. The ability to track consumers as they actually reach a buying decision is an intriguing part of this new platform.

The Game's Afoot

Ten years ago, we predicted that video games would outstrip movie (box office) revenue within the next ten years. We were wrong—it actually happened within four years of the release of our earlier edition of this book. Gaming is huge. The global video-game market was worth around $56 billion last year, more than twice the size of the recorded-music industry and nearly a quarter more than the magazine business.[1] The U.S. industry is projected to reach $25 billion by 2017.[2]

However, like every other entertainment platform, the digital disruption is taking the air out of current business models, deflating some sectors while others rise. Digital downloads and online gaming have weakened overall revenue for video games. Device and access, the same underlying earth-movers that are affecting other entertainment platforms, are having the same impact here: disrupting current business models while forming a base for new ones. Consumers are finding new devices to take their games where they want and new ways to access their favorites, heavily favoring mobile versus computer or console-based games.

---

[1] "All the World's a Game," *The Economist*, December 10, 2011.

[2] "New Reports Forecast Global Video Game Industry Will Reach $82 Billion By 2017," *Forbes*, July 8, 2012.

This shift is taking its toll, roiling hardware and software sales. But with mobile and online gaming charging up, forecasts for the overall growth of the platform are still rosy.

Consider the two charts in Exhibits 8-1 and 8-2.

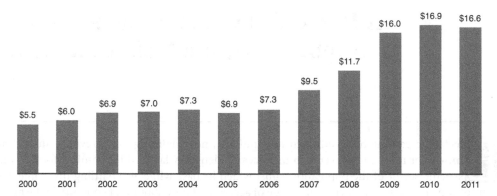

Exhibit 8-1 U.S. electronic game sales growth, 2000 to 2012

Source: The Entertainment Software Association, 2012

See the leap in 2009? That's the beginning of the digital onslaught. Exhibit 8-2 gives a closer look at the impact.

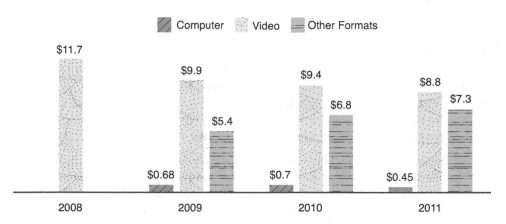

Exhibit 8-2 Electronic game sales by segment, 2008 to 2011

Source: The Entertainment Software Association, 2012

Those "other formats" include subscriptions, digital full games, digital add-on content, mobile apps, social network gaming, and other physical delivery—all of the new access models and platforms that have come on line in the four years, from smartphones to tablets to the cloud. Sales of video games, the classic hard disc/console-driven variety, have been steadily declining, while online delivery, social, and mobile games—the ones you play on your iPhone or Android—have been rising. Today, it's hard to find a device with a screen that doesn't offer an interactive entertainment experience.

So why are those traditional games slipping? First, consider the expense related to hard-core video gaming, the classic 37-year-old-guy variety: the game itself, the HDTV, the sound system or the premium headphones. It's an expensive hobby. With mobile/social gaming, there are expenses—the smartphone, the tablet—but they aren't necessarily specific to gaming per se; you're using that device for many other purposes. And the games themselves are far less expensive.

And then there's the content. The video game industry, long scrutinized for the violent "first-shooter" games that dominate the landscape, has been slow to move into other areas. They have a dedicated base that has kept the business growing for many years. But that base is saturated. The industry needs to move beyond those average 37-year-old males, or it will continue to contract.

Younger players—the ones who might normally be picking up the baton—are entering the gaming universe through different devices. They won't suddenly switch their mode of play just because they get a job, at least not in the numbers they did in earlier days.

This isn't lost on the game developers. Even such giants as Disney, which once believed that video games could have perfect synergy with feature releases, are shuttering some of their gaming divisions as they shift their focus to the mobile/social world, where gaming is ramping up at steeper angles than video ever did.

It isn't that we've stopped playing. Far from it. We've just moved on.

So who is playing these days?

Players by the Numbers

The Entertainment Software Association (ESA) offers plenty of interesting data in its recently published report, *Essential Facts about the Computer and Video Game Industry*.[3] Among the figures cited are these nuggets:

- The average U.S. household owns at least one dedicated game console, PC, or smartphone.
- Forty-nine percent of U.S. households own a dedicated game console, and those that do own an average of two.
- The average game player is 30; 32% are under 18; 31% are 18 to 35; and 37% are 36+.

Now let's talk gender—and this is where it gets interesting.

- Forty-seven percent of all players are women, and women over 18 years of age are one of the industry's fastest growing demographics.
- Today, adult women represent a greater portion of the game-playing population (30%) than boys age 17 or younger (18%).

---

[3] "2012 Sales, Usage and Demographic Data: Essential Facts about the Computer and Video Game Industry," the Electronic Software Association.

According to Flurry,[4] a consulting firm specializing in "the New App Economy," though the classic hardcore gamer was male (60% versus 40%), women are driving the rising revenue in social and mobile gaming, 53% to 47%. This same source tells us that this female gamer earns over 50% more than the average American and is more than twice as likely to have earned a college bachelor's degree.

A few more facts to add to the mix, again from the ESA:

- Sixty-two percent of gamers play games with others, either in person or online. Seventy-eight percent of these gamers play with others at least one hour per week.

- Thirty-three percent of gamers play social games.

Gaming Platforms: Video

Up until just recently, when we said "video games," we immediately thought of either the hard-disc variety that fit into a console, or the computer-based games that allowed for a massive multiplayer online (MMO) experience. These types of games typically fit into the following revenue models[5]:

- **Pay-to-play:** Requires players to pay a monthly subscription fee

- **Free-to-play:** Involves an upfront software cost but no additional payments

- **Freemium:** Allows players to access game content and play for free but offers options to pay for additional content and access

Some games have been around long enough to combine more than one model. *World of Warcraft* is the most profitable game in history, generating nearly $700 million in sales of the original game and expansions, with another $1.4 billion in subscription revenue.[6]

In addition, these games have created allied industries. The Entertainment Software Association estimates that 2011 content sales generated an additional $5.59 billion in hardware sales. Our old friend licensing and merchandising makes its appearance here as well, with $2.62 billion in accessories, including clothing. However, with the drop in content sales now hitting its fourth consecutive year, video games reflect the appearance of a maturing industry.

The marketing of video games has many similarities to the movie business. Games are advertised in all mediums, including TV and prior to trailers in movie theaters. Titles are released simultaneously across all platforms: Xbox, PS3, and PC. In addition, many games are released regularly once a year, or once every two years, like film sequels.

One of the most important trends now underway, from the perspective of our overall discussion, is the shift in gaming console usage. Today's gaming consoles are all Internet-enabled and allow

---

[4] Farago, Peter, "Mobile Social Gamers: The New Mass-Market Powerhouse," February 22, 2001, http://blog.flurry.com/.

[5] Chulis, Kimberly, "Big Data Analytics for Video, Mobile, and Social Game Monetization," July 17, 2012, www.ibm.com/developerworks/.

[6] Blizzard Entertainment Statistics, www.statisticbrain.com.

for over-the-top access to a wide variety of content, far more than just online games. Most of them come already preloaded with Netflix, Vudu, Hulu, and various social networking favorites. It is not out of the realm of possibility that set-top boxes could become a thing of the past, with what was formerly known as a gaming console being the media conduit in the typical home—which will also allow gamers to connect to the cloud, the quickly growing home of gaming software.

Gaming Platforms: Social

Social gaming refers to gaming that requires interaction with others, rather than gaming in solitude. Although this is certainly an attribute of video games, the term is most often used to describe games that are connected to social networking as the primary focus—in other words, you can't play the game alone.

Social games got their big start—revenue is predicted to reach $8.6 billion in 2014[7]—with Facebook, where Zynga, the game developer responsible for such hits as FarmVille and ChefVille, profited from allowing gamers to start for free but achieve higher status by buying up. Gamers can use actual money or Facebook credits to purchase in-game virtual goods to help them perform better, get premium access, and move to higher levels faster.

But social game developers are moving away from Facebook, primarily due to two factors:

- The potential growth of non-Facebook social gaming due to increased device ownership and use

- The restrictions that Facebook has placed on game developers, including higher revenue cuts for the site and an increasing inability for developers to post adverts on users' walls

Of that forecasted $8.6 billion, over $5 billion should be coming from non-Facebook social gaming by 2014, according to the same source. Like everything else, this growth will be facilitated in part by the ongoing move to mobile platforms.

Going Mobile

Even as the gaming console works to become the center of our home-media universe, the consumer is walking away: out of the family room, into the street, wherever they wish to go. The shift to mobile applications has all the makings of a tsunami, riding the currents of new devices, better access, and more content. And surfing along with it are the entertainment marketers, weaving content and advertising together in one seamless curl.

Gaming Platforms: Mobile

The one constant in entertainment is this: if it's good (and sometimes even when it's not), people want more. Entertainment platforms—movies, television, cable, even books and magazines—

---

[7] "Social Game Revenue Should Outgrow Facebook by 2014," www.allfacebook.com, via a study by SuperData Research, October 10, 2011.

have turned into huge industries to feed the public's desire for pleasure. As always, it is technology that moves the business forward, and in the digital disruption, the prime mover is the mobile device: smartphones and tablets. And when it comes to mobile content, games reign supreme.

What's 'Appening

What drives the mobile world are applications. The word itself generically applies to all types of software for all types of devices, but for the purposes of this discussion—and in the minds of more and more consumers—applications, or *apps*, are specific programs written to perform specific tasks for use on a mobile device.

There are currently over 500,000 apps available. By the time you read this, that number might have doubled. Unlike software packages such as Microsoft Office—broad-based programs that integrate into the operating system of a computer, which require hundreds of thousands of programming hours to create and maintain—applications can be (relatively) quickly developed by entrepreneurs hoping to hit it big.

That's a good thing because the consumer is clamoring for them and especially for entertainment, as shown in Exhibit 8-3.

Exhibit 8-3   Top Ten Mobile Application Categories[8]

RANK	CATEGORY
1	Games
2	Music and Entertainment
3	Communications
4	Social Media
5	Productivity and Tools
6	Sports
7	Books and Reference
8	Weather
9	News
10	Dating

The types of games that people are interested in cover a broad swath. In Exhibit 8-4, we can determine the ranking of the particular categories based on impressions: the number of times the app is located and loaded.

---

[8] "Mobile Game Applications: Special Report," January 2013, Millennial Media, www.millenialmedia.com.

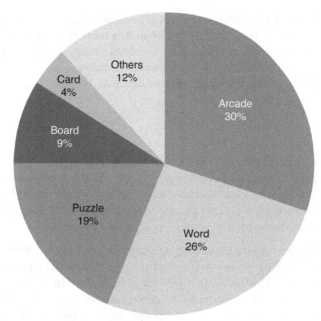

Exhibit 8-4 Types of Games, Ranked by Impression[9]

Monetizing Mobile

There are three basic forms of monetization in the mobile app world. The first, of course, is the revenue generated from the purchase of the application. Part of the appeal of apps is their pricing. Consumers seem to easily equate value to apps in the $.99 to $4.99 range, where they operate as inexpensive impulse buys.

The second stream comes from advertising. Gaming companies offer in-game banner ads, video offers, and full-page advertisements. In fact, ad-supported revenue in mobile gaming applications grew 119% year-over-year in 2012. More on the mechanics of this in just a moment.

The third and possibly the most rapidly growing form of revenue comes from in-game purchases. Though the original focus of gaming apps tended to be on the number of downloads a game might generate, at anywhere from $.99 and up, in-game purchases are...ahem...changing the game in gaming. Eighty percent of the 10 top-grossing iPhone apps in America—and 85% of the top 20—are now free. And why not? The real money is coming from what the gamer buys once he's in the game. Hooked on a driving game but unable to rise through the ranks? Purchase a more powerful race car. The buys aren't necessarily inexpensive, either: Top-grossing games like Rage of Bahamut offer in-app purchases ranging from $0.99 to $99.99.

Ka-ching, ka-ching.

---

[9] Ibid.

Gaming is a big business that will continue to get bigger. Industry analyst R.W. Baird estimates that this sector will continue to grow at a rate of 15% to 20% for the next several years.[10] There will be more devices, more ways to access games, but most important, it will continue to reach into new demographics. Gaming is becoming more small-d democratic and far more accessible, on all levels. But most of all, gaming taps into one great desire harbored by nearly every living being in one form or another: the desire to play.

Why We Game

Play is a critical element in human society. As children, we play to learn. The quote, "Play is the work of children," has been attributed to many people, but regardless of who said it first, it's true. Play teaches children how to be social and how to compete, creates a reward structure, and, oh yeah, it's fun. Play is something we spend a tremendous amount of time on when we are young, and with any luck, we find ways to bring it into our lives as we age.

Gaming is growing because it hits those long-ago-learned hot buttons. Some games allow for social interaction. Some allow for reward, and some give players the chance to become well-respected leaders or guides. Most tickle the need for competition. In short, games offer users a valuable personal experience, one tailored to the perceptions of the individual. One of the great fallacies of social interaction is the concept that people are only incentivized by money—many businesses have made this mistake, losing employees to competitors who offered a different type of reward: a sense of accomplishment based on the opinions of their peers; an ability to give value back to society. Gaming operates within these same principles.

Knowing that, how are savvy marketers increasing their connections with consumers? By increasing the use of games at all levels of marketing.

Gamification

In their excellent overview, KISSmetrics, an online analytics company, defines gamification as the use of gaming in marketing to engage and influence consumer behavior.[11] The concept isn't new; detergent companies kept their sales steady during the Depression by offering sets of dishes that could only be completed by buying enough soap. Those companies were appealing to the inner desire for reward, a key component of gaming.

But the growing use of devices that deliver games affords marketers an easy connection to the consumers they wish to reach, and gamification offers them the vehicle. Google offers an intriguing interactive graphic that continually charts the rise in interest in gamification over the last several years, with key markers, at www.google.com/trends/explore#q=gamification.

KISSmetrics goes on to outline the key attributes of gamification[12] as follows:

---

[10] "Game Industry Forecast Shows Solid Growth," October 12, 2011, www.industrygamers.com.

[11] "How to Use Gamification for Better Business Results," www.kissmetrics.com.

[12] Ibid.

- **Rewards:** A reward is something you receive and feel positive about. The feeling positive part is the key ingredient. Consumers should be rewarded with virtual goods (such as points) for specific behavior (that is, a purchase, filling out a form, and so on), and those virtual items should offer access to exclusive privileges and rewards, such as levels or prizes.

- **Loss Aversion:** Most people strongly prefer avoiding losses to acquiring gains. One way to get going with this is to give people something right away that they can lose (unless they keep playing). When you join Zynga's Farmville, you get a starter farm. If you don't visit the farm and care for your crops, they wither and die.

- **Status, Competition, and Reputation:** Most people inherently want a higher status not only to keep up, but to out-do the Joneses. This is why leaderboards are a good idea. Also, making achievements social encourages people to continually one-up and stay motivated to reach clear goals.

- **Feedback:** Feedback tells users that their intended action was registered and shows the outcomes of that action. Seeing points accumulate as actions are taken establishes a clear and instant reward system. It's also an immediate indication that the user is getting closer to her goal. Continually accomplishing small goals to reach a larger goal is often what makes games addictive.

Examples of gamification are rampant. Airline loyalty programs allow customers to build status and gain rewards. Nike sells shoes by inserting a device that allows runners to track their stats and compete against others. Trip Advisor builds loyalty by assigning badges to travelers who submit reviews and continues to pump the connection through ongoing emails that remind the travelers that they need to post more to reach a higher status. Local businesses have used gamification principles in posting questions on Facebook and then rewarding locals who answer with some type of prize. It seems almost impossible to accomplish any task these days that isn't pointing you toward a website or urging you to download an app.

Mobile Marketing

There are two constants in innovation as it relates to media. The first is any new media platform will eventually attract businesses based on sex. The second is any new media platform will soon become a handy marketing channel. After all, as we continue to discuss throughout this book, it's the monetization of media that builds a business, and marketing is a key component of that effort.

Mobile marketing has taken off in the past few years with, we would assume, much more to come. The following is a quick overview of the practice. Like everything else in the disruption, expect changes to occur momentarily, as devices multiply and standards are set.

The channels used by mobile marketing include

- **SMS:** Text messages to the device.

- **MMS:** Multimedia messaging, which will include text, audio, and video to the device.

- **Push Notifications:** Specific to particular apps on a device, alerting the user to information, including marketing, distributed by the creator of the app.

- **QR Codes:** The digitized, square glyphs that appear in the corner of ads in other media or as ads themselves. A user scans the glyph with his or her device and is directed to the website or mobile app of the advertiser.

- **Proximity System Messages:** If a device has GSM capability, the user might also receive messages that allow a specific location—a shopping mall, for example—to track his movements through the mall, offering him information about promotions of the stores nearest to his present location.

As a consumer, you may be aware that there are certain "opt-out, opt-in" protocols for mobile marketing. As a marketing professional, you will want to consider how your particular target market might or might not have interest in being on the receiving end of your message. Older consumers tend to relish privacy more than younger consumers, who seem to enjoy being aware of/sold on the latest trend.

Mobile Advertising

Mobile advertising is a hot topic. Proponents claim that the data now available through the give and take of the digital universe allows marketing firms to directly target specific consumers at the minute of their decision, thereby delivering the message to exactly the right person at exactly the right time. Others say that more traditional forms of advertising—which, in this case may include banner ads on websites—based on publications that focus on specific target audiences will still afford a better response. The practice is simply too new to fully vet.

The cost and frequency of mobile advertising is determined through complex algorithms; the "buy" occurs in real-time auctions that happen constantly.

Mobile advertising is facilitated though mobile advertising agencies who generally target specific networks, based on the clients' desired strategy. These networks differ by reach. The following description of the various networks is based on the work of dotMobi, a U.K. firm specializing in mobile marketing.[13]

- **Blind Networks:** The largest in terms of publishers, advertisers, and impressions. Serves a high volume of advertising to an extensive base of mostly independent mobile sites/apps, supplemented by premium publishers' unfilled inventory. Offer many options for targeting but might not allow advertisers to choose specific websites. Performance advertising is the norm, paid by cost per click (CPC). For marketers who want an active response to their ads: Clicking through a banner to the advertiser's site, click to download/call, and so on. CPC varies with supply and demand, determined through a self-service auction system.

---

[13] http://mobithinking.com/mobile-ad-network-guide.

- **Premium Blind Networks:** Medium-sized, with a higher proportion of premium publishers (big-traffic mobile sites of well-known brands; newspapers, broadcasters or operator portals). Some exclusive relationships. Attracts a higher proportion of brand advertising, paid for on a CPM basis. Advertising may still be blind or semi-blind (that is, targeted at a channel), but a premium price might buy a specific spot on a specific site. Costs vary considerably—as high as U.S. $20 CPM.

- **Premium Networks:** Limited number of prestige publishers—mobile operators and big-name destinations—serving as an extension of direct-sales teams. Example: Nokia and AOL's mobile inventory is sold on their own sites. Predominant pricing model is CPM; majority of campaigns are brand advertising. Attracts big brand advertisers who are willing to pay premium prices for prime locations. CPM will vary wildly from U.S. $5 to $75.

- **Local Mobile Ad Networks:** Focus on publishers where users are looking for local information (that is, restaurants, stores, or weather). Publishers include directory services, mapping/navigation, and other sites/apps where users enter their locations. More targeted, will cost more, but (might) deliver better results than normal mobile ads.

- **Cost-Per-Action (CPA)/Affiliate Networks:** Advertisers define the type of action they wish to achieve and specify the price they are willing to pay for each customer that fulfills this action, paying only when conversion is achieved. Defined actions could include subscriptions or registrations; downloads/installs/purchases; clicks to call; checks directions; uses coupon. Advertisers can specify the type of mobile sites/apps where ads will run (or cannot run) but not necessarily particular publishers. Campaigns can also target by geography, operator, handset, and demographic. Publishers select the advertiser campaigns they wish to run and decide where and when the ads will run. Publishers are only paid if users click through and perform the defined action.

Summary: Games, Mobile Applications, and Mobile Marketing

The ongoing convergence of devices, access, and content continues to drive entertainment forward, especially in the gaming platform. Revenue for the platform now exceeds that of movie box offices (but not extended movie revenue, a merchandising/licensing juggernaut all its own) and music. Gaming will continue to grow because it hits basic human triggers, including a desire for status, rewards, and interaction. Marketers can make use of gaming principles in all sectors, driving efforts across all device platforms. Hand-in-hand with the increase in mobile devices, mobile marketing and advertising offer an intriguing way to potentially reach consumers right at the moment of their buying decisions.

For Further Reading

Hasen, Jeff, *Mobilized Marketing: How to Drive Sales, Engagement, and Loyalty Through Mobile Devices,* John Wiley & Sons, Inc., 2012.

Krum, Cindy, *Mobile Marketing: Finding Your Customers No Matter Where They Are,* Pearson Education Inc., 2010.

McGonigal, Jane, *Reality Is Broken: Why Games Make Us Better and How They Can Change the World*, Penguin Press, 2011.

Zichermann, Gabe, and Christopher Cunningham, *Gamification by Design: Implementing Game Mechanics in Web and Mobile Apps*, O'Reilly Media, Inc., 2011.

9

The Universal Language: Music

Music is an industry that has been under digital assault for well over a decade: This platform struggles with the near-disappearance of its original business model, paradigm shifts in consumer's buying decisions, and a culture that seems to have less regard for the creator's—and publisher's—need to make a living.

In this chapter, we investigate the conditions that face music marketing professionals in the era of disruption: the shift to digital downloads, piracy, and a disturbing trend toward not owning music.

It's a complex business and still an important platform.

They're Playing Our Song

Music transcends borders, ignores rivalries, has no knowledge of political persuasions. At its best, music can create joy, heal pain, move us to tears, or stimulate a desire to reach further than we ever thought possible. Music is the one language that links all of us, no matter the age, gender, race, or politics of the listener. It is the one universal form of communication.

It is a whopper of a business, one that reaches billions worldwide.

It is also a business that struggles with new technologies. Though it is difficult to put absolutes on dollar figures—the music business is notoriously private—estimates show that the industry's revenue on recorded music have sustained a stunning hit in the last 10 years—and not the kind this business is usually looking for. Consider the data in Exhibit 9-1.

Exhibit 9-1   Total Spending on Recorded Music, in Billions

	2004	2010	2012
Physical	$13.0	$6.2	$2.5
Internet Download	$0.3	$1.9	$3.8
Mobile Download	$0.3	$0.9	$0.7
Total	**$13.6**	**$9.0**	**$7.0**

That's a nearly 50% cut in revenue. Does this mean that people have stopped listening to music? No—but they've certainly slowed down *buying* it. When that happens, it has an impact on all sectors of the industry, but especially on any form of *property*.

The Three Forms of Property

Going back to our original discussion of copyright and content, the music business focuses on three types of properties that can be monetized: publishing (compositions), recording, and media (CDs, MP3s). Each part of the industry has its own ecosystem.

Publishing

Songwriters or composers might or might not record their own songs and might or might not own their work, depending on how the work was created and for whom. For instance, a composer working on a Disney animated film is most likely working under a "work for hire" contract, which means Disney actually owns the song and the rights to sell it. On the other hand, an independent songwriter like Beth Nielsen Chapman might have her song recorded by Faith Hill. Chapman most likely assigned some of her rights to a publishing company, who will collect publishing royalties from Hill and pay a portion to Chapman.

Though publishing is an essential partner to the recording sector of the music industry, there are publishing companies that focus on nothing but placing music in television and movies, with little concern for releasing any recordings on an individual basis. The demand for music in other forms of media—movies, television, games—is high; publishing benefits from this demand.

Recording

When most lay people speak of the music industry, this is the segment they are referring to: the part of the business that consists of recording artists, record producers, recording studios, and the distribution of recordings, whether in physical form, over the airwaves, or downloaded digitally.

This is an area that has seen huge change in the last decade. Where developing an album (remember those?) once demanded a cadre of professionals—audio engineers, studio space, studio musicians, ranks of full-time publicists and marketing professionals, today's professional musician is every bit as likely to be recording his or her work in a home studio, thanks to huge leaps forward in software. The actual marketing of that music still depends on professionals, but they might be freelancers, brought in on each individual project. We look at this more closely in a minute.

Media

At one time, the physical distribution of media on CDs was a huge part of the business, with big box retailers such as Virgin Records or Tower Records reigning supreme as the buying hubs. The advent of digital downloads has relegated those two companies to the dustbin, while online retailers such as iTunes or Amazon now service the market. This is the segment of the market most likely to feel the next hit in the shifting business of music. After all, if you can stream your favorite music anytime and anywhere, why do you actually need to *own* a recording?

Make no mistake: CDs are still being sold, and we discuss this more when we talk about the changes in distribution. For now, let's stay focused on the business at large.

Major Players

The U.S. music market is split between three major players—Universal Music Group, Warner Music Group, and Sony Music Entertainment—and a large group of independents. Exhibit 9-2, current to the end of 2012, does not reflect the year-end sale of EMI to Universal Music Group. That deal was approved in late 2012 in both the U.S. and Europe.[1]

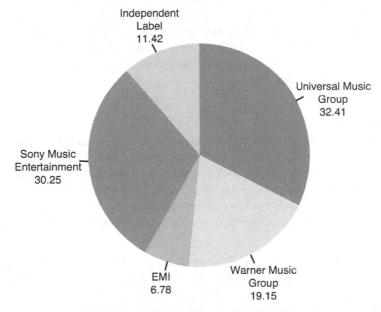

The Nielsen Company & Billboard's 2012 Music Industry Report
http://www.npr.org/blogs/therecord/2012/09/21/161560048/universals-
purchase-of-emi-gets-thumbs-up-in-u-s-and-europe

Exhibit 9-2 U.S. market share, total albums sold, 2012[2]

---

[1] "Universal's Purchase of EMI Gets Thumbs Up in U.S. and Europe," NPR, September 12, 2012, www.npr.org/blogs/therecord/2012/09/21/161560048/universals-purchase-of-emi-gets-thumbs-up-in-u-s-and-europe.

[2] The Nielsen Company & Billboard's 2012 Music Industry Report.

Each of the major labels often have its own publishing, recording, and media divisions. The independents might be more focused on the recording sector.

Music is a hit-driven business, pure and simple—the more hits, the more money. But it takes a *lot* of releases to make a hit. Over 11,000 nonclassical albums are released by the major labels every year, but now in the day of the individual download, it is unusual for more than 120 of those albums to sell more than 500,000 units (a "gold" record) in a physical format.[3] The major labels generate a high number of these hit releases, using both in-house and freelance talent to create, distribute, and promote the work—and they must, for it's the winners that cover the cost of releasing the losers.

Independents

During the last century, heavy consolidation in the industry resulted in many independent labels springing up. These labels joined forces with a few disenfranchised or new talents, using sales at concerts and free performances—or over the Internet—to cover the costs of their startups as they struggled to create the next important mini-label.

Today, independents as a whole are far from being small potatoes. Independent labels (as a group) generally have the largest share of prerecorded industry sales promoted by Sound Scan and released by NARM (National Association of Recording Manufacturers). These sales can represent anything from a garage band making its own limited release for companies like Rhino Records, TVT, and others who generate $50 to $100 million in sales. Many of these larger independents give the artist greater creative freedom and a greater share of the total revenue pie, including tour receipts, licensing, and merchandise.

Private Labels

With the rising availability of excellent recording software, today more than ever there is room in the music industry for the self-promoter. Ever since the early days of recording, there have always been those pioneering souls who had a 45 pressed or a CD burned, threw them in the car, and made the rounds of the radio stations. Liz Phair originally got her start releasing audio cassettes under her own label Girly Sound before signing with Matador. More recently, Justin Bieber put his videos on YouTube before being discovered by Scooter Braun, who went on to become his manager.

Today's budding artist can record a song or an album and throw it up on the Web, either in the form of a download or as a video posted on YouTube. But as with all other forms of entertainment media making its way to the Web—or to mobile devices—it takes more than simply hoping someone will notice. The entertainment marketing ecosystem is alive and well and ever-growing, servicing the hopes and dreams of those who would be stars.

Building momentum is difficult in a day when tens of thousands of new releases are shouting for attention. Advertising budgets, a full-time publicist, and a major tour manager are not part of

---

[3] Vogel, Harold L., "Entertainment Industry Economics: a Guide for Financial Analysis," Eighth Edition, Cambridge University Press, 2011.

most indies' experiences. Regardless of the accessibility of the Internet, it still takes a team to get you on top.

Let's take a look at the more established path to listeners.

The Music Development Process

As in every sector of the entertainment industry, each music career has its path. In a world where people believe they can make it big by posting a video to YouTube, in Major-Label-World, the typical trip to the top still looks like this:

An aspiring singer/songwriter

- Writes a few hot songs for a hot genre, forms a band or works solo, and builds a loyal fan base at music clubs and festivals.

- Hires a manager and/or producer.

- Makes a basic demo and sends it to music labels and scouts; they might hire a freelance public relations (PR) person.

- An A&R (Artist & Repertoire) professional hears the demo, likes it, makes a recommendation to produce a quality CD, and puts the act in front of a music label executive with decision-making authority.

- A senior executive at the label agrees to go forward, most likely in a demo deal, short for "let's see what you've got and how they respond." A budget is developed for the project.

- The label either hires or uses staff engineers, studios, back-up artists, songwriters, and an in-house producer to polish the work.

- A CD is mastered, and a major marketing push is developed.

- A publicist arranges talk shows, a tour manager books major concerts, magazine covers are planned, national radio play is organized. In the past, a music video might have been made, but tighter budgets have removed this from most deals.[4]

- Shipments go to wholesalers or to digital distributors, retailers are sent details on marketing push, and a media and publicity campaign is implemented.

From that point on, only the market will tell if the artist at the eye of this storm will be a one-hit wonder, a major superstar, or a comfortable career-type. Regardless of the star's status, he or she will become intimately familiar with the ways of the business—starting with the importance of intellectual property (IP).

---

[4] With the changing role of MTV—the network is now the home of reality shows, not music videos—the video-as-promotion has taken a deep slide in popularity. Thus does what was once a rock phenomenon become, literally, a footnote in music history.

The Rights Stuff

Once again, in the beginning, there is C: content. As in every other sector of entertainment, music content must be protected carefully. The music industry was one of the first to recognize the need for organizations that protected the IP rights of artists, as much (if not more) to protect the potential revenue due the recording company, as for the artist.

Two early pieces of legislation influenced the decision to create organizations that would protect these rights. In 1897, the U.S. granted performance rights to authors of nondramatic musical works (prior to this time, the performance had to be for profit), but an author of a musical work was hard-pressed to check up on every performance of his or her output. This was the rationale behind the 1914 formation of the American Society of Composers, Authors, and Publishers (ASCAP). The belief was that the author's rights could be protected better collectively. ASCAP became increasingly more powerful in the U.S. until 1939, when radio broadcasters, unhappy with ASCAP's monopoly, formed their own organization: Broadcast Music Inc. (BMI). BMI has become the other major performing rights association in the U.S., also representing composers, publishers, and songwriters.

ASCAP and BMI employ a blanket license, granted for a given period, which permits various institutions to perform any work in their repertoire. They then distribute royalties to members based on the popularity of their works. This allows the author to avoid handling each infringement of the copyright on an individual basis—a tremendous cost savings to the artist. It does, however, mean that these organizations must closely police the use of the works.

This became increasingly difficult as digital downloads became the standard of the industry. Certain moves by the U.S. government didn't help the problem. In the early part of this century, the Recording Industry Association of America (RIAA) led an effort to change the U.S. copyright law that designated sound recordings as "works for hire." This controversy began with language in the 1999 Satellite Home Viewer Improvement Act that might have prevented artists from reclaiming ownership of their master recordings. The RIAA worked with the Artist's Coalition (led by Don Henley, at that time formerly of the Eagles—they have since regrouped), the National Academy of Recording Arts and Sciences (NARAS), the American Federation of Musicians (AF of M), the American Federation of Television and Radio Artists (AFTRA), and the Music Managers Forum to create language that would have a long-term effect on the future IP rights of musicians.

Additional efforts in the last decade have included work with international organizations such as BUMA (Holland), GEMA (Germany), SACEM (France), and the Performing Rights Society (PRS, UK) on an International Joint Music Venture (IMJV) aimed at heading off music IP issues brought on by the globalization of the music marketplace and the move to digital downloads.

The 360 Deal

Legal ownership of rights is the heart of monetization. The biggest change in rights over the last decade came through the institution of what are known as 360 deals, in which the artist signs away a portion of the rights to everything connected with the work, including the traditional revenue-generating pieces—individual downloads or CDs—along with tour revenues, T-shirt sales, any appearance in a motion picture, the ownership of the website—in short, anything that adds to the revenue stream.

The philosophy behind this is based in brand-building. Because everything the label invests in—or even if it doesn't; even if it's something created by the artist to promote the work—is part of building the artist's brand, the label wants to share in the revenue from all of those sources.

More than one artist has looked at a 360 deal and decided to look elsewhere, but it's hard to walk away from the potential payoff of a major label's efforts.

The Changing Face of Distribution

The digital sale of music topped the physical sale in late 2011. As reported by *CNNMoney*,[5] based on reports from Nielsen and Billboard, digital music purchases accounted for 50.3% of music sales in 2011, with digital sales up 8.4% from the previous year and physical album sales declining 5%. That's still a lot of plastic being pressed—it's not time to turn the blank CDs into coasters—but it does speak to the future.

Digital downloads found their first foothold in Napster, which was shut down after protracted copyright infringement battles with the U.S. government. Napster returned as a digital retailer but was eventually bought out by Rhapsody, a music subscription service. Apple filled the gap with the now-giant iTunes, allowing users to purchase downloads but limiting them to the number of devices that could receive those downloads.

This rise in digital downloads cut the legs off any number of traditional retailers. The big box stores, as mentioned, disappeared. Columbia House, once a large buy-by-mail club, threw in the towel and focused on movies and books. Though you can still order a CD from amazon.com or buy one at Target or maybe find a few oldie compilations at Costco or Sam's Club, the hard disk is quickly becoming a small dot in the rearview mirror of the music business.

The trend to digital download continued on into 2012 but was joined by another force in the disruption: the rise of streaming versus downloads. As fast as individual downloads gobbled the market, we now have the rise of subscription services—Rhapsody and Spotify—that allow listeners to listen to music for a low monthly price with no individual download fees. Listeners are not buying the music; they are simply listening to it, whenever and wherever they want. And with the ever-growing rise in the ownership of mobile devices, the market for subscription services seems nearly unstoppable, especially when these subscription services allow you to download music (so that you can listen even when you're offline) as long as you're a member.

This is all based on the tsunami of tablets and smartphones, which are convenient and portable. As we said before, why own music when you can get it almost anytime you want it?

This shift to streaming is a global phenomenon. Consider the data in Exhibits 9-3 and 9-4.

And note the impact of mobile streaming versus digital.

---

[5] "Digital Music Sales Top Physical Sales," *CNNMoneyTech*, January 5, 2012.

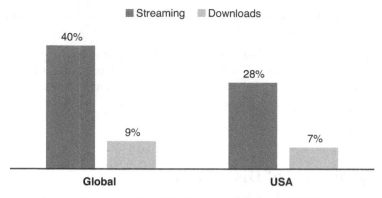

Source: Strategy Analytics Global Recorded Music Forecast 2012

Exhibit 9-3 The rise in online music

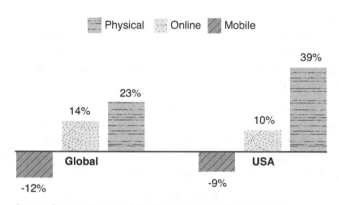

Source: Strategy Analytics Global Recorded Music Forecast 2012

Exhibit 9-4 The rise in mobile music revenue

But with the rise in digital distribution—whether downloaded or streamed—has come a con-current rise in piracy.

The Black Flag of Piracy

From the street corners of Manhattan, to the alleys of Hollywood, the back-street stalls of Beijing, and the beautifully appointed department stores of Sao Paulo, counterfeit CDs are still carefully reproduced, artfully packaged, and sold at greatly reduced prices—with no revenue going to either the original music labels or the artists. Now with digital downloads taking over distribution, the challenge has become even greater. There is far less cost for pirates to steal or allow for the distribution of downloads than in creating a CD.

The lack of global IP protection or copyright enforcement in many countries around the world has resulted in the loss of billions of dollars to the music industry. This situation is improving but is still not perfect.

We prefer to not give the pirates any publicity by naming their sites, but in general, the biggest threats came from sites that allowed listeners to share their own libraries by uploading content to the master site, then share it with whomever wanted to download it. Certain pirates claimed that they could not be held accountable for what subscribers did once the content was posted and even went so far as to encrypt the sites so that the site owner could legally claim that they didn't know what was stored there. The battle over this copyright infringement rages on.

In short, if you're downloading content from the Internet without paying a fee for it—be it per download or via subscription—you're stealing, plain and simple. Although you may never be caught, we hope that you ask yourselves how you might feel should someone walk into your apartment, dorm room, or home and simply walk out with whatever you value the most.

"Free" is not a word that works in the entertainment economy. If you're serious about making a living in it, make sure you respect the hard work of others.

Reaching the Masses

Regardless of how listeners eventually purchase or subscribe to a song, they still need to hear it somewhere first. Though social networking sites and subscription sharing services are certainly part of this discovery process, the long reach of radio still provides an initial boost to most new music.

The All-Important Airplay

Part of the standard promotion for any group or individual's success is getting airplay on radio stations. This poses a variety of challenges, as radio is an advertising-driven medium. Stations want to play the songs that are most likely to attract listeners to their format, the playlist of which has been carefully mapped out to grab the particular demographics advertisers are after.

To get airtime, the label's promoter must first get the new singles and albums in the hands of the appropriate stations. Advertising budgets can help in this regard; a mega-budget often signals to station programmers that a song can merit more playtime to the benefit of a station and its advertising.

However, there is more to getting airplay than just demographics and advertisers. Radio revenue is also dependent on independent promoters, the people who act as middlemen between record labels and radio stations. These *indies* offer a variety of payments to the stations to play certain songs—for instance, cash and promotional items—with the money to pay for such enticements coming from the record labels themselves.

These payments are not to be confused with "payola"—the term that grew out of the scandals that wracked the radio world in the 1950s, when disc jockeys (DJs) like Alan Freed were found to have received payments to play certain songs. Payola is only illegal when the listener is not made aware that payments are being made. The fact that indies are bona-fide businesspeople providing a "service" to the industry—up-front—keeps the practice from falling to the wrong side of the law.

Fredric Dannen's book, *Hit Men: Power Brokers & Fast Money Inside the Music Business*,[6] offers an intriguing insight into the practices—good and bad—of the music promotion business. As described in *Hit Men*, in the early days, the enforcers or distributors—financially supported and acknowledged by the labels—would buy "radio play" from DJs at radio stations all across the country with cash, drugs, and sex. When charges of racketeering and corrupt practices were brought against individuals at the labels and radio stations, the business cleaned itself up. Legitimate businesses were created under formal contract, with the labels to maintain constant contact with the radio stations, studio managers, DJs, and program directors, using full-blown marketing kits and promotional items to gain airtime. These practices include legitimate agreements to promote co-op advertising dollars to gain strong airplay support.

But what about the public, you might ask, and their desire to hear certain songs? Certainly those "request lines" lighting up must have some impact on airtime? The answer: maybe yes, maybe no.

The Bogus Request Scam

In the 1990s, country music radio stations in particular were plagued with floods of requests programmers soon began to suspect weren't genuine.[7] The calls came in clusters; hip DJs soon identified several specific labels they felt were responsible for hiring agencies to make bogus calls. This sort of promotion, unethical and as much a possible source of harm to performers as a help, began again in the new millennium, but radio stations are quicker to spot the patterns.

Because station programmers may skew their mix based on requests, a motive might have been to ensure more hits for a label's products. Some stations retaliate by boycotting all products from these suspicious labels. Record labels are quick to deny the allegations, often claiming overzealous fans. Radio stations, however, ultimately distrust labels associated with the practice, and a resulting diminished skew can result. This practice is much more difficult to perpetuate with Internet-generated station requests because email or text requests may be more readily screened.

Though it can be difficult to identify "real" listeners over the airwaves, it certainly isn't difficult to do at the heart of the music experience: the live performance.

Live Music

Live music happens in venues across America: Madison Square Garden in New York City, blues bars in San Francisco, the Newport Jazz Festival, honky-tonk dance ballrooms in Oklahoma, stadiums, outdoor amphitheaters, beach boardwalks, bandshells, open-air plazas, and, of late, in *boites*—New York/Paris-style cafes. Examples include the Carlyle in New York, where Bobby

---

6   Dannen, Fredric, *Hit Men: Power Brokers & Fast Money Inside the Music Business* (New York, NY: Vintage, 1991).

7   Stark, Phyllis, "Bogus Request Calls Hit Country Stations," *Billboard*, April 22, 2000.

Short reigned for decades. Since his death, the Carlyle has filled the room with random, high-profile acts.

Although some prefer to listen to music in intimate settings where they can actually see the artist, others crave the experience of being surrounded by thousands of other rabid fans.

The modern-day P.T. Barnum who brings the circus to town knows how to build interest, anticipation, and deliver a fanfare. The three rings in this particular case are the act or acts (think Lollapalooza or Lilith Fair, which is rumored to be starting up again), the associated retail sales of T-shirts, CDs, and full-color programs packed with photos, and the sponsorship dollars built on synergy with brands anxious to bring their messages to the artist's audience. These revenue streams enable the producer/promoter to gain a return on the significant investment necessary to stage these modern-day spectaculars. The promoter's marketing program will utilize local newspapers, local spot television, and heavy promotional radio featuring ticket giveaways to call-ins from listeners.

However, live music presentations have become more and more expensive due to many factors: the cost of venue rentals, housing for talent, equipment, special-effects, laser shows, special lighting, and large-screen projection. It has become essential to locate sponsors who can fund the bulk of the expense. Kool cigarettes became the founding sponsor of the Kool Jazz Concerts in New York and Newport, while Budweiser, Pepsi, and Coca-Cola all support warm–weather, outdoor concerts and provide seed money as well as outright sponsorship funds, balanced by obtaining exclusive pouring rights (the only brand of beverage poured at the event).

Hundreds of these sponsored events go on around the U.S. every year, including large-scale music-oriented events, like SXSW in Austin, Texas, or Summerfest in Milwaukee. They drive sales for both the artist and the sponsor and give live music fans a chance to feed their craving.

However, nothing gives the true live concert fan an experience like the "big top" of the music world: the megatour.

Megatours

There are many megatours each year, bringing groups and artists like Madonna, Coldplay, Jennifer Lopez, Lady Gaga, or Bruce Springsteen to the largest possible venues in the U.S. and around the world. Though tours were once orchestrated to promote the release of a new album, hoping for double-platinum-level sales, it is far more likely that today the touring artist(s) will release an album—often, a compilation of hits or previously unreleased tracks—to coincide with the tour.

Why? Because for many years, tours have been where the real money is made for an artist. Ticket sales, T-shirts, CD sales, all of it can go into the artist's coffers (after paying the associated costs to promoters and all the staff necessary to stage such an event)—unless the artist has a deal with their label, in which case the revenue has another split.

It was the ongoing success of tours that brought about the 360 deal mentioned earlier in our discussion. Labels wanted to make sure they had a slice of the pie, not only now, but forever after. Consider the revenue generated by worldwide tours, shown in Exhibit 9-5.

Exhibit 9-5   The Top Ten Worldwide Tours of 2012[8]

Rank	Gross Millions	Artist	Average Ticket Price	Average Tickets	Total Tickets	Average Gross	Cities/ Shows
1	296.1	Madonna	$140.38	31.481	2,109,234	$4,419,403	67/88
2	210.2	Bruce Springsteen & the E Street Band	$91.95	34,642	2,286,395	$3,185,269	66/81
3	186.4	Roger Waters	$110.96	34,997	1,679,856	$3,883,243	48/72
4	171.3	Coldplay	$86.88	40,239	1,971,692	$3,495,855	49/67
5	161.4	Lady Gaga	$102.09	31.628	1,581,423	$3,228,912	50/80
6	140.2	Cirque du Soleil: "Michael Jackson: The Immortal"	$104.44	7,805	1,342,397	$815,116	74/172
7	96.5	Kenny Chesney/ Tim McGraw	$88.87	49,336	1,085,382	$4,384,495	22/23
8	86.1	Metallica	$94.38	43,435	912,134	$4,099,536	21/30
9	69.9	Elton John	$117.25	7,643	596,162	$896,154	78/95
10	57.8	Red Hot Chil Peppers	$60.95	13,171	948,318	$802,778	72/77

What's interesting, when looking at the various acts in the top ten, is the wide variety of artists. Though some might think of popular music as the sole providence of a young crowd, it is evident that performers can extend their lives and their earning power for years, as loyal fans purchase tickets on, in some cases, a nearly annual basis. Mick Jagger of the Rolling Stones once said, "I'd rather be dead than singing 'Satisfaction' when I'm forty-five." Now, at the age of 70, he is a prime example of the enduring popularity of some rock icons, not to mention how one's opinions may change during the aging process.

A megatour is a high-water mark of success for a star or group and indicates a high level of trackable interest: the ability to fill the largest venues throughout America and the world. A promoter—such as LiveNation—orchestrating such a tour must make certain assurances regarding the artist's responsibilities, while the venue must also be able to assure the promoter that the seats will be filled. A typical tour contract is loaded with "riders," which ensure both sides other comfort levels. For instance, details may include the exact number and size of lights, sound capabilities, even the specific food or other entertainment that will be available to the artists.

Megatours are the perfect example of the medium becoming the message—the music itself is the main draw, but the message of the star's bankability that comes from such an event only serves to more firmly place that artist in the firmament of top performers.

---

[8]   Pollstar, "2012 Pollstar Year End Top 50 Worldwide Tours," December 31, 2012.

Marketing the Music

With a global audience always searching for a new beat, music offers marketers a tremendous ability to reach niche markets. Marketing the product to these eager ears has taken many forms, from pushing the personality to creating new mediums of delivery. But those new mediums—from LPs to 8-tracks to cassettes to CDs—may have masked an inherent weakness in the music industry, at least in the 1990s. With the introduction of the CD, many consumers raced to replace their damaged LPs with a medium touted as nearly indestructible, producing a healthy spike in sales. Then, with the introduction of digitization, another bump occurred, as fans filled their hard drives with downloads. But with the move to downloads and streaming, revenue creeps downward, now based on pennies rather than dollars.

So what's a product manager, assigned the task of walking a new artist from deal to domination, to do? Fall back on tradition while exploring new opportunities.

Marketing Personalities

Possibly more so than in any other entertainment sector, music depends heavily on the marketing of personality. The hype attendant to any on-stage appearance of a performer is part of the experience machine: getting the audience in a lather before they even enter the auditorium, creating a concert rush that energizes both the performer and the fan. Careers today are built on this phenomenon. But will the superstars of today go evergreen? Will they continue to sell out concerts with an advance? Cross over to movies, TV, books, and other entertainment media? Or will they flame out and disappear into the abyss, abandoned by fans and promoters?

How do they get to the top in the first place?

For the most part, they get there via the marketing machine that only the major labels can mount, selectively employed when everyone on the team believes this is "IT"—a superstar in the making, under contract. All the tactics required to achieve hit status will be employed with support from the top of the company. Multimillion dollar budgets, staffs of professionals in publicity, A&R, advertising, touring, and venue relationships build an enormous opening for a tour touting a new album. Those appearances are backed with countless talk show interviews, leading magazine cover stories, organized fan clubs, and TV appearances. Websites are built, social networking is set in motion—a Facebook page, Twitter, Pinterest. In some cases, a music video will still be produced, released to YouTube or available on Vevo.com, a music video subscription service. The executive in charge of gaining distribution will complete the deals necessary for both digital and hard-media release. Radio airplay will be negotiated. Finally, when the star's performance/marketing blitz is launched, a groundswell of hype, buzz, and CD purchasing hysteria leads to the reward: The release goes double platinum and pays for all the thousands of non-hits released by the label that year.

Cross-Promotion

Other methods widely used in the marketing of music are *cross-selling, tie-in programs*, and *music brand sponsorship*. For example, offering CDs of top performers at a bare bones price of $10.00 with the purchase of coffee at Starbucks is an effective promotion—and everyone wins. The labels get sales on a catalog of already released music; the talent receives a more modest royalty on the large volume sold; the coffee house builds traffic; and the stars receive advertising and display marketing. The ROI is acceptable and leads to sponsorship deals with stars, their managers, and labels.

The Country Music Association (CMA), in connection with Gaylord Entertainment and the Nashville Cable Network (now owned by CBS), holds an annual Country Music Marketing program where deals are brokered. The group helped Trisha Yearwood gain a multimillion-dollar deal with Discover Card and Brooks & Dunn with Lee's Wrangler Jeans. Garth Brooks and other country music stars "tie up" and receive concert and music video support in return for the endorsement of beverages, cereals, apparel, and automobiles. Music talent and sponsorship agencies put together these highly profitable and successful arrangements; marketing strategies and tactics are borrowed from one high-powered deal to the next. Like all such deals, success breeds higher financial commitments and bigger programs.

Television

Along with the awards shows—The Grammies, BET Awards, American Music Awards, Academy of Country Music Awards, Billboard Awards, and more—there are many possibilities for television exposure for new artists as well as the creative superstar.

One intriguing opportunity took flight in the early part of the century, with the rise of The Artist's Den. Founded by a young entrepreneur who saw an opportunity in live performance, *Live from the Artist's Den* is a three-time Emmy-award-winning PBS program that marries recording artists with interesting and important venues. Be it Ani DiFranco at the Pennsylvania Academy of the Fine Arts in Philadelphia, Crowded House at the Masonic Hall Grand Lodge of New York, or Dierks Bentley at the Ravenswood Billboard Factory in Chicago, the Artist's Den presents musicians in venues that may be every bit as intriguing as their music, with selectively invited fans who relish the idea of hearing their favorite artist—and possibly being in a video, available for download at the Artist's Den website.

Live from the Artist's Den is presented evenings on over 50 local PBS stations each year and has been marketed, licensed, and syndicated by Turner Broadcast in cities around the world.

Market Segments

Music truly is the universal language, but it still maintains specific fan bases, regardless of crossover appeal. To demonstrate the changes that digital downloads are bringing to the business, we present a look at the most popular music segments of today. In Exhibit 9-6, note the differences between total album sales on the right and digital album sales on the left. You'll see that while total album sales might have slipped between 2011 and 2012, digital album sales rose.

Exhibit 9-6 Music Genre Sales, 2012[9]

Genre Total Album Sales (in Millions)			Genre Digital Album Sales (in Millions)		
Alternative	52.2	54.6	Alternative	26.7	24.4
Christian/Gospel*	22.9	23.7	Christian/Gospel*	5.3	4.8
Classical	7.5	9.4	Classical	2.6	2.3
Country	44.6	42.8	Country	11.2	8.1
Dance/Electronic	8.7	9.9	Dance/Electronic	4.9	4.8
Jazz	8.1	11	Jazz	2.5	2.6
Latin	9.7	11.7	Latin	1.4	1.1
Metal	31.9	31.9	Metal	11.2	9.6
New Age	1.7	1.9	New Age	0.6	0.6
R&B	49.7	55.3	R&B	16.3	14.8
Rap	24.2	27.3	Rap	10.7	9.3
Rock	102.5	100.5	Rock	43.1	36.3
Soundtrack	12.3	13	Soundtrack	6	5.4

In the late twentieth century, as marketers discovered the power of niche products throughout the entertainment universe, the various sectors of the music world saw heightening popularity for a variety of different styles and tastes. When music labels realized the vein of gold running through these segments, they began to mine them for all they were worth—a considerable sum, as it turns out. Niches such as Latin, Hip-Hop, Rap, Techno, and House Music joined old standards such as R&B and Jazz in maintaining not only loyal bases, but in many cases, cross-over appeal.

As the various niches took off, other more traditional segments followed the trend toward new marketing techniques. Classical music got sexier with a focus on such handsome young stars as Joshua Bell (violin) and Josh Groban, a talented singer-songwriter who crosses over from classical to pop.

Opera Hits a High Note

Speaking of crossing over from classical to pop, we have to make mention of Peter Gelb, who brought new revenue to Sony as the head of its American Classical division. At Sony, Gelb mixed cellist Yo-Yo Ma with Americana (country) music and classical singer Charlotte Church with pop. The soundtrack to the movie "Titanic," the highest-selling film soundtrack in history, was also produced under Gelb's watch.

In 2006, Gelb took over as the general manager of the Metropolitan Opera, as traditional a venue as one could imagine. In his six years there, Gelb has caused controversy with new productions

---

[9] The Nielsen Company & Billboard's 2012 Music Industry Report.

of long-time favorites—testing the theory that even bad press is good—but raised awareness of the Met significantly by creating Live from the Met, with live performances broadcast in high-definition to movie theaters and, more recently, PBS. The broadcast has been a stunning success, and most important, has given people around the world access to an art form previously entrapped in staid buildings and upper-crust conformity.

Jesus Saves and Also Sells

To the surprise of many in this age of high-profile, highly-sexualized recording artists, religion is the driver behind one of the most popular music genres: Christian music. Live and prerecorded, it is unabashedly dedicated to Christianity and the celebration of Jesus. Christian/gospel digital music sales were up 11.1% in 2012 over the previous year.[10]

On major TV stations and local channels—especially on Sunday mornings and during Christian holidays—fresh-faced, wholesome, conservatively dressed, and respectful young adults sing rock & roll, middle-of-the-road, pop, and other contemporary rhythms and lyrics that praise Jesus and thank God for all that is good. Lead singers are attractive stars in their own right, while the back-up singers are more a reflection of a church choir than a typical star's musical entourage.

This category of music is sold as major CD issues through chains of Christian book and religious gift stores throughout the country, driving huge increases in sales revenue. Billboard tracks the "Top Contemporary Christian" albums, including re-entry items such as Elvis Presley's *He Touched Me: The Gospel Music of Elvis Presley*. There are few returns to the labels—usually smaller, specialized companies like Word and Spring House (though big labels such as Atlantic do weigh in now and then in the category with hits as well)—since the music is evergreen and has no fad or timing issues. It is unique in the music industry to have a nonperishable product. In addition, the singers are frequently paid minimal salaries and do much of their own marketing and promotion in the service of their beliefs.

Though the strongest sales are in the Bible belt, Southern Baptist strongholds, national Christian shows like Crystal Palace build sales of the music across the country.

Repackaging and Compilations

What late-night TV viewer isn't familiar with the constantly scrolling, heavily over-voiced commercials touting music compilations? Though this segment has gone through the same shifts as the rest of the music business—including to digital downloads—it's still a viable business, proving that perhaps it is true: The music never dies.

Entrepreneurs such as Richard Foos and Harold Bronson, who founded Rhino Records but moved on to Shout! Factory, purchase the rights to or license for reuse a variety of music, then repackage it in themes: Hits of the '70s, '80s, '90s; Romantic Love Songs; Party Music; Beach Songs. There is something for everyone, regardless of age, race, or gender. Rhino, now owned by

---

[10] Nielsen.

Warner Music Group, has taken the concept one step further by offering videos and books as well as films that are creatively packaged collections of materials from the past.

Legacy Recordings, a division of Sony Entertainment, discovered the formula of reissue and repackaging, utilizing catalogs from Columbia Records and Epic Records and the archives of Sony Music's RCA, J Records, Windham Hill, RCA Victor, Arista, Buddah Records, Philadelphia International Records, and Sony BMG Nashville. Legacy has access to a vast amount of underutilized properties and has reissued division multi-CD sets featuring Frank Sinatra, Miles Davis, Louis Armstrong, Dave Brubeck, Billie Holiday, the great ladies of early jazz, and many more. Though the marketing behind these releases is minimal, the basic tactics are always vibrant, and the loyalty of customers to the basic brand pays off handsomely.

Soundtracks

The soundtrack genre owes its success and shares its parentage with the movie industry, though it also requires cooperation from the music business to flourish. Usually the process begins with the postproduction of a film and falls into the following categories:

- Nonmusical film, utilizing music to heighten the tension or underscore the action, explosions, and random special effects; genres include action-adventure, horror, science fiction, and romance, using music from the public domain or composed by leading film music professionals, such as multiple Oscar winner John Williams. Some of the hundreds of examples include classics such as *2001: Space Odyssey* and *Sleepless in Seattle*, which continue to sell, long past the release of the movie. An ongoing example is the carryover theme from the long-running TV series *Mission Impossible*, remade for the Tom Cruise *Mission Impossible* movies.

- Musical film, featuring singing and dancing with new or already written songs to fit the characterization of the acting. This category also consists of films made from Broadway shows. A recent example of this is the soundtrack to the 2012 release *Les Misérables*. It also includes animated movies like *The Lion King, Beauty and the Beast*, and *Tarzan*.

- Movies featuring a leading singer, such as Whitney Houston in *The Bodyguard*. These movies have songs written or reorchestrated specifically for the film, with additional tracks by other artists. *The Bodyguard* soundtrack is one of the best-selling albums of all time, having sold over 45 million copies since the movie's release in 1992.

- Blockbuster films that feature unique soundtracks. For example, the *Titanic* soundtrack, which consisted primarily of orchestral music and featured one song by Celine Dion, became a surprise platinum CD success with worldwide sales of over 30 million copies. During the movie's first incarnation, the widespread distribution of the CD, the radio play of the theme song, and the huge displays in retail music stores helped to promote and market an extended run of the film. When the film was rereleased in 3D, in 2012, the album was repackaged and enjoyed another run on the charts.

- Soundtracks for games. The soundtrack for *Halo 4* actually debuted at number 50 on the Billboard Chart when the game and the soundtrack were released in 2012.

Soundtracks have become a large revenue stream and an excellent promotion and marketing opportunity, including the use of film clips from movie trailers on YouTube. This enlarges the simultaneous marketing of the film, music CD, and digital download.

To take advantage of this opportunity, most film studios work closely with their music divisions; for example, Warner Bros. Studios with WEA, Sony Entertainment with Columbia Music, and Universal Studios with Universal/Polygram Music.

On occasion, music producers or A&R professionals are hired by film producers to locate or develop saleable and marketable music produced years earlier that evokes a certain nostalgia for a period or historical movie.

Ringtones

Back in the Dark Ages—three years ago, in techno-time—pundits were actually predicting that mobile music was on the way out. Part of this doom and gloom was piracy, and part of it was due to the drop in ringtone sales, as consumers figured out ways to "sideways download" their own ringtones, using the music tracks they were downloading. Ringtone sales, you say? Could there really be that much money in those? In 2008, ringtones accounted for over $700 million in mobile music sales. They did in fact, slip, to $167 million in 2012, still nothing to sneeze at.[11]

Musical Theater

Music is not limited to records, radio, downloads, or ringtones. For those who seek a live performance with a story to match, there's musical theater, and most specifically, Broadway musical theater.

Broadway Baby Gonna Make a Billion

Who would guess that this headline could ever have been possible? For decades, Broadway musical theater has been considered the poor stepchild of the entertainment industry, a musty old convention that only attracted die-hard aficionados or tourists in New York. After all, who would want to spend a small fortune to see a staged musical—sitting in cramped seats, with poor air conditioning and ridiculous lines to the loo—when you could sit in a giant arena and have your ears blown out by the likes of Bruce Springsteen or Lady Gaga?

But make no mistake: Broadway musicals sell in the billions (see Exhibit 9-7).

---

[11] "Whatever Happened to the Ringtone?", CNN iReport, May 9, 2013, www.cnn.com/2013/05/09/tech/mobile/ringtones-phones-decline/index.html.

Exhibit 9-7 The Highest Grossing Broadway Musicals, as of February 2013

Rank	Show	Gross	Avg. Ticket	Run	Performances
1	*The Lion King*	$932 Million	$87.56	1997 – Present	6,322
2	*Phantom of the Opera*	$890 Million	$43.63	1988 – Present	10,409
3	*Wicked*	$710 Million	$87.56	2003 – Present	3,846
4	*Mamma Mia*	$527 Million	$81.60	2001 – Present	4,683
5	*Chicago* (revival)	$454 Million	$67.35	1996 – Present	6,733

Source: www.broadwayworld.com

This is a sector of the entertainment business that evolved from the early years of burlesque, slap-stick comedy, and small Yiddish theater on the lower east side of Manhattan, fueled by a rather small community of die-hard thespians, chorus kids, and pit musicians who could not imagine life without eight performances a week. Broadway theater is six nights and two matinees a week, repeating the same lines, playing the same notes, over and over—and yet still delivering a fresh experience to every wide-eyed guest in the seats.

The beauty of live theater is the fact that every single performance is different from the last—perhaps not noticeably, but it is, after all, live—no lip-synching or recording. Certain shows are revived over and over: *Gypsy* has been staged on Broadway five times, including twice in the decade of 2001 to 2010. Each new cast brings a new interpretation. Fans will argue over the great-est Rose: Ethyl Merman, Angela Lansbury, Tyne Daly, Bernadette Peters, Patti LuPone.

It is truly a love affair with an art form, now a huge business.

All the World's a Stage

The live theater thought of as "Broadway" is a bit of a misnomer, given live theater today is rep-resented by three major centers: Times Square in New York City, the theater district in Toronto, Canada, and the ever-famous, age-old West End in London, England. But even this is only a part of the total U.S. and global live theater picture. Successful—and even not so-successful—Broadway regularly hits the road in national tours, criss-crossing the U.S. in what the actors and musicians refer to as bus-and-truck productions. Add to that the hundreds, if not thousands, of performances put on in cities across the country under contract or license agreements with the folks who own the IP.

Just as important are the regional theaters, where new productions are mounted, sometimes moving to Broadway after successful runs. This could include the productions that are meant as Broadway tryouts at the La Jolla Playhouse in California or the original plays staged by the Step-penwolf Theater in Chicago, a mother lode of recent Broadway transplants.

Now add the staging of these shows in global cities. Imagine hearing *Miss Saigon* or *Phantom of the Opera* in Mandarin, German, Italian, French, or Hebrew, performed by a country's very own best-of-the-best theatrical talent. All of these shows are also under contract with local producer/presenters under tight supervision by the content owners.

Broadway Basics

What qualifies as "Broadway" shows are staged in forty theaters in New York's Times Square theater district, stretching from 42nd Street to 53rd. To the north, straight up Broadway, the newly renovated Vivian Beaumont at Lincoln Center and the extraordinarily beautiful Alice Tully Hall feature wonderful entertainment. Broadway theater also includes three nonprofit theater companies: Roundabout Theater, Manhattan Theater Club, and Lincoln Center Broadway Theater.

In today's live theatrical business there is a close relationship between the venue owners and the producers, often being one and the same. Important names in theater ownership include the Nederlanders, the Shuberts, the JuJamcyn organization, the Dodgers, and that "new" upstart, the Disney Theatrical Group. The rock stars of live musical theater continue to be the hyphenate producer-writers-lyricists-composers like Andrew Lloyd Webber, Cameron Mackintosh, Tim Rice, Elton John, and others who have the longevity and passion for this form of entertainment.

Broadway is not for the faint of heart. Though not statistically reliable, producers claim that three out of five shows brought to the stage close soon after, never recouping the initial investments. But those other two go on to make millions for their producers and the investors, keeping performers, musicians, stage hands, dressers, and the rest of the crew in salary checks for years, sometimes—but not always—guaranteed by winning a Tony Award, Broadway's version of the Oscars.

Today's Broadway does have its challenges and controversies. What years ago could be staged and presented for small budgets (and even smaller salaries) turned into multimillion dollar sets with crashing chandeliers, descending helicopters, and sinking ships. A most recent incarnation, *Spiderman: Turn Out the Dark*, cost over $75 million to produce—more than some blockbuster movies—and featured as much drama offstage as on but has still gone on to attract an audience, despite high price-point tickets.

Productions now flout well-known Hollywood names such as Tom Hanks, Scarlett Johannson, or Julia Roberts in an attempt to guarantee bigger payback. This doesn't always happen, of course; not all film actors are meant to be on stage. The cost associated with hiring these stars—often at salaries that are far higher than what is paid to notable Broadway icons such as Patty LuPone or Boyd Gaines—drive up the overall cost of the production.

Producers are constantly trying to economize in other areas, including the union contracts with stagehands or musicians. There has been an ongoing effort by producers to utilize what is known as a "virtual orchestra"—read, taped music—in place of the musicians who toil in the pit. This seems completely incongruous. After all, should Broadway patrons be forced to pay hundreds of dollars for the type of show they might see in some town in the sticks? Broadway is about *live* performance, by the professionals who bring the experience to life. And trust us, there are very few musicians who are getting wealthy in this area of entertainment.

Every hit Broadway show now includes a stand near the front door, selling T-shirts, coffee cups, posters and soundtracks. Something to note: The sound you hear from a soundtrack often sounds richer and fuller than what you heard coming from the orchestra pit. Broadway theaters are governed by strict regulations calling for a certain number of musicians in particular theaters. The orchestras that fill these pits are smaller than the orchestras used to record the soundtrack. This was not always so; the famous musicals of the Lerner and Loewe or Rodgers and Hammerstein era featured large orchestras and lush sound. When *South Pacific* was restaged in 2008—the first time on Broadway since 1949—the producers chose to use a full orchestra. The rich sound welling up during the overture took many theatergoers by surprise. It was Broadway music as it was meant to be heard.

From Stage to Screen

There was a time when a hit Broadway musical was sure to make it on to the silver screen. Notable examples include *South Pacific*, *The King and I*, *My Fair Lady*, *Oklahoma*, *Camelot*, and *West Side Story*. These movies were often presented in theaters in a format that mirrored the stage production: a long overture and an intermission. But the practice slowed down in the later part of the twentieth century, as audience tastes (and Hollywood's appetite for risk) changed. However, musicals as movies are now making a comeback, including *Chicago*, *Mamma Mia*, and most recently, *Les Misérables*. And, just as with movies, soundtrack sales add to the bottom line.

From Screen to Stage

What's good for the goose is *sometimes* good for the gander. Certain movies have been made into musicals with great success: *Sunset Boulevard*, *The Producers*, *The Apartment* (on Broadway as *Promises, Promises*), *Monty Python and the Holy Grail* (on Broadway as *Monty Python: Spamalot*), *Mary Poppins*, *Hairspray*, and the current all-time winner in the highest Broadway gross category, *The Lion King*. But movie success does not always translate to the stage. Disney fans might think that *The Little Mermaid* would be a natural for the same stage success as *The Lion King* and *Beauty and the Beast*, but no. Adam Sandler-style comedy, *The Wedding Singer*, also had a very short life.

On with the Show

Broadway, like every other entertainment platform, depends on the massive marketing machine to bring it to monetized life. For musical theater, this includes newspaper ads, small boxes in the theatrical ABC listings, billboards, radio promotions, the occasional TV commercial, and appearances in the annual Macy's Thanksgiving parade.

Ticketing strategies include occasional two-for-the-price-of-one or discounted tickets for same day performances at the TKTS booths found in Times Square, South Street Seaport, and downtown Brooklyn. TKTS is operated by the Theater Development Fund and offers up to 50% discounts on tickets for those who are willing to wait in line just prior to curtain. Not all shows are represented, but the offering is well worth the wait. Broadway.com also offers online ticket sales. In addition, Broadway shows have their own websites, performers have twitter feeds, and Facebook is employed.

For national exposure, there's the yearly Tony Awards, which offers a vignette of each of the nominated shows, along with the national tours. More than one audience member has sought out "the real thing" after seeing a performance in their home town—and as well they should.

This is not to discount the efforts of those touring companies. Those hardworking professionals bring Broadway to life across the country and often wind up on the big stage themselves. But there's nothing like the experience of sitting in a Broadway theater. Each of these venues has a story of its own: the famous shows that played for years; the understudies that went on to stardom; the ghost lamp that lights every deserted stage, every dark night. Broadway is a living thing and takes a living audience to bring it to life. Do yourself a favor: Go.

Billboard: The Bible of the Business

It would be impossible to close this discussion of the music platform without mentioning *Billboard*, the best-known publication in the business.

Founded in 1894, *Billboard* originally served as a weekly for the billposting and advertising business but evolved into the source for tracking trends and talent. The publication is read by everyone from fans to top executives and stretches into all areas of the business: legal, distribution, retailers, radio, publishing and, of course, the digital domain.

After many years of logging various trends in the business, Billboard launched its Hot 100 chart in 1958, charting all segments of the music business. It is still the standard by which all music popularity is judged in the United States, regardless of genre.

Although *Billboard* still exists in print, the publication made the transition to the Internet in 1995 and now attracts ten million unique visitors each month in more than 100 countries.[12] The site features charts that are both searchable and playable, along with news, interviews, and video.

Summary

As a universal language, music reaches all ages, cultures, and countries and is found in every sector of the entertainment industry. Whether it appears as a movie soundtrack, a live event, in a downloaded video, over the airwaves, or on the Internet, music reaches listeners in a language all its own. Music serves as both a marketing tool and a marketed medium, driving a multibillion-dollar industry.

For Further Reading

Dannen, Frederic, *Hit Men: Power Brokers & Fast Money Inside the Music Business*, Vintage, 1991.

Krasilovsky, M. William, Sidney Shemel, John Gross, and Jonathan Feinstein, *This Business of Music*, 10th Edition (This Business of Music: Definitive Guide to the Music Industry), Billboard Books, 2007.

Lathrop, Tad, and Jim Pettigrew, *This Business of Music Marketing and Promotion*, Billboard Books, 1999.

---

[12] Billboard.com.

Lendt, Chris K., *Kiss and Sell: The Making of a Supergroup*, Watson-Guptill Pub., 1997.

Passman, Donald S., *All You Need to Know About the Music Business*: Seventh Edition. Free Press, 2009.

Thall, Peter M., *What They'll Never Tell You About the Music Business: The Myths, the Secrets, the Lies (& a Few Truths)*, Billboard Books, 2010.

Wixen, Randall, *The Plain and Simple Guide to Music Publishing*, 2nd Edition, Hal Leonard, 2009.

10

Major Leagues, Major Money: Sports

I n this chapter, we look at the many faces of sport as an entertainment. Perhaps nowhere else in the world of entertainment is the impact of marketing felt so strongly as in sports. The supposedly simple act of kicking, catching, dunking, or chipping a ball forms a complex multibillion dollar business, with only a fraction of that from gate admissions.

This Sporting Life

Sports crossed the line from athletic competition to entertainment long ago, combining the event itself with technology that beams it everywhere, creating massive fan bases that have no real geographic boundaries. And, as sports embraced entertainment, entertainment embraced sports, utilizing a rising "jockocracy" to fill the media's analyst booths, desks, and sport sidelines with retired players. Well-known icons from other entertainment platforms have become so associated with certain teams—Spike Lee with the Knicks; Jack Nicholson with the Lakers—that they almost appear to be part of the brand.

Unlike the movies, sports are not scripted. There is no certainty of who might win or lose, and that's what keeps fans in front of their HDTVs, smartphones, websites, or radios, hoping, praying, and buying retail merchandise—today, even as they are watching or listening. In no other platform is such blatant hero-worship universally accepted or expected.

But one thing is for certain: As a business, it's a home run.

Radical Reach

This chapter focuses primarily on sports in the United States, but there is no denying the global impact of sports. The National Football League (NFL) is televised in 231 countries. Major League Baseball (MLB) reaches fans in 200 countries, with huge fan bases in Japan and Latin America. The National Basketball Association (NBA) is seen in 205 countries, utilizing 129 broadcasters and 42 languages. Even NASCAR (the National Association for Stock Car Auto Racing) reaches 150 countries. These numbers only include what we know from a broadcasting perspective; with the addition of the Internet and mobile media, the reach is nearly unknown.

Sports, as a business, can be hard to pin to specifics given that most of the franchises are privately held businesses. Most of the leagues do not allow for publicly held companies, with the exception of the NFL's Green Bay Packers, originally owned primarily by residents of Green Bay who fought to save the franchise back in 1950. Disclosure is not required, and there can often be multiple business entities involved.

However, when all potential revenue and marketing spending is taken into account, at least one resource estimates the size of the entire sports industry in the United States to be worth over $435 billion, far larger than movies, music, or any of the other entertainment platforms (see Exhibit 10-1).

Exhibit 10-1 Sports Industry Overview

	Amount	Units	Year/Season
Estimated Size of the Entire Sports Industry, U.S.	$435	Bil. US$	2012
Annual Company Spending for Sports Advertising, U.S.	$28.60	Bil. US$	2012
Major League Baseball (MLB)			
MLB League Revenue	$7.70	Bil. US$	2012
Overall Operating Income	$432	Mil. US$	2011
Average MLB Team Value	$605	Mil. US$	2011
National Football League (NFL)			
NFL League Revenue	$9.50	Bil. US$	2012
Overall Operating Income	$979	Mil. US$	2010/2011
Average NFL Team Value	$1.04	Bil. US$	2010/2011
National Basketball Association (NBA)			
NBA League Revenue (Basketball-Related Income)	$4.30	Bil. US$	2010/11
Overall Operating Income	$175	Mil. US$	2010/11
Average NBA Team Value	$393	Mil. US$	2010/11
National Hockey League (NHL)			
NHL League Revenue	$3	Bil. US$	2010/2011
Overall Operating Income	$127	Mil. US$	2010/2011
Average NHL Team Value	$240	Mil. US$	2010/2011
Sporting Equipment Sales			
Wholesale Revenues, U.S. Sporting Goods Manufacturers	$77.30	Bil. US$	2011
Retail Sporting Equipment Sales	$41.50	Bil. US$	2012

	Amount	Units	Year/Season
Other Sports Industry Revenue			
NCAA Sports Revenue (Including Div. I, II and III)	$777	Mil. US$	2011/2012
Spectator Sports**	$33.90	Bil. US$	2012
U.S. Health Club Revenue	$21.40	Bil. US$	2011
European Health Club Revenue	$31.40	Bil. US$	2011
NASCAR Revenue	$629.70	Mil. US$	2011

Source: Plunkett Research, 2012

The Key Cs

If we were to separate the elements of the sports industry—particularly the business and marketing of this entertainment sector—we would divide them between content (the activity or event itself) and conduit (the medium by which it is presented, be it live, TV, cable, PPV, Internet, or mobile). Consumption is as complex as any aspect of the entertainment industry since it is segmented by type of sport, gender of spectator, and even socio-economic factors.

Convergence occurs across all platforms. Many, many successful movies have been based on sports, including *Any Given Sunday*, *Bull Durham*, *Field of Dreams*, *Remember the Titans*, *The Natural*, and a plethora of classics that focus on biography of sports heroes. Sports-based electronic games, especially *Madden NFL*, now just known as *Madden*, have been very successful. Radio sports talk shows draw a loyal listener base and are found in every major metropolitan area, as well as on satellite radio networks. Books about sports provide content for the development of other sectors, including TV series and theatrical releases, as well as just plain reading enjoyment for hardcore sports fans. Entire cable networks are now devoted to sports, including ESPN and Fox Sports, along with league networks, which we discuss later. Websites abound. Mobile applications are appearing daily.

In short, sports fans can get their fix at any moment of the day, anywhere they like—and they do, by the millions.

Key Revenue Segments

When discussing the business of sports, PricewaterhouseCoopers (PwC) defines four key segments that create revenue for the industry[1]:

- Sponsorships, which include payments to have a product associated with a team, league, or event and naming rights. This is the fastest growing revenue segment, offering the widest availability to potential investors.

---

[1] "Changing the Game: Outlook for the Global Sports Market to 2015," PricewaterhouseCoopers, December 2011, www.PwC.com/sportsoutlook.

- Gate revenue for live sporting events. This is the segment that has the most constraint on growth, given that it is dependent on facility size. Keep in mind that many of the sporting events covered are already sold out, thanks to enthusiastic fan bases. Weather is also a factor.

- Media rights fees paid to show sports on broadcast and cable television networks, television stations, terrestrial radio, satellite radio, the Internet, and mobile devices. As in other platforms, mobile spend is rapidly growing, along with Internet access.

- Merchandising, which includes the selling of licensed products with team or league logos, player likenesses, or other intellectual property. This segment is especially strong in North America. It is of special interest to individual athletes, whose contracts often stipulate a percentage of the merchandising rights.

PwC bases its U.S. forecast on the following major sports leagues: football (NFL), baseball (MLB), basketball (NBA), hockey (NHL), soccer (MLS), and collegiate athletics (NCAA). PwC estimates that this combined market will grow substantially between 2012 and 2015[2]:

- Gate revenues will grow from $15.9 billion to $17.8 billion

- Media rights will grow from $11 billion to $12.8 billion

- Sponsorship will grow from $13.4 billion to $16 billion

- Merchandising will grow from $12.7 billion to $14.3 billion

Total growth for these combined sports segments? $53 billion to $60.8 billion. That's a *lot* of fan investment. When considering the business as a whole, we must also consider the associated marketing spend for each of the segments, taking this forecasted growth well over $100 billion.

Let's take a look at each of the major sports.

Major League Sports

Each of the principle sports shares a common structure, including

- Leagues, run by commissioners and their staffs, setting rules to define the parameters for the competitions

- Franchises, which are also known as teams

- Players, who are hired, fired, and compensated by the owners and are governed by contracts

- Championship games that attract a global audience

---

[2] Ibid.

In the new Media Millennium, they also share a reliance on huge revenue from broadcast and cable TV contracts, league-owned websites, and a move into the mobile universe. But before we investigate the impact of entertainment marketing, let's take a quick glance at the major sports leagues.

Major League Baseball (MLB)

The first baseball team to field professional players was the Cincinnati Red Stockings in 1869. In 1867, eight professional teams formed the National League. Competing leagues sprang up and folded, but Ban Johnson's Western League seized on franchise territories abandoned by the National League in 1900 and began luring National League players with higher salaries. Renamed the American League, it also began drawing away fans. The two leagues agreed to join forces in 1903 by having their champions meet in the World Series.

Today, MLB is composed of 30 teams in 28 cities. These teams are all independently owned but follow the rules and organization of the league. The league itself is divided into two leagues: the American and National Leagues. The champions of each league, determined in post-season play that includes certain wild-card spots, face each other every October in the World Series. Teams play 162 games in a season that lasts from April to October. Spring training is held in March when the teams play games against each other in addition to practicing for the regular season.

Value

According to *Forbes*, the value of the average MLB team rose to $605 million in 2011. Cable television is driving part of this growth: Aggregate cable television revenue for baseball's 30 teams has increased to $923 million from $328 million over the past 10 years.[3] Cable's desire for live television has a decided impact on the values of teams. The most valuable teams, as of March 2012,[4] are as follows:

- New York Yankees: $1.85 billion

- Los Angeles Dodgers: $1.4 billion

- Boston Red Sox: $1 billion

- Chicago Cubs: $879 million

- Philadelphia Phillies: $723 million

Note that the values stated here do not take into account the 2012 blockbuster deal, valued at over $2 billion, for the Los Angeles Dodgers. With the Dodgers inking a $7 billion deal with Time Warner Cable in January of 2013, you can be sure these numbers will go up, substantially, across the board.

---

[3] The Business of Baseball, 2012," www.forbes.com, March 21, 2012.

[4] "MLB Team Values," www.forbes.com/mlb-valuations/list/, March 2012.

Though the teams have profited from media revenue, so have the players, as shown in Exhibit 10-2.

Exhibit 10-2 Top MLB Player Salaries, 2012

RANK	PLAYER	TEAM	SALARY	POSITION
1	Alex Rodriguez	New York Yankees	$ 30,000,000	Third Baseman
2	Vernon Wells	Los Angeles Angels	$ 24,187,500	Outfielder
3	Johan Santana	New York Mets	$ 23,145,011	Pitcher
4	Mark Teixeira	New York Yankees	$ 23,125,000	First Baseman
5	Prince Fielder	Detroit Tigers	$ 23,000,000	First Baseman
5	Joe Mauer	Minnesota Twins	$ 23,000,000	Catcher
5	CC Sabathia	New York Yankees	$ 23,000,000	Pitcher

Source: USA Today Salary Databases, 2012

Baseball has the highest attendance of all major league sports, but this is based on the high number of games played each season in stadiums with large capacities.

Media

MLB media reflects the burgeoning world of entertainment media. Although local stations still broadcast local games, Fox, ESPN, and TBS also have contracts to broadcast various games under certain conditions. It would be difficult for us to report the exact state of affairs of these contracts because they are all under discussion at this time. However, MLB has had a decided impact on broadcasting, with the debut of the MLB Network on January 1, 2009, as the largest launch in cable television history. The network is currently distributed in 70 million homes throughout the U.S. and Puerto Rico.[5] The network broadcasts over 150 games, including two exclusive post-season League Division Series games, along with a host of other content: the SiriusXM All-Star Futures Game and the MLB All-Star Game Selection Show (starting in 2014); the MLB First-Year Player Draft; *MLB Tonight* (seven days per week), and other regular season and offseason studio programming including *Quick Pitch, The Rundown, Intentional Talk, Hot Stove,* and *Clubhouse Confidential.*[6]

Several of the teams in larger markets either own or have large stakes in their own cable networks, including the New York Yankees (YES), New York Mets (SNY), Boston Red Sox (NESN), and Cleveland (STO).

Major league baseball also owns and maintains the MLB.com website, which, like all the major leagues websites, offers news, stats, merchandise, and links to ticketing.

---

[5] "MLB Network to Televise Postseason and Regular Season Game Programming Through 2021," www.mlb.com, October 2, 2012.

[6] Ibid.

National Basketball Association (NBA)

Dr. James Naismith, a physical education teacher at the International YMCA Training School in Springfield, Massachusetts, invented basketball in 1891, nailing peach baskets at both ends of the gym. He gave his students a soccer ball, and one of the world's most popular sports was born.

Today's NBA is made up of 30 teams in 28 cities. The teams are divided into two conferences, Eastern and Western, and play each other for the NBA championship in June. The regular season lasts from October to June, with each team playing 82 games. NBA attendance is around 20 million people per season.

Value

Forbes estimates the average worth of an NBA team at $509 million, a 30% increase over last year. This increase is due to higher revenue from television—a $930 million-a-year deal with ESPN and TNT that runs through the 2015–16 season—new and renovated arenas, and the NBA's new collective-bargaining agreement, which reduced player costs from 57% of revenue to roughly 50%. The NBA also has a structure in which high-revenue teams provide money to low-revenue teams. The NBA expects league-wide revenue to top $5 billion this year.[7]

The value of the top five teams are estimated as follows[8]:

- New York Knicks: $1.1 billion

- Los Angeles Lakers: $1. billion

- Chicago Bulls: $800 million

- Boston Celtics: $730 million

- Dallas Mavericks: $685 million

Players have seen associated rise in wealth, as shown in Exhibit 10-3.

Exhibit 10-3   Top NBA Salaries, 2012–2013

RANK	PLAYER	TEAM	SALARY
1	Kobe Bryant, SG	Los Angeles Lakers	$27,849,149
2	Dirk Nowitzki, PF	Dallas Mavericks	$20,907,128
3	Amar'e Stoudemire, PF	New York Knicks	$19,948,799
4	Joe Johnson, SG	Brooklyn Nets	$19,752,645
5	Dwight Howard, C	Los Angeles Lakers	$19,536,360

Source: ESPN

---

[7] "Billion-Dollar Knicks and Lakers Top List of NBA's Most Valuable Teams," www.forbes.com, January 23, 2013.

[8] "The Most Valuable NBA Teams," www.forbes.com, January 23, 2013.

The average price for a New York Knicks ticket is $117.47. An average LA Lakers ticket goes for $99.25. Biggest bargain? Memphis Grizzlies, at $22.95.[9] Considering that Grizzlies fans get to see those same expensive teams play in the Memphis home court, that's a steal.

Media

The NBA also has a variety of media outlets. TNT televises 52 regular season games plus the All Star Game. ESPN and ESPN2 broadcast up to 75 regular season games and 29 playoff games. ABC broadcasts 15 regular season and playoff games; that deal is worth $4.6 billion for 6 years, paying the NBA $765 million annually. In addition, as with the NFL, social media, mobile outlets, and websites abound. Time Warner formed a marketing alliance to promote NBA.com. In addition, NBA TV broadcasts 90 regular season games, HD, and some first round playoff games. There are no exclusive games; all are subject to local blackout. There is a potential partnership in the works with Turner, who runs all NBA websites and is a rights partner.

Smaller Salaries, Bigger Dreams: The Women's National Basketball Association (WNBA)

While NBA players are raking in the big bucks, their sisters in the Women's National Basketball Association (WNBA) are not, but it hasn't affected the grassroots popularity of this league. The 12 teams of the WNBA play from June to September, during the NBA off-season, and attract an audience that is more than 50% women. It serves as interesting form of marketing for the NBA. NBA TV broadcasts all WNBA national games.

National Football League (NFL)

Descending from the English game of rugby, American football was developed in the late 1800s by Walter Camp, a player from Yale University, who is generally considered the "Father of American Football." He is credited with beginning play from scrimmage, the numerical assessment of goals and tries, the restriction of play to 11 men per side, set plays, and strategy features that have led to the development of the game played today.

Today's NFL is made up of 32 franchises that play in two conferences: the American Football Conference (AFC) and the National Football Conference (NFC). The Commissioner of the NFL is Roger Goodell. Teams play a 4-game exhibition season running from early August to early September; a 16-game, 17-week regular season running from September to December or early January; and a 12-team single-elimination playoff beginning in January. The NFL Championship, also known as the Super Bowl, is played in early February. The NFL equivalent of the All-Star Game is the Pro Bowl, which is played in Hawaii at the end of each season. Most NFL players enter the league from college.

---

[9] "NBA Ticket Prices Rise for First Time in Three Years," NBA, **www.nba.com**, February 1, 2012.

Value

Forbes estimates value of the average National Football League team at $1.04 billion and average revenue for the league's 32 teams at $261 million.[10]

Estimated value of the top five teams are as follows[11]:

- Dallas Cowboys: $2.1 billion
- New England Patriots: $1.635 billion
- Washington Redskins: $1.6 billion
- New York Giants: $1.305 billion
- New York Jets: $1.284 billion

Salaries in the NFL are dependent on the salary cap, which is the absolute maximum each club may spend on player salaries in a capped year. The cap is set each year at a specified percentage of the expected NFL gross team revenue for the next year, as determined by the NFL's auditors. For the year 2012, the salary cap was approximately $120.6 million.

Player salaries in the NFL reflect the parity the league has been working toward for years. The NFL has been successful with spreading the talent across all markets by creating balanced league revenue streams, the salary cap, and an aggressive strategy in negotiating media contracts. That effort is reflected in this list of top player salaries in Exhibit 10-4, considering that both major and less-than-major markets are represented.

Exhibit 10-4   Top NFL Salaries, 2012

Rank	Player	Team	Salary	Position
1	Peyton Manning	Denver Broncos	$ 20,000,000	Quarterback
2	Nnamdi Asomugha	Philadelphia Eagles	$ 15,000,000	Cornerback
3	Tyson Jackson	Kansas City Chiefs	$ 14,720,000	Defensive End
4	Brandon Carr	Dallas Cowboys	$ 14,300,000	Cornerback
5	Jared Allen	Minnesota Vikings	$ 14, 280,612	Defensive End

Source: Spotrac

Super Bowl

The Super Bowl is by far the largest championship match in major league sports and has become an almost-national holiday in the U.S. Even those who could care less about the game itself may be drawn to the commercials, many of which are viewed for the first time during the broadcast,

---

[10] "The Business of Football," www.forbes.com, September 7, 2011.

[11] "The NFL's Most Valuable Teams," www.forbes.com, September 7, 2011.

although this is not as standard as it once was. In today's wired and wireless age, many advertisers trotted their Super Bowl ads out via social networking weeks before the game. The idea was to create pre-buzz before the Super Bowl post-buzz.

The Super Bowl has a huge economic impact. In 2013, for Super Bowl XLVII, 30 seconds of commercial time went for $3.8 million, generating an estimated $220 million overall.[12] The economic impact on New Orleans was estimated at $439.4 million.[13] The Nielsen Company put viewer estimates at 108.4 million, roughly half of which are women.

Media

Regular season games are broadcast on five television networks: CBS, Fox, NBC, ESPN, and the NFL Network. The NFL Network came to life in 2003 as a wholly owned subsidiary of the league, funded by a $100 million investment. Along with eight Thursday Night football games, the NFL Network produces commercials, television programs (such as Showtime's *Inside the NFL*), and feature films for the league, utilizing a huge library of game film.

Sunday games are split between CBS (AFC games) and Fox (NFC games). Monday night games are broadcast by ESPN. Sunday night games are shown by NBC, and are also televised in Spanish on Telemundo, reaching a large and loyal fan base.

DirecTV offers a subscription-based program, NFL Sunday Ticket, that allows viewers to watch a host of regional games, further broadening the NFL's fan base beyond local metropolitan areas. Other cable subscribers may have access to the NFL's Red Zone, depending on their carriers. Red Zone features all the highlights of all games, including all scoring.

The NFL also has wide broadcast radio coverage, including Global Radio Networks, Compass Media Sports Network, and Univision (in Spanish). Sirius/XM Radio also carries local broadcasts of games, as a separate subscription price over and above the base price of the satellite carrier.

Games are also available via the Internet and via mobile application, but there is a separate charge for this, via applications available from each franchise.

The NFL operates NFL.com, which offers everything from news to merchandise to ticket links and includes full access to a fascinating football phenomenon: the fantasy league.

Fantasy Football

Although fantasy leagues are present in all major sports platforms—links appear on the website of every major league sport—fantasy football is probably the best known with the widest participant base. Fantasy Sports Trade Association estimates that 75% of the 35 million fantasy sports participants engage in fantasy football.[14]

---

12 "Super Bowl Ad Prices Rise: Worth the Cost?," www.cbsnews.com, January 31, 2013.

13 "New Orleans Is Stepping Up Its Game for Super Bowl XLVII," www.forbes.com, October 9, 2012.

14 "The Business of Fantasy Football," www.foxbusiness.com, August 31, 2012.

Fantasy leagues operate in a parallel universe to the NFL, with participants drafting and managing teams of players. Just like the real managers, participants design their starting lineups on a weekly basis to match the upcoming opponent. Though there are several leagues, by and large they operate under similar rules, with teams choosing position players, offense and defense, and a kicker.

Fantasy football has become widely accepted by the league and its supporting members, especially the media. Links for fantasy stats abound on websites, including at NFL.com. Cable programs such as RedZone are highly dependent on fantasy participants. Estimates on revenue generated by the fantasy leagues hover in the $1 billion yearly range, including cable deals, advertisements, draft guides, buy-in fees, and various endorsements.[15] There are even insurance brokers who will insure a fantasy participant against injuries to players.

None of these estimates include the amount of money that exchanges hands from the gambling engendered by fantasy leagues. This is a very gray area in American sports, made grayer still by the fact that the leagues are, by and large, supporting the concept by placing links for fantasy leagues on their websites.

National Hockey League (NHL)

The NHL traces its heritage to 1893, when the Stanley Cup (donated by Lord Stanley, Governor General of Canada) was first awarded to the Montreal Amateur Athletic Association hockey club of the Amateur Hockey Association of Canada. The National Hockey Association (NHA) was the first professional league to award the Cup (a large silver chalice with a new layer added each year, passed to the winning team and engraved with the names of that team's players) in 1910.

Today's NHL is organized into 30 teams—24 in the U.S. and 6 in Canada. The Commissioner of the league is Gary Bettman. There are two conferences, the Western and the Eastern, with three divisions each. Each team plays 82 regular-season games in a season lasting from September to June.

Value

Hockey is a sport facing some major challenges in terms of parity. According to *Forbes* magazine, these are the five most valuable teams:

- Toronto Maple Leafs: $1 billion

- New York Rangers: $750 million

- Montreal Canadiens: $575 million

- Chicago Blackhawks: $350 million

- Boston Bruins: $348 million

These teams are worth $605 million, on average. The five least valuable—the Carolina Hurricanes ($162 million), New York Islanders ($155 million), Columbus Blue Jackets ($145 million), Phoenix Coyotes ($134 million), and St. Louis Blues ($130 million)—are worth just $145 million,

---

[15] Ibid.

on average.[16] This does not bode well for creating a consistent product across all markets, even though the league boasts an average 95.6% capacity and a raft of new sponsor deals, including Discover, Geico, Honda, the Las Vegas Convention and Visitors Authority, McDonald's, Paramount Pictures, Tim Hortons, Verizon, and Visa.[17] It does not help that the league failed to play over half of its 2012–2013 season due to a lockout.

Player's salaries may not be as large as those in other major league sports, but the athletes at the top aren't hurting (see Exhibit 10-5).

Exhibit 10-5   Top NHL Player Salaries, 2012

Rank	Player	Team	Salary	Position
1	Brad Richards	New York Rangers	$ 12,000,000	Center
2	Ilya Bryzgalov	Philadelphia Flyers	$ 10,000,000	Goaltender
2	Christian Ehrhoff	Buffalo Sabres	$ 10,000,000	Defenseman
2	Vincent Lecavalier	Tampa Bay Lightning	$ 10,000,000	Center
5	Sidney Crosby	Pittsburgh Penguins	$ 9,000,000	Center

Source: *USA Today*

Media

Hockey has not historically fared well on U.S. television. It is currently carried by the NBC Sports Network. Sirius XM satellite radio also carries games for an additional subscription fee. The league co-owns the NHL Network with Comcast, featuring separate programming for American and Canadian audiences. The NHL Network broadcasts 75 live games a year including Hockey Night in Canada from CBC.

Major League Soccer (MLS)

Soccer—known as football outside of the United States—is one of the world's most highly watched sports, with huge, passionate fan bases around the world. The World Cup, held every four years under the auspices of the Fédération Internationale de Football Association (FIFA), the international association that governs the global game, is watched by hundreds of millions, with entire countries celebrating the victory of their teams. But in the United States and Canada, where Major League Soccer exists as a league, the sport has long struggled to get off the ground.

We include it here to recognize the global value, even as fans see the possibility of rising popularity in the U.S. This is as much based on the changing demographic of the U.S. as it is on the rapidly multiplying youth leagues that seem to appear on every wide patch of grass in the suburban

---

[16] "NHL Team Values 2012: Toronto Maple Leafs Are First Hockey Team Worth $1 Billion," www.forbes.com, November 28, 2012.

[17] Ibid.

America. MLS counts on those kids, imbued with the game as their parents and grandparents were with baseball, to carry the business of domestic soccer forward.

Soccer as a whole has an interesting structure. Unlike other major leagues, which are associations of independently owned and operated teams, MLS is single entity, where each team is owned and controlled by the league's investors. There are 19 teams that operate in a Western and Eastern Conference structure. U.S. teams compete for the U.S. Open Cup.

Value

The 10 original MLS investors kicked in $5 million each to fund the league. Recent expansion fees have increased from $10 million to $40 million, expanding the valuation of the teams.[18] But for MLS to gain the economic stature of other leagues, it will have to hit the big-time media money, something that has not yet happened.

Players' salaries—for everyone other than big-time international stars like David Beckham, who plays for the LA Galaxy—are at the bottom of the barrel, with many earning less than $50,000. Even Beckham makes peanuts ($6.5 million) when compared to a fairly run-of-the-mill position player in major league baseball.[19]

Media

MLS media dollars reflect the under-the-radar status of the league, currently generating about $27 million in annual TV revenue.[20] The big challenge for MLS is the fact that U.S. soccer fans—often transplants from other countries, where soccer/football is a near religion—can slake their thirst by satellite, watching their home teams play, instead of the American product.

The National Association for Stock Car Racing (NASCAR)

NASCAR came roaring up from the backwoods of the South in the 1990s, stealing the hearts of millions of fans, driving up the value of racing, and creating a plethora of new tracks across the country. But NASCAR blew a tire somewhere along the way, with declining viewership over the last decade.

The good news for the business is this: The decline has stabilized. NASCAR seems to be back on the road to health. It is the second-most watched televised sport (after football), but viewership had declined for five years, from a 2005 high of 8.5 million. But 2012 numbers are up, back to 2009 levels of just under 6.5 million.[21]

---

18 "Sale of D.C. United to Billionaire's Son Values MLS Team at Record $50 Million," www.forbes.com, July 11, 2012.

19 "M.L.S. Salaries: A Bigger Pot, but Still Half Full," *New York Times*, May 26, 2012.

20 Ibid.

21 "Nascar Gets Back on Track," *Forbes* magazine, March 12, 2012.

There are currently 30 teams in NASCAR, operating in 40 states and 135 tracks. Top teams are valued at[22]

- **Hendricks Motorsports:** $350 million
- **Roush Fenway Racing:** $185 million
- **Joe Gibbs Racing:** $155 million
- **Richard Childress Racing:** $147 million
- **Stewart-Haas Racing:** $108 million

Media

NASCAR's recent rise in viewership may help in the all-important sponsorship negotiations—a key component of NASCAR revenue—along with upcoming contract talks for television. Fox has recently agreed to an extension, from $1.76 billion for its current eight-year deal, which expires in 2014, to $2.4 billion from 2015–2022. Other media partners are ESPN and Turner, but NBC also seems prepared to get into the mix as the network continues to widen its reach in live sports.[23]

The Rest of the Story

Sports in the U.S.—or the world, for that matter—are not only about major league teams. The sporting universe has several other planets orbiting the big leagues.

Collegiate Sports

Although colleges around the country offer all sorts of sports, when we talk collegiate, we talk football, the powerhouse money-earner that often funds most or all of the other sports on any given college campus. Yes, there are great college basketball teams, but the fact is, that sport is driven by individuals who mostly have "one and done" careers in college. They opt for the NBA after playing the requisite one year at State U. College football, with its huge rosters, holiday bowl games, and now the controversial Bowl College Series (BCS) fabrication supposedly put in place to crown a national champion of sorts. It has a wide fan base that desires heavy media coverage.

College sports are a huge business all their own. Consider the data in Exhibit 10-6 regarding the athletic departments at the top 10 revenue earning schools.

---

[22] "The Most Valuable NASCAR Teams," www.forbes.com, March 12, 2012.

[23] "Fox, NASCAR Agree to Eight-Year, $2.4 Billion Contract Extension for Sprint Cup Races," www.aol.sportingnews.com, October 15, 2012.

Exhibit 10-6 Top Ten Colleges / Athletic Revenue

School	Conference	Revenue	Stated Expenses
Texas	Big 12	$150,295,926	$133,686,815
Ohio State	Big Ten	$131,815,821	$122,286,869
Alabama	SEC	$124,498,616	$105,068,152
Florida	SEC	$123,514,257	$107,157,831
Michigan	Big Ten	$122,739,052	$111,844,553
Penn State	Big Ten	$116,118,025	$101,336,483
LSU	SEC	$107,259,352	$91,796,925
Tennessee	SEC	$104,368,992	$97,580,406
Oklahoma	Big 12	$104,338,844	$94,363,928
Auburn	SEC	$103,982,441	$100,497,784

Source: *USA Today*

Where does it all come from? Gate revenue, of course (minimally). Then there's the media revenue, driven by television contracts, which in this day and age includes conference networks, like the Big Ten Network, jointly owned and operated by the Big Ten conference, and Fox Sports. Recently, conference switching has been all the rage; the Big Ten now has 12 teams happily sharing in the network revenue, while the 16-team Big East is now the Big Least, with 7 schools leaving. These teams left because they did not have football teams but have excellent basketball teams, which could form the basis of a new television network of its own.

Colleges benefit from sponsorship dollars as well as licensing. Bowl games, with the attendant media coverage, primes this pump significantly. Consider the history of Louisiana State University (LSU) and its participation in the BCS Bowl Championship Series: Prior to winning its first BCS championship in 2003, the school's licensing revenue had never exceeded $1 million. After winning the title, the Tigers' licensing income jumped 208% for the 2003–04 fiscal year, to almost $3 million. By the time the Tigers won again in 2007, they were grossing more than $5 million in licensing.[24]

The Olympics

The Olympics are for amateurs, except when they aren't. Today's Olympics include professional sports people who compete on national teams, basketball being the big draw. The Olympics might not generate revenue for the athletes—at least, not until afterward, when they may decide to drop their amateur status and cash in on licensing and sponsorships—but they do generate revenue for the networks that cover them, albeit not always enough to cover expenses. NBC paid $1.2 billion to cover the 2012 London Olympic Games and was reported to have broken even on the deal.

---

[24] "For BCS Winner, Licensing Boom Is Just the Start," www.sportsbusinessdaily.com, January 9, 2012.

Economic impact on the community can be a hard thing to judge, although estimates are always rosy. Londoners, however, did not fare well during the 2012 Summer Games. The organizing committee and the city spent huge amounts of time and dollars to inform people how to negotiate the central city, expected to be a mob scene. However, the powers that be did such an excellent job that central London was mostly a ghost town during the Games, resulting in a bust rather than a boom for hospitality and retail businesses located downtown, including London's famed West End, the heart of the theater district.

Individual Sports

Individual sports feature passionate fan bases as well as wide media coverage and intriguing, well-paid stars. Both professional golf and professional tennis have gained more exposure over the last decade, although golf has remained more popular in the public eye, at least from a television share perspective.

The economic impact of golf is huge. All of us duffers out there swinging (and sometimes cursing) drive an economy that has an estimated value of nearly $69 billion.[25]

Here's a fun fact that you may not know: the Professional Golfers Association (PGA), golf's overarching association, long ago established an interesting business model. It encouraged PGA Tour events to be set up as charities, returning net proceeds to the communities that hosted them. The staff at these events are mostly volunteers. This charitable status opened the door for wider corporate sponsorship, which not only funded the purses, but paid for a good portion of the television time,[26] creating a self-supporting media relationship. The sponsors get the benefit of aligning themselves with a charity, while getting their name (Honda Classic, AT&T Pebble Beach Pro-Am, Wells Fargo Championship) repeated over and over. Ah, repetition, the soul of advertising.

Cable television has blown the doors off the individual sports world, allowing for wide coverage of sports some of us didn't know existed. For example, we're willing to bet that you didn't know NBC Sports offers 29 (yes, you read that right, *twenty-nine*) sports fishing shows—and that's *just* NBC. Just like in the ads for Ginsu knives or the music compilations hawked on late night infomercials, a browse through the Internet for fishing shows seems perfect for a pitchman yelling, "But wait! There's MORE!!"

There *is* more. According to a new study, America's nearly 60 million anglers spend $48 billion per year on fishing equipment, transportation, lodging, and other associated expenses, generating a total annual economic impact of $115 billion. The industry supports over 828,000 jobs and generates $35 billion in wages and $15 billion in federal and state taxes. And when the going gets tough, the tough go fishing: Despite the economic difficulties in the U.S. economy over the past five years, the total amount spent on sportfishing, which encompasses tackle, travel, and other equipment, grew 5%.[27]

---

[25] "Golf 20/20: The 2011 Golf Economy Report," SRI International, October, 2012.

[26] "The Business of Golf: Beyond Tiger," *The Economist*, June 9, 2011.

[27] "Sportfishing in America: An Economic Force for Conservation," the American Sportfishing Association, January 2013.

Other highly popular sports include boxing, mixed martial arts, and extreme sports, as exemplified by the X Games, owned and controlled by ESPN, which features a series of contests that seem to balance on the possibility that someone could break their neck at any moment, doing the kinds of things mothers used to stand guard against.

Like the professional athletes who play team sports, professional individual sports stars often have the opportunity to grow wealthy from their pastimes/businesses. But rather than try to delve into the ever-changing specifics of who the recent heroes might be, it's more appropriate for the purposes of our discussion to focus on how that wealth is earned—not just for individuals, but for teams. This, after all, is the basis of this book: entertainment marketing, so let's get on with that fascinating side of the business.

The Business of Brands: Licensing and Sponsorship

One of the main thrusts of marketing is brand building, and sports are no exception to that rule. Through a combination of winning records, winning personalities, and hitting the jackpot in media rights, licensing, and sponsorships, sport brands add to their bottom line value (which includes actual holdings—stadiums and other real property—along with all revenue streams) with the often hard-to-specify sheer value of their brand. In the business world, when entities are bought and sold, this amorphous amount is called "good will." In marketing, it's known as brand value.

Forbes magazine uses an interesting set of factors to determine the brand value of what it calls its "Fab Forty,"[28] the most valuable brands in four distinct areas. The figures quoted in Exhibit 10-7 are the additional value a strong brand adds to the worth of a business, event, individual, or team.

Exhibit 10-7   Forbes Fabs: Top Brands in Sports

Rank	Brand	Brand Value
Businesses		
1	Nike	$15.9 billion
2	ESPN	$11.5 billion
3	Adidas	$6.8 billion
Events		
1	Super Bowl	$470 million
2	Summer Olympic Games	$348 million
3	FIFA World Cup	$147 million

---

[28] "The Forbes Fab 40: The World's Most Valuable Sports Brands," www.forbes.com, October 17, 2012.

Rank	Brand	Brand Value
Athletes		
1	Tiger Woods	$38 million
2	Roger Federer	$29 million
3	Phil Mickelson	$26 million
Teams		
1	New York Yankees	$363 million
2	Manchester United	$293 million
3	Real Madrid	$255 million

Source: Forbes

"Brands" have been described as everything from objects of love to religion, but in any case, brands offer a customer a type of emotional support in making buying decisions. Sometimes this support comes from the desire of the customer to identify with the brand: "Tiger Woods uses these clubs; they will help my game," or "If I use these clubs I will be more like Tiger." It's a complex assessment and a very personal one, but branding is a huge part of strategic revenue building.

Licensing

For athletes and teams—always cognizant of protecting their brands—one of the ways that results in higher revenue is through licensing. Leagues and franchises sell all sorts of products with their names and logos attached, everything from key chains to stadium seats removed from historic stadiums. The revenue for this merchandise, bought by a passionate fan base, is astounding, totaling $12.79 billion in 2011.[29]

Here's a look at how licensing revenue broke down by league in 2011[30]:

- **Major League Baseball:** $3.1 billion

- **National Football League:** $3.0 billion

- **Major League Soccer:** $394 million

- **National Basketball Association:** $2.0 billion (this, during a lockout that cut the season in half)

- **The National Hockey League:** $887 million

- **NASCAR:** $887 million

Collegiate licensing revenues rose to $3.32 billion during the same year.

---

[29] "Sports on the Rebound: Retail Sales of Licensed Merchandise Based on Sports Properties Rises 5.3% in 2011," The Licensing Letter, EPM Communications, Inc, June 2012.

[30] Ibid.

Endorsements

Endorsement occurs when an athlete licenses his name to be used as a type of testimonial for a product or service. This could be something directly related—Peyton Manning/Gatorade—or not related—Peyton Manning/MasterCard. The product or service hopes that customers, both present and potential, will link the qualities of that star with its product or make the emotional leap connecting the two.

Endorsements are a gigantic pot of gold for athletes. Consider the numbers in Exhibit 10-8 and how endorsements are often a far larger portion of overall earnings than salary or winnings.

Exhibit 10-8 Top Athlete Earnings with Endorsements[31]

Athlete	Sport	Salary / Winnings	Endorsements	Total Earnings
Manny Pacquiao	Boxing	$56 million	$6 million	$62 million
Tiger Woods	Golf	$4.4 million	$55 million	$59.4 million
LeBron James	Basketball	$13 million	$40 million	$53 million
Roger Federer	Tennis	$7.2 million	$45 million	$52.7 million
Kobe Bryant	Basketball	$20.3 million	$32 million	$52.3 million
Phil Mickelson	Golf	$4.8 million	$43 million	$47.8 million
David Beckham	Soccer	$9 million	$37 million	$46 million
Cristiano Ronaldo	Soccer	$20.5 million	$22 million	$42.5 million
Peyton Manning	Football	$32.4 million	$10 million	$42.4 million
Lionel Messi	Soccer	$20 million	$19 million	$39 million

Source: Forbes

Sponsorships

Sponsorship occurs when a company pays to have its name associated with a team, individual, or event. This is done not only to extend brand awareness, but to deepen the emotional ties with the fan base in hopes of increasing revenue for the company's products or services.

Sponsorship continues to provide an increasing source of revenue for sports. Pricewaterhouse-Coopers estimates that by 2015, sponsorship will actually overtake gate as the largest source of revenue for sports.[32]

---

[31] "The World's Highest Paid Athletes," www.forbes.com, June 8, 2012.

[32] "Changing the Game: Outlook for the Global Sports Market to 2015," PricewaterhouseCoopers, December 2011, www.PwC.com/sportsoutlook.

But the question is always out there: What real impact does sponsorship have? A recent survey conducted for SportsBusiness Journal/Daily by Turnkey Sports & Entertainment[33] produced some interesting results. Among many results, the Major League Soccer Sponsor Loyalty survey demonstrates

- The number of fans who correctly identified AT&T as an MLS sponsor was three times higher than the number of fans who thought Verizon had the league's wireless rights—despite the fact that Verizon holds a slightly greater market share of U.S. wireless subscribers than AT&T.

- Visa, MLS's official payment services partner since 2007, had a 39.8 percent overall recognition rate in 2012, the highest mark for any credit card in the history of the survey across all leagues. More than 44% of avid fans recognized the relationship, the highest rate of any of the league's sponsors among avid fans.

- Anheuser-Busch, an MLS sponsor since the league's inaugural 1996 season, had its best survey ever, netting 38.3% of fan mind-share, a year-over-year increase of 13 percentage points.

Although this data is specific to soccer, other surveys have shown similar results for other leagues and teams. Live sports reaches avid fans, and avid fans support their teams—and those products and services associated with those teams.

Naming Rights

Naming rights is a practice by which corporations assign their names to stadiums, arenas, and other facilities for a specific length of time. From a marketing perspective, it creates great exposure for the brand, as the name of the stadium appears in all advertising, during game broadcasts, and even from the signage, visible to passersby day and night. It is a lucrative deal for the owners of the facilities, which in many cases may be team owners or municipalities.

The practice can occasionally backfire when a company goes out of business or faces some sort of public challenge that a team would prefer not to have associated with its brand.

Exhibit 10-9 provides a sampling of recent deals made for naming rights. Keep in mind that this covers just a few; there are 72 U.S. facilities that utilize naming rights.

Exhibit 10-9 Top Ten Naming Rights Deals

Stadium Name	Sponsor	Home Teams	Avg. $/Year	Expires
Phillips Arena	Royal Phillips Electronics	Atlanta Hawks, Thrashers	$9.3 million	2019
FedEx Field	Federal Express	Washington Redskins	$7.6 million	2025
Bank of America Stadium	Bank of America	Carolina Panthers	$7 million	2024

---

[33] "MLS Partners Run the Table in Fan Recognition," *Sports Business Daily*, December 10, 2012.

Stadium Name	Sponsor	Home Teams	Avg. $/Year	Expires
Lincoln Financial Field	Lincoln Financial Group	Philadelphia Eagles	$6.7 million	2022
American Airlines Center	American Airlines	Dallas Mavericks, Stars	$6.5 million	2031
Invesco Field at Mile High	Invesco Funds	Denver Broncos	$6 million	2021
Minute Maid Park	Coca Cola	Houston Astros	$6 million	2030
Staples Center	Staples	Los Angeles Lakers, Kings, Clippers, Sparks	$5.8 million	2019
FedEx Forum	Federal Express	Memphis Grizzlies	$4.5 million	2023
Gaylord Entertainment Center	Gaylord Entertainment	Nashville Predators	$4 million	2018

Source: ESPN

Technology Trends

Like all other entertainment marketing platforms, sports is highly involved in the use of new technology to reach its audiences. As demonstrated earlier, each of the leagues has a complex website, offering fans a deep reach into everything they need to know or want to buy, at least in terms of league-licensed merchandise. The sites offer the ability to get that merchandise up for sale quickly—memorabilia for championships (League Championships, World Series, Super Bowl, NBA Championship, Stanley Cup, you name it) is available literally seconds after the game is over, creating a wonderful opportunity for impulse buying.

Social Media

Social networking, such as Facebook pages for all major sports and sports stars, is also a huge part of the mix, allowing fans what appears to be a closer interaction with their favorites than ever before. Fans can join a global community even as games are being played, posting their thoughts and comments online, whether through Facebook or the team's own website.

Teams reach out to fans, staying top of mind, even when the season is over, with email blasts and Facebook posts regarding off-season moves such as trades, contract negotiations, schedule updates—whatever might connect with the fan.

Many teams have taken the social connection one step further, launching "fan ambassador" sites that connect with fans through exclusive media releases and game play.[34] The Indianapolis Colts have the Colts Stampede; the Detroit Pistons have Fast Break. Fans can earn points by sharing

---

[34] "Social Media: Rewards Programs Sprout Up," www.espn.go.com, November 30, 2012.

information and gain recognition/status as their names climb up the leaderboard. Remember our discussion on this back in the gaming chapter? What better place to link games with consumers than through sports, a natural fit.

Other examples of reaching out through social media include the U.S. Olympic Basketball team posting pictures—just like any other tourist—on Instagram. And who could forget (or get the song out of their head) the various teams, including the U.S. Olympic swimmers, that posted YouTube videos of themselves lip-synching/acting out Carly Rae Jepson's "Call Me Maybe?" Or Linsanity, the craze that erupted across the social media universe when Jeremy Lin, an unheralded New York Knicks benchwarmer, suddenly became the star sensation?

And then there's Twitter, a mixed blessing if ever there was one. There was a time when people were urged to think before they spoke, but this doesn't seem to apply to Twitter—perhaps because tweeters aren't thinking of it as speech. Whatever the case, the rapid deployment of one's inner thoughts and feelings doesn't always make for good fan relationships, and all leagues are now concentrating on making sure that players—and team/league employees—understand the potential damage that can be wreaked at any given moment.

Mobile media is huge in the sports world, as it is everywhere else today. Apps abound for the die-hard fan. Every team has apps that connect the fan with stats and info, and many allow the fan to tune into radio broadcasts for a fee. Every major network aligned with sports broadcasting—ABC, NBC, CBS, Fox, ESPN—has not just one, but a variety of applications ready to be downloaded to smartphones and tablets, allowing for everything from stats, videos, league trackers, and fan interaction to fantasy league play.

Social Stadiums

The public's fascination with all things smartphone has had an impact in another area. Stadiums, filled to the brim with people checking email, watching replays, tweeting, posting on Facebook, and listening to play-by-play, are being forced to upgrade the technology they might have only recently installed.

Technology provider Cisco recently announced StadiumVision Mobile. The following is taken directly from the release[35]:

> When integrated with an in-venue app, the solution delivers live video and data feeds with minimal delay and offers multiple channels of unique content such as a replay channel, an alternate-view channel (a view of the bench during timeouts), and a data channel (for stats, trivia contests and multi-player games). These options create a more interactive and personalized experience and open business opportunities for the venue and teams through targeted advertising, sponsorship activations, promotions, branding and more.

Increasing the overall in-stadium fan experience is an important issue in sports; gate receipts are still a huge part of revenue. With new stadiums adding luxury boxes, private clubs, special

---

[35] "Cisco Introduces StadiumVision Mobile," Cisco press release, February 1, 2013.

upgraded seating sections, and personal seat licenses—essentially an additional fee layered on top of your season ticket cost—teams are making a big effort to keep fans coming to the stadiums.

Consider the NFL: After peaking in 2007, the NFL has faced declining ticket sales. 2012 saw a slight increase, to an average paid crowd of 67,579, but still on the downside of 2007's 69,661. (re-did footnote 36 with new source).[36] This could be due to many factors, not the least of which is the excellent experience of watching football on television. Today's technology allows for a thoroughly analyzed, well-tracked game featuring instant stats and graphics that clearly describe the current position of the ball, along with great replays. Even though there are still teams, such as the Green Bay Packers, that boast a loyal fan base that continues to brave the coldest weather, stadiums by and large must find new ways to draw crowds. The stadium experience is key to the health of league sports.

Old Media: Cable Deals

Speaking of television, let's take another look at a chart we reviewed in Chapter 5, "The Rising Tide of Technology: Television Content Delivery in a Digital Age." All of the money we've been discussing in this chapter comes from somewhere, and a good portion of it comes from the media rights negotiated with cable providers. Take a look at Exhibit 10-10.

Exhibit 10-10   Recent Major Sports Cable Deals

Deal	Amount ($Billions)	Date	Term (Years)	Increase over Prior Deal
CBS/Fox/NBC–NFL	$28.0	12/15/2011	9	63%
ESPN–NFL	$15.2	9/8/2011	10	73%
Fox/Turner	$6.8	10/2/2012	0	100%
ESPN–MLB	$5.6	8/8/2012	8	100%
ESPN–BCS	$5.6	11/21/2012	12	100%
Time Warner Cable–LA Lakers	$3.0	2/14/2011	20	400%
ESPN/Fox–Pac 12	$3.0	5/4/2011	12	320%
Fox–LA Angels	$3.0	12/8/2011	20	200%

Source: Will Richmond, "80 Billion Reasons Why Pay-TV Will Become Even More Expensive," www.videonuze.com, 2012.

Teams, leagues, and athletes might be getting wealthier by the minute, but it's the fan that is paying the price. The TV deals you see posted here will be coming out of your pocket, whether you watch sports or you don't. In some areas, this can amount to as much as $3 to $5 on your monthly cable bill. But as we've discussed, live sports is one of the last bastions of live TV, a platform that allows for the traditional advertising that helps pay for programming. After all, how many people

---

[36] http://espn.go.com/nfl/attendance.

truly wish to DVR a game, other than for convenience? In most cases, the avid fan will already know the outcome, and that takes all the fun out of the experience.

New Deals from Existing Players

The importance of live sports is also reflected in the continuing evolution of new sports channels, especially among the recognized leaders of sports coverage. This includes

- **ESPN:** ESPN2, ESPN Classic, ESPN News, ESPN Deportes (in Spanish), ESPN U, ESPN 3
- **Time Warner:** Turner Sports, TNT, TBS, RSNs
- **Fox Sports:** Fox Sports RSNs, Fox Sports Net, Fox College Sports, Fox Deportes (in Spanish), Fox Soccer Channel
- **Comcast:** RSNs, Versus (rebranded NBC Cable Sports), the Golf Channel
- **CBS:** CBS College Sports (originally CSTV) rebranded (again) to CBS Sports Network

Marketing Challenges

Any form of relationship marketing (sponsorships, licensing, endorsements) has an inherent risk associated with it. Should the athlete be found doing something controversial, or worse yet, illegal, the product or service associated runs the risk of being tarred with the same brush, or at least gets a negative response from the audience. If the league or owners do something perceived to not be in the interest of the fans, ticket sales take a beating. Sports marketing professionals have a wide variety of challenges they must face with speed and decorum.

Strikes: Marketing Backlash

Of the many issues that can create havoc for the sports marketing executive, the one that generates true panic is a players' strike. When well-paid, well-perked athletes decide to strike for increased pay, it becomes a strong negative image for everyone involved. Player strikes typically evoke little sympathy from fans, few of whom share in the athlete's lifestyle.

The result can be an economic blackballing of the teams and the leagues, with fans voting with their pocketbooks and staying home, at least for some period of time. Sports, after all, is about brand management, and fan relationships are a big part of that. Though sports fans tend to be some of the most loyal consumers, the ever-widening gap between rich and poor can lead to a situation in which the fan stops identifying with the team. This situation is exacerbated by the free agency that has resulted in the constant change of players, leaving little "team" left to root for.

Steroid Scars

In 1994, prompted by Major League Baseball owners' decision to unilaterally restrict free agency and withdraw salary arbitration, the players started a 232-day strike, which caused the cancellation of the entire post-season, including the World Series. Play resumed in 1995 when the owners and the MLBPA approved a new collective-bargaining agreement.

The strike had a deleterious effect on baseball. National media coverage fed the growing rancor of the fans, who threatened to stage their own strikes, staying away from the game. With the golden goose near death, the owners resuscitated the commissioner's office, electing one of their own—Bud Selig—as the game's ninth commissioner.

Fans continued to show their displeasure but returned in droves in 1998, when Mark McGwire and Sammy Sosa battled it out for Roger Maris' 37-year-old single-season 61-home run record. The fans and the press were transfixed, watching each at-bat with breathless anticipation. McGwire, muscles bulging, powered his way to 70 dingers, and the national crowd went wild. Later that year, MLB signed a new six-year, $800 million TV contract with ESPN. Sport-tainment was born, with owners and players now receiving riches for their role as entertainers.

Records continued to fall in the next several years, as one bulging player after another took a swing at a legend, building big stats for huge new contracts or extensions. But this era is now marked by much controversy, given the discovery that steroids and other performance-enhancing drugs had played a big role in the races. Purists argue that the MLB turned a blind eye to the problem to rebuild revenue. The players are paying the price. Sosa, McGwire, and several others have been denied access to the Hall of Fame, with many doubting that they will ever be seriously considered.

Performance-enhancing drugs are found in all types of sports, at all levels. A huge debate continues about the problem, with some saying that drugs are a sort of new technology, a boon that allows all athletes to perform at higher levels, while others point to the risks, including early death, which can result from their use.

The bottom line is that for the present, they are illegal, and each time a player is found to have been using them, scandal erupts, fans shake their heads, and sponsors back away. Lance Armstrong's 2013 admission that he used performance-enhancing drugs during his Tour de France days cost him his reputation and an estimated $75 million, losing deals with Nike, Anheuser-Busch, Radio Shack, Oakley, and Trek Bicycle Corp., his major sponsors.

Player (Mis)Behavior

Sports executives must also deal with the individual athlete's transgressions off the field, another type of minor or major earthquake that can send sponsors flying. But the sports sponsor is an odd duck, and many athletes have weathered financial storms. Kobe Bryant makes an additional $32 million annually from an endorsement portfolio of global brands including Nike, Smart Car, Panini, and Turkish Airlines—this in spite of settling a high-profile sexual assault case in 2003 before the case went to trial.[37]

Right or wrong, it seems that time and distance heal many of the sponsors' scars. Is it good for the health of sports? Hard to say. It does seem to be good for the health of sports *business*. One challenge in all of this lies in the fact that modern-day athletes have based the argument for higher earnings on the fact that *they* are the entertainment. If that's the case, it would seem that there

---

[37] "Kobe Bryant Sexual Assault Case," Wikipedia, http://en.wikipedia.org/wiki/Kobe_Bryant_sexual_assault_case.

needs to be an increased recognition that all those concerned—players, league, coaches, owners—have a responsibility to those who wish to be entertained and who pay admission.

One recent dustup in the NBA came about when Coach Gregg Popovich chose to send four of his top San Antonio Spurs starters home for a rest instead of playing them on a nationally televised game with the Miami Heat—the only game the Spurs would play at Miami during the 2012–2013 season. The Spurs had an upcoming home game with the league-leading Memphis Grizzlies, and Popovich wanted them ready for that game. The league wound up fining the Spurs $250,000 for their (in)action.

David Stern, possibly more than any other commissioner in sports, understands that his is an entertainment product and that the fans expect to see the stars play. He expressed his displeasure in this statement[38]:

> The result here is dictated by the totality of the facts in this case. The Spurs decided to make four of their top players unavailable for an early-season game that was the team's only regular-season visit to Miami. The team also did this without informing the Heat, the media, or the league office in a timely way. Under these circumstances, I have concluded that the Spurs did a disservice to the league and our fans.

In other words, those stars and coaches are being well paid as the entertainers they claim to be, and the league's stance is that they must perform.

Summary

From the major leagues to soccer, golf, polo, tennis, bowling, fly fishing—nearly any sport imaginable—sports hold a valuable place in the integrated marketing of entertainment content. The loyal fan base of each sport is a ready and willing target for a wide variety of sponsorship, licensing, and merchandising opportunities, as well as convergence with other forms of entertainment, including television, movies, and games. Most important, sports offer an inroad to all ages, races, socio-economics, and genders.

For Further Reading

Davis, John A., *The Olympic Games Effect: How Sports Marketing Builds Strong Brands*, John Wiley & Sons, 2012.

Lee, Jason W., *Branded: Branding in Sport Business*, Carolina Academic Press, 2010.

Rein, Irving, *The Elusive Fan: Reinventing Sports in a Crowded Marketplace*, McGraw Hill, 2006.

Shank, Matthew D., *A Strategic Perspective* (4th Edition), Prentice Hall, 2008.

---

[38] "NBA Fines San Antonio Spurs $250K for Resting Stars," *USA Today*, December 1, 2012.

11

On the Road: Travel and Tourism

ravel and tourism are two key revenue generators in the economy, adding nearly $1 trillion to United States coffers alone. But more than any other platform, travel and tourism rely on relationship marketing—the good word of others—to generate great results. Marketing professionals must be highly aware of all the factors influencing the consumer's decision. In a world where one destination is looking increasingly like every other, the approach to this product must be carefully strategized, hitting all the motivating factors.

In this chapter, we examine the key components of marketing to travelers, while examining the wide variety of destinations that draw visitors in droves.

Travelin' On

To some, the terms "travel" and "leisure" have absolutely no business being anywhere near one another in a sentence. To these people, the concept of travel is fraught with missed airplanes, fleabag hotels, and skies that never offer anything but a constant downpour. But in spite of the little glitches here and there, the public still seems willing to pack their bags and get onboard—heading to hotels, resorts, theme parks, ski slopes, islands, cruise ships, casinos, and cities large and small—thanks to great marketing and promoting the fact that most successful destinations work hard to offer the wonderful experience they promise.

Whatever motivates the choice, travel and tourism—integrated with the hospitality industry—represent an important growth sector for the U.S. economy, so much so that the current administration has thrown considerable resources into launching an initiative to grow this industry, the Task Force on Travel and Competitiveness. The task force, co-chaired by the Secretary of the Interior and the Secretary of Commerce, has published the *National Travel & Tourism Strategy*.[1] According to this report

---

[1] *National Travel & Tourism Strategy*, Task Force on Travel & Competitiveness, 2012.

- The leisure and hospitality sector is the fifth largest employer in the United States and one of six priority sectors likely to drive domestic employment growth over the next 10 years.

- In 2011, real travel and tourism spending (adjusted for changes in pricing) grew 3.5%, outpacing the 1.7% growth rate of the economy as a whole.

- U.S. and international travelers spent $807 billion, generating $1.2 trillion in total economic activity and supporting 7.6 million American jobs.

- The United States received more than 11% of global spending on travel and tourism, with 62 million international visitors who generated travel and tourism exports of $153 billion, lowering the trade deficit by $42.8 billion.

Add the data found in Exhibit 11-1 into the mix, and you have an industry that is not only projected to grow, but could be a key factor in restarting a lagging domestic economy.

Exhibit 11-1 Travel Expenditures and Visitors, U.S., Domestic, and International

Measurement	Unit	2011	2012	2013	2014
Total travel expenditures in the U.S.	Billions	$817	$851	$893	$933
U.S. residents	Billions	$704	$728	$762	$797
International visitors	Billions	$113	$123	$131	$137
Total international visitors to the United States	Millions	61.8	64.9	67.9	70.7
Total domestic person trips	Millions	2,005.9	2,043.1	2,089.2	2,137.1
..Business	Millions	453.2	459.3	466.5	474.5
..Leisure	Millions	1,552.6	1,583.8	1,662.7	1662.7

Source: Travel Forecast Summary, United States Census Bureau, September 30. 2011

But before we all join in on *Happy Days Are Here Again*, it needs to be noted that travel and tourism pose some intrinsic challenges to marketers, the chief being inconsistency. Bad weather or bad employee attitudes—or, heaven forbid, both—can lead to bad experiences for dream-seeking guests. When you add the rest of the possibilities—strikes, change in the value of the dollar, political upheaval, rise and fall of crime rates—you begin to see the peculiarities of travel and tourism marketing. Good marketing offers the promise of customer satisfaction, but the actual satisfaction must come from the experience itself.

This challenge of inconsistency is the great difference between marketing travel and other types of entertainment, which, barring a sore throat for Lady Gaga or stale popcorn for *Iron Man*, tends to deliver what you paid for.

In any case, building a successful strategy for destination entertainment requires a specific approach.

The Promise of Paradise

Although other entertainment platforms create mental transportation for consumers, the travel and tourism business is all about actually going there, affording the guest something other than her day-to-day life: relaxation, leisure activity, possibly some form of personal renewal. Marketing and sales efforts must tantalize consumers with factors that best meet the consumer's objectives, which might include convenience, location, amenities, sports and recreation, emotional and physical assets, and packages that are priced well.

But this is a crowded and intensely competitive arena. Remember that you are vying for one thin slice of your customer's time. Your offering must be better than anything else he or she might choose—including doing nothing. To do this, you must understand the three potential motivators for travel:

- The wish to visit someplace exotic or different
- Stimulation and the gathering of new knowledge
- The pursuit of a hobby

Some destinations strive to meet all of these motivators: Think Walt Disney World, with its parks, golf courses, the foreign allure of EPCOT, the intellectual stimulation of the Disney Institute. But for the most part, creating a strategic plan for a travel destination will find you focusing in on a narrower field of options. And while you and your team are doing that, you'll have your own set of challenges in creating a plan that works, including

- The number of constituencies that must pass judgment on the strategy and tactics, including advertising, PR, and promotions
- Subjective evaluation by management with little or no experience in marketing or the ability to judge the merits of effective advertising
- The need to react to many external and uncontrollable issues, including economics, crime, poverty, violence, and political instability

Marketing to prospective tourists is an exciting, volatile, creative, and extremely rewarding pursuit that offers enormous financial returns when it is done well. But it does take a careful approach so that your clients secure their share of the vacation pocketbook.

Building the Plan

The marketing of travel and tourism must hit three levels of decision-making: impulse, planning, and dreaming for another day. Done correctly, marketing will entice all parties at all levels. But enticement is only half the battle; once the happy traveler reaches his or her destination, the dream must be delivered, full on. Doing so builds repeat visits and great recommendations to friends, family, and social networking sites such as Trip Advisor or Kayak. This level of satisfaction is only achieved when the guest arrives with clear expectations.

Keep in mind that the final success in this industry is based on the customer's experience. Marketing professionals must understand the strengths and weaknesses of their product to match the traveler's expectations with reality. Failing to do so can result in a wildfire of negative word of mouth.

After the motivator most closely associated with the potential consumers of a product or destination is identified, the plan to reach those consumers should be built on the traditional basics: research, strategy, and marketing to desire.

Know Thy Destination: Research

You cannot create an effective marketing plan for a destination if you don't know that destination yourself. Research is critical in

- Identifying the lifestyle of the prospective vacationer for the product.
- Assessing the discretionary budget required to pay for the trip.
- Matching expectations with core advantages.
- Recognizing the media considered most frequently by the target customer as credible sources of vacation information.
- Defining how destinations deal with travelers of varying abilities, a consumer segment with very special needs.

Simply put, not every traveler wants (or can afford) to spend a week at the Ritz-Carlton. Some may prefer a grass shack at the edge of the beach, where loud Hawaiian shirts are the dress of the day—and night. Your job is to match the destination with the correct client base.

The best research of a destination is done through an actual site visit. One of the perks of the travel and leisure industry is what is known as a *fam trip*—a familiarization trip, offered to qualified professionals to initiate them into the unique attractions and characteristics of a particular destination. This intra-industry marketing tool—a respected and classic motivation and appreciation reward system—is often offered at no cost to travel agents, travel writers, and marketing professionals. There may occasionally be a small fee attached to weed out those who might be more interested in their own travel than in creating a unique selling proposition for the destination.

One special note: In doing site research on more exotic locations or those where there are potential issues of danger or unpleasant surprises, researchers might want to bring a professional guide or tour leader along to prevent mishaps.

There are many other ways to gather information for communications campaigns and target audience identification. Every sector of the travel and leisure industry has a particular approach to gathering and evaluating data.

- Conde Nast does continuing surveys with its readership.
- Credit card companies, especially American Express, invest heavily in research and tourism marketing to capture discretionary budgets for vacation travel.

- The magazines people read/use for travel information send out reporters to compile editorial and visual content that hopefully qualifies and reinforces the image their advertisers present.

- Every hotel, cruise line, travel agency, and time-share company of substance has a visitor survey that gauges customer satisfaction, complaints, and attributes that make for positive or negative reactions.

- Advertising agencies use leading research firms to gain insights into the positioning, slogan, and image that best represents an idealized version of the site being sold.

- Travel agents, now under pressure to prove their relevance as consumers turn to the Internet for information and travel bookings, rely on the American Society of Travel Agents (ASTA), which has developed proprietary studies over the years.

Even the smallest of locations, once they have identified the type of tourist that is attracted to their location, might do some rough, inexpensive focus group research to gain responses to proposed ads and radio commercials. There are also numerous travel consultants, usually former convention bureau executives or marketing directors for destinations, airlines, and hotel chains, who offer their services to prepare research.

In addition, there are academic journals that offer thoughtful approaches to researching the needs and wants of the potential consumer. The *Journal of Travel Research* and the more recently established *Journal of Vacation Marketing* (JVM), from Henry Stewart Publications in London, provide considerable support for travel research methodology. Some of the research papers presented in JVM include "Evaluating Vacation Destinations Brochure Images," by Annette Pritchard and Nigel Morgan; "How to Develop a Strong Hotel Branding Strategy with a Weak Branding Budget," by Hugh Taylor; and "Methods Used by Airlines to Determine Ticket Prices," by Janice Chapman. The JVM is available online at http://jvm.sagepub.com/.

Positioning

Having researched the destination, we must now focus on positioning it among the thousands of other choices. In the very competitive arena of travel and leisure, a location's image and its halo effect are critical elements of differentiation.

Travel destinations fall into one of three basic images: positive, negative, or neutral. Many locations enjoy positive positioning due to movies and the media consistently celebrating their positive attributes—think Paris or Rome. Others might not be so fortunate; travel packages to the Middle East are a tough sell in the early part of the twenty-first century. Subjective as these images may be, it is important to consider them when preparing a marketing plan, for if the image is basically negative, no amount of expensive marketing strategies will be cost-effective. Unfortunately, the image might never be resolved or improved, even if it is due to a misperception or some perceived flaw.

If, on the other hand, the image is neutral, the game is wide open. This blank slate offers a huge opportunity to build on. For years, the island of Aruba and the city of Philadelphia had little or no image. Marketing their strengths and adding to their infrastructure enabled them to become destinations of choice. Aruba became known for rain-free holidays and easy access to casinos. Philadelphia created events like "The Book and The Cook," 10 days of best-of-show house tours, and an expanded promotion of the most successful flower show outside of Chelsea Gardens, England.

The ever-evolving tastes of travelers have helped many far-away places become hot boutique destinations. Environmentalism brought us eco-tourism, which in turn brought cross-promotion with National Geographic, which now offers green vacations to Brazil, Kenya, and Belize, among other exotic locations. The rise of extreme sports created demand for heli-skiing and extreme surfing.

The Importance of Integration

When addressing positioning, integrated marketing communications become important in creating message consistency and affordable impact on the consumer's decision-making process—both conscious and unconscious. At every level, the standard of excellence in achieving the desired positioning for a location requires working with the same strategy, the same goals, and the same presentation of the image in every media and at every contact point with all audiences. This is imperative when trying to expand the consumer base or to reposition an existing destination.

A great example of this is Las Vegas. Once known as "Sin City," Las Vegas actually used the lingering whiff of adult-oriented entertainment to build itself into one of the primary convention markets in the country. However, its mid-1990s effort to broaden its base by promoting itself as a center of family entertainment almost backfired, when adults started to avoid the locations on the Strip that offered child-oriented activities. Las Vegas not-so-quietly returned to its roots with its "What Happens in Vegas, Stays in Vegas" approach, refocusing on its image as a theme park for adults. By the way, what's played in Vegas also stays in Vegas. Sales tax, hotel tax, casino gaming, and restaurant and bar taxes all have a local component that goes directly to support the marketing effort of the city, all adding up to a sizable number: $115 million in 2012.[2]

The integration of an umbrella image and individual tactical outreach—with individual emotional motivators—might not have an immediate impact, but they help to implant an image for future planning. Advertising, direct marketing travel agent communications, PR, booklets, brochures, contests, and hospitality messages must be consistent, utilizing repetition to build a strong message. It is then that delivery on the promise is important. To sustain tourism growth, the destination *must* also market the program internally as well as externally. Buy-in from the client is critical. If the store clerks, hotel staff, restaurant waiters, tour guides, and thousands of locals who derive their income from tourism are resentful, feel put upon, dislike meeting and greeting visitors, or are sending out negative interchanges based on culture, politics, race, or religion, the marketing plan is doomed.

---

[2] "Tourism Marketing and Management," *Houston Chronicle*, http://smallbusiness.chron.com/tourism-marketing-management-43669.html.

Advertising, Publicity, and Promotion

Travel and tourism form a specialized niche in the marketing world. Many communication consultants or advertising executives who have managed multimillion-dollar budgets for leading packaged goods companies, automotive brands, and leading retail chains have no understanding at all of this major category.

The Role of the Agency

The marketing managers of hotel chains, resorts, island destinations, cities, countries, cruise lines, leisure airline travel, and ski slopes tend to seek out specialized boutiques with prior experience. Thus, the chicken and egg syndrome is alive and well in this segment, with the inevitable musical chairs as one specialized agency loses Jamaica and picks up Barbados, or the loss of Delta is replaced by the arrival of United Airlines.

But these agencies know how to overcome the problems of crime, corruption, anti-Americanism, terrorism, typhoons, monsoons, and government instability. Advertising and marketing budgets may be cut or eliminated for a period of time until the new government cabinet or long-suffering local business community decides to run a "come back to Paradise" campaign. Then the PR machinery begins to spin stories about the reduction of the pre-existing problem and how peace and safety have returned.

Though it might sometimes seem difficult to be truly innovative in the marketing of travel—the "beauty shots" of sand, sea, and sky all seem to look like one another—the professionals who populate this sector occasionally find intriguing ways to do so. Those best equipped to do so often come from the travel industry or have trained at universities specializing in the practice like the Cornell University Hotel Management School and the Culinary Institute of America (CIA) in upstate New York, which are both accredited schools in the industry. In addition, some agencies sponsor client research, analyze, and evaluate the results and make intelligent recommendations. Most notable are several agencies in Florida, including Crispin Porter + Bogusky and YPartnership (formerly known as Yesawich, Pepperdine, Brown & Russell).

It's best to update your scorecard on the players and their professional communications agencies in any given season frequently, as moves are made as often as government cabinets change and marketing directors are replaced. No new broom sweeps cleaner than the tourism advertising business.

Creating an Identity

To be a draw for tourism, a destination (large or small) must have a focus, an identity. Familiar identities range from the simple "Virginia is for Lovers," to the extreme with New York as "The Entertainment Capital of the World," to the sublime such as "Paris, the City of Lights." Every destination wants to compete for attention, and the discretionary vacation budget eventually strives for the marketing equivalent of a selling proposition or unique sales claim.

Here again, external factors can wreak havoc on long-standing identities. If you said the words "New Orleans" prior to 2005, your mind might fill with images of Bourbon Street, the French

Quarter, Mardi Gras, and great Cajun and Creole food. Post Katrina, the city was left with shots of grief, despair and chaos from the Superdome to the Ninth Ward. But it was tourism—aided by pictures of happy travelers in an intact French Quarter—that helped bring the city back, actually breaking records in 2011.[3]

Destinations with a successful tourist trade almost always share certain attributes:

- Extensive and varied lodging accommodations
- A variety of dining choices, including a unique regional cuisine
- Shopping
- Wide selection of activities for all ages
- Architectural wonders and/or cultural destinations (museums, for example)

But above all is at least one identifying characteristic that makes the destination—big or small—worth a trip: its own unique personality. The challenge to the travel and leisure marketing professional is to find that voice and then shout it to the world through product branding, market positioning, and delivering on guests' expectations.

Following are a few examples of destinations that have successfully marketed their unique personalities.

Nashville, Tennessee

Nashville was still a relatively sleepy regional city when the Grand Ol' Opry first started broadcasting out of Ryman Auditorium. The sounds emanating from radios across the hills and hollers of Tennessee lured many a picker and grinner, their eyes focused on stardom. Before long, acts such as Minnie Pearl, Patsy Cline, and Hank Williams found a national following, which unleashed a river of talent flowing right back to the source. The city spawned spanking-new music studios and bus tours of stars homes. It wasn't long before television realized the potential of that audience, and The Nashville Network (TNN) was born. Nashville is now the "Country Music Capital of the World."

Along with the traditional methods of destination marketing, Nashville has a strong showcase in the Country Music Awards, which give the viewer a great sense of the attractions in the city. Additionally, the Country Music Association (CMA), which markets country music stars as an important ingredient in contemporary brand promotions, sponsorships, and licensing arrangements, sponsors a three-day conference every year in Nashville for opinion leaders and marketing professionals. A great mid-sized convention center lures business travelers happy to take part in a little down-home atmosphere.

Nashville also realized that tourists visiting music destinations want to hear great music, from blues, to country, to gospel. There are several U.S. cities where this can happen. In the spirit of

---

[3] "New Orleans Tourism Breaks record in 2011," *New Orleans Times Picayune*, March 27, 2012.

co-opetition—in which natural competitors draw strength from one another by creating mass to drive visitation—Nashville joined New Orleans and Memphis to form a marketing package called The U.S. Music Trail Tour.

Also included in that partnership is a tiny town in Missouri: Branson.

Branson, Missouri

High in the hills of Southern Missouri, in the middle of the Ozarks, sits a town of 10,520 full-time residents that has become a music tourism mecca. Branson serves up to 70,000 visitors daily, all of whom pump almost $2 billion dollars annually into the local economy. The town has over 40 theaters with more than 60,000 theater seats, 175 lodging facilities with over 18,000 rooms and 200 restaurants with over 38,000 seats. It is a destination of choice for visitors from a rectangular slice of America that runs north to Minneapolis, east to Chicago, west to cities all across Texas, and south to Arkansas.

Branson is an example of the primacy of proper targeting of age, religion, race, and socio-economic demographics. Every single week, 10 months per year, buses, vans, and shuttles arrive with visitors who fall into the following demographic categories: average age of 60 plus, retired, high school education, mostly blue collar occupations, generally white Christians who enjoy packaged vacations. They purchase five or six nights of relatively inexpensive tickets, head to the all-you-can-eat buffets, target the discount shopping, and revel in the chance to talk to the performers whose names light up the marquees of Branson.

These entertainers either own their own multimillion state-of-the-art theaters or have naming and exclusive performance rights with long-term contracts. Once primarily focused on Andy Williams, Jim Stafford, Tony Orlando, Bobby Vinton, John Davidson, Kenny Rogers, Yakov Smirnoff, Wayne Newton, and Charlie Pride, Branson now features many of those same entertainers, along with everything from the Acrobats of China to a Titanic Museum.

Tourism revenue from Illinois, Minnesota, Nebraska, the Dakotas, and other distant locations gets to Branson due to its marketing success. The fleet of huge, 40-ton buses parked discretely at the edge of each theater represents access for well over 65% of the visitors. For 30 years, the bus companies have actively marketed in their own geographic areas and are definitely responsible for the origins of the early visitors and today's long-distance audience.

Branson is a terrific example of the power of marketing. The roots of this entertainment phenomenon are in a local theme park, Silver Dollar City. As the park developed its following and people became familiar with Branson, the entertainment offering increased, taking advantage of a visitor population that was left with little to do after theme park closing hours. As the selection of venues grew, the city leadership decided to form a Branson Marketing Committee, operating separately from the Chamber of Commerce. They named an experienced marketing executive as the Director of the Marketing Committee to work with all the theater, motel, restaurant, and themed attractions. He in turn hired an experienced PR professional. The PR plan was to get a major story about this unique location placed nationally. In 1990, the town was featured on 20/20—primetime television—and the rest was music, and marketing, history.

Austin, Texas

Visitors arriving at Austin's Bergstrom International Airport are greeted with signs in the jetways and banners across the airport lobby that make the claim that Austin is "The Live Music Capital of America."

Greater Austin, with a population of slightly under a million people, is driven chiefly by a large university (University of Texas), a large community college (Austin Community College), and software and hardware manufacturers like Dell Computer, Motorola, IBM, and Advanced Micro Devices.

The average Austin resident and business visitor is young, educated, and ready to be entertained, and Austin's Sixth Street is the place he or she heads. Much like Bourbon Street in New Orleans, this area is a strip of music nightclubs and restaurants featuring jazz, rock, blues, country, and other varied forms of entertainment. The several hundred venues range from open-mike bars to bookstores/coffee shops, full-scale nightclubs specializing in blues, rock, and country, to huge venues featuring national and international roadshows. The city's daily newspaper, *The Austin American Statesman*, has a regular Thursday insert, Xlent, that covers nothing but entertainment, particularly live music.

Each year, the city celebrates its self-proclaimed status by hosting a week-long music festival, South by Southwest (SXSW). The festival brings thousands of visitors to the city and presents an opportunity for performers to be discovered by agents and producers. In the synergistic tradition discussed throughout this book, this entertainment event spawned a sister SXSW film festival, growing in importance and popularity each year.

Big Cities, Big Challenges

There are locations throughout the world that have become self-propelled marketing machines— cities that are so intimately connected with entertainment that it would seem that marketing these destinations would be a slam dunk. However, the question of "guest perception" certainly had an impact on two of the premier entertainment cities of the U.S.: Los Angeles and New York.

Los Angeles

Mention the initials "LA," and entertainment junkies around the world will immediately conjure up visuals of palm trees, Beverly Hills, sunny beaches, and movie stars. More specifically, they target Hollywood. From the fifty-foot-high letters in the Hollywood Hills to the pressed-in-cement footprints outside of Mann's Chinese Theater, the images and icons of Hollywood are burned into minds around the globe. In fact, "Hollywood" is one of the most widely recognized brands in the world. Mention the word anywhere, and anyone who has ever seen a movie, whether in a 1,000-seat state-of-the-art theater or projected onto a bed sheet, will know what you are talking about—at least how they perceive it.

And that was the perplexing part of the Los Angeles brand. In the words of Dorothy Parker, when it came to this major destination, there was no "there" there—at least the "there" so many visitors seem to expect. Visitors to Los Angeles often left disappointed, especially when searching for a movie mecca. An ambitious "Hollywood and Highland" project was launched years ago, but the only feature of any note is the Dolby Theater, where the Oscars are held every year. The surrounding area still has little else other than some shops, a wax museum, and down the street, Mann's Chinese Theater. Other than that, it quickly shifts into less than interesting surroundings.

Los Angeles finally turned to its most important business, using entertainment to renovate and upgrade the city's image. LA Live, a multiplatform entertainment destination, was built adjacent to the Staples Center, reinvigorating the entire area. The 27-acre site features bars, restaurants, a multiplex cinema, concert theater, ESPN Zone and studio, apartments, condos, and a Ritz Carlton hotel. The Grove, a retail/entertainment development adjacent to the historic Farmers Market at Third and Fairfax, gave tourists a destination shopping area other than tony Rodeo Drive. And of course the studios, with back-lot tours and Universal's CityWalk, have upped the amperage for fun.

Sports remain an important draw, with the Lakers and Clippers and the Dodgers. Soccer enthusiasts have the LA Galaxy. The city is also actively seeking the return of an NFL football team.

New York

New York City had a problem: Times Square, the so-called "Crossroads of the World," had disintegrated into a gathering place for pimps, prostitutes, hustlers, drug addicts, muggers, and assorted other nontourist types. But still the tourists came, looking for a fantasy that had been burned into the collective consciousness, through fading black-and-white shots of V-J Day Celebrations and smoke rings emanating from the Camel cigarette sign.

In a fabulously successful clean-up campaign in the last decade of the twentieth century, Times Square took a 180-degree turn back toward glamour. Developers razed porno shops and refitted theaters that had drifted to XXX films. Disney bought the New Amsterdam Theater, once the home of Florenz Ziegfield's reviews (and in the roof garden, notorious parties) and did a stunning renovation, building a home for their theater division. The entire area became a key tourist destination that actually reflected the glitz tourists were looking for.

The city's constant exposure through various forms of media and entertainment continues to drive tourism. Many New Yorkers (and not all of them happy, by the way) point to this clean-up as the genesis of New York's grime- and crime-reduction, which has brought a new verve to the city, with rock-star chefs creating empires of extended brands, newly renovated museums, sports teams in all major leagues and—well, just all that is New York, the most Some and the biggest Where in world.

The Dynamics of Travel and Tourism Marketing

Like every other entertainment platform we've discussed, travel and tourism have felt the impact of the Internet. Travel and tourism, being relationship-based in general, benefits from a huge social networking link. The simple fact is this: People like to talk about their travels, and social networking gives them ample opportunity.

Social Networking

In a report prepared for interactive digital marketing agency Stikky Media, author Stacey Santos presents the following aggregated data on social media in tourism,[4] demonstrating the incredible rapport between tourism and technology.

Mobile Usage

By 2015, 9 out of 10 consumers will have a mobile subscription.

- 29% of travelers have used mobile apps to find flight deals
- 30% have used mobile apps to find hotel deals
- 15% have downloaded mobile apps specific to upcoming vacations
- 85% of leisure travelers use their smartphones while abroad
- 72% post vacation photos on a social network while still on vacation
- 46% check in to a location (for example, Facebook and FourSquare) while on vacation
- 70% update their Facebook status while on vacation

Top Five Uses of Smartphones While Traveling

- Take photos
- Use map features
- Search restaurants
- Search activities and attractions
- Check in prior to flight

Consumer Trust

- 92% of consumers around the world say they trust earned media, such as word-of-mouth and recommendations from friends and family, above all other forms of advertising, an increase of 18% since 2007.
- 70% of global consumers say online consumer reviews are the second most trusted form of advertising, an increase of 15% in four years.
- Only 47% of consumers around the world say they trust paid television, magazine, and newspaper ads, and confidence has declined by 24%, 20%, and 25% respectively since 2009.

Despite these numbers, the majority of ad dollars are still spent on traditional or paid media.

---

[4] "2012 Social Media and Tourism Industry Statistics," Stacey Santos for Stikky Media. Ms. Santos cites her sources as: The World Travel Market (WTM) Industry Report and Global Trends Report; Nielsen: Global Consumers' Trust in 'Earned' Advertising Grows in Importance; Lab42: Techie Traveler; Facebook Key Facts; TripAdvisor Fact Sheet.

Reviews

Post-vacation, 46% of travelers post hotel reviews.

- 40% post activity/attraction reviews

- 40% post restaurant reviews

- 76% post vacation photos to a social network

- 55% "liked" Facebook pages specific to a vacation

Influence

Social media has a huge influence on travel bookings. Of those who used social media to research travel plans, only 48% stuck with their original travel plans.

- 33% changed their hotels

- 10% switched resorts

- 10% changed agents/operators/websites

- 7% vacationed in a different country

- 5% switched airlines

TripAdvisor

- 69 million monthly visitors.

- More than 60 million travel reviews and opinions from travelers around the world.

- More than 90% of topics posted in the TripAdvisor forums are replied to within 24 hours.

Destinations around the world now sport TripAdvisor decals and ask guests to review them. In turn, TripAdvisor encourages contributors to keep right on commenting, awarding "badges" and assigning status levels, a very seductive way to get travelers to build the site and app.

In addition, social media has allowed individual businesses—small and large resorts, bed and breakfasts, tour operators—to present themselves to an ever-widening group of travelers, presenting photographs, rates, room layouts—nearly anything the inquiring traveler might need to make a decision. With social media, Il Cardo Resort, a lovely Tuscan inn near Anghiari, Italy, can reach potential customers across the globe. The Pelham Hotel, a fabulous boutique hotel in London, is now visible to potential clients who might never have known of its existence. In travel and tourism, the consumer is king, and the Internet is the key to the kingdom.

However, as we have warned in every chapter, social networking can be both a boon and a bust. Good news may travel fast, but bad news spreads like lightning. When you add the warp speed of the Internet, the need to carefully integrate marketing with reality becomes ever more apparent. If all the reviews feature words like "terrific" or "fabulous," the guest isn't likely to expect rude or dilapidated. In the relationship-heavy travel and tourism sector, image—and delivery—are everything.

Ta Ta to the Travel Agent?

The arrival of the Internet, as in every other platform, has wreaked havoc on existing business models—in this case, the travel agencies.

Back in the old days—about a decade ago, although it feels as if we might be talking about *Mad Men* time—travel agencies were important partners to airlines, railroads, bus companies, cruise lines, hotels, resorts, and theme parks. A travel agent was a sole-source supplier for the American dream of going on the road. Housed in offices across the country, the agents of American Express, Carlson Wagonlit, Ask Mr. Foster, and Liberty Travel created dream packages for the adventure-bound.

A free service for the traveler, agencies collected their revenue from the modes of travel and destinations themselves. Their marketing campaigns—full-color spreads in the Sunday travel sections, complete with photos of sandy beaches and international landmarks—helped fuel the desires of the traveling public and were an important part of the overall marketing of the industry. The packages the agencies offered—so many nights of hotel rooms, cheap airfares, and meal plans—made travel affordable for the general public.

However, as the economics of travel began to change, so did the travel agency industry. The deregulation of the airlines, which fueled price-cutting wars, began to erode the profit margins of airlines. One cost-cutting measure was to decrease the fees paid to the agencies. Agents tightened their belts, sat down at their computers, and continued to price out the best packages they could for their clients—little knowing, in the mid1990s, that they were staring straight into the screen of the enemy: the computer.

First SABRE, the online booking site for airlines, began to allow consumer access. Then came Orbitz, Travelocity, Expedia, Travel Advisor, and Kayak—any number of online offerings. Airlines and hotels began allowing booking online. September 11, 2001, put a huge crimp in the travel industry, as did the economic downturn of the mid-2000s. Mobile apps delivered one last roundhouse punch right to the side of the industry's jaw.

You would think travel agents would be down for the count—but not so. According to Questex Media/Travel Group—publishers of travel magazines and conference providers to the industry—travel agents are still responsible for 77% of all cruise bookings, 73% of all package travel bookings, and 55% of all airline travel bookings.[5] They may not be making as much money, but they are still providing a service for those travelers—including busy business people who either don't want to spend their time figuring out their travel or would prefer to have an expert make the suggestions for anything more than a quick flight to visit Aunt Helen. Who better to plan a multidestination travel package, including flights, transfers, hotels, tours, and all the assorted details—than a travel agent? After all, the final success in this industry is based on the customer's experience with the product, and a travel agent can help that be a positive one.

---

[5] "Impact of Technology on the Travel Agency Business," *Houston Chronicle*, http://smallbusiness.chron.com/impact-technology-travel-agency-business-57750.html.

Relationship Marketing

Customer retention is a huge concern in the travel and tourism industry. The goal is not just to get people traveling; it's to bring them back, over and over. Customer satisfaction is key. Because travel is such a personal thing, a more personalized, face-to-face approach is needed to make sure the correct message gets out to the various distribution channels. There is a heavy emphasis on relationship marketing in this industry, promoting personal touches and hassle-free services, at both the B to B (business to business) and B to C (business to consumer) levels.

Intra-Industry Trade Shows and Associations

There are trade shows and associations for every segment of the travel industry—from the destinations market to the individual traveler(s), to travel agents, to business planners looking for potential conference sites and rewards for their sales force or executives.

IT&ME

An excellent example of the diverse nature of the travel industry is the Incentive Travel & Meeting Executives Show (IT&ME), which focuses on what is known as "incentive travel"—rewards for a busy sales force, harried employees, or top executives. Also known as "The Motivation Show," its objective is to act as a marketplace for the diverse products within the tourism industry, including premiums, incentives, business gifts, and incentive travel services.

The show exhibits thousands of suppliers of merchandise and travel services, representing the service categories of more than 60 countries. Representatives of major hotel chains, accredited tour operators, and travel companies specializing in incentive travel, chambers of commerce, and individual resorts—all of these can be found at IT&ME, which attracts potential decision-makers in the field of incentive travel. With a strong educational component—workshops and lectures—shows such as IT&ME are also an excellent place for novices in the travel and leisure industry to get a handle on how the industry markets itself.

SITE

The Society of Incentive & Travel Executives (SITE) is an association whose membership is made up of business professionals dedicated to the recognition and development of motivational and performance improvement strategies, of which travel is a key component. SITE serves as a networking and educational opportunity for its members, with a variety of local chapters, conferences, and one main conference held each year in an incentive destination such as Las Vegas, Hong Kong, or London.

ASTA

Another key association in the industry is the American Society of Travel Agents (ASTA), the world's largest association of travel professionals. Over 26,000 travel agents and the companies whose products they sell—such as tours, cruises, hotels, and car rentals—are members of ASTA, which also serves as the advocate for travel agents, the travel industry, and the traveling public.

ASTA benefits its membership through representation in industry and government affairs, providing education and training, and identifying and meeting the needs of the traveling public. Reflecting ASTA's stance on the necessity of travel agents, their current motto is: "Without ASTA, you are on your own." Cheery thought.

CLIA

The Cruise Lines International Association (CLIA) contributes strongly to generic information on the pleasures and positive attributes of cruising in an attempt to increase the audiences for this experience. The association also acts as the spokes-group and lightning rod for criticism regarding lapses by member cruise companies. They organize special trade shows where companies can gather, talk about new techniques in every aspect of running a line, and showcase new, successful marketing offers and packages. Cruisefest, which runs in conjunction with ASTA, offers opportunities for travel industry professionals to network and benefit from seminars and workshops. Because Cruisefest is typically held in ports such as Miami or Vancouver, industry professionals also have the opportunity to tour some of the latest cruise ships afloat.

Each of these associations also publishes its own newsletters and magazines, available not only to the industry, but to the traveling public.

Cuddling the Consumer

Relationship marketing must extend well beyond intra-industry efforts. Though courting industry professionals is critical, reaching out directly to the consumer is paramount. After all, when push comes to shove, it's the traveler who will be standing in line in front of the ticket counter or checking in at the hotel—not the agent or webmaster.

Customer Loyalty Programs

Loyalty programs have exploded over the last decade, with what seems to be every retail outlet possible—the corner gas station to the local grocer—asking you if you've signed up. The biggest challenge with these is customer perception regarding return: What am I getting for giving you my personal data? In most instances, the answer seems to be nothing. This is not the case in the travel industry, where frequent flier and hotel programs actually do return a reward.

With airlines, it may be a free flight; an upgrade to first class; free baggage check-in; or a trip to the airline club, where stranded passengers loll about in relative comfort while everyone else is knocking knees in crowded seating areas next to the gate. Hotels offer upgrades to suites or special discounted rates. But a real motivator in these programs seems to be status. The 2009 George Clooney movie *Up in the Air* let the cat out of the bag: There really are black-card VIP programs out there, which allow the most loyal customers the best services, and frequent travelers—the real road warriors—want them.

But how about the rest of us? How important are the loyalty programs? The jury is still out when it comes to the not-so-frequent traveler, the people who don't use the programs often enough to see any impact. To build those numbers, airlines now offer branded credit cards that allow nonfliers to accumulate the same points they might earn if they were flying, even if they're just buying groceries. Although it takes a lot of groceries to add up the baseline 25,000 miles for a free trip, many consumers seem to believe the investment (the cards typically have a fee) is worth it.

Within the provider side of the industry, the current conversation is focusing on how to better use the data being collected, for that's the real prize in these programs. When you sign up for a card, you're sharing your preferences with the brand by allowing them to track you through all of your stays. The question is, will the providers actually use the data to create a better benefit, one that will actually create true loyalty? The answer remains to be seen.

One thing we do know about customer loyalty programs is that if the provider makes a promise, it needs to stick with it. Ending programs without paying off or changing the rules midway leaves a bad taste in the consumer's mouth, and risks customer flight.

Branding Beds

Major hotels chains have successfully built national—and, in many cases, global—brands with strong, persuasive marketing, constant upgrading of their facilities and loyalty programs, built on the 80/20 rule: 20% of the guest population represents 80% of chains' sales revenue. To entice repeat visitation of that all-important 20%, most chains now offer reward programs built on frequency of stays, frequent flyer synergy programs, their own newsletters, and relationships with credit card and telephone companies, which support the accumulation of miles/points.

The desire to stamp "you are special/we are unique" on these establishments has resulted in design-friendly room decor and high levels of services, including Wi-Fi, branded amenities in the bathroom, and luxury linens on the bed. Westin, the hotel chain now owned by Starwood, started a revolution in the industry with its Heavenly Bed program. Westin wisely honed in on the fact that the main thing most travelers do in a hotel room is sleep, and the better the sleep, the happier the customer. Westin invested millions of dollars in upgrading all the mattresses and linens in their rooms to something often far better than what the traveler had at home, and the result was skyrocketing retention—and imitation by all its major competitors. But Westin didn't stop there; it built a side business on the Heavenly Bed, offering all of it—mattress, linens, duvet, pillows—in catalogs placed in the room and a special website. Now its brand recognition extends to Pottery Barn marketing, where the Heavenly Bed is prominently offered.

Hotel chains have stretched their brands in all directions. Starwood offers something for everyone, from the super-plush St. Regis and Le Meridien to the dorm-room setting of the aLoft brand, with Sheraton, W, Element, and Westin in between. For the boutique hotel fancier, Starwood chains offers the Luxury Collection, a group of high-end one-off hotels around the world. Industry giant Marriott offers the Ritz Carlton on the top end, with JW Marriott, Marriott, Courtyard, Springhill Suites, and Fairfield Inn, among several other brands, capturing nearly every niche possible. This is just a sampling; there are literally hundreds of hotel chains around the world, and each of them has its own focus on building a bigger brand.

Even Disney and Universal, who, for a period of time were willing to place visitors to their entertainment parks in other properties, hired leading architects to fashion hotels that reflect popular themes, appeal to their primarily family audiences, support their major brands, and enhance the total experience of being in Orlando, Anaheim, Paris, or Tokyo.

On the technology side, hotel chains have launched new efforts to offer better choice to consumers. Choice Hotels International, Hilton Worldwide, Hyatt Hotels, InterContinental Hotels, Marriott International, and Wyndham Hotel Group have joined together in launching a search site called Room Key, which will allow travelers to search across all brands and price points. In addition, the site will offer—you guessed it—social networking, allowing customers the chance to share their plans and opinions with friends, family, and complete strangers.

Along with social media, hotel chains use websites, mobile applications, and constant repetition of newspaper ads in travel sections throughout the country. The variety of travel channels now available via cable gives hotels a great niche in which to run TV commercials reinforcing the ambiance of the brand and the romance factor. Chains also carefully market to travel agents, with glossy, expensive booklets and brochures, window posters, and familiarization trips for high-sales producers.

Other Destination Entertainment

Travel and tourism extend well beyond the boundaries of cities, national parks, and hotel beds. Adventure is the soul of travel, and many consumers are interested in experiencing destinations that offer them something other than the standard cityscape or hotel room.

Circus

The circus is a form of popular entertainment that dates back hundreds of years, when traveling companies of performers would delight locals with all forms of physical prowess, from acrobatics to stunts with wild animals. For many nineteenth, and even early twentieth century people, living far away from metropolitan areas, the circus was quite possibly the most exciting form of entertainment they might see in their entire lives. Ringling Brothers, Barnum and Bailey (later merged), and even Buffalo Bill, with his touring Wild West Show, brought thousands of people inside the Big Top.

In the early 1980s, two former Quebec street performers, Guy Laliberté and Gilles Ste-Croix, formed Cirque du Soleil as a modern version of this ancient entertainment. Using a theatrical, character-driven approach and a synthesis of circus styles from around the world, Cirque took the world by storm. The company now has 19 shows in 21 cities, with permanent performance venues in many locations. Nearly 15 million people have experienced a Cirque show,[6] generating over $7 billion[7] in revenue. Las Vegas alone houses six Cirque shows in six of the major casinos.

However, that presence in Vegas—a microcosm of the extended Cirque brand—makes one wonder how much further that brand can be stretched. Cirque is dependent on its unique flavor, its special appeal. Key components of "special" are limitation and exclusivity. At what point does enough turn into too much? A recent Cirque offering, set to run at Radio City in New York for three years (with an option for five), was cancelled after two. Could the balancing act be teetering?

---

[6] Cirque du Soleil website, www.cirquedusoleil.com.

[7] "Run Away to the Circus? No Need. It's Staying Here," *New York Times*, April 28, 2009.

Hard to say. For the time being, they're still one of the greatest shows on earth.

Cruises

There was a time when cruising was thought to be a world of blue-haired old ladies and tottering old men, all lined up at the constant buffets. Studies in the early 1990s presented these statistics: the average customer was over 65 years of age, the percentage of the U.S. population that had ever cruised was under 4%, and the business model was based on those same senior citizens taking more cruises. The industry also suffered from the perceptions that there was too much so-so food, too much motion on the ocean, not enough diverse activities, and cruising was too expensive.

Not such a great outlook, right? The cruise industry didn't think so either. They encouraged CLIA to do research and then followed the recommendations. Today, the cruise industry sports these statistics:

- Twenty million people cruised in 2012.[8]

- The average age has dropped to 48.[9]

- The median income is $97,000.[10]

- Twenty percent of the U.S. population has taken a cruise.[11]

- First-time cruisers frequently report exceeded expectations for food, entertainment, accommodations, and overall quality of their vacation.[12]

In short, a marketing miracle: The industry took the pulse of potential passengers, created a product that would appeal to them, and got the message to the masses. This charge was originally led by Carnival Cruise Line, the first in the cruise industry to utilize the powers of marketing and audience identification for their company. Carnival's in-residence marketing wizard, Robert Dickerson, engineered a change in the demographics of the cruise customer from 100% senior citizen retirees to a mix of couples with children, young single adults, and empty nesters, all with time and disposable income.

The industry now offers a wide variety of ship choices, from luxury lines with less than 300 passengers to what appear to be floating cities, carrying over 4,000 people. Ships now offer surf pools, planetariums, on-deck LED movie screens, golf simulators, water parks, demonstration kitchens, self-leveling billiard tables, multiroom villas with private pools and in-suite Jacuzzis, ice skating rinks, rock climbing walls, bungee drops, and trampolines.[13]

---

[8] CLIA.

[9] Cruise Industry Overview 2012, Florida-Caribbean Cruise Association.

[10] Ibid.

[11] CLIA.

[12] CLIA.

[13] Cruise Industry Overview 2012, Florida-Caribbean Cruise Association.

Like hotels, some cruise lines offer extension and differentiation within their own brands. Carnival, the largest of the lines, owns AIDA Cruises (Germany), Carnival Cruise Lines (U.S.), Costa Cruises (Italy), Cunard Line (United Kingdom), Holland America Line (U.S.), Ibero Cruises (Spain), P&O Cruises (United Kingdom), P&O Cruises Australia (Australia), Princess Cruises (U.S.), and Seabourn Cruise Line (U.S.).

In addition, cruising offers a wide variety of specialty trips for all manner of interests. There are jazz cruises, literary cruises, celebrity cruises featuring radio talk show hosts, gourmet cruises. Olivia offers cruises for gay women, catering to less affluent cruisers on large (2,000+ passengers) Caribbean trips as well as a more moneyed clientele on smaller (200+) cruises in the Mediterranean or the rivers of Europe.

As a final note, possibly the best example of the importance of branding in cruising was the arrival of the Disney Cruise Line. Investing over a billion dollars in two brand-new ships and their very own island, Disney's Castaway Cay, all purpose-built for the mantra of a "seamless guest experience," Disney's venture into cruising has been an unqualified success, luring not only families with children, but senior citizens and singles as well. The Disney fleet has now expanded to four ships and sails to Alaska, the Bahamas, the California Coast, the Caribbean, Europe, the Panama Canal, and Transatlantic crossings.

Consumers who align themselves with the Disney brand have high expectations that they will have a comfortable, safe, entertainment-filled experience, and Disney has parlayed this brand equity into a business that is actually pulling from the first-time cruiser demographic.

Part of Disney's success in the market was a strategy that called for creating specific spaces and programs for children. Given that Disney recognized that childless couples and singles would think of Disney Cruise Line as a floating playroom, the company created a revolutionary program that draws children to their own cruising experience, while creating a level of guilt-free comfort for their parents—and a restful experience for childless travelers. Disney's Oceaneer Adventure, custom tailored to specific age groups, has been successful in meeting the goals of the company and the expectations of all its cruising guests.

The All-Inclusive

In a period when cost was more important than comfort, one leisure company was created to serve up exotic locales for consumers in Europe who were on tight post-war budgets and in need of a getaway. Club Med, originated by a French company, provided a complete one-week vacation for one inclusive cost. This eliminated any concern about constant payments for additional services, the fear of running out of money, or not being able to pay the bills after the vacation was over. It offered the middle-class French family—and later the European family—a complete holiday experience at a remote beach at extremely low prices, made affordable by providing very basic amenities. The accommodations were usually family-sized tents, with outdoor showers, shared bathrooms, and family-style dining, usually in a tin hut—rustic, but in a warm climate with little or no rain.

The marketing concept was simple and eminently successful: "One price for a complete vacation for the whole family." There were always several young, attractive male or female general organizers (GOs), who were in charge of the sports activities during the day and the entertainment in the evening. These adult camps or clubs were usually accessible by car or train.

This is a far cry from today's modern Club Med. Under the same management, but with a new generation of marketing executives, today's Club Med serves up a streamlined and upscale offering in handsome, comfortable bungalows, with hotel-style cuisine, and state-of-the-art sports equipment, managed by the always helpful GO. Club Med can now be found at exclusive beach locations all over the world, accessible by plane and then car, bus, or van.

The marketing proposition is still the same, appealing to a similar family-oriented, budget-conscious consumer. The advertising presents $949 and up for plane, accommodations, all meals, beer and wine, and most sports. The closing promise or positioning line is "The World Is On Sale." In addition to making a persuasive marketing offer, the facilities deliver exactly what is promised and expected, resulting in a firm relationship with a great number of loyalists and returnees.

However, in a period of sales downturn, Club Med discovered through research that the Club had gotten a reputation as a "swinger's paradise," with nude sunbathing and licentious behavior as the main attractions. Management quickly changed whatever was driving that perception, given the desire was to stick with a family-oriented business, a much more sustainable and attractive model.

But one man's pain is another's pleasure. In this case, the latter man was an entrepreneur and appliance retailer named Butch Stewart, who gave birth to the next level of "all-inclusive," the beach resort: Sandals, on the Caribbean island of Jamaica. His offer of plane, luxury hotel, gourmet meals, cocktails, and sports all for one fixed fee per person (with couples prices at a promotional offering during off-season periods) brought capacity crowds from major metropolitan cities. The chain expanded to other islands in the Caribbean and was imitated by the Hedonism chain; soon, other all-inclusive resorts followed as it became a vacation rage. These resorts have even managed to avoid the liability of real or perceived dangers from local crime, due to their nature of being self-contained and secure worlds. Clearly, in this case, an industry was reinvented by a marketing idea, supported by the needs it fulfilled for the target audience: conveyance, one price, quality, and reliability.

Time Share—Coming of Age

At the beginning, time-share marketing appealed to those Americans who wanted the dream of a two-week vacation, not in a hotel or motel, but in place they could own. The attraction of a fully-furnished one- or two-bedroom apartment, with kitchen, swimming pool, picnic tables, and barbeque, in close proximity to a tourism destination like Miami, Orlando, or Tampa, made for easy selling. However, most of the sales were to gullible, lower middle-income purchasers, who were duped into buying a share of a motel for one or two weeks for their lifetime ownership, making time-shares a shady business at minimum.

In a discussion of place and relationship marketing, this was a low-class sale at its most highly skilled, with glossy booklets, special deals for early confirmations, and unique financing at exorbitant rates. All this was under the stewardship of commissioned salespeople applying high-pressure tactics, weaving stories of the opportunity and nature of the units, without a twinge of conscience or moral restraint—*Glengarry Glen Ross* in Bermuda shorts.

The major selling point was the "exchange privilege"—the thrill of being able to trade two weeks in Orlando for another destination like California, Arizona, New Orleans, or even New York. Unfortunately, in the early years of this marketing concept, exchanges were difficult, cumbersome, and often unrealized. Because the concept grew rapidly and unsuspecting purchasers became a large group, the complaints became thunderous. The Attorney General stepped in, along with many state officials responsible for preventing consumer abuse.

Fast forward to the present, where we see a remarkable change in the timeshare environment. Leading hotel brands have entered the field, providing credibility and a reassurance that previously did not exist. Unfortunately, the marketing executives assigned to rebuild the image first had to wipe out 20 years of bad press and wholesale bilking of the public. The worst challenge in marketing is to reverse a negative or shady image. The best opportunity is when there is no image—not even a positive halo effect—in this case, the brand can be built from the ground up in a guided process.

Marriott, Hyatt, Disney, Sheraton, and Westin have all entered the time-share market and have named this special hospitality product the Vacation Club. This time period has also seen the development of two major exchange companies, Interval International and RCI, which handle the time-share exchange process. Both exchange companies issue books with small photos of possible exchange properties all over the world. The books list and display about 1,200 to 1,300 properties in many U.S. vacation spots, with as many as five or ten in locations such as Orlando or Southern California. There is roughly a $123 ($199 for international) charge for making an exchange, which covers administrative costs.

Consumers might still have some difficulty getting exactly the exchange they want, but flexibility, certain special marketing bonuses, and trading in points earned with hotel partners enable owners to take advantage of the program. Time-sharing has overcome its past and become a vacation marketing miracle. In fact, many resort developers are now creating properties especially designed for time-share purposes—they then rent out any excess "inventory" as condos.

A final note to affirm that brands are important in every part of the travel and tourism industry: The Four Seasons, Ritz-Carlton, and the St. Regis, three of the premier hotel chains in America, now offer residences—whole ownership of a residence within the hotel or resort. The marketing is careful, complex, and includes branding reassurance, along with access to all or most of the services at existing Four Seasons, Ritz Carlton, and St. Regis properties. As these leading chains expand to Europe, wealthy patrons will be able to have homes in many destinations without the responsibility of caretaking. These chains also offer fractional ownership, which allows for a one-twelfth ownership of a residence.

Theme Parks

In the early 1950s, Walt Disney grew dismayed by the lack of venues he could take his young family to for an outing. Amusement parks of the time were relatively shady places, hangouts for teenagers and con artists. Disney decided to take a shot at creating the kind of amusement park families could enjoy. Thus the dream of Disneyland began—and with it, today's multibillion dollar theme park industry.

Walt Disney's first attempts to establish his dream were initially laughed at, frowned upon, and refused financing. In an interesting twist of fate that would come full circle decades later when the Walt Disney Company would purchase the broadcasting network, ABC, which backed his idea, giving him the funds needed to create Disneyland, the first in the empire that now includes Walt Disney World in Orlando, Euro Disney, Tokyo Disneyland, Disney Hong Kong, and soon, Disney Shanghai. The Disney theme park empire has been an engine of revenue for all other Disney ventures and has always been a target of synergy between the businesses: give them a taste of Disney elsewhere, but get them to the parks.

The parks are a destination for a wide swath of the international public, offering a vacation the entire family can enjoy. But more than that, they are a self-propelled marketing machine. Visitors to Disney properties spend their days and nights completely enfolded in the brand, interacting with story lines and characters and being led out of each attraction through a retail outlet, packed with Disney merchandise to remind them of their trip. In a perfect example of synergy, new releases from the Disney studios become attractions at the parks, driving visitation; the park experience drives trust in the Disney brand, promoting future releases in all sectors of the company's business.

Furthermore, Disney has also perfected the concept of synergy partners, including other major brands through various deals in which the company shares in revenue while offering the halo effect of their own brand's goodwill. In the Innoventions pavilion in Epcot, where brands such as Taylor-Morrison Homes, Microsoft, and Honda demonstrate new technologies, Disney brings consumers face to face with products aplenty. However, families are happy to be a part of the promotion process, as Disney's world-famous eye for operational detail assures them of a safe, memory-filled experience.

Technology is playing a huge role at Walt Disney World. Starting in the spring of 2013, guests will be offered the use of a vacation management system called MyMagic+, in the form of a bracelet that allows them to bypass turnstiles and leave credit cards at home: Simply wave the bracelet in front of a reader, and you're done. Although Disney believes that this will promote a better guest experience—the holy grail of all places Disney—it will also allow them to collect scads of data on actual guest interaction with the park: where they go and what they buy.

Although Disneyland and Walt Disney World are paeans to the most famous animated characters in the world, Universal Studios pays homage to the movies—Universal movies. Located in Los Angeles, Orlando, Japan, and Singapore, Universal Studios is another example of synergy between the silver screen and the entertainment-hungry consumer. When sitting in a seat in a dark room with 300 strangers isn't enough, Universal offers you the opportunity to sit in a specially designed tram, surrounded by animatronics, and get tossed around with 16 strangers in a motion-based simulator—don't just see the movie, ride it. And while you're at it, stay in a hotel on the property, visit the retail shops, and eat in the restaurants.

The recent addition of the Wizarding World of Harry Potter—a multiacre recreation of everything from Hogwarts to the Hogwart's Express—has brought visitors by the millions.

These two park concepts have spawned an entire industry of attractions that can best be described as amusement parks on steroids. With their cousins—Six Flags, Paramount Parks, Dollywood, Silver Dollar City, and the rest—theme parks offer a day's or week's-worth of entertainment to a public that wants to do more than just ride a roller coaster.

As an industry, theme parks are one of the largest employers in the country and are rapidly spreading throughout the world. The main association for the industry, the International Association of Amusement Parks and Attractions (IAAPA), holds a yearly show that covers over one million square feet of exhibit hall space, drawing over 50,000 attendees over a four-day period.

B2C marketing for the industry is accomplished through the use of all forms of media; B2B marketing is accomplished through yearly trade events such as IAAPA, as well as websites and applications—over 100, offering everything from tickets to weather information. In addition, IAAPA publishes an excellent trade magazine, *Fun World*.

Casinos

Earlier in this chapter, we spoke of Las Vegas and how changing its marketing strategy nearly throttled its personality. Fortunately for adults of all ages, that didn't work.

Vegas is possibly the greatest theme park for adults ever created, with reproductions of Paris, New York, Venice, and Monte Carlo—all in the form of casino resorts—and a newly retro return to the days of the Rat Pack with luxury offerings such as Wynn, Encore, and the Cosmopolitan. When you add the gourmet food—nearly every major chef in the world has his or her own five star restaurant here—and the top-name entertainers, you're talking a very good time, indeed. Good news for the millions of conventioneers who flow through town every year.

But the heart of Vegas is gaming. Vegas is the best known of the casino towns, which include Atlantic City, Reno, Lake Tahoe—and locations in 33 other states.

Yes, you read that right. Casino gambling, once limited to a few very specific locations in the U.S., has now spread across the country. In an era of shallower tax bases and tightening budgets, states across the nation have jumped on the casino bandwagon, taking is as much as 55% of the slot machines "hold"—the money dumped in that isn't returned to gamblers in the form of winnings. Iowa has 17 casinos. Mississippi's Gulf Coast has 12, with more on the way. Maryland has a $1 billion casino on the boards, which would be built about 10 miles from Washington, D.C.

In addition to these commercial casinos are the Indian casinos. The Indian Gaming Regulatory Act, passed by Congress in 1988, first permitted legal gambling by Indian tribes in their home states. By 1993, the National Indian Gaming Commission had finalized rules for the casino, bingo, and/or other gambling venues available at about one-third of the 557 federally recognized Native American reservations. The need for revenue first drove the formation of such locations, and a test case in Florida in 1979, when the Seminole tribe had a prize that exceeded the state lottery total, paved the way. Success stories from Minnesota to Connecticut helped increase the number of Class III facilities (those able to offer the full array of casino games). There are now over 450 Indian casinos across the country.[14]

---

[14] "Foxwoods Is Fighting for Its Life," *New York Times*, March 14, 2012.

The biggest winner in gambling revenue? You might say Nevada (Las Vegas, Reno)—but you'd be wrong. It's Pennsylvania, which in 2010 collected $1.3 billion from slots and table-game revenue from the state's 10 casinos,[15] owing to its 55% take of the hold. (Most other states are in the 25% range; credit the Pennsylvania state government with some great wheeler-dealing.

This increase in gambling destinations has had a huge impact on many of the traditional gambling meccas. The math is pretty simple: More casinos means fewer people traveling to get their fix. Many casinos are suffering from casino-overload in their marketing areas, and with new states legalizing gaming, it isn't going to get better. A case in point is the Foxwoods Resort and Casino in Ledyard, CT, operated by the Mashantucket-Pequot tribe, which was one of the first to offer the kind of glitz available at the Nevada or Atlantic City casinos. Foxwoods is the largest resort casino in the U.S., built at a time when the future seemed great. The facilities include a $225 million, state of the art museum that honors the history of the tribe. But that same tribe has recently had to negotiate terms on $2.3 billion in debt, mostly due to recession and over-building.

What this means, of course, is that the marketing techniques used to draw gamblers are more important than ever. You're never going to get repeat Vegas visitation from the guy who'd just as soon go to the local "racino"—race track/casino, such as Aqueduct in New York—the big casinos still shoot for the "whales"—the big fish that casinos carefully cultivate through complimentary ("comped") rooms, flights, and food. But you don't have to spend that big to be comped—not at one sitting anyway. Casinos are happy to comp those loyal guests who come regularly and spend often.

Guests hungry for this kind of recognition typically sign up for the "slot clubs" that are a part of every casino. Members are issued cards that are used at the slots (where 70% of casino revenue is derived), so the casino keeps track of their activity. The Luxor in Las Vegas, as an example, has a block of 300 rooms set aside for comping on weekdays and as many as 500 rooms it can comp on a weekend. Those rooms aren't filled with millionaires. The Luxor also uses direct mail campaigns in addition to advertising to obtain regulars. In addition, the casino employs casino hosts, each of whom is responsible for 250 regular customers. Every guest at the Luxor gets a letter within three days of his or her visit; a host is responsible for keeping in touch with each of his or her 250 regulars at least once every three months. For instance, if a player hits a jackpot, the player also receives an Egyptian good luck pin. All of this attention and communication go toward maintaining a customer base, and the goal is to make them feel needed and wanted.[16]

Resort casinos also use other strategies to bring in customers. In Vegas, Caesar's built Celine Dion her very own theater, which has since housed Bette Midler as well as Elton John while Celine took a world tour. Gourmet food is also a draw. In addition, large resort casinos often offer luxury shopping.

Most marketers understand that getting new customers is more expensive than retaining repeat ones. This is certainly true for casinos. The needs, wants, and desires of people drawn to a

---

[15] "Foxwoods Is Fighting for Its Life," *New York Times*, March 14, 2012.

[16] For more detail, see the thorough coverage in: Rudd, Denis P. and Lincoln H. Marshall, *Introduction to Casino & Gaming Operations*, 2/E (Englewood Cliffs, NJ: Prentice Hall, 2000).

gambling environment must be motivated by more than an attractive price on an airline ticket to get there. The marketing mix must reflect the fundamental components of product, price, and distribution. The casinos themselves systematically market to audiences through the use of clubs, tournaments, headliner acts, and other special events. Like much of the hospitality industry, gaming operations are people-oriented businesses; they require strong communications from PR departments and promotional support from the entire company.

Experiential Branding

The 20th Century saw the birth of "The Brand" as the keystone of consumer outreach. This somewhat ephemeral concept grew in importance throughout the last century. Now, it is commonplace for people to display the brand, loudly, on their clothes, their accessories, their cars. We have become a nation of walking billboards, and we pay the brand for the privilege.

In theory, brands establish an identity by association with meaningful ideas, values, and a quality position that people can readily understand. In other words, "I know it, I trust it, and it fits my particular take on life." During the evolution of branding, to fully entice the consumer, differentiation was key: Create unique selling propositions that would translate into immediate benefits for the customer—"If I put that stuff in my hair, I'll be the sexiest man alive; if I use the other brand, I'll just look greasy."

Traditionally, marketing professionals would then march the brand out to the public through the use of print or broadcast advertising—utilizing actors, spokespeople, or clever copy to lock the brand into the consumer's consciousness. The message was delivered through the traditional media outlets appropriate to the campaign. Finally, the brand was then attached to as many products as possible.

As technology has expanded, more media can be utilized to promote a brand. Consumers are now bombarded with thousands of messages per day. How to cut through the clutter? Create an *experience* of the brand. Bring the brand to life so that consumers can connect with it, claim it as part of their lifestyle. To do this, marketers tie the brand to an entertainment-driven experience—one that creates a pleasant memory or educational offering.

Experiential marketing helps brands connect with the consumer as human—not just as product user. It takes the core values of the brand and introduces them into an actual environment—one that gives the visitor a visceral experience of what the brand means and offers. Experiential branding is the intersection of entertainment and marketing.

The concept first hit the retail side of branding with individual brands. Manufacturers such as Nike (with Niketown) discovered the power of exhibiting their product in environments that included merchandise combined with museum-like exhibits, state-of-the-art audio-visual technology, online interfaces, and themed decor to support—but not define or overpower—the brand image. Niketown offers products for sale, but it does not necessarily compete with other retail partners in the area that also offer their merchandise; instead, these brand facilities act as yet another marketing effort for local retailers, by promoting the brand image.

Other manifestations of experiential marketing are found in corporate heritage centers, which took the place of plant tours in the late twentieth century, due to liability, and sometimes espionage, concerns. In retail, "pop-up" stores bring the brand to town like an old-fashioned carnival, appearing for a few days, weeks or maybe months, before disappearing like a Ray Bradbury character, leaving just a whiff of marketing behind. The same is true of traveling road shows, such as the NFL Experience, which allow wannabee footballers to immerse themselves in their iconic brand.

High-touch sensory experiences are often seen as the leading edge of a "brand narrative" that speaks over many channels. Today, marketing strategies are designed as a sophisticated choir of environmental, online, print, and broadcast voices.

Summary

Travel and tourism are integral to the entertainment industry, providing the destinations that showcase entertainers, as well as offering relaxing getaways that are a form of entertainment in themselves. In addition, brands often create their own destinations, either permanent or temporary, that allow the consumer to experience a brand as entertainment.

For Further Reading

Kotler, Philip R., John T. Bowen, and James Makens, Ph.D, *Marketing for Hospitality and Tourism* (6th Edition), Prentice Hall, 2013.

Pike, Stephen, *Destination Marketing*, Elsevier Inc., 2008.

12

What's Next: A Global Snapshot

In the last 11 chapters, we have primarily focused on the United States, both in terms of entertainment consumption and creation. But entertainment is a global phenomenon, driven by changes in economies and technology. New opportunities for entertainment marketing are opening up around the globe.

An in-depth investigation into the state of entertainment marketing in each country of the world would fill the entire shelf of the local library. In this chapter, we take a 50,000-foot view of how these growing entertainment economies are shaping up: what the trends are and where we see continuing opportunities, paying attention to the influences of government control, the development of content, and the rapidly changing access to conduit.

Global Growth

In early 2012, the global census hit a milestone as the world's population reached 7 billion. This growing population has provided massive opportunity for the mega-media and entertainment conglomerates we've been discussing. Major studios, television networks, phone companies, cable operators, and programmers have experienced enormous growth from their content export, including subrights agreements, licensing contracts, and syndication auctions to every available distributor in every country in the world. These efforts have produced nearly $750 billion of media-driven entertainment throughout the planet. When we add in all the potential sponsorship and merchandising revenue, the number streaks into trillion-dollar territory.

U.S. entertainment can now be found in over 150 countries, translated into 16 major languages and hundreds of local dialects. The advent of new technologies and the appearance of a middle class in once-under-developed regions have created huge new audiences—and some backlash. After years of being fed large quantities of U.S. pop music, television, film, and other entertainment products, global entrepreneurs are beginning to develop their own content, using local talent. The success of these ventures has generated film schools and arts programs in nearly every entertainment-consuming country, paving the way for even more local growth in the coming years.

The entertainment economy is on the move.

Global Regions

In discussing the global market for entertainment, we break the world into four regions. Each of these regions has its own peculiarities and opportunities, which we discuss throughout the chapter. Before we do that, however, let's take a quick look at the global revenue generated in each of the regions. A projection of 2016 revenues helps define potential growth.[1] Do note that North America is still, by a longshot, the king of entertainment content and associated revenue.

- **North America:** 2012, $335.5 billion. Projected 2016, $339.4 billion.

- **EMEA (Europe, Middle East, Africa):** 2012, $431.8 billion. Projected 2016, $509.5 billion.

- **Asia Pacific:** 2012, $386.8 billion. Projected 2016, $494.3 billion.

- **Latin America:** 2012, $66.9 billion. Projected 2016, $97.4 billion.

This adds up to a whopping $1.2 trillion in 2012, with a 2016 projection of $1.5 trillion. Keep in mind that these figures do not include anything but the basics: no licensing (except for television), product placement, or extended profits from merchandising and retail—all of the very important revenue sources that make up the entertainment economy as a whole. We estimate that total to be nearly $760 billion in 2012, taking us tantalizingly close to $2 trillion.

Now *that's* a market.

2012 global entertainment content breaks down by platform as follows[2]:

- **Internet access:** $351 billion

- **Cinema (Box Office Only):** $87.8 billion

- **TV Subscription and Licensing:** $229.1 billion

- **Music:** $51.1 billion

- **Consumer Magazines:** $75.3 billion

- **Video Games:** $62.3 billion

- **Newspaper Publishing:** $168.6 billion

- **Radio:** $49.6 billion

- **Out-of-Home:** $33.8 billion

- **Consumer and Educational Book Publishing:** $112.2 billion

Note who the champ is in these revenue figures: Internet access. As we've discussed throughout the book, the Internet is a crucial development in emerging business models.

---

[1] "PwC Global Entertainment and Media Outlook: 2012–2016, www.pwc.com/outlook

[2] Ibid

Digital Developments

Before we move on to our discussion of the various regions, we must once again discuss the impact of the *digital disruption*.

Had you studied the projections for entertainment revenue even as recently as five years ago and then compared them to the charts we present now, you would see a fairly hefty change to the negative. The gloomy economy of the post-crash years has certainly played a part in this, but so has the rise of digital media. Traditional platforms have suffered as they've struggled to find ways to charge for online content, while new forms of delivery slashed old profit margins. After all, selling 10,000 e-books at $3.99 is vastly different than selling 10,000 hardcovers at $22.95. Music was nearly brought to its knees by piracy and a generation that believes that sharing is not stealing. Millions of movies are downloaded illegally.

However, there now seems to be greater clarity. With digital the new normal, entertainment and media companies are beginning to right the ship, stabilizing and growing revenue. A good thing, because with the huge shift to mobile consumption, digital delivery is going to keep right on growing. PwC estimates total 2012 global Internet Access revenue at $351 billion, growing to $493.4 billion in the next four years.[3]

The increase in digital spending could ramp up even faster, especially in the United States, where the federal government has recently proposed making a large portion of high-frequency spectrum available for unlicensed use, which could increase the download rates of Wi-Fi devices by up to one hundred times their current speed.[4] This not only bodes well for mobile; it opens the door for technology that we haven't even seen yet. In other words, look for another widely divergent set of revenue results five years from now.

For now, let's start with a baseline. We begin with the United States and Canada.

Global Regions: North America

We've laid the groundwork for the United States throughout the book, so while we present the outlook for entertainment growth for North America, our discussion in this section of Chapter 12 focuses primarily on Canada.

Canadians feel strongly about establishing and maintaining a separate identity from the U.S., even though the Canadian economy is closely integrated with that of its neighbor to the south. The technology of Canadian media and entertainment is similar to that found in the U.S. The Canadian Broadcasting Corporation (CBC) is Canada's national public broadcaster. It was created in 1936 through an Act of Parliament, brought on by about the growing American influence in radio. The CBC operates both English-language and French-language national television networks. Both languages are broadcast on two separate channels: one with regular programming and one with all-news programming. There are also two private national television networks: CTV and Global Television.

---

[3] Ibid

[4] "F.C.C. Moves to Ease Wireless Congestion," *New York Times*, February 20, 2013.

Currently, the CBC reaches its international markets via five avenues:

- Radio Canada International

- Sale of television programs

- CBC websites

- Newsworld International

The fifth avenue, TV5, is a globally distributed, French-language general interest network, created in 1985. TV5's region-specific programming reaches 120 million homes via six satellites, reaching Europe; Quebec, Canada; Africa; Latin America and the Caribbean; the Orient; the United States; and Asia.

Canada's largest piracy problem has been in the area of software. Finally on the decline, estimates of lost revenue were running as high as $450 million per year.

Moving to the south, let's look at Latin America.

Global Regions: Latin America

Over the last decade, Latin America has experienced economic growth, attracting increased foreign investment and tourism. The region is also progressing in the battle to alleviate poverty, creating a larger and more demanding middle class.

Mexico

Like Canada, Mexico is similar to the U.S. in terms of its conduit base, with more than 300 TV stations and 25.6 million televisions. However, of that market, one broadcaster, Grupo Televisa SA de CV (Televisa), holds a nearly 90% share. Unlike Canada, this primary provider is not a government-owned entity and therefore operates under a more marketing-driven mandate than the CBC.

Televisa has interests in the following businesses:

- Television production and broadcasting

- Pay television programming

- Direct-to-home satellite services

- Cable television

- International distribution of television programming

- Feature film production and distribution

- Publishing and publishing distribution

- Music recording and distribution

- Radio production and broadcasting

- Professional sports and show business promotions

- An Internet portal, EsMas.com. An equity interest in Univision Com, Inc., a U.S. Spanish-language television broadcaster that commands an 84% share of Spanish broadcasting within the United States

- A 51% stake in a cable joint venture with Cablevision and a 60% stake in Innova, which operates the SKY direct-to-home satellite, known as Sky Latin America

Televisa is the heavyweight in Spanish-language television: It produces, broadcasts, and distributes Spanish language television programs to 85 countries throughout North and South America and Europe, with its main international outlets being the U.S., Spain, and other Latin American countries.

Copyright piracy remains a major problem in Mexico, with U.S. industry loss estimates remaining high. Pirated sound recordings and videocassettes are widely available throughout Mexico. The International Intellectual Property Alliance (IIPA) estimated that trade losses due to copyright piracy in Mexico totaled over $500 million in 2011. The Business Software Alliance, a trade association representing the packaged software industry, estimates that the Mexican piracy rate in 2010/11 was 60%, which resulted in losses of approximately $264 million. The International Federation of the Phonographic Industry, a music trade association, estimates the piracy rate for music in Mexico to be approximately 40% and growing particularly among the youth.[5]

Cinemex, the first Mexican screen ownership group to modernize the country's theaters, began as a college business plan. Adolfo Fastlicht, Miguel Angel Dávila Guzmán, and Matthew Heyman, Harvard classmates, saw an opportunity in Mexico and followed up on it, finding venture capital to modernize seating, increase screen size, introduce digital-ready screens, enhance sound quality, and provide restaurants within the Cinemex theaters. In addition, they exploited the potential for screen advertising to local and global marketers and soon added $20 million a year in additional revenue. In 2002, Cinemex was sold to Onex Corporation and Oaktree Capital for $300 million. Two years after that, the new owners sold Cinemex to the Carlyle Group, Bain Capital, and Spectrum.

Of special note in Latin America is Brazil, one of the economic powerhouses in what is now known globally as the BRIC nations: Brazil, Russia, India, and China.

Brazil

After decades of challenges, Brazil welcomed its first democratically elected president, Luiz Inácio Lula da Silva, known popularly as "Lula." Lula was successful in using the country's oil reserves, rebuilding the country's infrastructure, and expanding the middle class, while nearly eliminating hyperinflation. He also eliminated unproductive government mandates and provided an atmosphere that was consumer supportive and comfortable for foreign direct investment (FDI). Brazil has dominated the entertainment landscape in Latin America.

---

[5] www.ustr.gov/html/2001_mexico.pdf, Office of the United States Trade Representative, *Foreign Trade Barriers: Mexico*, p. 310.

Globo Cabo, a holding company based in Sao Paulo, is the largest operator of cable television in Brazil, serving 3.5 million subscribers with over 8.5 million homes passed in 67 cities of Brazil.

Globo Cabo acquired VICOM, a privately held company with over 3,000 ground-based satellite transponders in Brazil, early in this past decade. The company explored ways to exploit synergies between its extensive urban cable network and VICOM's vast satellite network. The company also collaborated with Microsoft to develop a broadband Internet platform in Brazil. Microsoft bought a 9.6% stake in the company and together they launched Virtua, a high-speed residential broadband service. Virtua is available exclusively to its cable TV subscribers. The company is also investigating broadband offerings to facilitate the convergence of interactive and digital TV.

Globo also has an edge in the area of content. The parent holding company has interests in newspapers, magazines, and TV; this provides a cornucopia of content to be leveraged across the board. Additionally, the Globo network, through Globo TV International, is beamed from Brazil to a myriad of countries. Household penetration is split into two groups of nations: the United States, Australia, and most South and Central American countries are home to numerous Brazilian expatriates; the second group of nations, such as Portugal, Angola, and Mozambique, share Portuguese as its its common language and is equally receptive to the programming.

Video piracy continues to be the main source of piracy in Latin America. Brazil, the largest market in the region, also has one of the highest piracy rates, with piracy losses topping $250 million in 2011. It is the position of the MPA that the Brazilian Government has, to date, demonstrated inadequate commitment and attention toward protection of Intellectual Property rights.[6]

In many countries in the region, piracy is linked to organized crime, thus complicating both investigation and enforcement. Signal theft is also common in the region, while Internet piracy has not yet posed a real threat due to lack of bandwidth in the region.

Argentina

Argentines have a reputation of being extremely flexible about politics, economics, and the crises that seem to occur about every seven to ten years. The last major setback was in 2001. There is a definite trend toward a reoccurrence, with inflation at over 25% of the GDP.

Despite all this, the entertainment and media sectors are doing very well. With a population of 37 million, the entertainment industry in 2011 exceeded $37 billion with over 50% spent on cable and network television. Magazines and newspapers represent another 40%, and the remaining 10% is in radio and the Internet. There is a healthy business in book sales both online and in very large and attractive stores throughout the major cities, primarily directed at women. Theater and events thrive because there is a Broadway style street called Corrientes, where talented and well-connected producers stage a mix of locally developed shows as well as touring shows from the U.S., London, and Canada. In this sector there is effective collaboration between the theatrical producers in Argentina and Brazil. Triple play from the cable and the telephony companies offer broadband, Internet, speedy connections, with access to chat rooms, shopping, and online games.

---

[6] www.mpaa.org/anti-piracy/, The Motion Picture Association of America.

Four out of 10 Argentines rent movies from existing stores, and over 40% visit movie theaters over a three-month period.

The largest media conglomerate is Clarin, with ownership in network TV (Telefe), cable, (Klaxon), newspapers, (Clarin), popular women's magazines, growing online book publishing, and movie production. This has become another political issue as the president, Christine Kerchner, who was also the wife of the deceased former president has begun to chafe under the constant criticism by the Clarin organization on her political party and the running of the country. As a reaction, she has passed legislation restricting the growth of media conglomerates and is actively pursuing passing legislation that will force Clarin to sell off their cable holdings and restrict their potential growth and political leverage.

Moving across the Atlantic, let's examine the area known as EMEA: Europe, the Middle East, and Africa.

Global Regions: EMEA

The next region we visit is also the largest, in terms of the countries that make up the segment. It includes one of the most mature markets—Western Europe—as well as an area that is expected to grow quickly, the Middle East and North Africa, known as MENA, which includes Algeria, Bahrain, Egypt, Jordan, Kuwait, Lebanon, Libya, Morocco, Oman, Qatar, Saudi Arabia, Syria, and the United Arab Emirates.

Western Europe has contributed greatly to the growth of the entertainment economy, acting as the earliest importing countries of American entertainment content. Western Europe now regularly exports its own talent, throughout the European Union and beyond.

EMEA: *Germany*

Germany is the home of Bertelsmann, one of the most important companies in entertainment. Over 80% of Bertelsmann is majority owned by the Bertelsmann Foundation, a nonprofit organization founded by the Mohn family. That family also owns the remaining 19.1%. Among its expansive media holdings, Bertelsmann owns Random House and BMG.

Bertelsmann is a leader in Europe in the publication of major consumer and business magazines; has major holdings in the television industry with RTL; and has become the pre-eminent direct marketing company with direct-to-the-consumer book clubs, record clubs, and direct sales of DVD products. Although it made some forays to launch a U.S. version of its very successful magazine division Gunnar & Jahr, it failed and closed the operation.

The most notable contribution to Germany's film making industry is the renaissance of Studio Babelsberg, once the home of the revolutionary German cinema, a prime mover in the early motion-picture industry. Studio Babelsberg came under the control of the Nazis during the war years. Hundreds of propaganda films were churned out, including Leni Riefenstahl's *The Power of the Will*. It is now the home of all major German, and some international, film productions. Located a short distance outside of Berlin, in Potsdam, it is close to the World War II museum.

Piracy control in Germany has been through better enforcement of existing German legislation. It has led to a decline in piracy in all areas except the Internet.

EMEA: *Russia*

Russia has proceeded rapidly to embrace Western culture and its entertainment economy through a combination of capitalism and authoritarian politics. It has used its leverage and pressure to expand local film production, using oil profits to license good quality TV programming from the U.S., the U.K., and Latin America. There is a ready source of acceptable content from some of the former USSR countries as well as content production companies in Eastern Europe, including Hungary, Poland, and the Czech Republic.

Recently the major television system has also licensed children's programming from RGB, an experienced production company in Argentina and RTL, the private network in Germany.

EMEA: *The Middle East*

The Middle East is a complex region of the world and has the greatest disparity in language, religion, customs, and goals. Yet the area is linked by an important ambition: to share in global entertainment revenue and participate in the digital revolution.

The Middle East: Israel

Television is a government tool in Israel. It was established in 1967, the year of the Six Days War between Israel and its neighboring Arab countries. Israeli television was first broadcast by Channel One, overseen and administered by the Israel Broadcasting Authority; it retains control of the channel today.

According to the Israel Broadcasting Authority Law, the Authority's responsibilities rest in three main areas:

- To broadcast television (and radio) as a public service

- To broadcast educational and entertainment programs, as well as information in the areas of social, economic, monetary, cultural, scientific, and arts policy

- To ensure that the broadcast gives suitable expression to various opinions and transmits reliable information

Today, Channel One is divided into two divisions. The first, the News Division, directs news, sports, special local and overseas broadcasts, and current affairs magazines. The second, the Program Division, is made up of five departments. They include the documentary department, entertainment department, drama department, children's and youth department, and Israel heritage department.

Channel Two was created in 1993. Unlike Channel One, Channel Two is funded by the sale of on-air advertising. Channel Two is not entirely separate from the government, however. Educational TV, a branch of the Ministry of Education, has been incorporated into Channel Two and is supported by government funds.

Israel's Arab population is not neglected. Channel Three, which is also government-owned, is a satellite/cable-only channel that broadcasts news and entertainment in Arabic or with Arabic subtitles. The content includes cultural and sports programs, news features, and "open studio" live broadcasts. Channel Three can be picked up in all Middle Eastern countries, North Africa, the Persian Gulf, and some southern European nations.

On the cable front, Israel has three major operators: Golden Channels, Matav, and Tevel. In the areas of music and film, though Israel has some domestic production, most content is imported from the United States.

Both advertisers and most consumers still prefer imported content from satellite. They are now buying a great deal of children's programming from Argentina and Brazil and always fill the channels with American top films and television series.

Over the past decade the government has supported the Israeli Film Festival in the U.S., now presented on both coasts. This has enhanced the prestige of Israeli film makers and contributed to greater quality of content, increasing viewership of Israeli film in the home country as well as in the U.S. and abroad.

Israel's lack of transnational development in entertainment may offer a monstrous opportunity for the Israeli entertainment industry. However, the opportunity for marketers remains to be seen, both from a cultural and a political perspective. Middle East unrest continues to depress the opportunities available in the entertainment marketing sector. Additionally, the Middle East has not been known for strict sentencing for copyright violations.

Middle East/North Africa: Dubai and Abu Dhabi

Abu Dhabi represents 86% of the UAE territory, one-third of its population, and 90% of its oil production. Dubai represents 5% of the UAE territory, one-third of its population, and has transferred to a trade and services economy due to depleting oil reserves. Dubai has maintained a certain autonomy from the capital (Abu Dhabi).

In 2012, The UAE was ranked 114th out of 195 countries in the world press freedom index, falling in the group of countries that are "Not Free." Topics such as homosexuality, drugs, prostitution, abortion, and religion are taboo in Media in the UAE. Even discussion of lifestyles, such as dating, is sensitive in a country that outlaws kissing in public. Economic news can be deemed sensitive, such as when Dubai World announced it was $40 billion in debt. Violations of media laws can lead to jail or swift deportation.

Few media outlets offer pan-Arab marketers true regional coverage. Satellite TV is currently the only advertising medium that reaches the whole MENA region.

The digital platform is creating a unique opportunity for local media players to expand regionally both in terms of audience and relevance to advertisers. The biggest recent news regarding Arab media was the purchase of Al Gore's Content cable television channel by the government of Qatar for $500 million to expand the footprint of Al Jazeera in the U.S.

EMEA: South Africa

South Africa, emancipated by Mandela who used the World Cup to ease the way toward the end of apartheid (as presented in the 2009 Matt Damon film, *Invictus*), has slowly entered the global entertainment economy. South Africa's entertainment center is focused in Johannesburg and Cape Town. Through significant foreign investment, particularly from the Japanese and the Chinese, South Africa has reached important milestones in broadband penetration of homes, enabling middle class families to increase utilization of the Internet, including Skype for communications and streaming media for entertainment.

Global Regions: Asia Pacific

The Asia Pacific region is the single greatest example of the direct relationships among the growth of the middle class, improving GDP, and increased average per capita income. This powerhouse combination of factors has led to the expansion of theatrical box office, television viewership, device acquisition, and overall out-of-pocket consumption for media.

India and China have led the conversation over the last decade, but we start our discussion with Japan, a big story since the end of World War II, but now a mature market.

Asia Pacific: Japan

NHK (Nihon Hosokyokai or Japan Broadcasting Corporation), the only TV/radio broadcasting station authorized by law to provide universal services, operates five channels. Two are terrestrial channels: one provides news, movies, dramas, sports, and entertainment; the other, educational programs. The remaining three channels are Direct Broadcast Satellite (DBS) channels, offering, respectively, sports/news, old movies, and High Definition Television (HDTV) broadcasts.

On the cable front, Japan's notoriously rigid isolationist practices have worked against the full development of cable TV. Between the fact that the government has limited the number of channels, and the practice of limiting foreign ownership of stations to 33% (just recently increased from 20%), there are hurdles facing MSOs in this market. Additionally, Japanese consumers are still in a mindset similar to that of American consumers in the early days of cable; they believe there is enough programming available for free and that cable is too expensive.

From a piracy perspective, the Japanese market suffered from an influx of pirated films emanating from Vietnam. Vietnam's government-owned film distributor routinely distributed illegal copies of foreign films; however, action by the MPA and the Japanese government has slowed this problem.

Asia Pacific: India

An overview of the global entertainment and media scene—even a cursory one—could not be complete without mention of India, especially due to the overwhelming success of the Indian cinema industry known as Bollywood. The term is a derivation of combining Hollywood with Mumbai, formerly known as Bombay, the center of Indian film production.

Indian cinema has produced over 27,000 feature films and thousands of documentary short films, produced in 52 different languages; today, India makes more than 800 feature films every year, making it the largest film-producing country in the world. These films are distributed worldwide to an audience that eagerly awaits each new release featuring a raft of popular stars.

On the TV scene, the big player in today's India is ZEE TV. The channel turned India's mostly staid TV industry on its head with its forward-looking philosophy. ZEE TV provides viewers with innovative programs: talk shows, game shows, discussion, situation comedies, and dramas—broadcast in Hindi, created by Indians for Indians. ZEE TV also continues to serve the needs of India's myriad linguistic groups (there are 15 major languages spoken in India) by producing a variety of shows in different languages.

STAR TV, which pioneered satellite television in Asia, became ZEE's partner in India on December 1993, when STAR purchased 50% of Asia Today LTD, the Hong Kong-based broadcaster of ZEE TV. ZEE TV is now watched daily by an average of 180 million viewers across the world, and meets the prime time requirements of both the Eastern and Pacific time zones. Aimed at serving the needs of South Asians living abroad, the channel airs 24 hours a day.

On the cable TV scene, a government effort to clean up private broadcasters has resulted in the banning of tobacco and alcohol advertisements, "adult shows," and advertisements containing references that might offend religious sentiments. The government-controlled channel Doordarshan does not broadcast such advertisements.

According to a report prepared by PricewaterhouseCoopers for the Confederation of Indian Industry, the Indian entertainment and media industry is expected to exceed revenues of 805 billion INR (17.2 billion USD) in 2013. Robust growth is expected as a result of steady macroeconomic growth, rising spending power, and positive demographic indicators. Industry revenues are expected to reach 1,764 billion INR (37.6 billion USD) by 2016. The same report states that India is only the 14th largest E&M market in the world with industry revenues contributing about 1% of its GDP.[7]

Asia Pacific: China

Conducting business in China is one of the biggest challenges—and opportunities—facing western countries today. In the midst of a struggle for political control, combined with the opening of trade and some investment, the Chinese entertainment industry is aggressively searching for a path. With its roots in the propaganda past, as well as art house films stressing traditional Chinese values and mores, the Chinese film industry is as much an opportunity and challenge as anything else in this intriguing economy.

Early in the prior decade, the Chinese government announced it would permit foreign companies to collaborate with domestic companies to make movies and manufacture moviemaking and recording equipment. In 2011, the total box office in China reached over US$2.67 billion, with at least two-thirds of the revenue coming from foreign imports, including U.S. films. However, the

---

[7] http://cii.in/WebCMS/Upload/em%20version%202_low%20res.PDF, *India Entertainment and Media Outlook 2012*, PwC, 2012

protection afforded local content production for the last decade resulted in domestic productions making up 60% of the total movies *shown* in China—lots of viewings but not as much revenue.

This government interaction had an impact upon both the production of movies and the content. Violence and sex have long been targets of censorship in Chinese-made movies. Although that is slowly changing as foreign sensibilities become involved in the process, the government remains active in policing how China is represented in film. Movie makers are now allowing Chinese censors to view their work early in the process or risk being blackballed. Paramount recently submitted a 3D version of *Top Gun* for review. The film fell into a black hole. When Paramount learned that it was being rejected, it realized that showing MIG fighter planes as the enemy aircraft was a very large no-no.[8]

However, piracy has been a problem in China—and continues to be. At times, the figure released by the government has suggested that the piracy rate was running as high as 90%. There were large-scale imports of pirated products from surrounding areas, and the number of production lines in-country had also increased. However, the government has been obliged to take more determined enforcement actions against pirates after the official WTO accession of China.

The Chinese cable industry is big—100 million cable-TV users—but supposedly totally home-grown. Because many foreigners have struck deals with China's local cable operators, who have merrily ignored the central government's ban on same, it appears that a crackdown may be on its way. In any case, foreign entertainment marketers have yet to see what the outcome will be and who will be able to take advantage of any opportunities that present themselves.

Summary

Entertainment marketing, once primarily the domain of U.S.-based studios, has expanded into all sectors of the global entertainment industry. As technology joins discretionary time and disposable income in creating a global marketplace eager to consume entertainment product, today's marketing professionals must be aware of a variety of new challenges and opportunities. The continued development of content and conduit around the world creates an increasingly competitive entertainment economy, filled with consumers who have almost instantaneous access—either legally or illegally—to product. Marketing professionals must learn how to harness today's technologies to create new strategies for product rollout and maintenance.

---

[8] "To Get Movies into China, Hollywood Gives Censors a Preview," *New York Times*, January 14, 2013.

Conclusion

Where Do We Go from Here?

There seems to be very little that might cause the entertainment industry to stop dead in its tracks. The combination of technology, available data, ease in communication, rising global economic equality—all of it supports a continuation in the incredible growth of entertainment marketing.

Not that it doesn't have its challenges. Digital disruption is the norm of the day, with old business models teetering and new ones not quite set. Piracy threatens copyright. Renting undermines owning. Technology makes the new obsolete overnight. The entire industry seems to move at the speed of a fiber-optic network. Our world is in the throes of a disruption and transformation not seen since Gutenberg pulled the first pass on his printing press.

Entertainment today covers not only what we do with our free time, but how we work, how we gather and share information, and how we connect on the most personal basis. It is a huge and rapidly growing opportunity for those with the intelligence, interest, and stamina to make it in a very competitive business.

You, as a potential entertainment marketing professional, can best prepare for your future by following a traditional journalistic practice: asking who, what, why, where, and when.

Who: The Consumer

Today's consumer demands three things: choice, choice, and choice. As always, consumers will choose what content will become popular and profitable, aided by your work as a marketer. But now, consumers will choose where they consume it and what device they will consume it on. That means that you, in developing that content, must be prepared with a product that will work on all platforms. Because technology is changing at a stunning rate of speed, you must be aware of every trend, of all possibilities, to stay ahead of the competition.

Read, listen to, watch *everything* that can give you an indication of where all this is going. Your audience demands this of you. This immersion mirrors their own experience of the content and the conduit: constant, unceasing.

Keep. *Up*.

What: Technology and Trends

Throughout our discussion, we have attempted to provide a cursory overview of the technology that is shaping the world of entertainment (and therefore entertainment marketing); "attempted" because the lifespan of today's technology is a blink. It is nearly impossible to be totally current with all of the changes. The old technologies of research, writing, and editing are bound by the pace of human ability—it requires huge amounts of time and energy to create a text, formulated from ideas and concepts. And in that time, new technologies come and go, leaving their imprint on the advances that follow. In the time it took to create this book, changes—some stunning—have occurred in all three areas of concern to the entertainment marketer: production, distribution, and consumption.

The digital disruption has only begun, and it will continue, roiling all business models. You will experience the same onslaught of "new" as every generation before you; only yours will be coming faster. As an entertainment marketer, you need to be even more technologically savvy than your audience, for *you* need to create the concepts, molded to the audiences and their technologies, that will satisfy consumers.

And then there is the question of what is entertainment. A one time, it was reading, then it was reading and radio, then reading, radio, and movies, and now it includes social media and digital music. The process never stops. We cannot forecast what the next generation will consider entertainment because it will be built around the precepts of their own experience of the world. But more and more, it will be marketing professionals who create those concepts because entertainment is a conduit all its own. It takes the audience away from its humdrum world. In the process, it sells, through name recognition, sponsorship, and product tie-ins. Entertainment is the road to the subconscious, reaching the consumer while the consumer is happy, relaxed, alert, or excited, tying the message directly to a memorable experience—regardless if that experience is adrenaline-produced or serotonin-stimulated.

Why: The More Things Change...

Entertainment is a global phenomenon, fed by the digital technology that allows it to stream 24/7, downloaded into countries rising in economic power, discretionary time, and disposable income. Entertainment, media, and technology not only connect the world, affect how people view their own cultures, their own opportunities, their own economies, and even their own political structures.

The ways of both the Western and the Eastern worlds cross-pollinate as populations become aware of other lifestyles and consumables. This may happen, initially, via entertainment. This access feeds curiosity and a desire for more. This is the predominant force in the growth of entertainment and entertainment marketing, as they enter new frontiers around the world. Global media conglomerates meet this demand for more with an ever-expanding range of new products.

Entertainment marketing is a significant part of the new global economy, creating products that answer a previously unstated need of this new mass audience. In the process, entertainment marketing creates new revenue streams around the world.

Where: Where Do You Want It?

So now we have the who—the global population; the what—the technology; the why—revenue streams. Where?

Everywhere. Anywhere.

Where do you want it? Gobi Desert? No problem. Rainforests of the Amazon? Be right with you. Polar icecap? Been there, done that. Technology makes it possible; the desire of multinational populations makes it probable; and synergy, mentioned throughout this book, makes it pervasive.

The ability to create digital content will continue to create new avenues for the multiplexing of the message. Entertainment is streaming everywhere, all the time.

When: Get Onboard

The changes that will affect entertainment marketing are happening now, in the technologies, the audiences, the media conglomerates, and the international desire to know more, right now. Marketing professionals who desire to become part of the entertainment phenomenon are challenged to more clearly understand the world around them and the tools with which they can reach the consumer—as they always have been.

For as long as humankind has gathered around the community fire to rub elbows, entertainment has been part of the draw. We thrive on the opportunity to drop our day-to-day troubles, experience new sensations, broaden our interests, and learn something new. Today's entertainment industry offers all of this and more, launching an entertainment marketing revolution in every corner of the world.

However, the ever-expanding role of technology continues to create new challenges for the industry. Today's entertainment business far outdistances any geographic boundaries. It must rely on courts outside the U.S. to maintain a healthy marketing environment by upholding IP laws and treaties. Fortunately, the presence of entrepreneurs and governments active in the growth of the global entertainment industry is helping to work toward a necessary balance.

As marketing professionals take hold of this phenomenon, becoming part of entertainment's trillion-dollar worldwide economy, they must keep in mind that what *sells* entertainment *is* entertainment. Consumers connect with those messages that most massage their desire to be swept away. It's up to you to do the sweeping.

Finally, if you're following our advice, remember this: have some fun. After all, you're part of the most entertaining business ever invented.

Contribute. Prosper. But most of all, enjoy!

Index

D

Dallas, 79
Damon, Matt, 274
Dannen, Fredric, 196
data collection, 195
DBO (domestic box office), 57
DDB Worldwide, 34
deals, marketing teams, 36-37
Dear John, 158
decisions, 29-30
  large decisions, 30-31
  no-decision-at-all decision, 31
  researching, 31-32
  small decisions, 30
decline in subscriptions, cable TV, 135
demographics
  cable TV, 85
  gaming, 177-178
  Nielsen ratings, 85
destination entertainment, 254
  all-inclusive vacation, 256-257
  casinos, 260-262
  circuses, 254-255
  cruises, 255-256
  experiential branding, 262-263
  theme parks, 258-260
  time shares, 257-258
destinations, 239-241
development process, music, 191
DeVito, Danny, 158
digital disruption, 6
  conveyance versus content, 7-8
  global regions, 267
  technology, 8
digital distribution, 55-56
  hardware, 140
    laptops, 141
    smart TVs, 140
    smartphones and tablets, 140-141
  over the top (OTT), 139-140
digital downloads, music, 193
digital media receivers, 142
Digital Millennium Copyright act of 1998, 107
digital self-publishing, 147
digital transmission, 55-56
Diller, Barry, 38, 143
Dion, Celine, 203, 261
direct broadcast satellite companies, 115
direct marketing, books, 159-160
DirectTV, 67
Discover Card, 200
discoverability, books
  author as marketer, 163-164
  populist reviews, 162
  social networking, 162-163
DISH Network, Hopper, 126

Disney branding hotels, 253
  Iger, Bob, 38
  music, publishing, 188
  Netflix, 141
  Oceaneer Adventure, 256
  Pixar, 52
  strategic development (SD), 14
  Time Warner, 120
  Toy Story, 60
Disney, Roy, 38
Disney, Walt, 13, 51
Disney Cruise Line, 256
Disneyland, 258-260
disruptive content, 144-145
distribution
  book publishing, 153-154
  movies, 55
    digital distribution, 55-56
    piracy, 56-57
  music, 193-194
    airplay, 195-196
    live music, 196-197
    megatours, 197-198
DMA (Designated Market Area), 83
Dolan, Charles, 118
Dore, Kathy, 124
DreamWorks, distribution, 55
Dubai, 273
Dubai World, 273
DVRs, 87, 126
Dynasty, 79

E

Eastwood, Clint, 158
Eat, Pray, Love, 158
e-books, 149
  Amazon, 154-155
  romance publishing, 150
EDI-Neilsen, 31
Ehrhoff, Christian, 222
Eisner, Michael, 38, 51
EMEA (Europe, Middle East, Africa), 266, 271
  Germany, 271-272
  Middle East, 272
  Russia, 272
  South Africa, 274
endorsements, sports, 229
entertainment industry, Internet, 138
entertainment marketing, 25-26,
  Four Cs, 11-12
  future of, 278
  history of, 24-25
  over the top (OTT), 11
  perishability, 12-13
entertainment moguls, 37-38
entertainment spending, 2-5
Epcot, 259
Epic Records, 203

Gutenberg, Johannes, 147
Guzman, Miguel Angel Davila, 269

H

halo effect, relationship marketing and, 91-92
Hammett, Dashiell, 149
Hannon, Ezra, 165
Happy Days, 79
hardware, digital distribution, 140
    laptops, 141
    smart TVs, 140
    smartphones and tablets, 140-141
Harlequin Romances, 150
Harry Potter, branding, 165-166
Hathaway, Anne, 64
HBO (Home Box Office), 118, 139, 144
HBO GO, 139
HD Radio, 109-110
HDNet, 72
heads of subsidiaries, 33
Heavenly Bed program, 253
Heaven's Gate, 54
Herweg, Ashley, 104
Herweg, Godfrey, 104
Heyman, Matthew, 269
high concept movies, 48
    Jaws, 48-49
    versus not high concept, 49
Hildick-Smith, Peter, 163
Hill, Faith, 188
hispanics, cable TV, 122
history, of entertainment marketing, 24-25
home videos, 47-48
Hopper, DISH Network, 126
hotels, branding, 253-254
House, 79
House of Cards, 145
household ratings, 84
Howard, Dwight, 217
Hulu, 142, 145
Hulu Plus, 142
Hunter, Evan, 165
HUT (households using television), 84

I

I Am Number Four, 159
I Love Lucy, 79
IAAPA (International Association of Amusement Parks and Attractions), 260
identifying target niches (radio), 104-105
identities
    Austin, Texas, 246
    Branson, Missouri, 245
    Los Angeles, 246-247
    Nashville, Tennessee, 244-245
    New York City, 247

Iger, Bob, 38, 51
independent book stores, 167
independent films, 67-68
    film festivals, 70-71
    independent screens, 72
    independents, 70
    Internet, 70
    market for, 68
    marketing, 68-69
    wild postings, 71-72
    word of mouth, 69-70
independent producers, 53-54
independent screens, independent films, 72
independents
    independent films, 70
    local television stations, 81
    music, 190
India, 274-275
Indian casinos, 260
individual sports, 219-227
influence, travel and tourism, 249
in-game purchases, monetizing mobile gaming, 181
In-House Agency, 34
in-house producers, 53
integrated communications, 26
integration, travel and tourism, 242
intellectual property
    music, 192-193
    television, 98
Internet, 16, 266
    convergence, 18
    entertainment industry, 138
    growth in broadband, 136
    independent films, 70
    movie trailers, 63
Internet Essentials, Comcast, 137
internet radio, 107-108
intra-industry marketing, 91
    relationship marketing, 251
Invictus, 274
IPTV, 126
Israel, 272-273
Israel Broadcasting Authority Law, 272
IT&ME, relationship marketing (travel and tourism), 251
iTunes, 193
iTunes Tagging, 109

J-K

Jackson, Tyson, 219
Jagger, Mick, 198
James, E.L., 152
James, LeBron, 229
James Bond movies, product placement, 50-51
Japan, 274
Jaws, 48-49
Johnson, Joe, 217